Evgeny Sveshnikov · French Defenc

ProgressinChess

Volume 19 of the ongoing series

Founded and edited by
GM Victor Korchnoi
GM Helmut Pfleger
GM Nigel Short
GM Rudolf Teschner

2007
EDITION OLMS

Evgeny Sveshnikov

French Defence Advance Variation

Volume 1: Basic Course

WHITE REPERTOIRE

With a Foreword by Anatoly Karpov

2007
EDITION OLMS

THE AUTHOR: Evgeny Sveshnikov (born 1950) is an active international player who currently represents Latvia. This Russian Grandmaster is widely recognised as a great openings expert. He has worked as a trainer for the 12th FIDE World Champion Anatoly Karpov, among others. He is especially known for having developed the system with ...e5 in the Sicilian defence which now bears his name, as well as for his work on the 2 c3 system for White against the Sicilian and the Advance Variation against the French Defence.

Bibliographic Information published by Die Deutsche Bibliothek

Die Deutsche Bibliothek lists this publication in the Deutsche Nationalbibliografie; detailed bibliographic data is available in the internet at http://dnb.ddb.de.

Copyright © 2007 Edition Olms AG
Willikonerstr. 10 · CH-8618 Oetwil a.S., Switzerland
E-mail: info@edition-olms.com
Internet: www.edition-olms.com

Printed in Germany

Editor: Ken Neat
Translator: Phil Adams
Photographic Acknowledgement: Dagobert Kohlmeyer, Russian Chess House
Typesetting and Index by: Art & Satz · Ulrich Dirr, D-80331 Munich
Printed by: Druckerei Friedr. Schmücker GmbH, D-49624 Löningen
Cover: Eva König, D-22769 Hamburg

ISBN 978-3-283-00523-8

Contents

Foreword by Anatoly Karpov   6

Introduction   8

Symbols 10

1 For and against 3. e5 11

2 The plans for each side, linked to the pawn structure 24
   2.1 Attack on the king 25
   2.2 Advantage in space and/or development, typical endgame 42
   2.3 For and against the blockade, weak colour complex 68
   2.4 Play on both wings 82

3 The many facets of the blockade 108
   3.1 Aaron Nimzowitsch: theoretician, practical player and romantic 108
   3.2 The classical blockade 111
   3.3 The modern view of Nimzowitsch's theory 119

4 What would you play ? 134
         Check your solutions! 146

   Appendix 157
         Index of themes 157
         Index of names 158
         Index of games 160
         Index of variations 175

Foreword

It gives me great pleasure, for several reasons, to introduce the author of this book. In the first place, not only are we contemporaries but we also come from the same area: he comes from Cheliabinsk and I from neighbouring Zlatoust. So "Zhenya" Sveshnikov and I have known each other from childhood. We often played together in the junior teams of the Russian Federation, and then the Soviet Union. We both had the same trainer: Leonid Aronovich Gratvol, who was fanatically devoted to developing junior chess. It is perhaps thanks to him that the future grandmaster grew to love not only the work of chess analysis but also coaching, which he started relatively young. Usually, active players prefer tournament play to spending time and energy on other chess activities. Yet Evgeny Ellinovich has managed, not only to win over seventy international tournaments during his long career, but also to bring on the talents of dozens of grandmasters and masters.

Secondly I should mention the high quality of analysis of my old comrade, his conscientiousness and his basic honesty, which I came to appreciate many times in the years when Grandmaster Sveshnikov was one of my trainers during my difficult matches against Garry Kasparov.

Thirdly, I am anxious to stress that our collaboration continues in various ways. Evgeny Ellinovich helps me prepare for important events, teaches in the Anatoly Karpov School and willingly assists when I fly with colleagues to promote the game of chess in distant regions of Russia. I should add that he often does this on his own initiative as well; it is thanks to him that chess schools have revived in the Altai and South-Urals regions.

Finally I must mention his fanatical and stubborn work in researching the openings, which eventually brought him brilliant success. I recall that thirty years ago, during a USSR championship event, I said to him pityingly: "Zhenya, why do you keep torturing yourself by playing that Sicilian with …e7–e5? Choose something simpler and you'll play much more easily!" Today I have to admit that I was wrong: he was right not to listen to me: today everybody plays the Sveshnikov Variation! And as a fellow native of the Urals, I am pleased that this system is also known as the "Cheliabinsk Variation".

Unfortunately, his monograph on the Sveshnikov Sicilian has until now remained practically the only publication by this grandmaster in the Russian language. But now finally this new theoretical work of Evgeny Sveshnikov is available. It is devoted to the popular 3. e5 system against the French Defence. Its popularity is once more largely due to its constant adoption by Sveshnikov, who has developed a fantastic feel for its nuances. It has helped him amass a plus-score (70% from over 150 games!) against such French Defence experts as Evgeny Bareev. The author believes that Black cannot equalise against the Advance Variation and to date no-one has been able to prove the contrary.

I consider this book to be a real manual, original in its conception and excellent in its execution. It not only teaches you how to play a specific variation of the French Defence, it also helps you understand many strategic ideas and their practical application in the middlegame, which for the majority of players is even more important.

A book by such an outstanding grandmaster and theoretician should prove useful to a wide readership. Club, Internet and weekend tournament players will find that Volume 1 will quickly give them a good grounding in what is really a very unpleasant (for Black) plan of attack. Masters (and even grandmasters) will find in Volume 2 a real master-class by the world expert in this variation.

Anatoly Karpov
Many-times World Champion

* * *

Evgeny Sveshnikov and Anatoly Karpov

Introduction

I have been using the 3. e5 system against the French Defence for about thirty years. How did this weapon become part of my arsenal? In the 1970s chess information was not as readily available as it is in today's computer age; it was difficult to obtain it and process it. I got into the habit of self-reliance, trusting solely my own ideas. I understood that the move 3. e5 was not objectively the strongest, but I had no desire to compete with such experienced French-specialists as, for instance, Vaganian, in the long and complex lines that arise after the main continuation 3. ♘c3. Thus I chose the 3. e5 system against the French (and similarly 2. c3 against the Sicilian) for practical reasons, since I understood that my opponents would be focusing their attention on the moves 3. ♘c3 and 3. ♘d2 which were much more popular at that time.

By the end of the 1980s I had accumulated enough theoretical and practical material on the 3. e5 system. I prepared a talk for my pupils which I ended up giving to over a thousand people. What I found interesting was this: when I tried to teach concrete variations to players of 2nd or even 1st Category, they just looked bored and remembered nothing. On the other hand, if I explained a typical idea by means of an illustrative game, they learnt it for ever. So for learning a new pattern it is best to use well-annotated games, in which the main ideas and plans of both sides can be clearly explained. When the pupil understands the general idea he can memorise the concrete variations more easily.

At the start of the 1990s I wrote a quite extensive article on 3. e5!? for *New in Chess Year Book*. The very positive response to that article prompted me to undertake the present book project, well aware that it would require not just a lot of time …

It is well known that the choice of a plan is based on the pawn structure in the centre and the dynamic placement of the pieces. In my opinion it is not very useful to talk about a particular pawn structure without placing it in the context of a concrete opening. A student who has not reached at least the minimum level of candidate master will have difficulty in assimilating such material. My teaching experience tells me that the material can be assimilated much better if it is taught in the context of an actual opening.

I decided to begin this book with an explanation of the main ideas for each side; each plan is illustrated with games and extensive commentary. Other things being equal, I have given preference to games by the players who were the first to employ a particular plan. Incidentally, most of the annotations were made without consulting a computer, and in this lies their chief merit, since all the ideas are "human". Of course, the variations were then checked later with analysis engines, to eliminate crude oversights. The computer is a valuable assistant for the technical work but in the realm of ideas it is actually, with rare exceptions, of little use.

Further on we present the reader with a series of test positions and solutions to reinforce what has been learnt. Since one of the most common themes of the Advance Variation is to blockade the centre and play against the weakened dark squares, I have included a chapter on this topic.

I wanted to write a book that would be interesting and instructive not just to ordinary players but also to candidate masters, masters and even grandmasters. The practical strength of a player and his understanding of the opening are often at different levels. It often happens that even experienced players go astray in unfamiliar positions. That is why even for them it is useful to reflect once again upon the "why", the general bases underlying the concrete variations that they have memorised.

For advanced players who have studied the first two chapters of Volume 1, I have provided in Volume 2 some reference material in tabular "Encyclopaedia" format, plus theoretically important games with light notes only – to encourage independent analysis. I have also drawn attention to what at present appear to be the most critical positions.

Chess is not just a sport – it is also an element of culture, which is why I usually begin my opening studies with a historical review. I consider it essential to pay tribute to all those who have contributed to the development of this variation, and to trace its development.

Volume 1 (Basic Course) consists of:

1) Historical overview

2) Explanation of the plans for both sides through games annotated in detail

3) A chapter on blockade

4) Test positions

After assimilating this material you can move onto a more professional study ("one step at a time").

Volume 2 (Advanced Course) consists of:

1) Theoretically important games for independent analysis

2) Encyclopaedia

3) Conclusions: the likely future development of the 3. e5 system

4) Games for further study

5) The latest theoretical developments

Naturally I hope that this two-volume work will become not only a manual for club, Internet and weekend tournament players, but will also prove a useful reference for masters and even grandmasters.

* * *

That I have been able to bring this immensely time-consuming but equally interesting work to a successful conclusion is very much due to the efforts of International Master Vladimir Barsky, whom I should like to thank sincerely here for his collaboration in the development and completion of this book project.

Symbols

Symbol	Meaning	Symbol	Meaning
♔	King	♗	Bishop
♕	Queen	♘	Knight
♖	Rook	♙	Pawn
+	Check	#	Mate
×	captures	N	new move
0–0	short castling	0–0–0	long castling
∞	unclear position	⯮	compensation for the material
±	White has a slight advantage	∓	Black has a slight advantage
±	White has a clear advantage	∓	Black has a clear advantage
+−	White has a decisive advantage	−+	Black has a decisive advantage
1–0	Black resigns	0–1	White resigns
=	equal position	½–½	Draw
→	with attack	↑	with initiative
⇄	with counterplay	□	only move
!?	interesting move	?!	dubious move
!	good move	?	bad move
!!	brilliant move	??	very bad move
ICC	Internet Chess Club	ACP	Association of Chess Professionals
PCA	Professional Chess Association		
⇧	White to move	⬇	Black to move

Chapter 1

For and against 3. e5

I am convinced that one of the most interesting positions in chess is the initial position. Therefore I advise you to think about your actions from your very first moves; do not just thoughtlessly follow the advice of the 'authorities'.

1. e4 e6

Strictly speaking, this is not the strongest of moves; after all White can immediately capture the centre by means of the move 2. d4. Furthermore, Black will find it difficult to develop his light-squared bishop. On the other hand, Black presents no weaknesses; if Black plays 1...e5 instead, the e-pawn immediately becomes a target. It is possible that the best move is 1...c5! hindering 2. d4. Nevertheless, recently Black has been achieving decent results with the French Defence and many young grandmasters have adopted it as a part of their opening repertoire.

2. d4 d5

Now White has three main continuations: 3. ♘d2, 3. ♘c3 and 3. e5. In the 19th century 3. e×d5 e×d5 4. c4 was often played, aiming for a very rapid opening of the position, but practice has shown that after 4...♘f6 5. ♘c3 ♗b4! White cannot count on any advantage.

3. ♘d2 – is the move played by grandmaster Siegbert Tarrasch, which reached the peak of its popularity during the 1970s and 1980s. However, on close analysis we can see that this move breaks the principles of opening development. Specifically, White is not really fighting for the centre (note that the

d4 pawn is weakened), no attention is being paid to development (the knight blocks the c1 bishop and the queen) and in fact the only principle being observed is that of safety. But safety should really be Black's concern and White, with the advantage of the first move, ought to attack, otherwise the advantage evaporates. Thus, having somewhat paraphrased Wilhelm Steinitz, can one characterise the move 3. ♘d2.

Why then was this move so popular; didn't the grandmasters understand its shortcomings? Fashion is mostly to blame, since the then champion of the world, Anatoly Karpov was a supporter of this line at the highest level. But his encounters with Victor Korchnoi, in which Karpov did not win a single French, together with recent practice, have shown that with 3...c5! Black practically equalises. Further proof of the strength of 3. ♘d2 c5 can be found in the games of Evgeny Bareev, in which he regularly obtains good counterplay as Black with this line. In 1984 when Karpov played 3. ♘c3 against Agdestein, the attention of other grandmasters was also drawn in this direction.

Undoubtedly, 3. ♘c3! is the most principled and also the strongest move, obeying all the principles of development in the opening. I played this line when I was a master at the end of the 1960s and the beginning of the 1970s, but then I switched to 3. e5. After 3. ♘c3, positions arise which are very complex, both strategically and tactically. At that time many tense games were played with it. By playing 3. ♘c3 therefore, you are giving a head start to a well-prepared and knowl-edgeable opponent. But 3. e5 is quite an-other matter.

3. e5

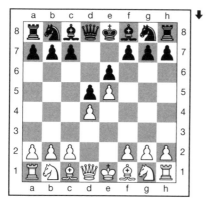

This move has been known since the time of Gioacchino Greco (1600–1634). Its advan-tages are obvious:

1) it gains space;

2) the light-squared bishop on c8 is blocked in;

3) the e5 pawn takes away the important f6 square, after which it is not easy for Black to develop his kingside, whilst there is the potential for White to generate an attack in this area of the board.

But there are also disadvantages:

1) by making a second move in succession with the same pawn White loses time;

2) pawn chains are formed and the pos-ition acquires a semi-closed character, which means that White will find it more difficult to use the advantage of the first move.

3) Black does not have a weak pawn in the centre, and so White does not have an im-mediate target to attack.

Now I propose to make a short excursion into history. Have a look at the course taken by one of the earliest surviving games in which White adopted the 3. e5 plan against the French Defence.

Game 1
Greco – N.N.
1620

1. e4 e6 2. d4 d5 3. e5 c5 4. c3 c×d4?!

Of course, the exchange on d4 is prema-ture, as now White acquires the c3 square for the knight. However, we should not reproach N. N. for this mistake as Black repeated it in much later games.

5. c×d4 ♗b4+ 6. ♘c3 ♗×c3+

The exchange of dark-squared bishops is one of White's main ideas in this system, since such an exchange seriously weakens the dark-square complex in the black camp. And here Black voluntarily parts with this key defender.

7. b×c3 ♘c6 8. ♗d3 ♘ge7 9. f4± ♘f5 10. ♘f3 0–0 11. g4 ♘h4 12. 0–0 ♘×f3+ 13. ♕×f3± ♗d7

It is interesting to see how this "prehistoric" position looks through the eyes of an un-sentimental computer: 13...♕a5 14. ♗b2 b6 (14...f5 15. e×f6 ♖×f6 16. g5→) 15. ♕h3 (15. ♕e2 f5 16. e×f6 ♖×f6 17. g5±) 15...h6 (15...g6 16. f5+−) 16. g5+−.

14. ♕h3 g6

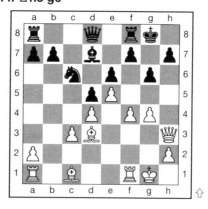

15. f5

White has a decisive attack: his opponent is simply powerless to defend the dark squares.

15...e×f5 16. g×f5 g×f5 17. ♖×f5 (17. ♗h6+−) 17...♗×f5

17...♔h8 would not have saved the game: 18. ♔h1 ♖g8 19. ♕×h7+ ♔×h7 20. ♖h5+ ♔g7 21. ♗h6+ ♔h8 22. ♗f8#.

18. ♗×f5

Black resigned.

* * *

Louis Paulsen and Aaron Nimzowitsch each made an enormous contribution to the development of this system. You will find a detailed appreciation of Nimzowitsch in the chapter devoted to the problems of blockade, but we shall talk about Paulsen now.

The German chess player Louis Paulsen (15.01.1833–18.08.1891) was born in Nassengrund (Germany) into a chess-loving family. His older brother was a strong player and a participant in many international chess congresses. His sister Amalia was also a good player. Louis was a merchant by profession. In 1854 he and his brother emigrated to America.

One of Louis Paulsen's first tournaments in his new country was the American Chess Congress of 1857; he lost in the final to Paul Morphy, 2–6. This defeat should be counted as a success rather than a failure for Paulsen. He was only twenty-four years old and his development as a player was slow, unlike that of the "meteor" Morphy. Paulsen reached his peak in his late forties.

In 1860 Paulsen returned to his homeland. Two years later he played his first match with the "uncrowned world champion" Anderssen. The duel became a dogged battle and ended in a draw (+3 –3 =2); with a huge effort of will Anderssen won the last two games and saved the match. These eternal rivals met in matches twice more and on both occasions Paulsen was victorious: in 1876 (+5 –4 =1) and again in 1877 (+5 –3 =1). He also finished above his distinguished rival in many tournaments. The total count

of their meetings is +20 –17 =7 in favour of Paulsen.

Whilst Anderssen is considered an unsurpassed master of attack, Paulsen can be called the founder of the modern approach to studying the openings. He was a chess theoretician, a chess scientist if you wish. His opening schemes were studied not just by his contemporaries but also by many later generations of chess players. Some of the systems introduced into practice by Paulsen remain relevant to this day (!). This applies to the French Defence with 3. e5 and the system in the Sicilian Defence named after him (1. e4 c5 2. ♘f3 e6 3. d4 c×d4 4. ♘×d4 a6). Paulsen used the Boleslavsky System (1. e4 c5 2. ♘f3 ♘c6 3. d4 c×d4 4. ♘×d4 ♘f6 5. ♘c3 d6 6. ♗e2 e5!) five times: seventy years before Boleslavsky!

If Chigorin is justly considered the foremost nineteenth century exponent of the open games, it was Paulsen who undoubtedly possessed the deepest understanding of the Sicilian and French Defences; in this respect he was ahead of his time by a whole century. In modern databases you can find more than twenty of Paulsen's games as White featuring the 3. e5 variation of the French Defence. White's play in the following game is impressive. Seventy-three years later Wolfgang Unzicker repeated Paulsen's first ten moves, and after 115 years the position after 10. ♘a4 became an opening tabia!

Game 2
Paulsen – Schwarz
Leipzig 1879

1. e4 e6 2. d4 d5 3. e5 c5 4. c3 ♘c6 5. ♘f3 ♕b6 6. a3 ♗d7 7. b4 c×d4 8. c×d4 ♘ge7 9. ♘c3 ♘f5 10. ♘a4

(see next diagram)

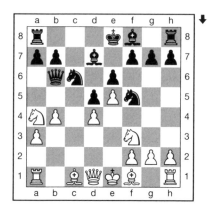

10...♕c7

10...♕d8 was played in Unzicker–Gligorić, Saltsjöbaden 1952.

11. ♗b2 ♗e7 12. ♖c1 a6 13. ♘c5 ♗xc5 14. ♖xc5 0–0 15. ♗d3 (with the threat 16. ♗xf5 exf5 17. ♖xd5) **15...♘fe7**

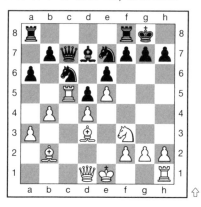

White has cramped Black on the queenside and Black's last move is a mistake that allows Paulsen to launch a direct attack on the black king.

16. ♗xh7+! ♔xh7

If 16...♔h8 White's pressure continues unabated, e.g. 17. ♘g5 g6 18. ♕f3 ♘g8 19. ♗xg8 ♔xg8 20. ♕h3 ♖fd8 21. ♕h7+ ♔f8 22. ♕xf7#.

17. ♘g5+ ♔g6

The alternatives are no better: 17...♔g8 18. ♕h5 ♖fe8 19. ♕h7+ ♔f8 20. ♖c3! or

17...♔h6 18. ♗c1 (with the threat ♘xe6+) 18...♕c8 (18...♔g6 19. ♕g4 ♕c8 20. ♘xe6 ♔h7 21. ♕xg7#) 19. ♕g4 ♔g6 (19...♘f5 20. ♕h3+ ♔g6 21. ♕h7#) 20. ♘xe6+ ♔h7 21. ♕xg7#.

18. ♕g4 f5 19. ♕g3 ♕c8 20. ♖c3

Time to bring up the reserves. The premature 20. ♘xe6+? does not work: 20...♔f7 21. ♕xg7+ ♔xe6 (21...♔e8?? 22. ♕xf8#) 22. ♕h6+ ♔f7 23. ♕f6+ ♔e8–+.

20...f4 21. ♕g4 ♘f5 22. ♖h3 ♖h8 23. ♘xe6+ ♔f7 24. ♕xf5+ ♔e7

The king has no safe square: 24...♔e8 25. ♖xh8+; 24...♔g8 25. ♖xh8+ ♔xh8 26. ♕h5+ ♔g8 27. ♘g5 ♗f5 28. g4 fxg3 29. hxg3 ♔f8 30. ♕h8+ ♔e7 31. ♕xg7+ ♔d8 32. ♖h8#.

25. ♕g5+ ♔xe6

Or 25...♔f7 26. ♕xg7+ ♔xe6 (26...♔e8 27. ♖xh8#) 27. ♕f6#.

26. ♕g6+ ♔e7 27. ♕xg7

and Black resigned in view of 27...♔d8 (27...♔e6 28. ♕f6#) 28. ♖xh8+. A classical example of play on both wings!

Paulsen carried out the idea of blockading the black centre pawns many years before Nimzowitsch!

Game 3
Paulsen – Blackburne
Berlin 1881

1. e4 e6 2. d4 d5 3. e5 c5 4. c3 ♘c6 5. ♘f3 ♗d7 6. ♗e3 ♕b6 7. ♕d2 ♖c8 8. dxc5 ♗xc5 9. ♗xc5 ♕xc5 10. ♗d3 f6 11. ♕e2 fxe5 12. ♘xe5 ♘xe5 13. ♕xe5 ♘f6 14. 0–0 0–0

If 14...♕b6!? would prevent White from controlling d4 and e5.

15. ♘d2 ♖ce8 16. h3 ♗b5

(see next diagram)

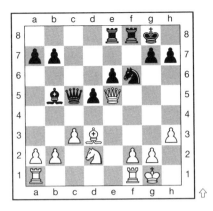

17. c4

It would have been more consistent to bring about the central blockade by 17. ♘b3! ♕b6 18. ♗×b5 ♕×b5 19. ♖ad1±.

17...♕b4?! (17...♘d7 ∞) **18. ♕e2**

And here 18. c×b5 ♕×d2 19. ♖ad1 ♕a5 20. a3± was preferable.

18...♗c6 19. ♖ab1 g6 (19...e5!∓) **20. a3 ♕d6 21. b4 b6 22. ♖fe1 ♘h5 23. ♕e5 ♕d7 24. ♗f1 ♖f5 25. ♕b2 ♖ef8 26. f3**

The game would be unclear after 26. b5 ♗b7 27. ♘f3 ♖×f3 28. g×f3 d×c4 29. ♗×c4 ♘f4 ∞.

26...♕d6 27. c×d5 e×d5 28. ♕d4 ♘f4?! 29. ♘e4 ♕d7 30. ♘f2 ♘e6 31. ♕e3 ♘f4 32. ♘g4± ♕g7 33. ♕e7

White could have achieved a decisive advantage by 33. g3 d4 34. ♕e7 ♖5f7 35. ♕d6. Paulsen managed to lose this game, but the result takes nothing away from his opening strategy.

Paulsen's games against Adolf Schwarz became a real theoretical duel in the then popular line 3. e5 c5 4. c3 ♘c6 5. ♘f3 f6 6. ♗d3 f×e5 7. d×e5 g6. They exchanged points until finally in the Vienna tournament of 1882 Paulsen employed the plan of 8. h4! ♗g7 9. h5 and it was clear that the variation favoured White.

White played the entire following game at the level of a present-day master, bringing all debate about this variation to an end.

Game 4
Paulsen – Schwarz
Vienna 1882

1. e4 e6 2. d4 d5 3. e5 c5 4. c3 ♘c6 5. ♘f3 f6 6. ♗d3 f×e5 7. d×e5 g6 8. h4! ♗g7 9. h5± ♘ge7 10. h×g6 h×g6 11. ♖×h8+ ♗×h8 12. ♕e2 ♕c7 13. ♗f4 ♗d7 14. ♘a3! a6 15. 0-0-0 0-0-0 16. ♖h1 ♖g8 17. ♖h7 b5 18. ♗g5! ♗g7 19. g3 c4 20. ♗b1 ♔b7 21. ♗f6+- ♗f8 22. ♘c2 ♔a8 23. a3 (prophylaxis!) 23...♘f5 24. g4 (restriction!) 24...♘fe7 25. ♘cd4 (blockade!)

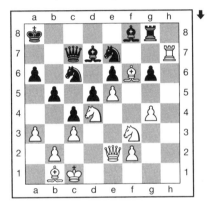

25...♕c8 26. ♕e3 ♘×d4 27. ♕×d4 ♘c6 28. ♕b6 ♘b8 29. ♕e3 ♗c5 30. ♕d2 ♘c6 31. ♘g5 ♘a5 32. ♔d1 ♕c6 33. ♕f4 ♗c8 34. ♘e4 ♗b6 35. ♘d6 ♕c5 36. ♗h4 g5 37. ♕f7 ♖d8 38. ♗×g5 ♖d7 39. ♕f8 ♖×h7 40. ♗×h7 ♔b8 41. ♗e3

Black resigned. An excellent performance by Paulsen!

Paulsen's contributions to the development of this variation are so great that I think that 3. e5 against the French should be called the Paulsen-Nimzowitsch system. Thirty to fifty years later Aaron Nimzowitsch added many new ideas.

The 3. e5 system is often linked with the name of the first World Champion Wilhelm Steinitz. Indeed, he used 3. e5 three times in the great tournament of Vienna 1898, but in the first two games against Burn and Maróczy he did not even manage to equalise.

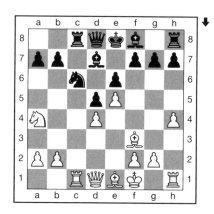

Game 5
Steinitz – Maróczy
Vienna 1898

1. e4 e6 2. d4 d5 3. e5 c5 4. c3

In his third 3. e5 game in this tournament Steinitz gave up the centre in return for piece pressure on the squares d4 and e5: 4. d×c5!? ♘c6 5. ♘f3 ♗×c5 6. ♗d3 ♘ge7 7. 0–0 ♘g6 8. ♖e1 ♗d7 9. c3 a5 10. a4 ♕b8 11. ♕e2 ♗b6 12. ♘a3 0–0 13. ♘b5 ♘a7 14. ♗e3 ♗×e3 15. ♕×e3 ♘×b5 16. a×b5 b6 17. ♘d4 f5 18. f4± (Steinitz–Showalter, Vienna 1898). Later this plan was adopted by many players, including Nimzowitsch and Keres, but Louis Paulsen got there first!

4...♘c6 5. ♘f3 ♕b6 6. ♗e2

6. ♗d3?! c×d4! 7. c×d4 ♗d7 8. ♗c2 ♘b4 9. 0–0 ♘×c2 10. ♕×c2 ♘e7 11. ♘c3 ♖c8 12. ♗e3, and now instead of 12...♘c6?! (Steinitz–Burn, Vienna 1898) 12...♘f5∓ would have been stronger.

6...c×d4

A later game by Steinitz went: 6...♗d7 7. 0–0 ♖c8 8. b3 (Here White could have gained an edge with 8. d×c5 ♗×c5 9. b4 but, having neglected this possibility, for the entire game he had to struggle for equality.) 8...c×d4 9. c×d4 ♘ge7 10. ♘a3 ♘f5 11. ♘c2 ♘b4 12. ♘e3 ♘×e3 13. f×e3 ♗e7 14. ♘e1 0–0 15. a3 ♘c6 16. b4 f6 17. e×f6 ♗×f6∓ (Steinitz–Showalter, London 1899).

7. c×d4 ♘h6 8. ♘c3 ♘f5 9. ♘a4 ♕a5+ 10. ♔f1 ♗d7 11. ♗d2 ♕d8 12. ♗e1 ♖c8 13. ♖c1 ♘h4 14. ♘c3 ♘×f3 15. ♗×f3 ♕b6 16. ♘a4 ♕d8∓ (16...♕×d4? 17. ♖×c6±) **17. h4**

(see next diagram)

17...♘×e5!∓ 18. ♖×c8 ♕×c8 19. ♗e2 ♘c4 20. b3 ♗×a4 21. b×a4 ♗e7.

White's position is lost, but Steinitz managed to save it. As we can see, the first World Champion had more pain than pleasure with this variation.

The picture presented by Nimzowitsch is quite different. He further developed Paulsen's and Steinitz's idea of giving up the pawn centre d4/e5 after 3. e5 c5 4. d×c5 with the aim of occupying (blockading) the central squares with his pieces. Thanks to Nimzowitsch the 3. e5 system rose considerably in popularity.

His games against Salwe and Levenfish at the tournament in Carlsbad 1911 are well known; they have become cornerstones of the theory of blockade. They can be found in the chapter on blockade later in this volume. And now I should like to bring to your attention another game from the same tournament, a game in which Nimzowitsch had to solve difficult problems. This was a confrontation between two of the greatest openings experts of the early twentieth century. Rubinstein was at the height of his powers, whilst Nimzowitsch was still gaining experience and was not yet as strong in the opening as his redoubtable opponent. This was one of the rare occasions when Nimzowitsch lost the battle of the opening.

Game 6
Nimzowitsch – Rubinstein
Carlsbad 1911

1. e4 e6 2. d4 d5 3. e5 c5 4. c3 ♘c6 5. ♘f3 ♕b6 6. ♗d3?!

Nimzowitsch was experimenting creatively. Modern theory frowns on this move and prefers 6. a3!? or 6. ♗e2.

6...c×d4!

Black is familiar with the subtleties of this system; weaker is 6...♗d7?! 7. d×c5 ♗×c5 8. 0–0 ±.

7. c×d4 ♗d7! 8. ♗e2

Nimzowitsch decides against sacrificing a pawn with 8. ♘c3!? ♘×d4. Modern theory agrees with this decision. Now we have a well-known position with White a tempo down, since he could have played 6. ♗e2.

8...♘ge7 9. b3 ♘f5 10. ♗b2 ♗b4+ 11. ♔f1 h5

Rubinstein has played the opening well and has a slight advantage.

12. g3 ♖c8 13. ♔g2 g6?!

Black could have played more actively with 13...h4!? ↑.

14. h3 ♗e7 15. ♕d2 a5

15...♗f8!? was also interesting: 16. g4 h×g4 17. h×g4 ♖×h1 18. ♔×h1 ♗h6 19. ♕d1 (19. ♕d3 ♘b4 20. ♕d1 ♖c2 ∓) 19...♘fe7 ⇄.

16. ♖c1

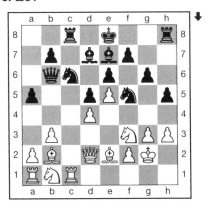

16...♗f8!

Rubinstein makes the right decision and brings the bishop to h6 to exploit the vulnerable white heavy pieces on the c1–h6 diagonal.

17. ♕d1 ♗h6 18. ♖c3 0–0?!

Black should have considered the more active 18...g5!? with the possible continuation 19. g4 h×g4 20. h×g4 ♘h4+ (20...♘fe7 21. ♘a3 ♘g6 22. ♘b5) 21. ♘×h4 g×h4 22. ♘a3 ♘e7 23. ♖×c8+ ♘×c8 ⇄. Rubinstein decided simply to complete his development, after which Nimzowitsch outplayed his adversary. Yet at this time Rubinstein was one of the best players in the world!

19. g4 ♘fe7

White is not threatening to capture on h5, since then the e7 knight could return to f5.

20. ♘a3 ⇄ ♘b4 21. ♘c2 ♖×c3 22. ♗×c3 ♘×c2 23. ♕×c2 ♖c8

Black has seized control of the c-file but he lacks an entry square.

24. ♕b2

24. g5 ♗f8 25. ♕d2 ♘c6 =.

24...♗b5 25. ♗×b5 ♕×b5 26. ♗d2 ♗f8 27. ♖c1 = h×g4 28. h×g4 ♖c6 29. ♕a3!? ♖×c1 (29...♘c8!? 30. ♕b2 ♘e7 ⇄) 30. ♕×c1 ♘c6 31. ♗h6 ♗e7 32. ♗g5 ♕e2

It would have been better to withdraw the bishop to f8; then White could not really hope for more than a draw.

33. ♗×e7 ♘×e7 34. ♕f4± ♕e4?!

Rubinstein commits an error: the queen exchange creates a weakness on e4, and leaves Black with a difficult knight ending. The correct continuation was 34...♘c6! 35. ♘g5 ♘d8 36. ♕f3 ♕×f3+ 37. ♔×f3 ±.

35. ♕×e4 d×e4 36. ♘d2 ♘c6 37. ♘×e4 ♘×d4 38. f4

38. ♘d6!? b5 39. f4 g5! 40. f×g5 ♔g7 41. ♔g3 ♔g6 42. ♔f4 ♘e2+ =.

38...b5?!

38...♘e2!? 39. ♔f3 ♘c1 40. ♘c3 g5!?
41. f×g5 ♘d3 42. ♔e4 ♘f2+ 43. ♔d4 ♘×g4±.

39. ♔f2± a4 40. b×a4 b×a4 41. ♘c3?!

Nimzowitsch has outplayed Rubinstein but
this allows counterplay. 41. ♔e3±, was correct, e. g. 41...♘c2+ 42. ♔d2 ♘b4 43. ♘f6+
(43. a3 ♘d5 44. ♘f6+ ♔×f6 45. e×f6 g5⇄)
43...♔g7 44. a3 ♘c6 45. g5 ♘d4 46. ♔c3
♘e2+ 47. ♔b4 ♘×f4 48. ♔×a4 ♔f8 49. ♔b5
♔e7 50. a4 ♔d8 51. a5 ♔c8 52. ♘e8+−.

41...g5!

The only way to create counterplay. Instead
41...a3 would have lost: 42. ♔e3 ♘c2+
43. ♔d2 ♘b4 44. g5 ♔f8 45. ♔e3 ♔e7
46. ♔d4 ♘c2+ 47. ♔c4 ♘e1 48. ♘e2 ♔d7
49. ♔b4 ♔c6 50. ♔×a3 ♔d5 51. ♔b4 ♔e4
52. a4+−.

42. ♔e3

Also good was 42. ♘×a4 g×f4 43. ♘c5 ♔g7
44. ♘d3 f6 45. e×f6+ ♔×f6 46. ♘×f4 ♔g5
47. ♔g3 e5 48. ♘h3+±.

**42...♘c2+ 43. ♔d3 ♘b4+ 44. ♔c4 ♘×a2
45. ♘×a2 g×f4 46. ♘c3**

But not 46. ♔d4 because of 46...♔g7
47. ♔e4 f6 48. e×f6+ ♔×f6 49. ♔×f4 e5+
50. ♔f3 a3=.

46...♔g7

If 46...a3 47. ♔b3!+− (47. ♔d3 ♔g7 48. ♔e4
f6 49. e×f6+ ♔×f6 50. ♔×f4 e5+=) 47...♔g7
48. ♘e4 f3 49. ♔×a3 ♔g6 50. ♔b4+−.

**47. ♘e4 ♔g6 48. ♔b4 f3 49. ♔×a4 f2
50. ♘×f2 ♔g5 51. ♘d3??**

This lets the victory slip. Instead White could
have won with 51. ♔b4 ♔f4 52. ♘d3+
♔×g4 (52...♔e4 53. ♔c4+−) 53. ♘c5 ♔f5
54. ♘d7+− f6 55. e×f6 ♔g6 56. ♔c5 ♔f7
57. ♔d6+−. It must be said that Nimzowitsch's results would have been much better if he had not slipped up like this on a fairly
regular basis.

**51...f6!= 52. e×f6 ♔×f6 53. ♘f2 ♔g5
54. ♔b4 e5 55. ♔c4 e4 Draw.**

Three years later in one of the strongest
tournaments of the early twentieth century
the second world champion Emanuel Lasker
was faced with the 3. e5 system for practically the only time in his long career. Lasker
demonstrated a good method against the
plan of 3. e5 c5 4. d×c5.

Game 7
Tarrasch – Lasker
St. Petersburg 1914

1. e4 e6 2. d4 d5 3. e5 c5 4. d×c5

Tarrasch was often considered to be a disci-
ple of Steinitz, a populariser of his ideas. Perhaps Tarrasch chose 4. d×c5 because Steinitz had played it. However, as we know, the
real inventor of this plan was Louis Paulsen!
Incidentally, Steinitz often highlighted the importance of Paulsen's ideas in the opening
and said that he (Steinitz) and his contemporaries had learnt a lot from Paulsen. From
the modern point of view, 4. d×c5 is prema-
ture, since it considerably simplifies Black's
development problems.

4...♘c6 5. ♘f3 ♗×c5 6. ♗d3 f5!?

This interesting continuation reduces White's
attacking chances on the kingside. On the
other hand it permanently weakens the e6
pawn. Now even losing the e5 pawn would
not be so tragic for White.

7. c3 a6

Prophylaxis: Lasker hinders the manoeuvre
b4–b5 and creates a haven for the bishop on
a7.

**8. ♘bd2 ♘ge7 9. ♘b3 ♗a7 10. 0–0 0–0
11. ♖e1 ♘g6⇄**

(see next diagram)

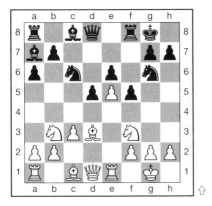

Both sides have made very natural moves and a position offering chances to both sides has arisen. White must now concern himself with the safety of his e5 pawn. Black has solved his opening problems, so Lasker's plan deserves attention.

12. ♘bd4 ♗b8 13. ♘×c6 b×c6 14. ♔h1?! (14. b4, 14. c4) **14...a5 15. b3 c5 16. ♗a3 ♛b6 17. ♕d2 ♗b7 18. ♕g5 ♗a7 19. h4 ♕d8 20. ♕g3 ♕e8 21. ♘h2?!** (21. ♘g5↑) **21...♘e7 22. f4 ♖c8 23. ♘f3 ♔h8 24. ♘g5 ♘g8 25. ♗e2 ♕e7 26. ♖ad1 ♖df8 27. ♖d2 ♘h6 28. ♖ed1 ♕e8 29. ♔h2 ♖c7 30. ♔h3 ♖dc8 31. ♗b2 ♗c6 32. ♗f3 ♖b8 33. ♗a3 ♘g8 34. ♗e2 ♘h6 35. ♕e1 ♖d8 36. ♕g3 ♖b8 37. ♕e1 ♖d8 38. ♕g3 ♖b8 39. ♕e1 ♖d8 Draw.**

The 3. e5 system has appeared in the games of other world champions. On the white side we find Capablanca, Smyslov, Tal and Kasparov; for Black – Botvinnik and Petrosian; Alekhine, Euwe and Spassky played it with both colours. You will find examples of their skill in Volume 2 in the chapter "Theoretically important games for independent analysis". As we can see, the variation's history goes back more than a century and the names of the players mentioned above testify to its quality. Nevertheless the world champions played it only sporadically and thus their role in developing its theory was limited.

A huge number of ideas, some of which we are already familiar with, stem from Aaron Nimzowitsch. He worked on the variations 3...c5 4. c3 ♘c6 5. ♘f3 ♕b6 6. ♗e2 and 6. ♗d3 and also invented the gambit 1. e4 e6 2. d4 d5 3. e5 c5 4. ♘f3 ♕b6 (4...♘c6) 5. ♗d3 c×d4, introduced in the game Nimzowitsch-Leonhardt, San Sebastian 1912 (game 35 on page 68). This gambit was played by such well-known theoreticians as Rauzer, Alekhine, Levenfish, Keres, Bondarevsky and Pachman – surely an impressive list! That is why in the near future it can be expected that this sharp variation will once more attract the attention of chess players.

I consider the Soviet master Vsevolod Rauzer to be a real chess scientist. He was well versed in the principles of opening play and generally handled the openings superbly. It is sufficient to recall his attack against the Sicilian Defence and his deep manoeuvres in the Ruy Lopez. Today's players still use these ideas of his, which no computer can refute. His ideas have become pure chess science, classical models which are incapable of improvement. However, this cannot be said about the following game, which was simply an interesting experiment.

Game 8
Rauzer – Grigoriev
Odessa 1929

1. d4 e6 2. e4 d5 3. e5 c5 4. ♘f3 ♘c6 5. ♗d3!? c×d4

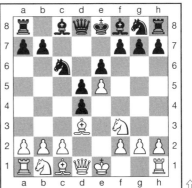

Nimzowitsch employed this gambit four times, scoring four wins! The sacrifice brought Paul Keres five wins, and only a single loss against Euwe. I think this gambit could be named after Keres, who played it about ten times.

6. 0–0 f6

A logical move – Black immediately attacks the white centre. It is also possible to play 6...♘ge7 7. ♖e1 ♘g6 8. ♘bd2 (or 8. a3 ♗e7 9. ♘bd2 0–0 10. ♘b3 f5⇄) 8...♗e7 9. ♘b3 0–0 10. ♘b×d4 ♗d7⇄.

7. ♕e2 f×e5 (7...♕c7!?) 8. ♘×e5 ♘f6 9. ♗g5

White's free development looks very attractive, but his priority should have been to hold the e5 square. However, the alternatives also seem to give Black the edge: 9. ♗f4 ♗d6 10. ♘d2 0–0 11. ♖ae1 ♕c7, 9. ♗b5 ♕c7 10. c3 d3!, 9. ♘d2 ♘×e5 10. ♕×e5 ♗d6 11. ♕×d4 e5. Thus instead of 7. ♕e2 it would have been better to play 7. ♗b5!?, as Alekhine did against Euwe in the next game.

9...♗d6?

Now White establishes firm control of e5 and gains a clear advantage. Instead 9...♘×e5! 10. ♕×e5 ♗d6! 11. ♕×d4 (11. ♗b5+? ♔f7∓) 11...0–0 12. ♘d2 ♕c7 13. ♕h4 h6∓) would have left him fighting for equality.

10. f4 0–0 11. ♘d2 ♕c7 12. ♖ae1± ♗b4 (12...♕b6) 13. a3 ♗×d2 14. ♕×d2 ♗d7 15. ♕f2

15. ♘×d7 ♕×d7 16. b4⊞.

15...♖ae8?

(see next diagram)

Correct was 15...♘×e5 16. ♖×e5 (16. f×e5? ♘e4 17. ♕h4 ♖×f1+ 18. ♖×f1 ♕×e5∓) 16...♕b6 17. ♕h4 ♘e4⇄. Now White launches a decisive attack.

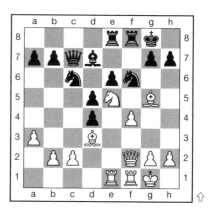

16. ♗×f6 ♖×f6 17. ♘g4! ♖ff8 18. ♕h4+– h6 19. ♖f3 ♖e7 20. ♘×h6+ g×h6 21. ♖g3+ ♖g7 22. ♕×h6 ♖ff7 23. ♕h7+ ♔f8 24. ♕h8+ ♔e7 25. ♖×g7 ♕×f4 26. ♖f1 ♕e3+ 27. ♔h1 ♖×g7 28. ♕f8#.

It is well known that Alexander Alekhine attentively studied Soviet chess books and magazines and he was surely familiar with Rauzer's game. But despite White's impressive victory in the above game, the fourth world champion preferred another plan at an early stage.

Game 9
Alekhine – Euwe
Nottingham 1936

1. e4 e6 2. d4 d5 3. e5 c5 4. ♘f3 ♘c6 5. ♗d3 c×d4 6. 0–0 f6 7. ♗b5!?

Immediately fighting for the e5 square.

7...♗d7 8. ♗×c6 b×c6

It would have been bad to recapture with the bishop 8...♗×c6 in view of 9. ♘×d4 f×e5? (9...♗d7±) 10. ♕h5+ g6 11. ♕×e5+–.

9. ♕×d4

9. ♘×d4 c5∓.

9...f×e5 10. ♕×e5 ♘f6

10...♕b8 11. ♗f4±.

11. ♗f4 ♗c5 12. ♘c3

The knight is going to fight for control of the c5 square, but 12. ♘bd2 looks more logical.

12...0–0 13. ♗g3 ♕e7

The manoeuvre 13...♘g4!? 14. ♕e2 e5!? ⇄ deserved consideration, as did the idea of deploying the queen on the light squares with 13...♕e8⇄.

14. a3 a5 15. ♖fe1 ♖a7?

This seems unnatural; 15...♘g4 16. ♕e2 ♖f5 was better.

16. ♘a4 ♖b7 17. ♕c3 ♗a7 18. ♕×a5 ♘e4

Black has definite compensation for the pawn. Also interesting was 18...♖a8⊞.

**19. ♕a6 ♗e8 20. b4 g5 (20...♗h5!? ⊞)
21. ♘c5 ♗×c5 22. b×c5 ♘×c5 23. ♕e2
♘e4 24. ♕e3 ♗g6 25. ♘e5**

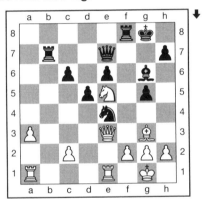

In this game Alekhine teetered on the edge of the precipice but it all worked out for him. He returned the pawn in order to control the dark squares and gain a slight advantage. Euwe never managed to make use of the active position of his pieces.

**25...c5 26. ♘×g6 h×g6 27. f3 ♘×g3
28. h×g3 ♔f7 29. a4 ...**

... and White won on the 81st move.

These games show that White cannot count on an advantage from the gambit. Alekhine's play is obviously sufficient for equality, but Rauzer's plan not even that. It is interesting that databases show White scoring about 60% with this gambit, compared with a 50% score for the 3. e5 system as a whole. These statistics indicate that you should include this gambit in your repertoire for practical reasons rather than for its objective strength.

Another interesting idea of Nimzowitsch's involves the early development of the queen: 1. e4 e6 2. d4 d5 3. e5 c5 4. ♕g4!?. The exclamation mark is for the originality of the idea, the question mark for its objective value. This line is examined in more detail in Volume 2 in the annotations to the game Sveshnikov – Komarov, Vrnjačka Banja 1999 (game 28 on page 57). We should acknowledge Nimzowitsch's analytical work and his efforts to promote the 3. e5 variation among other chess players. You can learn more about this in the chapter "The many facets of the blockade".

After Nimzowitsch's death the move 3. e5 was forgotten for a long time and appeared only sporadically. It was only in the 1960s–1970s that the future grandmasters Igor Zaitsev and Victor Kupreichik enriched this ancient variation with new ideas.

Game 10
Kupreichik – Korchnoi
Sochi 1970

1. e4 e6 2. d4 d5 3. e5 b6

This move, also used by Petrosian, is rather passive.

4. c3 ♕d7 5. a4 a5 6. f4?!

In my opinion the diagonal c1–h6 should be kept open for the bishop. I prefer the simple 6. ♘f3.

6...♘e7 7. ♘d2

I also dislike this move, since the knight has the excellent square a3. Thus 7. ♘f3 should be played. But Kupreichik would like to deploy this knight on the kingside.

**7...h5 8. ♘df3 ♗a6 9. ♗×a6 ♘×a6
10. ♗e3 ♘f5 11. ♗f2 ♗e7 =**

I assess this position as roughly equal, since Black has no weakness. His plan is simple: play g7–g6 and ♔f8–g7. In this situation White should become active on the queenside, but he has withdrawn his pieces from that sector.

12. ♘e2 h4 13. 0–0 0–0–0?

But this is going too far! Obviously we can understand Korchnoi's desire to play for a win against his young opponent (this was a training tournament for masters against grandmasters), but queenside castling is too risky. What's more, it seems that Korchnoi was unaware that he was up against an outstanding attacking player! As I mentioned earlier, the correct plan consisted of transferring the king to g7. Hence the move 12…h4 was also questionable.

14. ♕d2 (14. b4!?) **14…♖dg8 15. ♖fb1 ♘b8 16. b4**

Kupreichik is in his element!

16…♘c6 17. ♘c1 g5 18. f×g5 ♖g7

18…♕d8 19. b×a5 ♘×a5 20. ♘b3 ♗×g5 21. ♕d3±.

19. ♕d3 a×b4

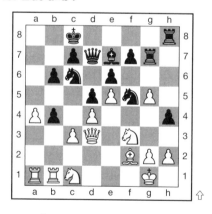

20. a5 ♔b8 21. a×b6+– c×b6 22. ♖a6 ♕b7 23. ♖ba1 b×c3 24. ♕×c3 ♗b4 25. ♕d3 ♗a5 26. ♕b5 ♘b4 27. ♖1×a5

Black resigned. White conducted the attack brilliantly, giving his opponent no chance.

Game 11
I. Zaitsev – Pokojowczyk
Sochi 1976

I witnessed this game and I must say it made a great impression on me. I used the same system myself on various occasions but I never managed to win as convincingly as this.

1. e4 e6 2. d4 d5 3. e5 c5 4. c3 ♘c6 5. ♘f3 ♕b6 6. a3 c4 7. ♘bd2 ♘a5 8. g3 ♗d7 9. ♗h3!?

Igor Zaitsev's move. It is directed against the …f6 break. Another idea is to leave the g2 square free for the knight transfer ♘f3–h4–g2–e3.

9…f6?!

Black goes along with his opponent. Stronger was 9…0–0–0 10. 0–0 h6 11. ♘h4 g5 12. ♘g2 h5⇄.

10. e×f6! g×f6 11. 0–0 0–0–0 12. ♖e1 ♗g7

Instead 12…♖e8 13. ♖b1 ♕c7 14. b3 c×b3 15. ♘×b3 ♘c4 (15…♗a4 16. ♖×e6+–) 16. ♗f4± was also insufficient for equality. Black could have considered 12…♘e7!? to bring the knight into play.

13. ♖b1 ♔b8

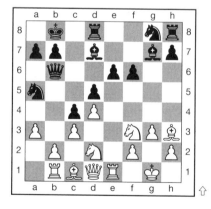

14. b4!±

With this typical advance White begins to harvest his advantage.

14…c×b3 15. ♘×b3 ♘×b3

Or 15...♗a4 16. ♖xe6 ♗xb3 17. ♕e2 ♘c6 18. ♗f4+ ♔a8 19. ♘d2+−.

16. ♖xb3 ♗a4 17. ♖xb6 ♗xd1 18. ♖bxe6+− ♗xf3 19. ♗f4+ ♔a8 20. ♗c7 ♘h6 21. ♗xd8 ♖xd8 22. ♖e8

Black resigned.

* * *

I recommend that anyone who wishes to learn to play the 3. e5 system for White should make a detailed study of the games of Kupreichik and Zaitsev! The endeavours of these two players were supplemented by those of Sveshnikov, Malaniuk, Romanishin, Sax and others. Yet for a long time Black did not take the move 3. e5 seriously, because it was not used by the elite. This situation persisted until the end of the 1980s, when I chalked up no less than ten victories with it against grandmasters. A systematic theory of 3. e5 began to be developed, and today it is no longer a simple variation but a complete system, one in which Black is finding ever more difficult problems in obtaining an equal game.

As we discussed earlier, in recent years Black has been safely solving his problems against 3. ♘d2?! with 3...c5, while after 3. ♘c3! White has to be prepared to face long forcing variations arising after 3...♗b4 4. e5 c5, 3...♘f6 or 3...dxe4!?. And although White can retain the advantage in all these lines, it is not so easy to covert this into a win. This is perhaps the reason why in recent years the move 3. e5 has grown sharply in popularity among the chess elite as well as among amateur players. In this line Black has fewer possibilities for counterplay.

These are the most important plans for Black:

1) Exchange of the light-squared bishops by 3...b6 or 3...♘e7 and 4...b6, or by the manoeuvre 3...c5, 4...♕b6, 5...♗d7 followed by ♗b5.

2) Counter-attack on the d4 pawn by c5, ♕b6, ♘c6, followed by ♘ge7–f5 or ♘h6–f5.

3) Counter-attack on the white centre by 3...c5 4. c3 ♘c6 5. ♘f3 f6!?.

4) The flexible system (according to Botvinnik) 3...c5 4. c3 ♘c6 5. ♘f3 ♗d7!? 6. ♗e2, and then

a) 6...♘ge7 (or even 6...♖c8) followed by ♘f5 or ♘g6. Or

b) 6...f6!? attacking the e5 pawn.

But after 5...♗d7!? Black must also be prepared for 6. dxc5?!, 6. ♗e3!? (Paulsen, Kupreichik), 6. ♘a3 and especially 6. ♗e2!, after which he can gain nothing from an attack on the d4 pawn and must switch to an attack on e5 with f7–f6.

In any case the position after 3. e5 is objectively favourable for White – his advantage is not smaller than in the initial position.

According to my records, I have played the 3. e5 system in more than 150 (!) games as White, with a score of more than 70%. Among players of the young generation, Alexander Grischuk stands out as having scored a number of wins against grandmasters with 3. e5. Peter Svidler, Alexey Shirov and Alexander Motylev also play this system regularly and successfully.

For many years the chief expert on the black side was Wolfgang Uhlmann. Victor Korchnoi (who has also started playing this with White), Boris Gulko, Yuri Razuvaev, Artur Yusupov, Alexander Chernin, Mikhail Gurevich, Smbat Lputian, Igor Glek and Sergey Volkov have fought and continue to fight successfully against the 3. e5 variation. In *ChessBase* Lev Psakhis is the specialist commentator on this system.

Nowadays Black has considerable problems in this opening; hence I would recommend playing the Paulsen-Nimzowitsch-system 1. e4 e6 2. d4 d5 3. e5!? as White, not only to those starting on their study of chess theory but also to experienced players. To anyone who studies this book carefully I promise an improvement in playing strength in this system of roughly 200 Elo points. I wish you great success!

Chapter 2

The plans for each side, linked to the pawn structure

As I have already remarked in the introduction, it is best to illustrate a new scheme with the help of a good selection of well annotated games. Just presenting a single game, won convincingly by using a particular scheme, can make an impression but is not completely convincing. It is only when you demonstrate two or three games played following the same standard pattern that young chess players begin to understand that there are certain laws which cannot be broken.

In contemporary chess it is very difficult to win a game simply by carrying out a single plan, even if it is implemented energetically and consistently. Usually you have to vary the ideas according to the countermeasures employed by the opponent. Hence the following list of plans for each side is offered with the caveat that it should only be thought of as a rough guide. The list consists of plans which, in this or that game, might have played an overwhelming role whilst other ideas remained in the background. Furthermore, the plans for each side are directly linked with pawn structure and piece activity.

Plans for White:

1) Attack on the king making use of the space advantage on the kingside and a lead in development.

2) Use of the space advantage to cramp the opponent as much as possible and to force a transition to an advantageous endgame.

3) Release of the tension in the centre (d×c5, e×f6) followed by a blockade on the squares d4 and e5.

4) Exchange of dark-squared bishops, followed by exploitation of the weakened dark squares.

5) Play on both wings.

6) If Black forms a locked pawn chain with c5–c4 then White prepares to undermine it with b3 and c4 (after b×c4) and (or) carries out a typical piece sacrifice on c4, d5, f5, e6, or g6.

Counterplay for Black:

1) Pressure on the d4 pawn.

2) Exchange of light-squared bishops by means of ♗d7–b5 or b6 and ♗a6.

3) The undermining of the e5 pawn by means of f7–f6.

4) Attack on the queenside by b5, a5, b4 plus counterplay along the c-file.

5) Counterplay on the kingside linked to g7–g5 and pressure on the f-file (a rare plan).

To be able to present the material more conveniently we have divided the games into four large groups:

1) Attacking the king.

2) Advantage in space and (or) development, the sacrifice of a pawn for space, and standard endgames.

3) "For" and "against" the blockade, weakness of one or other colour complex.

4) Play on both wings.

As the author plays this system mainly with the white pieces and considers that it gives White the advantage, the division into themes is carried out mainly from the point of view of White's play. Black appears in the role merely of an opponent but his plans and counterplay are nevertheless examined in some depth. The heading of each game shows the idea, or ideas, which played a dominant role in the game.

2.1 Attack on the king

As a rule, the prerequisites for an attack are a lead in development and a space advantage. In our case, however, one other peculiarity of the position is present – the white pawn on e5. This pawn denies Black's pieces the use of the very important f6 square, which makes it more difficult for him to protect his king, especially if it takes up residence on the kingside. Alekhine was absolutely right when he noted that the white pawn on e5 is the signal for an attack on the enemy king. This is characteristic not just of the French with 3. e5, but also of the Sicilian with 2. c3, for instance, and of many other openings.

An attack by White on the queenside relies above all on having a lead in development. This plan, as we have already said, is one of the most important in White's arsenal.

In the first chapter we saw several nice attacks by White, in the games Greco – N. N., 1620 (game 1 on page 12), Paulsen – Schwarz, Leipzig 1879 (game 2 on page 13) and Kupreichik – Korchnoi, Sochi 1970 (game 10 on page 21). We shall now move on to some other examples.

Attack on the king

Game 12
Sveshnikov – Faragó
Hastings 1984/85

A model game, the theme of which is the attack on the king and play against the knight on f5.

1. e4 e6 2. d4 d5 3. e5 c5 4. c3 ♘c6 5. ♘f3 ♘ge7 6. ♘a3 cxd4 7. cxd4 ♘f5 8. ♘c2 ♗e7?

This is a mistake; correct is 8...♘b4 9. ♗d2±. Now my bishop arrives at d3 in a single move.

9. ♗d3 0–0

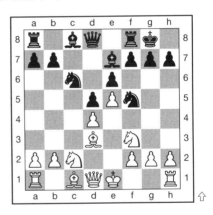

What are the prerequisites of White's attack? As usual, he has an advantage in space, but there is no lead in development. However, both white bishops are aiming at the enemy king and the f5 knight is not secure. After White's next move, play becomes forced.

10. g4! ♘h4

In the case of 10...♘h6 the simple capture 11. ♗xh6 is possible, as well as the preliminary 11. ♖g1!, after which the move f7–f5 is not possible, because after White captures on f6 all Black recaptures lose material. The knight is therefore stranded on h6.

11. ♘xh4 ♗xh4 12. g5!

Now it is the bishop that finds itself in an awkward situation. Black must capture the g5 pawn, which will involve opening the g-file and coming under a strong attack.

12...♗xg5 13. ♕h5 h6 14. ♖g1 ♗xc1 15. ♖xc1 f5

Again the only move. If 15...♔h8?!, then 16. ♔e2+−.

16. ♕xh6 ♖f7 17. ♔e2! ♕b6 18. ♕h4 ♗d7

18...♕xb2?! loses to 19. ♖b1 ♕xa2 20. ♖a1 ♕b2 21. ♖gb1 ♕c3 22. ♖a3 ♘xd4+ 23. ♕xd4 ♕xd4 24. ♘xd4+−.

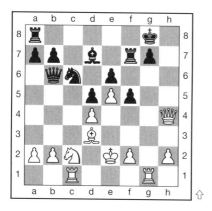

19. ♖g5 ♕xb2 20. ♔d2?!

An inaccuracy which nevertheless does not let Black off the hook. More precise is 20. ♖h5! ♘xd4+ 21. ♔d1!+− ♖ff8 22. ♕xd4+−.

20...♘e7

20...♖e7 21. ♖cg1+−.

21. ♖h5 ♘g6 22. ♕g3 ♘f8 23. ♕h3 ♖e7 24. ♖h8+ ♔f7 25. ♖g1 ♗a4 26. ♕h5+ g6 27. ♖xg6

Black resigned. In many variations the insecure position of the knight on f5 is the precondition for active play by White on the kingside.

Attack on the king

Game 13
Sveshnikov – Gulko
52nd USSR Championship, Riga 1985
It should be said that Boris Gulko was one of my main adversaries in the French Defence with 3. e5. It is true that this was in the 70s and early 80s, when I had only just begun to play this system. I should add that even today Boris Frantsevich is one of the main specialists in this variation for Black. He was one of the first to suggest interesting ways for Black to play, and more than one generation of chess players has learnt from his games. Nor must we forget the contribution towards the theory of this variation by his friend Boris Zlotnik, a master and distinguished trainer who, in the mid-80s, wrote an important theoretical article on the French with 3. e5.

1. e4 e6 2. d4 d5 3. e5 c5 4. c3 ♘c6 5. ♘f3 ♗d7 6. ♗e2
Here 6. a3!? is interesting. The game Sveshnikov – Chernin, Riga 1985, continued 6...♖c8 7. ♗d3 cxd4 8. cxd4 ♕b6 9. ♗c2 g5!? 10. h3 ♘xd4!? 11. ♘xd4 ♗c5 12. ♘e2 ♗xf2+ 13. ♔f1 f6 14. ♗a4 fxe5, and here 15. ♘bc3! (instead of 15. ♗xd7+?) would have cast doubt on the correctness of the piece sacrifice (exercise 59 on page 144).

6...♘ge7 7. ♘a3 cxd4
In our previous meeting (Tashkent 1985) Gulko responded with 7...♘g6 and after 8. h4 cxd4 9. cxd4 ♗b4+ 10. ♔f1 h6 11. h5 ♘f8 White had the better chances.

8. cxd4 ♘f5 9. 0–0!?
Here 9. ♘c2 ♗b4 10. ♘e3 ♘xe3 11. fxe3 ♗e7 12. a3 ♘c6 13. b4 a6 14. ♖b1 ♘a7 15. a4 ♘c6!? 16. ♗d2 a5 17. b5 ♘b4 leads to approximate equality.

9...♕b6
Here 9...♗xa3 10. bxa3 ♕b6 11. ♗e3 0–0 deserves attention. Saddling White with doubled pawns on the a-file might have enabled Black to show the downside of White's ninth

move. This happened in the game Sveshnikov – Luther (Nova Gorica 2000) – see Volume 2, game 38 on page 33.

10. ♘c2 a5

Black takes control of the b4 square and seeks an exchange of light-squared bishops my means of the manoeuvre ♘a7, ♗b5. However, this involves a considerable loss of time and besides, on 11...♘a7 12. a4! is possible, preventing Black from carrying out his plan. Both 10...♖c8 11. g4 ♘fe7 and 10...♘a5 should be considered, e. g. 11. g4 [11. ♘e3 ♘xe3 (11...♘e7 12. b3 ♗b5 13. ♗a3±) 12. fxe3 ♗e7⇄] 11...♘e7 [11...♘h6 12. b4 ♘c4 (12...♗xb4 13. ♖b1 +−) 13. ♗xh6 gxh6 14. ♗xc4 dxc4 15. ♘d2±; 12. ♗xh6 gxh6 13. b4 ♘c6 (13...♘c4±) 14. b5 ♘a5⇄] 12. ♘fe1 ♗b5 13. ♘d3 h5 14. gxh5 ♘f5 15. ♗e3 ♖c8 (15...♘c4 16. a4 ♘cxe3 17. fxe3 ♗c4 18. ♘f4∞, Sveshnikov – Dolmatov, Naberezhnye Chelny 1988) 16. b4 ♘c6 17. a4 ♗c4 18. ♖b1 ♕d8 19. ♘f4 ♗xe2 20. ♕xe2 ♕h4 21. h3 with complex play (Sveshnikov – Kiriakov, Elista 1994, Volume 2, game 52 on page 45).

11. g4 ♘fe7 12. ♘h4

Also possible was 12. ♘fe1, and on 12...h5 (after 12...♘g6 13. f4 ♗e7 14. ♗e3 White can, without losing time on 13. ♘g2, prepare the immediate f4–f5 advance) – 13. gxh5 ♘f5 14. ♗e3 and compared with the game Sveshnikov – Skalkotas (Athens 1983) instead of the useful 10...♖c8 Black has played 10...a5.

12...♘g6 13. ♘g2 ♗e7 14. f4 0–0 15. ♗e3 f5

There is no other defence against the threat of 16. f5.

16. exf6

The game would have had a less forcing character after 16. h3, followed by ♖b1 and ♗d3.

16...♖xf6

17. h4

On this occasion White's attack was successful, but on examination of the following games, played by Gulko and myself, it becomes clear that White's position is not really so good.

17. ♗d3 ♗d6 18. h4 ♖af8 19. g5?! ♖6f7 20. ♗xg6 hxg6 21. h5 gxh5 22. ♕xh5 g6! 23. ♕xg6+ ♖g7 24. ♕d3 ♘e7 25. ♕b3 ♕xb3 26. axb3 b6, when Black has good compensation for the sacrificed pawn (Benjamin – Gulko, USA 1992).

17. ♗d3 ♗d6 18. h4 ♖f7 19. h5 ♘ge7 20. ♕e2 ♖af8 and Black has a good position. After 21. ♖ad1 g6 22. h6 ♘b4 23. ♘xb4 axb4 24. b3 ♘c6 25. ♖f2 ♖f6 26. ♕d2 ♕c7 27. ♖df1 ♘a7 28. ♖c1 ♕b8 29. ♕e2 ♕e8 the game Sveshnikov – Mencinger (Finkenstein Open 1994) ended in a draw.

Thus White's attack should not be winning against correct play. However, this game very clearly demonstrates the method of attack. Of course theory continues to develop and I can now say that the variation with 12. ♘h4 with ♘g2 to follow is clearly insufficient for an advantage. Nevertheless White's method is very instructive.

17...♗d6 18. h5 ♘ge7 19. ♗d3 ♖c8 20. ♕e2 ♖ff8

A useful move. Now the advance 21. g5 will not come with tempo.

21. ♘h4 h6

Black tries to bring the game to a crisis: he has no obvious active counterplay, and treading water is not to his taste. After 21...♘b4 22. ♘xb4 ♕xb4 23. ♖ad1 Black will find it difficult to generate threats against d4, for example after 23...♘c6, apart from the calm 24. ♗b1, there could also follow 24. ♗xh7+ ♔xh7 25. ♕d3+ ♔g8 26. h6 with a strong attack.

22. g5 hxg5

22...♘f5 is bad in view of 23. ♗xf5 exf5 24. gxh6 gxh6 25. ♕g2+.

23. fxg5 ♘f5!

24. h6

Of course the prosaic 24. ♘xf5 exf5 is also possible, with somewhat better prospects, but the continuation in the game is very tempting.

24...♘ce7

The best move. It would be dangerous to take the piece, for instance: 24...♘xh4 25. ♕h5! g6 26. ♗xg6 ♘e7 (26...♘f5 27. ♗xf5 ♖xf5 28. ♖xf5 exf5 29. ♕g6 etc.) 27. ♗f7+ ♔h8 28. ♕xh4 ♘f5 29. ♕h5 with a strong attack.

25. ♕h5 ♗g3?

The decisive error. Also bad was 25...♗h2+ 26. ♔xh2 ♖xc2+ 27. ♗xc2 ♕c7+ 28. ♔g1 ♕g3+ 29. ♘g2 and 29...♘xe3 loses to

30. ♗h7+ mating. However, Black has at his disposal an interesting resource 25...♘g3!, the power of which White did not fully appreciate when he played 25. ♕h5. Black apparently rejected 25...♘g3 because of the variation 26. ♖xf8+ ♖xf8 27. ♗h7+ ♔xh7 28. hxg7+ ♘xh5 29. gxf8♕, but in fact he is not forced to capture the queen (with 28...♘xh5) and can instead play 28...♔xg7 with the better prospects. So in this variation White would have to respond with 27. ♕g4 or 27. ♕d1, after which a very sharp position would be reached offering chances for both sides.

The ensuing play is pretty forced.

26. g6! ♗xh4 27. hxg7 ♔xg7 28. ♕h7+ ♔f6 29. ♕xh4+ ♔g7

If 29...♔xg6, then 30. ♕xe7 threatening 31. ♖f2 and ♖g2.

30. ♕h7+ ♔f6 31. ♗h6

Black resigns. A nice finish is possible: 31...e5 32. ♕g7+ ♔e6 33. ♕xe5#.

After the game Mikhail Tal came up to me and said: "What a great attack on the h-file!" I shall remember the praise of that attacking genius for the rest of my days!

The next game shows the dangers that lie in wait for Black's king if he lags behind in development.

Attack on the king

Game 14
Grischuk – Bareev
17th EU Cup, Panormo 2001

1. e4 e6 2. d4 d5 3. e5 c5 4. c3 ♘c6 5. ♘f3 ♘h6

(see next diagram)

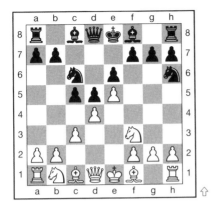

In the event of White capturing on h6, Black is relying on being able to develop quickly with ♗g7, 0–0 and f6, when his bishop pair and active piece play will be compensation for the defects in his kingside pawn structure.

6. ♗d3

Other options are:

6. dxc5 ♗xc5 7. b4 ♗b6 8. b5 ♘e7 9. ♗d3 ♘g4 10. 0–0 ♘g6 11. ♗xg6 fxg6∓, Grischuk – Bareev, Cannes 2001 (Bareev won this game);

6. ♘a3 ♘f5 (6...cxd4 7. cxd4 ♗xa3 8. bxa3 ♘f5 9. ♗d3 ♕a5+ 10. ♗d2 ♕xa3 11. ♕b1 a6 12. 0–0 h6 13. ♖c1 ♕e7 14. ♗xf5 exf5 15. ♕b6 0–0 16. ♖ab1 ⯑, I. Zaitsev – Mesropov, Moscow 1996) 7. ♘c2 ♗d7 8. ♗e2 cxd4 9. cxd4 ♗e7 10.0–0 ♖c8 11. ♔h1 h5 12. a3 ♘a5 13. ♘e3 ♕b6 14. b4 ♘c4 15. ♘xf5 exf5 16. h4 a5⇄, Jonkman – Sadvakasov, Philadelphia 2003;

6. a3 ♘f5 7. b4 cxd4 8. cxd4 ♗e7 9. ♗b2 0–0 10. ♗d3 a6 11. 0–0 f6 12. ♗xf5 exf5 13. ♘c3 f4 14. ♖e1 ♔h8 15. ♕b3 ♗e6 16. ♖e2±, Grischuk – Najer, St. Petersburg 1999.

6...cxd4 7. ♗xh6!?

After the exchange on d4 this move makes more sense, since it is easier for White to play for a lead in development: his knight can come to c3 and his rook to the c-file.

7. cxd4 ♘f5 8. ♗xf5 exf5 9. ♘c3 ♗e6 10. h4 h6 11. h5 ♗e7 12. ♘e2 ♕a5+ 13. ♔f1 ♖c8 14. ♔g1 ♔d7 15. ♘f4 ♖c7 16. ♖h3 ♖hc8 17. ♖g3 ♗f8∞, Khalifman – Akopian, Dortmund 2000.

7...gxh6 (7...dxc3? 8. ♗c1 +–) **8. cxd4 ♗d7**

8...♗g7 9. ♘c3 0–0 10. ♕b1?! (10. 0–0 f6 11. ♖e1 fxe5 12. dxe5±) 10...f5 (10...f6) 11. exf6 ♕xf6 12. ♗xh7+ ♔h8 ⯑.

9. ♘c3 ♕b6 10. ♗b5

10. 0–0!?

A) 10...♕xb2 11. ♘b5 ♖c8 12. ♖b1 (12. a4!?) 12...♕xa2 13. ♖a1 ♕b2 14. ♘xa7 ♘xa7 15. ♖xa7 ♗g7 16. ♕b1 ♕xb1 17. ♖xb1 ♖c3 18. ♗e2 ♗c6 19. h3 ♔d7 20. ♗a6 ♖b8 21. ♗xb7 ♔d8 22. ♔h2±;

B) 10...♘xd4 11. ♘xd4 ♕xd4 12. ♘b5 (12. ♕e2 ⯑) 12...♕b6 13. a4 a6 14. a5 ♕d8 15. ♘d6+ (15. ♘d4 ⯑) 15...♗xd6 16. exd6 ♗c6±.

10...♖g8

The alternative plan of kingside castling would have been more expedient.

11. 0–0

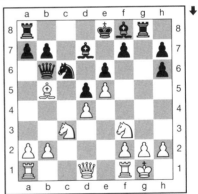

11...♘xe5?!

A very dubious decision: Black opens lines in the centre with his own king still on e8.

12. ♘xe5 ♗xb5 13. ♕h5 ♖g7

13...0–0–0 14. ♘xb5 ♕xb5 15. ♕xf7 +–.

14. ♖fe1↑ ♖d8?

The computer also suggests this suicidal move at first, but quickly spots a decisive combination for White and gives instead the only defence 14...♗e7. But in that case White is still better, e.g. 15. ♕×h6 (15. ♖e3!? Golubev) 15...♔f8

A) 16. ♖ac1?! ♔g8 (16...♗g5 17. ♘g6+ h×g6 18. ♕×g5±) 17. ♘f3 (17. ♘×b5? ♗g5) 17...♗c6 18. ♘e2 ♕×b2∓;

B) 16. ♖e3 ♗g5 (16...♔g8!?) 17. ♘g6+ h×g6 18. ♕×g5±.

15. ♘×b5 ♕×b5

16. ♘×f7! ♖×f7 17. ♖×e6+

Black resigned because if 17...♗e7 18. ♖×e7+! wins: 18...♔×e7 19. ♖e1+ ♔f8 (19...♔d6 20. ♕×f7 ♕d7 21. ♕f6+ ♔c7 22. ♖e7+−) 20. ♕×h6+ ♔g8 21. ♕g5+. Also 18. ♖ae1 ♔f8 (18...♖d7 19. ♖f6+−) 19. ♕×h6+ ♔e8 20. ♕h5 ♔f8 21. ♕e5+− would be good enough.

Attack on the king

Game 15
Motylev – Hort
Essent Open, Hoogeveen 2003

1. e4 e6 2. d4 d5 3. e5 c5 4. c3 ♘c6 5. ♘f3 ♕b6 6. a3 c4 7. ♘bd2 ♗d7?!

This allows the immediate break b2–b3, which favours White with his superior development. Black should be giving priority to developing his kingside, after first pausing to clamp down on White's active play by means of 7...♘a5, e.g. 8. g3 ♗d7 9. h4 ♘e7 10. ♗h3 (10. ♘g5 h6 11. ♘h3 0-0-0 12. ♘f4 ♔b8 13. ♗e2 ♕c7 14. ♔f1 ♘c8 15. ♗h5 g6 16. ♗e2 ♘b6⇄, Ivanchuk – Bareev, Monte Carlo 2003) 10...f5 11. 0-0 h6 12. ♖b1 ♖g8 13. ♗g2 g5 14. h×g5 h×g5 15. b3 c×b3 16. ♘×b3 ♗a4 17. ♘fd2 0-0-0 18. ♕c2 ♕c6 19. ♕d1 ♗×b3 20. ♘×b3. Draw (Potkin – Vysochin, Cappelle la Grande 2004).

8. b3

8. ♗e2 ♘ge7? 9. ♗×c4! ♘g6 10. ♗d3 ♘f4 11. ♗f1 ♖c8 12. g3 ♘g6 13. h4 ♘a5 14. ♗d3 ♗b5 15. ♕e2 ♗×d3 16. ♕×d3 h5 17. 0-0± (Panarin – Nepomniashchy, Vladimir 2002).

8...c×b3 9. ♘×b3 ♘a5 10. ♘×a5 ♕×a5 11. ♗d2 ♘e7

11...♕a4 Sveshnikov – Timman, Tilburg 1992 (game 29 on page 60).

12. ♗d3 ♕c7 13. 0-0 h6

14. ♘h4!?

A novelty: White opens a route for his queen to the kingside, hinders ...♘f5 and clears the way for an advance of his f-pawn. Another good move is 14. ♕e2!?, when Black has serious problems in developing his kingside pieces, e.g. 14...♘c8, and now:

A) 15. c4!? d×c4 (15...♘b6 16. c5±) 16. ♗×c4 ♘b6 17. ♗d3 ♗c6 18. ♖fc1 ♕d7 19. ♗e4 ♘d5 20. ♘e1± ♘e7 21. ♘c2 ♗×e4 22. ♕×e4 ♕d5 (22...♘d5) 23. ♕×d5 ♘×d5 24. ♘e3 ♔d7 (24...♖d8 25. ♘×d5 ♖×d5

26. ♖ab1 b6 27. ♖c8+ ♖d8 28. ♖bc1 ♗e7
29. ♖1c7 ±) 25. ♘xd5 exd5±;

B) 15. ♗e3 ♘b6 16. ♘d2 ♗c6 17. f4 g6
18. ♖fc1 ♕d7 19. a4!? ♘xa4 20. c4 ♘b2
21. cxd5 exd5 22. ♗b1 ♗b5 23. ♕f3⯮, Charbonneau–Bluvshtein, Montréal 2003.

White can also consider 14. ♘e1 ♘c6 15. f4
g6 16. g4 0–0–0 17. f5 gxf5 18. gxf5 exf5
19. ♗xf5 ♗e6 20. ♕h5 ♔b8∞, Vlassov–
Ilyushin, Chigorin Memorial, St. Petersburg
1995.

Even so, the move chosen (14. ♘h4) seems
to me to be too direct; White reveals his hand
too early.

14...g6

14...♘f5? 15. ♘xf5 exf5 16. ♕f3±;

14...♘c6 15. f4 ♗e7 16. ♕g4 (16. ♕h5 ♘a5
17. f5 ♗xh4 18. ♕xh4 ♘b3 19. fxe6 ♗xe6
20. ♗b5+ ♔f8⇄) 16...g6 17. ♘xg6 ♖g8
18. ♕h5 fxg6 19. ♗xg6+ ♔d8 20. f5⯮.

15. g3 ♘c8?!

To be considered was 15...♘f5 16. ♘g2
(After 16. ♘xf5 gxf5 it would be difficult for
White to exploit the weak f6 and h5 squares
without any knights.) 16...h5 17. h4!?±.

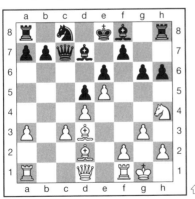

16. ♗xg6!? ♗b5

16...fxg6 17. ♘xg6 ♖g8 18. ♕h5 ♔d8
19. ♘xf8 ♖xf8 20. ♕xh6±.

17. ♕g4

17. ♖e1 fxg6 18. ♘xg6 ♖g8 19. ♘xf8
(19. ♕h5? ♕f7) 19...♖xf8 20. ♗xh6 ♖f5±.

17...fxg6

17...♖g8? 18. ♕xe6+.

18. ♘xg6

Another strong idea would be 18. c4!? ♗xc4
19. ♘xg6 ♕g7 20. ♕xe6+ ♘e7 21. ♘xh8
♗xf1 22. ♖xf1 ♕xh8 23. ♖b1↑.

18...♗xf1

18...♖h7 19. ♕xe6+±.

19. ♕xe6+ ♘e7

19...♔d8 20. ♕f6++−; 19...♗e7 20. ♔xf1
♖f8 21. ♘xf8+−.

20. ♘xh8 ♗d3 21. ♘f7

21. ♕f7+ ♔d7⇄.

21...♕d7 22. ♘d6+ ♔d8 23. ♕f6 ♔c7 24. ♕f3!

Taking aim at the weak point in the black
camp – the b7 square. White has three
pawns and a strong attack for the piece, so
it is not surprising that he ends up the victor.

24...♗a6

24...♗b5 25. c4! ♗xc4? 26. ♘xc4 dxc4
27. ♗a5++−.

25. ♖b1 ♕e6?!

(see next diagram)

Black could have set White more difficult
problems with 25...♕a4!?, after which it
would not have been easy to choose the right
path. The line 26. ♗f4!? ♕c2 27. ♖e1 (27. ♖c1
♕e2) 27...♕d3 28. ♕g4∞ would be unclear,
as would 26. c4 ♕c2 27. ♖d1 dxc4 28. ♗a5+
b6 29. ♖e1 (29. ♕xa8 ♕xd1+ 30. ♔g2
♘c8!−+) 29...♖d8 30. ♗b4∞. The only way is
with 26. ♕f6! ♕c2 27. ♘b5+ ♗xb5 28. ♕d6+
♔c8 29. ♖xb5 b6 30. ♗xh6±.

Another interesting defensive try would have
been 25...♖b8!?

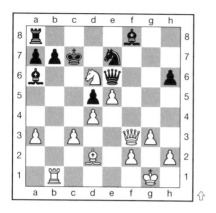

26. c4! ℤd8?

26...ℤb8□ 27. ♘b5+ (27. cxd5 ♘xd5
28. ℤc1+ ♚d7 29. ℤc5 ♘f6 30. ♕xf6 ♕xf6
31. exf6 ♗xd6 32. ℤd5 ℤd8 33. ♗b4 ♚e6
34. ℤxd6+ ℤxd6 35. f7 ℤd8 36. f8♕ ℤxf8
37. ♗xf8 h5 38. f3±)

A) 27...♗xb5 28. ℤxb5 dxc4 (28...ℤd8
29. ♗b4+−) 29. d5±;

B) 27...♚d7 28. cxd5 ♕xd5 (28...♘xd5
29. ♘xa7!?+−) 29. ♕g4+ ♚d8 (29...♕e6?
30. ♕xe6+ ♚xe6 31. ♘c7+ ♚d7
32. ♘xa6+−) 30. ♘c3±.

**27. ♘xb7!+− ♗xb7 28. ♗a5+ ♚c8
29. ♗xd8 ♘f5**

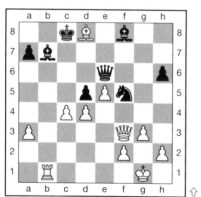

30. ℤxb7!? (30. ♗a5!?+−) **30...♚xb7
31. cxd5 ♕c8**

31...♘xd4 32. ♕xf8+−.

**32. d6+ ♚a6 33. ♕d3+ ♚b7 34. ♕b5+
♚a8 35. ♗c7 a6 36. ♕c6+**

36. d7 ♕xc7 37. ♕d5+.

36...♕b7 37. d7

Black resigned, in view of 37...♗e7
(37...♕xc6 38. d8♕+ ♚b7 39. ♕b8#)
38. d5+−.

Attack on the king

Game 16
Kupreichik – Vaganian
Russian Cup, Kiev 1984

Fearing an attack on the kingside, Black often castles on the queenside. But even then
White, with his space advantage and lead in
development, can give the black king a hard
time. Black's counter-attack on the kingside
usually comes too late.

**1. e4 e6 2. d4 d5 3. e5 ♘e7 4. ♘f3 b6
5. c3 ♕d7 6. ♘bd2 a5 7. h4**

Revealing quite clearly his aggressive inten-
tions on the kingside.

**7...h5 8. ♘g5 ♗a6 9. ♗xa6 ♘xa6 10. ♘f1
♘f5 11. ♘g3!?** (11. ♘e3) **11...♘xg3
12. fxg3 f6!? 13. exf6 gxf6 14. ♘h3
0-0-0 15. 0-0**

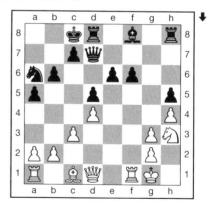

The symmetry of the two knights on opposite
edges of the board is striking. But the white
knight has various interesting routes back
into the fray, whilst its opposite number will
be stuck out of play for some considerable
time.

15...e5!?

Black sacrifices a pawn to open lines on the kingside and activate his bishop. Instead 15...♗g7 would be passive, e. g. 16. ♘f4 ♔b7 17. ♘xh5±.

16. ♖xf6 ♗g7 17. ♖f3 (17. ♗g5!?) **17...exd4 18. cxd4 ♖de8 19. ♗e3 ♘b4 20. ♗f2 ♔b7 21. ♖c3 ♗h6!?**

Intercepting the white knight's route to the centre. Instead 21...♖e4 22. ♘g5± would be weaker.

22. a3 ♘c6 23. b4

A tempting pawn sacrifice. Besides, if this is not played it is difficult to see how else White can make progress.

23...axb4 24. axb4

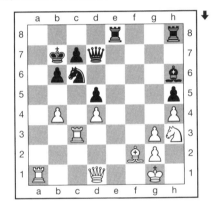

24...♘a7

Perhaps Black was wrong to decline the sacrifice. On 24...♘xb4 Kupreichik gave this variation: 25. ♖ca3 ♘c6 26. ♖a6!? ♘a5 27. ♖6xa5 bxa5 28. ♕b3+ ♔c8 29. ♖xa5 ♕c6 30. ♖xd5 ⩲. It is understandable that Vaganian did not fancy defending such a position against Kupreichik, but here anything can happen.

25. ♖ca3 ♘b5 26. ♖a6 ♕g4 27. ♕d3

27. ♕a4 ♕e2 28. ♖a2 ♕c4∞.

27...♕e2 28. ♕f5! ♕c4

28...♕e4 29. ♕d7+−; 28...♕e6 29. ♕xh5!?

29. ♕xh5 ♖e2

Black's counterplay comes too late.

30. ♕g4 ♖f8 31. ♔h2

31. ♕d7!? ♖fxf2? 32. ♘xf2 ♕xd4 33. ♔h1!+−.

31...♖exf2 32. ♘xf2 ♖xf2

32...♗e3!? 33. ♕g7 ♖c8 (33...♖xf2 34. ♕g8++−) 34. ♕f7+−.

33. ♕e6!+− ♗c1

33...♕xd4 34. ♕e8!+−; 33...♗g7 34. ♖a8 ♖f8 35. ♖xf8 ♗xf8 36. ♕e8+−; 33...♖e2 34. ♕g8 ♔c6 35. ♕g6+ ♘d6 (35...♔b7 36. ♖a8 ♕c2 37. ♖b8+! ♔xb8 38. ♕g8+) 36. ♕xh6 ♕xd4 37. ♕f8+−.

34. ♖a8 ♗a3 35. ♕c8+ ♔c6 36. ♕e8+ ♔b7 37. ♖8xa3 ♖xg2+ 38. ♔xg2 ♕c2+ 39. ♔h3 ♘xa3 40. ♖xa3 ♕f5+ 41. ♔g2

Black resigned.

We frequently find that different plans complement one another and indeed flow from one to the next. For example, if we have a kingside attack and the opponent suddenly weakens his dark squares, then we would be justified in choosing a different target.

Attack on the king, play on the dark squares

Game 17
Grischuk – M. Gurevich
French League 2003

1. e4 e6 2. d4 d5 3. e5 c5 4. c3 ♗d7 5. ♘f3 ♕b6 6. a3 ♗b5 7. b4

7. c4!?

A) 7...dxc4!?, Sveshnikov – Vysochin, Yugoslavia 1998 (Volume 2, game 27 on page 26);

B) 7...♗xc4 8. ♗xc4 dxc4 9. d5 ♘e7 10. ♕a4+ (10. ♘c3 ♘xd5 11. ♘xd5 exd5 12. ♕xd5 ♗e7 13.0-0 ♘c6 14. e6 0-0 15. exf7+ ♖xf7 16. ♗g5 ♕d8 17. ♖ad1. Draw, Sveshnikov – Osmanović, Sarajevo 1983) 10...♘d7 11. dxe6 ♕xe6 12. ♘bd2 ♘c6 13. ♘xc4 ♗e7 14. 0-0 0-0 15. ♗f4 a6

16. ♘d6 b5 17. ♕e4 ♘cxe5 18. ♗xe5 ♘xe5
19. ♖ad1 ♘xf3+ 20. gxf3 ♗xd6 21. ♕xe6
♗xh2+ 22. ♔xh2 fxe6∓, Heinz – Linder, Se-
lestat 2002.

7...cxd4 8. ♗xb5+! ♕xb5 9. cxd4 ♘d7

9...a5 10. ♘c3 ♕c6 11. ♗d2 axb4 12. axb4
♖xa1 13. ♕xa1 ♕a6 14. ♕b1 b5 15. 0–0 ♘e7
16. ♕d3± Shirov – Ljubojević, Monte Carlo
2002.

10. ♘c3 ♕c6

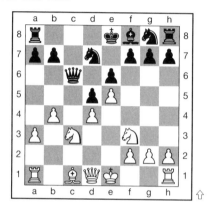

11. ♘a4!?

11. ♗b2 ♘b6 12. ♘d2 ♘e7 13. 0–0 ♘f5
14. ♖c1 ♕d7 15. ♘e2 ♗e7=, Alekseev –
Rustemov, Russian League, Tomsk 2001.

11...♘e7?!

11...♘b6 12. ♘xb6 (12. ♘c5 ♘c4) 12...axb6
13. ♗b2 ♘e7 (13...♘h6 14. ♖c1 ♕d7 15. ♖c3
♗e7 16. ♗c1!?±) 14. 0–0 ♘c8 15. ♖c1 ♕d7
16. ♖c3±, Torre – Bagamasbad, Greenhills
1997;

11...a5, Sveshnikov – Grosar, Slovenian Club
Championship 2003 (game 21 on page 42).

12. ♗e3

12. 0–0!? ♘f5 (12...♖c8 13. ♗b2 ♕c2
14. ♕xc2 ♖xc2 15. ♖fc1 ♖xc1+ 16. ♖xc1 b5
17. ♘c3 a6 18. a4±) 13. g4!? (13. ♗g5 h6
14. ♖c1 ♕b5 15. ♗d2±) 13...♘e7 14. ♗e3±.

12...♘b6 (12...♘f5!?) 13. ♘xb6 ♕xb6
14. 0–0 ♘c6

14...♕b5!?;

14...♘f5 15. ♖c1 ♕d8 16. ♕a4+ ♕d7 17. ♕a5
♗e7 18. ♖c7 b6 19. ♖xd7 bxa5 20. ♖b7
axb4 21. axb4 0–0 22. g4 ♘xe3±, Carlsen –
Rustemov, Moscow 2004.

15. ♘e1!?

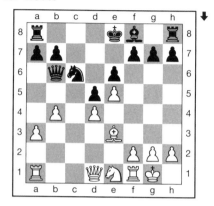

A new slant on a manoeuvre that we have already come across several times: the knight
opens a route for the queen and at the same
time heads for a better position (in this case
c5).

15. ♖b1±; 15. ♕d3±.

15...♗e7

15...a5 16. ♕a4 ♗e7 17. ♘d3 0–0 18. b5 ♘a7
19. ♖ab1↑.

16. ♕g4 g6 17. ♘d3 0–0

17...a5!? 18. ♘c5 (18. bxa5 ♖xa5 19. a4
0–0⇄) 18...axb4 19. axb4 ♖c8 (19...♖xa1!?
20. ♖xa1 ♕xb4 21. ♖a8+ ♘d8 22. ♕d1 0–0
23. ♗h6 ♖e8 24. ♘d7⩲ ♕b5) 20. ♘xe6!?
fxe6 21. ♕xe6 ♕d8 22. b5 ♘b4 23. ♖fc1
♖b8 24. ♗h6 ♕d7 25. ♕b6 ♗d8 26. ♕a7
♖c8 27. ♖xc8 ♕xc8 28. ♖c1 ♕d7 29. ♕b8
(29. ♕a3) 29...♔f7 30. ♗d2⩲.

18. ♘c5 ♕c7

18...♗xc5 19. bxc5 ♕b2 20. ♖ab1 ♕xa3
21. ♕h4±.

19. ♖ac1± ♖fc8 20. h4!? b6 21. ♘d3
♕d7 22. h5

The pawn formation (e5 pawn) indicates that
White should attack on the kingside. It is not

easy for Black to transfer pieces across to defend.

22...♗f8 23. ♘f4 ♗g7

23...b5!? (Psakhis) 24. ♘d3 a5 25. ♘c5 ♕e8⇄.

24. h6!?

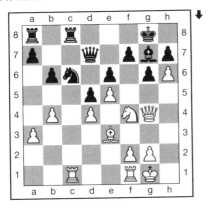

24...♗xh6?

Black allows himself to be provoked. After 24...♗f8!? (24...♗h8?!) 25.♘h5 ♗e7∞ 26. ♗g5!? (otherwise it is difficult for White to attack: 26. ♖c3 is ineffective: 26...a5 27. b5 ♘a7 28. ♖xc8+ ♖xc8 29. a4 ♖c4⇄; perhaps 26.♖fd1!?±) 26...gxh5 27. ♕g3 ♔f8 28. ♗e3 ♕d8 29. ♕g7+ ♔e8 30. ♕xh7 White's compensation for the piece might not be enough.

25. ♘h5!

Possibly Black reckoned only on 25. ♘xg6 fxg6 26. ♗xh6 ♘e7∞ when the knight would take up a fine post at f5.

25...♗g7 26. ♘xg7 ♔xg7 27. ♕h4

Now the dark squares can no longer be defended.

27...♔g8

27...h5 28. ♕f6+ ♔h7 29. g4 ♕e7! (29...hxg4?? 30. ♔g2+−) 30. ♕f4 (30. ♖xc6? ♕xf6 31. ♖xc8 ♕h4 32. ♖xa8 ♕xg4+=) 30...g5 (30...hxg4 31. ♔g2+−) 31. ♕h2 h4 32. f4→; 27...♘e7 28. ♕f6+ ♔g8 29. g4+−.

28. ♗g5 f5

28...h5 29. ♗f6 b5 30. ♖cd1 a5 31. g4 ♔h7 32. gxh5 g5 33. ♕g3 (33. ♕xg5?? ♖g8) 33...axb4 34. ♕d3+ ♔h6 (34...♔g8 35. h6+−) 35. axb4±.

29. exf6 ♘d8 (29...e5!?) **30. ♕h6**

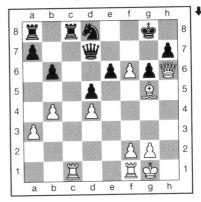

30...♖c4?!

30...b5!? 31. ♖fe1 ♖c4 32. ♖xc4 bxc4 33. b5 a6⇄.

31. ♖xc4 dxc4 32. d5! a5

32...exd5 33. ♖e1 ♘c6 34. ♖e7+−; 32...e5 33. ♖e1+−.

33. ♖e1 ♖a7 34. f7+!

Black resigned in view of 34...♘xf7 (34...♕xf7 35. ♗xd8) 35. dxe6 ♘xh6 36. exd7 ♖xd7 37. ♗xh6.

Attack on the king, play on the dark squares

Game 18
Motylev – Rustemov
57th Russian Championship
(Qualifier), Tomsk 2004

1. e4 e6 2. d4 d5 3. e5 ♗d7!?

A rare move which has never been used at the highest level. However, the idea is a typical one in the closed positions of the French Defence. Black wants to exchange his light-squared bishop. He plans to play a7–a6, so that if White exchanges bishops on b5 the a-file will be open for the black rook.

4. c3

White does not react to his opponent's move, contenting himself with strengthening his centre and developing his pieces. Of course a more active plan is also possible, for instance 4. ♘f3!? a6 5. ♗g5 ♘e7! (as opposed to 5...♕c8?, see Bronstein – Kärner, Tallinn 1981, Volume 2, game 21 on page 23) 6. ♗d3 (6. ♘c3±) 6...c5 (6...♗b5 7. ♗×b5+ a×b5 8. ♕d3±) 7. d×c5 ♘bc6 8. 0–0 h6 9. ♗e3 ♕c7 10. c3±.

4...a6 5. ♘d2 ♗b5 6. ♗×b5+ a×b5

Black has achieved his first objective – the bishops have been exchanged and the a-file opened. But what now?. The advance c7–c5 is difficult to implement, since in that case both b-pawns would be weak. Meanwhile White has the advantage in space and force on the kingside.

7. ♘e2

A characteristic manoeuvre: the knight heads for h5 via f4 or g3.

7...♘d7 8. 0–0 h5?!

A controversial decision. Black seizes a bit of space and secures a base for his knight at f5 but at the cost of weakening the dark squares and more or less renouncing king-side castling.

9. ♘f4 g6 10. ♘f3 ♘b6 11. h4!?

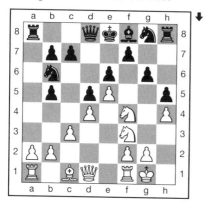

White fixes the kingside and prepares to post his bishop to g5. 11. ♘d3!?± would also have been good.

11...♘h6 12. ♘d3 ♘f5 13. g3 ♗e7?!

It is hard to see how else Black could complete his development. But now White can exchange the bishops and obtain comfortable bases for his knights at f4 and g5. So 13...♕d7 14. ♗g5 ♗g7± would have been better.

14. ♗g5 ♖a7 15. ♕c1 ♔f8

Black castles artificially, leaving the rook on h8 to defend against the possible breaks with g3–g4 and h4–h5.

16. ♔g2 ♔g7 17. ♖h1 ♘c4 18. ♕f4 ♖a8 19. a3 b6 20. ♖ae1 ♖c8

Everything is ready for White to begin his attack.

21. g4! h×g4

21...♘h6?! seems dubious in view of 22. g×h5 (or 22. ♗f6+ ♗×f6 23. e×f6+ ♔f8 24. g5±) 22...g×h5 23. ♖eg1±.

22. ♕×g4 ♔f8 23. b3!?

White wants to involve the d3 knight in the attack, but is reluctant to let the b2 pawn go, after which the a3 pawn might be lost and there would also be problems with the c3 pawn. But White is quite willing to let just the a3 pawn go as fodder for the horse, since the knight would take a good while to get back into play from a3.

23...♘a5

In the hope than the return journey from b3 will be a bit shorter.

24. ♘f4 ♖g8

24...♘×b3?! 25. h5 g×h5 26. ♖×h5 ♖g8 27. ♖eh1 ♔e8 28. ♖h7! ♗×g5 29. ♖1h5!+–.

25. ♗f6!

White is willing to sacrifice another pawn to open the e-file and exploit the e5 square.

25...♘×b3

25...♗×f6 26. e×f6 ♕×f6 27. ♘g5 with the unpleasant threats of ♘h7+ and ♘×e6+.

26. ♘g5 ♔e8

The only move, since 26...♕d7 27. h5 ♘h6 28. ♕d1 +− loses.

27. h5 g×h5

27...♗×f6 28. e×f6 ♔d7 (28...♕×f6 29. ♘g×e6+−) 29. h×g6 ♕×f6 30. ♖h7 ♖g7 31. ♖×g7 ♕×g7 32. g×f7 +−.

28. ♕×h5 ♔d7

The king tries to escape.

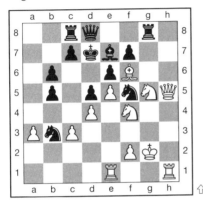

29. ♘×d5!

This nice shot forces Black into an unfavourable endgame and is stronger than 29. ♕×f7 ♖×g5+ 30. ♗×g5 ♕g8⇄.

30...e×d5 30. ♕×f7 ♖×g5+ 31. ♗×g5 ♕c6

Now 31...♕g8 32. ♕×f5+ would be pointless.

32. ♗×e7 ♘×e7

32...♕g8+!? would have been a better try: 33. ♕×g8 ♖×g8+ 34. ♗g5 ♖×g5+ 35. ♔f3±.

33. ♖h7

Or 33. ♕f6+!? ♔d7 (33...♔b7 34. ♖h7±) 34. ♖e3±.

33...♕g8+ 34. ♖g7

34. ♔f1 ♕×f7 35. ♖×f7 ♔d7 36. ♔e2±.

34...♕×f7 35. ♖×f7 ♖g8+ 36. ♔f3 ♘g6

Formally speaking, Black even has a slight material advantage: two knights for a rook and pawn. But the black pieces are completely lacking in coordination, the b3 knight is out of the game and the white passed

pawns are charging down the board. Thus the black position can hardly be salvaged. The best chance lay in 36...♔d7 37. ♖h1 ♘d2+ 38. ♔e3 ♘e4 39. ♖hh7 ♖e8 40. f4 ♔e6 41. ♔d3 c5 42. ♖fg7±.

37. ♖h1 (37. ♔e2!? ±) **37...♘d2+ 38. ♔e2 ♘e4 39. ♖hh7**

With the "simple" threat of mate in one.

39...♖c8?

39...♘×c3+ 40. ♔e3 b4 41. ♖×c7+ ♔b5 42. a×b4±.

40. ♖h6+− ♖g8 41. f3 ♘×c3+ 42. ♔d3 ♘b1

The fate of this knight has been an unfortunate one.

43. ♖f6+ ♔b7 44. ♖h×g6 ♖e8 45. ♖g7 ♘×a3 46. ♖ff7 ♖c8 47. e6

It's all over.

47...♔c6 48. e7 ♖e8 49. ♖f8 ♔d7 50. ♖×e8 ♔×e8 51. f4

Black resigned.

Counterplay on the kingside

Game 19
Sveshnikov – Rublevsky
Russian Championship, Elista 1994

Comments by Sergey Rublevsky are in italics.

1. e4 c5 2. c3 e6 4. d4 d5 4. e5

It wasn't easy for me to decide to enter this line for the first time in my life and, in doing so, take on Sveshnikov in "his" variation of the French. But it seemed to me that the black position was solid and safe enough. After playing and analysing this game I began to understand that things were not so simple.

4...♘c6 5. ♘f3 ♗d7 6. ♗e2 ♘ge7 7. ♘a3 c×d4 8. c×d4 ♘f5 9. ♘c2 ♘b4 10. 0-0 ♘×c2 11. ♕×c2 ♕b6 12. ♕d3 ♖c8 13. a4!

At the time I knew only the game Sveshnikov – Dreev (Rostov on Don 1993), on which I was basing my play: 13. ♗d2 ♗b4! 14. ♗f4 a6 15. a4 ♘e7 16. h4 ♗a5 17. ♖fc1 ♖xc1+ 18. ♗xc1 h6, Draw. In my opinion the immediate 13. h4!? is stronger, not giving up any queenside squares to Black.

The move in the game is stronger than 13. ♗d2. With this variation I have played two other theoretically important games – against Brumen (Bled 2000, Volume 2, game 56 on page 48) and Dizdar (Bled 2002, Volume 2, game 57 on page 49).

13...♗b4 14. h4

Play on both wings. White has defended against an exchange of bishops by ♗b5 and he now launches an offensive against Black's kingside.

14...h6!?

This is more accurate than 14...♘e7, when White would have the possibility of becoming immediately active on the kingside with 15. ♕e3!?.

Also 14...h5 is worth considering, after which it would be very difficult to dislodge the knight from f5. Probably I would have played 15. ♗g5 with the idea of ♖ad1, ♘h2 and g4, which would have led to a sharp and uncompromising struggle.

15. h5 ♘e7 16. ♘d2

As soon as Black has released the pressure on d4, White transfers his knight to the queenside. But the main point is to open a route for the queen across to the kingside, after which it will be obvious that the g7 pawn is weak.

16...0–0 17. ♘b3

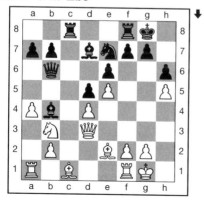

17...f5

Black is compelled to close the kingside, since otherwise White will begin an attack against the black king: 17...♘c6? 18. ♗xh6! gxh6 19. ♕g3+ ♔h8 20. ♕f4 ♘e7 21. ♕xh6+ ♔g8 22. g4, or 17...f6? 18. ♗f4 with the idea 18...fxe5 19. ♗xe5 ♘c6 20. ♗xg7 ♔xg7 21. ♕g6+ ♔h8 22. ♕xh6+ ♔g8 23. ♕g6+ ♔h8 24. ♗d3.

Black could also have played 17...a5 18. g4!? with chances for both sides.

18. a5

An equal game would result from 18. exf6 ♖xf6 19. ♗e3 ♘f5.

18...♕d8!?

I wanted to keep the queen close to the kingside, seeing that I couldn't penetrate down the c-file: 18...♕c7 19. ♕g3 ♔h8 20. ♖d1 with the idea of 20...♕c2 21. ♗d2!.

19. ♗d2

The exchange of bishops highlights the weakness of the dark squares in the enemy camp.

19...♗xd2 20. ♕xd2 b6

Restricting the b3 knight.

21. axb6 axb6 22. ♕b4

The queen is looking for a way into the black camp. After 22. f4 ♘c6 that would be impossible and Black would have counterplay.

An interesting move, but I think playing on the queenside was not the right plan. After 22. f4 ♘c6 23. ♖a3± White's advantage is obvious.

22...f4 23. ♖fc1 ♖xc1+ 24. ♖xc1 ♘c6 25. ♕d2

25. ♕d6 f3! 26. ♗xf3 ♖xf3 leads to either perpetual check – 27. gxf3 ♘xd4! 28. ♘xd4 ♕g5+ 29. ♔h2 ♕xh5+, or an equal endgame: 27. ♖xc6 ♖xb3 28. ♖c7 ♖xb2 29. g3 ♕f8

30. ♕xf8+ ♔xf8 31. ♖xd7 ♖b4 32. ♖d6 ♔e7
33. f4.

25...♕g5 26. ♖c3 ♘e7

Better than the immediate attack on the h5
pawn: 26...♗e8?! 27. ♕d3 ♘e7 28. ♕h3 ♘f5
29. ♗g4 ♗a4 30. ♗xf5 ♖xf5 31. ♘d2!, since
after its capture the black pieces are tied up:
31. ... ♕xh5 32. ♕xh5 ♖xh5 33. ♖c8+ ♔h7
34. ♖b8.

27. ♖c7 ♗e8 28. ♕b4 ♘f5

Black fails to solve all his problems with
28...♗xh5 29. ♕xe7 (29. ♗xh5?! ♕xh5
30. ♕xe7 ♕d1+ 31. ♔h2 ♕h5+ with a draw)
29...♗xe2 30. ♕xe6+ ♔h7 31. ♕xd5 f3
32. ♕e4+ ♔h8 33. g4 ♗a6 34. ♖a7 (34. ♖c3?
♖f4!) 34...♗c4 35. ♖a8 ♖xa8 36. ♕xa8+ ♔h7
37. ♕xf3 ♗xb3 38. ♕xb3 ♕g4+ 39. ♔f1
♕xd4 40. ♕c2+ ♔g8 41. e6 ♔f8 42. ♕f5+ ♕f6
43. ♕d5, and Black will still have to work hard
to draw.

After 28...f3 29. ♗xf3 ♖xf3 30. ♕xe7 ♕xe7
31. ♖xe7 ♖xb3 32. ♖xe8+ ♔f7 33. ♖b8 ♖xb2
33. f4± White would have found it hard to
win the endgame.

29. ♕xb6 ♗xh5 30. ♕xe6+ ♔h7

The other king move was clearly weaker:
30...♔h8? 31. ♖c8 ♖xc8 32. ♕xc8+ ♔h7
33. ♗d3 ♗g6 34. ♕e6.

31. ♗xh5 ♕xh5 32. ♖c3

The other defensive try would fail: 32. ♘d2??
♘g3! 33. fxg3 fxg3 34. ♘f3 ♖xf3, and now
35. ♕h3 loses to 35...♖f1+ 36. ♔xf1 ♕d1#.

32...♕e2!?

Black has a slightly inferior endgame after
32...♘xd4?! 33. ♘xd4 ♕d1+ 34. ♔h2 ♕xd4
35. f3, but 32...♘e3! was stronger, and White
has to give perpetual check by 33. fxe3 f3!
34. ♖c2! f2+ 35. ♖xf2 ♕d1+ 36. ♔h2 ♖xf2
37. ♕xd5 ♖f1 38. ♕e4+ ♔h8 39. ♕a8+ since
33. ♖c1? fails to 33...♘g4 34. ♕xd5 f3.

33. ♕xd5

(see next diagram)

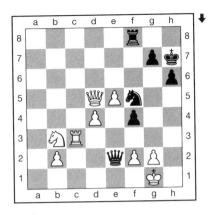

33...♘g3!

An excellent tactical resource, taking advantage of the weak white king. If Black
tries 33...♕e1+? 34. ♔h2 ♕xf2 instead then
he falls under an attack with 35. ♕e4! e.g.
35...♕xb2 36. ♖c8! ♖f7 37. e6 ♕xb3 38. exf7
♕xf7 39. ♕d3.

34. fxg3

After 34. ♖c1? ♕h5! 35. f3 ♖b8! (but not
35...♘e2+ 36. ♔f2 ♘xc1 37. ♕e4+ ♔h8
38. ♘xc1, and White is better) 36. ♔f2 ♕h4
only Black can play for a win.

34...fxg3 35. ♖xg3 ♖f1+ 36. ♔h2 ♕e1 37. ♖xg7+

This leads immediately to perpetual check.
A king march behind enemy lines achieves
nothing: 37. ♔h3 ♖h1+ 38. ♔g4 h5+ 39. ♔f5!
(39. ♔f4? ♖h4+ 40. ♔f3 ♕f1+ 41. ♔e3 ♕f4+)
39...♕xg3 40. ♔e6 ♖h2 41. ♔d7 ♖xg2 42. e6
♕g4 43. ♔d8 ♖e2 44. ♘c5 ♖d2 45. ♘e4
♖e2 46. ♘c5 ♖d2, and now certainly not
47. e7?? because of 47...♖xd4 48. ♕xd4
♕xd4+ 49. ♘d7 ♕h4!.

37...♔xg7 38. ♕d7+ ♔g6 39. ♕e8+ ♔g7 40. ♕d7+ ♔g6 41. ♕g4+ ♔h7 42. ♕d7+ ♔h8

Draw.

Counterplay on the kingside

Game 20
Sveshnikov – Balashov
44th USSR Championship, Moscow 1976

Comments by Yuri Balashov are in italics.

1. e4 c5 2. c3 e6 3. d4 d5 4. e5 ♘c6 5. ♘f3 ♗d7

By transposition a well known position in the French Defence has arisen. The move 5...♗d7, recommended by the former World Champion Mikhail Botvinnik, is considered these days to be the main line for Black in this position. In 1976, however, this move was practically unknown and it took my opponent by surprise.

Of course, Botvinnik's authority is widely respected, yet I would not say that 5...♗d7 is the strongest move in this position. 5...♕b6 is certainly not weaker. The advantage of 5...♗d7 is its flexibility, yet in no way does it solve all of Black's problems.

When this game was played, I had only just taken up the 3. e5 system and I did not handle the opening in the best manner. My opponent showed the good possibilities for counterplay available to Black.

6. d×c5

A dubious move. The f8 bishop immediately reaches a good position. White's best continuation here is 6. ♗e2.

The main move here is 6. ♗e2.

6...♗×c5 7. ♗d3

Of course the most logical move here is 7. b4 which I played subsequently:

7. b4 ♗b6 8. b5 (to ease Black's pressure on the e5 pawn) 8...♘a5 9. ♗d3

9...♕c7 10. ♕e2 ♘e7 11. 0–0 ♘g6 12. ♖e1 0–0–0 13. ♘a3 ♔b8 14. ♗d2 f6 15. ♗×g6 h×g6 16. ♗f4 ♗c5 17. ♘c2 ♘c4 18. a4 ♖hf8 19. ♗g3 f5 20. ♗f4 ♕a5 21. ♖ec1 ±, Sveshnikov–Shabalov, Riga 1990 (see also exercise 45 on page 141, solution page 152).

9...♘c4 10. a4 ♕c7 11. ♕e2 a6 12. b×a6 ♖×a6 13. 0–0 ♘e7 14. ♘a3 ♖×a4 15. ♘×c4 d×c4 16. ♖×a4 ♗×a4 17. ♗×c4 0–0 18. ♗d3

♘g6. Draw. Kharlov–Dreev, Russian Championship, Moscow 1991.

The following game was the last word concerning this variation: 9...♕c7 10. ♕e2 ♘c4 11. a4 a6 12. b×a6 ♖×a6 13. 0–0 ♘e7 14. ♘a3 ♖×a4 15. ♘×c4 d×c4 16. ♖×a4 ♗×a4 17. ♗×c4 0–0 18. ♗d3 ♘g6 19. h4 ♗c6 20. h5 ♗×f3 21. g×f3 ♕×e5 22. h×g6 ♕g3+ 23. ♔h1 ♕h3+. Draw. Sveshnikov–Kharlov, Böblingen 1992.

7...♘ge7

7...f6 8. b4 ♗e7 9. b5 ♘×e5 10. ♘×e5 f×e5 11. ♕h5+ ♔f8 12. ♕×e5 ♗f6 13. ♕d6+ ♘e7 14. 0–0 e5 15. ♗a3 ♔f7 16. ♘d2 ♖e8 with a complicated game, Sveshnikov–Savon, Zonal Tournament, Lvov 1978.

8. 0–0

Grandmaster Sveshnikov is famous for steadfastly sticking to his principles in defending his own opening lines. A year and a half after this game he tried to strengthen White's play by 8. b4 ♗b6 9. b5, but after 9...♘a5 10. 0–0 ♖c8 11. a4 ♘g6 12. ♗a3 ♗c5 13. ♗×c5 ♖×c5 14. g3 ♕c7 Black had the better chances (Sveshnikov–Balashov, Zonal Tournament, Lvov 1978).

In my opinion, White's chances are not worse in the final position of this variation; the computer agrees with me.

8...♘g6 9. ♖e1 ♕c7

White has played the opening inaccurately and allowed Black to seize the initiative.

10. ♗×g6?!

If 10. ♕e2 0-0, followed by f7–f6, and Black obtains a satisfactory game.

Of course White should not have given up his bishop, after which he has problems. 10. ♕e2 = was better.

10...f×g6!

This capture is much stronger than 10...h×g6. Now Black has excellent prospects on the kingside thanks to the half-open f-file.

The normal move here is 10...h×g6, after which Black stands a little better. 10...f×g6 is interesting but questionable. I must admit that in 1976 I didn't suspect that Black could be planning h6, g5 and ♗e8 – for me this was a real revelation. Today of course I would try to prevent its execution, but at that time I did not fear it – because I didn't know it existed!

11. ♗f4?

White does not sense the danger he is in. He fortifies his e5 pawn by transferring the bishop to g3, but this manoeuvre is ineffective. On g3 the bishop will just be a spectator for the rest of the game. It was necessary to offer an exchange of dark-squared bishops by 11. ♗e3, which corresponds to the needs of the position. White could also consider sharpening the game with 11. c4.

An unnecessary and dubious move. Instead 11. ♘bd2 was better, with an unclear position.

11...0–0 12. ♗g3 ♘e7

Black has a stable advantage now.

13. ♘bd2 ♘f5 14. ♘b3

After this further error Black is able to activate the d7 bishop.

14...♗a4

A very interesting move, but 14...♖ac8 was also good.

15. ♔h1?

An obvious error. I was stuck for a move. After 15. ♕d3 it was still a game.

15...♕b6∓ 16. ♕c2 ♖ac8 17. ♖e2 h6 18. h3 g5

Black's initiative is growing, and it is hard to see what White can do about it.

19. ♗h2 ♖c7 20. ♘e1 ♗e7

The threat is 21...♘d4. Whilst White is obliged to deal with tactical threats, Black improves the position of his pieces.

21. ♕d1 ♖c4 22. ♖d2

The time for decisive action has arrived!

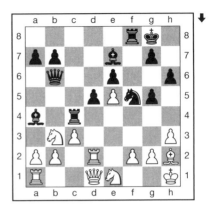

22...g4! 23. h×g4 ♘e3 24. ♕e2

The knight is taboo because of 24. f×e3 ♖f1+ 25. ♗g1 ♕×e3.

24...♘×g4 25. f3

Or 25. ♗g1 ♖e4 26. f3 ♖×e2 27. ♗×b6 ♖×d2 28. ♘×d2 a×b6 29. f×g4 ♖f4.

25...♘×h2 26. ♘d4

If 26.♔×h2 ♖h4+ and the white king is in peril.

26...♗c5 27. ♔×h2 ♗×d4 28. c×d4 ♖×d4 29. ♖c1

White's main problem is not so much being a pawn down as having a weak king. Here he should have sought exchanges with 29. ♕f2.

29...♖h4+ 30. ♔g3 ♗b5!

The decisive manoeuvre.

31. ♕f2 ♕d8 32. ♕e3 d4 33. ♖cd1 ♖hf4 34. ♕×f4 ♖×f4 35. ♔×f4 ♕g5+

White resigned.

2.2 Advantage in space and/or development, typical endgame

Advantage in space and development, transition to the endgame

Game 21
Sveshnikov – Grosar
Slovenian Club Championship 2003

1. e4 e6 2. d4 d5 3. e5 c5

Occasionally Black chooses the plan 3...♘e7 4. ♘f3 b6 – with the idea of exchanging the light-squared bishops [Kupreichik–Vaganian, Russian Cup, Kiev 1984 (game 16 on page 32); Sveshnikov–Vaganian, Moscow 1985 (game 42 on page 82); Grosar–Zugaj, Ljubljana 1992; Moiseenko–Erashchenko, Togliatti 2000].

4. c3

A reliable move; you rarely see 4. ♕g4?! (Sveshnikov–Komarov, Vrnjačka Banja 1999, game 28 on page 57), but 4. ♘f3!? ♘c6 5. ♗d3∞ deserves attention.

4...♕b6

There is another interesting plan connected with the exchange of light-squared bishops: 4...♗d7 5. ♘f3 a6!? 6. ♘bd2± (Sveshnikov–Dražić, Ljubljana 1997).

5. ♘f3 ♗d7

The alternative is 5...♘c6.

6. a3!?

At one time 6. ♗e2 ♗b5 7. 0–0 ♗xe2 8. ♕xe2 ♕a6 9. ♕d1 (or 9. ♕xa6 ♘xa6; 9. ♕e3) was played, but Black easily solved his opening problems. Then Igor Zaitsev came up with a sharper plan for White, based on the pawn sacrifice 7. c4!?. You can study this variation by looking at Zaitsev's games with it. Three critical positions in this line should be noted:

1) 7...♗xc4 8. ♗xc4 dxc4 9. d5 exd5 10. ♕xd5;

2) 7...♗xc4 8. ♗xc4 ♕b4+ 9. ♘bd2 dxc4 10. a3 ♕b5;

3) 7...dxc4 8. d5 exd5 9. ♕xd5 ♘e7 10. ♕e4 ♕g6!

6...♗b5!?

Black has one other possibility to fight for equality: 6...♘c6 7. b4 cxd4 8. cxd4 ♖c8 with two variations: 9. ♗e3 (Sveshnikov–Piskov, Bled 1990, Volume 2, game 50 on page 42) and 9. ♗b2 (Sveshnikov–Nevednichy, Bled 1991, game 43 on page 84). 9. ♗e2? is insufficient because of 9...a5! 10. b5 ♘xd4! 11. ♘xd4 ♖xc1! 12. ♕xc1 ♕xd4 and now 13. ♕c7! (weaker for White is 13. ♕c3! ♗c5∓, Sveshnikov–Hoàng, Cheliabinsk 1990) 13...♕xa1 14. ♕b8+ with perpetual check; however, Black can carry on the fight with 13...♗c5 14. ♖a2! ♕xf2+ 15. ♔d1 ♕e3⇄.

7. b4 cxd4

Here 7...♗xf1 would be bad because of 8. bxc5±, but 7...cxb4 is playable, transposing, since 8. ♗xb5+ ♕xb5 9. axb4 ♘d7 10. ♖a5 ♕c4⇄ 11. ♘fd2 (11. ♕a4 a6) 11...♕d3 12. ♕f3 ♕xf3 13. ♘xf3= is not dangerous for Black.

8. ♗xb5+

White achieves nothing with 8. ♕xd4 ♕a6 9. ♗xb5+ ♕xb5 10. a4 ♕d7⇄.

8...♕xb5 9. cxd4

9. ♘xd4 ♕d7 10. ♘d2 ♕c7 11. ♘2f3 ♕xc3+ 12. ♗d2 ♕d3 13. ♕a4+ ♘d7 14. ♖c1 a6 15. ♖c3 ♕e4+ 16. ♗e3 ♕b1+ 17. ♗c1 ♕e4+ 18. ♗e3 ♕b1+=.

9...♘d7

9...a5!? 10. bxa5 ♘c6 11. ♘c3 ♕c4 12. ♘e2 ♖xa5⇄.

10. ♘c3 ♕c6

Inadequate for equality is 10...♕c4 11. ♘e2 a5 12. bxa5 ♖xa5 13. ♗d2 ♖a8 14. 0–0 ♘e7

15. ♖b1 ± (Alavkin – Driamin, Russian Cup, Tula 1999).

11. ♘a4 !?

Here 11. ♗d2 ♘b6 12. 0–0 ♘c4 or 11. ♗b2 ♘b6 12. ♘d2 is interesting, but I didn't want to allow the black knight to settle on c4.

11...a5 !?

A new try. The game Torre – Bagamasbad, Greenhills 1997 (see page 34) continued 11...♘b6 12. ♘xb6 axb6 13. ♗b2 with advantage for White. In Grischuk – M. Gurevich, France 2003 (game 17 on page 33) 11...♘e7 ?! was played.

12. ♗d2 axb4 13. axb4

Here 13. ♖c1 ? is unfavourable because of 13...♕a6! 14. ♕b3 b6.

13...♕a6 14. b5 !? (14. ♖a2 !?) **14...♕xb5 15. ♘c3 ♖xa1 16. ♘xb5**

After 16. ♕xa1 ♕a6 *Fritz* assesses the position as slightly better for Black.

16...♖xd1+ 17. ♔xd1

(see next diagram)

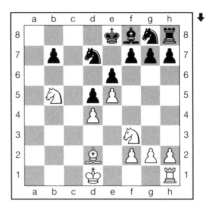

The critical position of the variation 11. ♘a4 a5 !?: White has a marked initiative for the sacrificed pawn, certainly enough to reach a draw at least, but is it sufficient to win?

17...♘b8 ?!

In my opinion the natural 17...♘b6 18. ♔e2 ♘c4 !? would have given Black good counterplay.

18. ♔e2 ♔d7

18. ♘c6 19. ♖b1 ± (19. ♖a1 !?).

19. ♖b1 !

The rook belongs precisely on this file!

19...♘c6 20. ♘a7 !?

Pretty, but more convincing was 20. ♘d6! ♗xd6 21. exd6 ♔c8 (21...f6 22. ♖xb7+ ♔xd6 23. ♗c1! e5 24. dxe5+) 22. d7+!? ♔xd7 23. ♖xb7+ ♔e8 24. ♖b6 ♘ge7 25. ♘e5, or 23...♔c8 24. ♖xf7 ±.

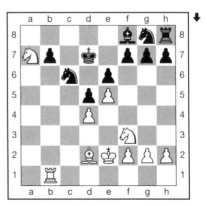

20...♘xa7?

The decisive error.

Good drawing chances were offered by 20...♔c7! 21. ♘xc6 bxc6 22. ♗a5+ ♔c8 23. ♖b6 ♔c7!, and there is no way that White can profit from the discovered check.

21. ♖xb7+ ♔e8

Here 21...♔c6 22. ♖xa7 ♗e7 23. ♘g5 ♗xg5 24. ♗xg5 f6 25. ♗d2 is no help.

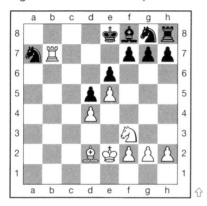

22. ♖b8+!

After this important check everything is clear.

22...♔d7 23. ♖xf8 ♘c6 24. ♗c1!?

I had no desire to let my opponent have any counterplay whatsoever, even for two pawns. I wanted more – to win a pawn without allowing Black any freedom. Of course, 24. ♖xf7+ ♘ge7 25. ♖xg7 h6 26. h4 would have won without too many problems.

24...h6

If 24...♘ce7 then 25. ♘g5 ♘g6 26. ♖xf7+ decides.

25. h4

The does not jeopardise the win, but 25. ♖xf7+ ♘ge7 26. ♖xg7 was simpler.

25...g6

There is nothing else.

26. ♗xh6

Here 26. ♗a3!+− was more logical.

26...♖xh6 27. ♖xg8 ♖h5 28. g4 ♖h7 29. ♔e3 ♘e7

If 29...♔e7 then 30. ♔f4 decides.

30. ♖f8 ♘c6 31. ♘g5 ♖xh4 32. ♖xf7+ ♔e8 33. f3!

The final precise move.

33...♖h1 34. ♖f6

Black resigned, since both pawns are lost.

Space advantage, play on both wings, pawn sacrifice

Game 22
Shirov – Anand
FIDE World Championship,
New Delhi/Teheran 2000

1. e4 e6

Normally Anand plays 1...c5 or 1...e5. The choice of the French Defence was possibly based on the expectation that Shirov would play the 3. e5 system, which Anand did not consider dangerous for Black.

2. d4 d5 3. e5 c5 4. c3 ♘c6 5. ♘f3 ♕b6 6. a3 a5 (6...c4) **7. ♗d3**

I think the defects of the move 6...a5 can be highlighted by the reply 7. b3!. Nevertheless, the pawn sacrifice offered in the game is well worth consideration, and has much more justification here than in the variation without the insertion of the moves 6. a3 a5. Black has weakened the squares b6 and b5, whilst White has brought the square b4 under his control. These factors play an important role; for instance Black can hardly consider castling queenside now.

7...♗d7 8. 0–0!

White sacrifices a pawn, in exchange for a big lead in development. Less promising are the continuations 8. dxc5 ♗xc5 9. 0–0 a4 10. ♘bd2⇄ or 10. c4?! dxc4 11. ♗xc4 ♘a5.

Also playable is the plan with 8. ♗c2 (although it does not appeal to me very much), e.g. 8...h5 9. 0–0 ♘h6 10. b3 ♗e7 11. ♗e3 cxd4 12. cxd4 ♘g4 13. ♘c3 ♖c8 14. ♘e2 ♘xe3 15. fxe3 g5 16. ♕d2 ♘d8 17. ♘e1 ♗b5 18. ♗d3 ♗xd3 19. ♕xd3 ♖c6 20. ♘c2 g4 21. b4 ♗g5 22. ♘c3 ♖c4 23. ♘e4! ♗e7 24. ♘d2 ♖c8 25. ♖fc1 ±, Sandipan – Barua, Raipur 2002.

8...cxd4 9. cxd4 ♘xd4 10. ♘xd4 ♕xd4 11. ♘c3 ♕b6

The inclusion of the moves 6. a3 a5 alters the evaluation of the pawn sacrifice: White now has an advantage, and the only question is whether it is sufficient to win. Black cannot really accept the second pawn, e.g. 11...♕xe5 12. ♖e1 ♕d6 (12...♕b8 13. ♘xd5 ♗c6 14. ♗f4 ♗d6 15. ♕g4→) 13. ♘b5 ♗xb5 14. ♗xb5+ ♔d8 15. ♕h5 ♘f6 16. ♕xf7 ♕e7 17. ♕xe6 ♕xe6 18. ♖xe6 ♗c5 19. ♗g5 ♗d4 20. ♖d1 ♗xb2 21. ♖xd5+ ♔c8 22. ♖c5+ ♔d8 23. ♖c2, and Black resigned (Prié – Villeneuve, Paris 1990).

12. ♕g4

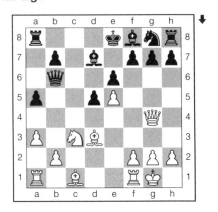

This move is typical of Shirov – as usual he plays the opening very actively and probably in the strongest manner. The queen sortie to g4 nevertheless has some disadvantages: Black's reply compels White to force matters, otherwise Black will pile up on the unprotected e5 pawn and quietly complete his development. If White immediately begins play against the weakened queenside with 12. ♕e2 (the idea is ♘b3, ♗e3, ♖c1) then Black has the strong reply 12...♘e7!, e.g. 13. ♘b5 ♘f5 14. g4 (14. ♖d1 ♗c5!∓) 14...♘d4 15. ♘xd4 ♕xd4 16. ♗e3 ♕xe5 17. f4 ♕d6 18. ♗d4 ⩲ or 13. ♗e3 d4 14. ♘b5 (14. ♗b5 ♗c6∓) 14...♗xb5 15. ♗xb5+ ♘c6 ⇄.

12...g6

It is interesting that Anand queries the soundness of this move and suggest 12...f5 instead. But then the move 13. ♕e2 would gain in force, since the g8 knight then has only one possible development square, namely c6.

13. ♗e3 ♗c5

13...♕d8 14. ♘b5 h5? 15. ♕xg6! ±; 13...♕xb2? 14. ♗d4 ♖c8!? (14...♕d2 15. ♖fd1 ♕h6 16. ♘b5 ⩲) 15. ♖a2 (15. ♖fb1 ♕d2 16. ♖d1 h5 ⩲) 15...♕b3 16. ♖b1 ♖xc3 17. ♖xb3 ♖xb3 18. ♕d1 ♖xa3 19. ♖xa3 (19. ♖b2 ♗b4) 19...♗xa3 20. ♕b3 ♗b4 21. ♗c3 ±.

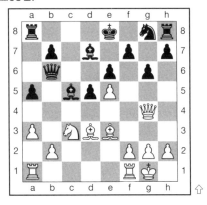

14. ♘a4?!

Here White could have taken advantage of the weakness of the dark squares on the kingside by 14. ♕f4! (Anand). Let us consider Black's possible defences:

If 14...♘e7 15. ♕f6 ♖g8 16. ♗xc5 ♕xc5 17. ♖ac1 ♕b6 18. ♖c2! ⩲ White increases his dynamic advantages – and what can Black do?

If 14...d4 15. b4!! neither 15...d×e3 16. b×c5 ♕×c5 17. ♘e4+− nor 15...a×b4 16. a×b4 ♖×a1 17. ♖×a1 d×e3 18. ♖a8+ ♔e7 19. b×c5 ♕b2 (19...♕×c5 20. ♕g5+ f6 21. e×f6 ♔d6 22. ♘e4+) 20. ♕h4+ f6 21. e×f6+ ♔f7 22. ♘e4± is any good.

The only defence was indicated by Anand: 15...g5 16. b×c5 (16. ♕g4 h5; 16. ♕×g5 ♗f8!) 16...g×f4 17. c×b6 d×c3 18. ♗d4±.

Black has an unpleasant position after 14...♗×e3?! 15. f×e3 0−0 16. b4↑, or 14...♖c8 15. ♘a4! ♗×a4 (15...♗×e3 16. f×e3 ♗×a4 17. ♕×a4+ ♔f8 18. ♖×f7+! ♔×f7 19. ♕d7+ ♘e7 20. ♖f1+−) 16. ♕×a4+ ♔d8 (16...♔f8 17. ♖ac1!+−) 17. ♗×c5 ♖×c5 18. b4±.

14...♗×a4 15. ♕×a4+ ♔f8 16. ♗×c5+

16. ♕f4!? ♔g7 17. ♗×c5 ♕×c5 18. ♖fc1 ♕b6 19. ♖ab1 (19. b4 a×b4 20. a×b4 ♖×a1 21. ♖×a1 f5⇄) 19...♕d8 (19...h5 20. b4 a4 21. ♖c5±) 20. ♖c3 h6 21. ♖e1∞.

16...♕×c5 17. ♖ac1 ♕b6 18. ♕d7!

White now threatens to penetrate with the rook to c7, so the following moves for Black are forced. If 18. ♖c2!? ♔g7 (18...♘e7) 19. ♕f4 ♖f8 20. ♖fc1 ♕b3 21. ♗e2∞.

18...♖d8!

In his annotations to this game Anand suggests other variations such as 18...♘h6 19. ♖c7 ♕×b2 or 19...♕d4, but it is difficult to believe that he seriously considered these variations during the game; it is very dangerous just to allow Shirov to attack you.

19. ♕c7 ♕×c7 20. ♖×c7 ♖b8!

Anand has calculated precisely that Black's counterplay is sufficient to draw.

21. ♖fc1 ♘e7 22. f4 (22. ♗b5 ♘c6=) **22...♘c6 23. ♖c5**

(see next diagram)

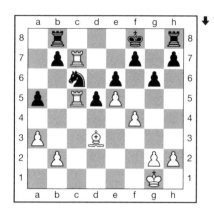

The rook comes to b5, after which White wins back the pawn, but Black will be able to simplify the position.

23...♔g7

Any Black attempt to seize the initiative is liable to rebound, e. g. 23...g5 24. f5! (Anand) 24...♘×e5 25. f6 ♔e8 26. ♗b5+ ♔d8 27. b4! (protecting the c5 rook) 27...a×b4 28. a×b4 ♖f8 29. ♖e7! ♖c8 30. ♖×b7±.

24. ♖b5 g5! 25. g3 h5!=

White retains a slight advantage after 25...♖hc8 26. ♖×c8 ♖×c8 27. ♖×b7 ♘d4 28. ♔f2±.

26. ♖b×b7

26. h4?! g×f4 27. g×f4 ♘d4! 28. ♖×a5 ♘f3+ 29. ♔f2 ♘×h4⇄.

26...♖×b7 27. ♖×b7 h4 28. ♔g2 h×g3 29. h×g3 g×f4 30. g×f4 ♖h4 31. ♔g3 ♖h1 32. ♔g2

White must acquiesce to the repetition of moves, since he cannot capture on f7: if 32. ♗b5 ♘d4 33. ♗e8 ♔f8! 34. ♗×f7? ♖h7−+; or if 32. ♖c7 ♘d4 33. b4 ♖a1! 34. ♖c3 a×b4 35. a×b4 ♖a2∓.

32...♖h4

Black is equally unable to avoid the repetition since otherwise White will win the important f7 pawn: 32...♖d1 33. ♗b5 ♘d4 34. ♗e8.

33. ♔g3 ♖h1 34. ♔g2

Draw.

Typical endgame

Game 23
Anand – M. Gurevich
Interzonal Tournament, Manila 1990

**1. e4 e6 3. d4 d5 3. e5 c5 4. c3 ♘c6
5. ♘f3 ♗d7 6. ♗e2 ♘ge7 7. ♘a3 c×d4**

7...♘g6 8. h4 c×d4 9. c×d4 h6 10. h5 ♗×a3
11. b×a3 ♘ge7 12. ♖b1 (12. 0–0, Grischuk–
Graf, 35th Olympiad, Bled 2002, game 50
on page 99) 12...♘a5 13. ♗d2 ♗c6 14. ♗b4
♘c4 15. ♘d2 ♘f5 16. 0–0 ♘×d4 17. ♗×c4
d×c4 18. ♘×c4 ♘f3+! 19. g×f3 ♕g5+
20. ♔h2 ♕h4+ 21. ♔g1 ♕×c4∓, Stević–
Nikolić, Slovenian League, Celje 2003 (see
also exercise 28 on page 138, solution
page 149).

**8. c×d4 ♘f5 9. ♘c2 ♘b4 10. ♘×b4
♗×b4+ 11. ♗d2 ♕a5**

11...♕b6! 12. ♗×b4 (12. a3 ♗×d2+ 13. ♕×d2
♗b5=) 12...♕×b4+ 13. ♕d2 ♕×d2+=.

12. a3!

12. ♗×b4 ♕×b4+ 13. ♕d2 ♕×d2+ (13...a5
14. a3 ♕×d2+ 15. ♔×d2 a4 16. h4 ♘e7 17. h5
h6 18. ♔e3 ♘c6 19. g4 ♘a5 20. ♘d2 b5†,
Wempe–Glek, Essent Open, Hoogeveen
2003) 14. ♔×d2 ♘e7 (14...f6 15. ♗d3 ♘e7
16. b4 0–0 17. ♖ac1 ♖ac8 18. b5 ♗e8
19. ♖×c8 ♘×c8 20. ♖c1 ♘b6 21. ♖c7 ♖f7
22. ♖×f7 ♔×f7 23. h4±, Margoline–Ulibin,
Cappelle la Grande 1995) 15. ♖hc1 (15. ♖ac1

♘c6 16. ♔e3 f6 17. ♗b5 ♘b4 18. a3 ♗×b5
19. a×b5 ♔d7 20. ♖c3 ♖hc8=, R. Popov–
Morozevich, Krasnodar 1997) 15...f6 16. ♖c5
♔d8 17. ♗d3 ♖c8 18. ♖ac1 ♖×c5 19. ♖×c5
♗e8 20. ♘e1 ♘c6 21. e×f6 g×f6 22. ♔e3 ♔e7
23. f4 ♔d6= (Sieiro González–M. Gurevich,
Havana 1986).

**12...♗×d2+ 13. ♕×d2 ♕×d2+ 14. ♔×d2
f6**

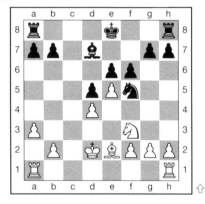

This endgame is not as simple as it looks at
first sight. Gurevich lost it to Anand, but a
few years previously, as we saw, he played
it slightly differently and won against Sieiro
González. I consider that White maintains
a slight advantage, but he has to act energetically, as otherwise the position can turn
against him.

On the theme of "Typical endgame" see
also the game Sveshnikov–Donchev, Lvov
1983 (see exercise 48 on page 142, solution
page 152).

15. ♖ac1 ♘e7 16. b4± ♔d8

It makes no sense to provoke White with
16...♘c6 into playing 17. b5, since that would
fit in with his plan to gain space on both
wings and restrict the black bishop.

17. ♗d3 ♖c8 18. ♖×c8+ ♘×c8 19. g4

After 19. h4?! h5 it would be difficult for White
to prepare a kingside break.

19...h6?!

This weakens the light squares and Anand
eventually takes advantage of this. Instead
19...♘b6 would be better, with the idea of

playing ♘c4+ and, if White exchanges on c4, deploying the bishop on the long diagonal.

20. ♘h4! ♘e7

Obviously Black cannot allow the white knight to settle on g6, since then White could easily organise his kingside breakthrough. Exchanging on e5 is unfavourable for Black, since the white king would gain the central square d4 as a base from which to threaten constantly to invade the queenside.

21. f4 a6 22. ♖f1 ♗b5!?

An interesting try. Exchanging on b5 would be unfavourable for White, since it would be easier for Black to attack the a3 pawn than for White to attack the b5 pawn. The exchange of bishops in itself is no cause for anxiety for White; he maintains a great advantage in space and Black lacks counterplay.

23. f5?

Hasty. It was better to prepare this with 23. ♖e1±.

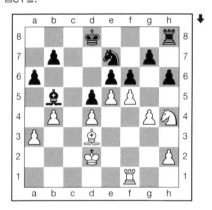

23...h5?!

Black fails to take advantage of White's error: 23...♗xd3! (Anand) 24. ♔xd3 h5 25. ♘g6

A) 25...♘xg6 26. exf6

A1) 26...gxf6 27. fxg6 ♔e7 28. g5 f5 29. ♖c1 (29. ♖f3 h4 30. ♔e3±);

A2) 26...♘f4+ 27. ♖xf4 gxf6 28. fxe6 hxg4 29. ♖xg4=.

B) 25...♖h6!?

B1) 26. g5!? fxg5 27. ♘xe7 ♔xe7 28. ♖c1 exf5 (28...♔d7 29. fxe6+ ♖xe6 30. ♖c5±) 29. ♖c7+ ♔f8 30. ♖xb7 ⩱;

B2) 26. ♘f4 hxg4 27. ♘xe6+ ♔e8 28. ♘xg7+ ♔f7±.

24. ♘g6

24. ♗xb5 hxg4!? (24...axb5 25. exf6 gxf6 26. ♘g6 ♖h6 27. ♘xe7 ♔xe7 28. ♖e1 hxg4 29. ♖xe6+ ♔f7 30. ♖b6 ♖xh2+ 31. ♔e3 ♖h3+ 32. ♔f4 ♖xa3 33. ♖xb7+ ♔e8 34. ♔xg4±) 25. ♘g6 ♖xh2+ (25...♘xg6 26. fxg6 axb5 27. exf6 gxf6 28. ♖xf6±) 26. ♗e2 ♘xf5 27. exf6 gxf6 28. ♔d3∞.

24...♘xg6?

It would have been better to play 24...♗xd3! with transposition to the lines analysed above.

25. exf6! gxf6

25...♘h4? 26. fxg6 ♖g8 27. f6 ♗e8 28. ♗h7+−.

26. fxg6 ♔e7?!

26...♗xd3 27. ♔xd3 ♔e7 (27...hxg4 28. ♖xf6 ♔e7 29. g7 ♖g8 30. ♖g6+−) 28. g5 f5 (28...fxg5? 19. ♖f7+), and White continues 29. ♖c1 as in the game, although Black has a pawn on a6 instead of b5, or 29. ♖f3±.

27. g5! f5 (27...♗xd3 28. gxf7+) **28. ♗xb5 axb5 29. ♖c1**

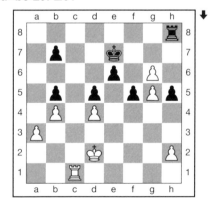

White has the more active pieces and the better pawn structure.

29...♔d6 30. ♔e3 ♖g8 31. ♔f4 b6

31...♖×g6 32. ♖c8!± (32. ♖c5!?).

32. ♖c3 ♖×g6 33. ♖h3 ♖g8 34. ♖×h5 ♖c8 35. g6 ♖c4 36. ♖g5! ♖×d4+ 37. ♔e3

37. ♔f3? ♖g4! 38. ♖×g4 f×g4+ 39. ♔×g4 ♔e7 =.

37...♖e4+ 38. ♔f2

Black resigned.

Space advantage, play on both wings, typical endgame

Game 24
Najer – Totsky
Cappelle la Grande 2004

1. e4 e6 2. d4 d5 3. e5 c5 4. c3 ♕b6 5. ♘f3 ♗d7 6. a3 ♘c6 7. b4 c×d4 8. c×d4 ♖c8 9. ♗e3±

The move 9. ♗b2± is also very strong. At least I am not aware so far of any way that Black can equalise against it.

9...♘h6 10. ♗d3 ♘g4

This is safer than 10...♘f5, after which Black must always take into account the possible exchange on f5, e.g. 11. 0–0 ♗e7 12. ♘bd2 (12. ♗×f5 e×f5 13. ♘c3 ♗e6 14. ♘a4 ♕d8 15. ♕d2 h6 16. ♘e1 0–0 17. ♘d3 ♔h7 18. ♘ac5 b6 19. ♘b3 ♕d7 20. ♘b2±, Jonkman – Stevanović, Lissabon 2000) 12...0–0 13. ♗×f5 (13. ♘b3 ♘×e3 14. f×e3 f5 15. e×f6 ♗×f6 16. ♘c5 ♕c7 17. ♖c1 b6 18. ♘×d7 ♕×d7 19. ♗a6 ♖c7 20. ♕c2±, Jonkman – Dittmar, Saint Vincent 2002) 13...e×f5 14. ♘b3 ♗e6 15. ♕d2 ♖c7 16. h4 ♖fc8 17. h5 h6 18. ♘c5±, Najer – Soćko, Internet (Blitz) 2004. Furthermore, after 10...♘g4 Black can prepare f7–f6 without having to exchange on e3 first.

11. 0–0

11...♘×e3

11...♗e7 12. ♘bd2!? (12. ♕d2 f5 13. e×f6 ♗×f6 14. ♘c3 ♘×e3 15. f×e3 0–0 16. ♖f2 ♕c7 17. ♖c1 ♘e7 18. ♕c2 h6 19. ♕b3 ♔h8∞, Movsesian – Heberla, Czech League 2003/04) 12...♘×e3 13. f×e3 ♘b8 14. ♕b1 ♗a4 15. e4 ♘c6 16. ♕b2 a5 17. e×d5 e×d5 18. b5 ♘d8 19. ♖ac1 ♖×c1 20. ♖×c1 0–0 21. ♘b1 ♘e6 22. ♔h1 ♘g5 23. ♘c3 ♘×f3 24. ♘×d5 ♕d8 25. ♘×e7+ ♕×e7 26. g×f3±, Balashov – Belozerov, Russian Championship, Elista 2001.

12. f×e3 g6

12...♗e7

A) 13. ♘bd2

A1) 13...♘b8 14. ♕e2 ♗a4 15. e4 ♘c6 16. ♕e3 0–0 17. ♖ab1 a5 18. b×a5 ♕a7 19. e×d5 e×d5 20. ♖b6 ♘×a5 21. ♖h6 (this interesting manoeuvre shows the imagination and potential of the young player; but his equally young opponent succeeds in defending himself) 21...♗c2 22. ♖h3 ♗×d3 23. ♕×d3 h6⇄, Motylev – Rychagov, Russian Championship U20, Kolontaevo 1997;

A2) 13...♘d8?! 14. ♕e2 ♖c3 15. ♖fe1?! (15. ♖ab1!?, 15. ♖fc1!?±) 15...0–0 16. g4 a6 17. ♘b1 ♖c8 18. ♕d2 ♕c7 19. ♖a2 ♗a4 20. ♕g2 f6⇄, Baklan – Moskalenko, Zonal Tournament, Donetsk 1998;

B) 13. ♕e2 0–0 14. ♘bd2 f6 15. b5 ♘d8 16. e×f6 ♗×f6 17. ♘e5 ♗e8 18. ♕g4 ♖c3

19. a4!?∞, Smirnov – Belozerov, Novosibirsk 1999;

12...f6 13. ♘bd2 fxe5 14. ♘xe5 ♘xe5 15. ♕h5+ ♔d8 16. ♕xe5 ♖c3 17. ♕g5+ (17. ♘f3±) 17...♗e7 18. ♕xg7 ♖e8 19. ♗xh7 ♖xe3 20. ♗g6 e5 21. ♗xe8 ♗xe8 22. ♖ad1 +−.

13. ♘bd2

13. ♕e1 ♗g7 14. ♘c3 ♘b8 15. ♔h1 0–0 16. e4 f6 17. exd5 fxe5 18. dxe5 exd5 19. ♘xd5 ♕e6 20. ♕e4 ♔h8 21. b5±, I. Zaitsev – Laine, Finland 1994 (Volume 2, game 32 on page 29).

13...♗h6 14. ♕e2 (14. ♕e1 !?) **14...♘e7**

14...0–0 15. ♘b3 ♕d8 16. ♘c5 ♖c7 17. h4 ♘b8 18. g4 b6 19. ♘xd7 ♕xd7 20. g5 ♗g7 21. ♘h2 ♘c6 22. ♗b5±, Ibragimov – Volzhin, Katowice 1992.

15. g4

15. ♘b3 a6 16. ♘c5 ♗b5 17. ♘e1 ♕c6 18. a4 ♗xd3 19. ♘exd3 0–0 20. a5 ♕b5 21. ♖f3 ♖c7 22. ♖af1 ♘c6 23. ♕f2 (23. ♕e1!±), Hendriks – Dgebuadse, Helmondsee 2000.

15...♖c3

15...♗a4 16. h4 ♖c3 17. ♘e1 0–0 18. ♖a2 ♖c1 19. ♘df3 ♗g7 20. ♕h2±, Gafner – Snatenkov, Orsk 2000.

16. ♖fc1

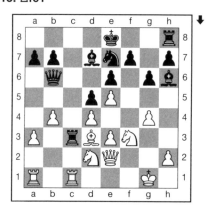

16...♖xc1+

According to my database, this is the first new move – an example of how far theory extends these days. The position has become clearly better for White: he has a big space advantage, and Black finds it difficult to create counterplay.

16...♕c7 17. ♘b3 b6 18. ♕d2 ♖xc1+ 19. ♖xc1 ♕b8 20. g5 (20. h4 0–0 21. g5 ♗g7 22. h5 ♗a4 ⇄) 20...♗g7 21. ♕c3 ♗a4 22. ♘bd2 ♔d7 23. ♕b2 ♖c8 24. ♘b1 ♖xc1+ 25. ♕xc1 ♕c8 26. ♕xc8+ ♘xc8 27. ♘c3±, Heberla – Moskalik, Poland 1999.

17. ♖xc1 0–0 (17...♗a4!±) **18. ♘b3 ♖c8 19. ♘c5± ♕d8 20. ♖f1 ♖c7**

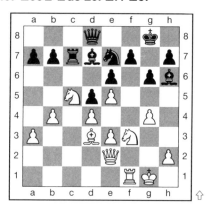

21. ♕e1

The queen covers the c3 square and, if need be, can transfer quickly to the kingside.

21...b6

Perhaps it was better to play 21...♗c8, ready to take immediately on a6 after ... b6, ♘a6.

22. ♘a6 ♖c8 23. b5!

Soon Black will not be able to move.

23...♗e8 24. a4 g5?!

A sad move. Black gains the g6 square for the knight, but switches off his bishop's "oxygen". It would be better to play 24...♗g7 25. h4 h6 26. h5±.

25. ♕b1 ♘g6

(see next diagram)

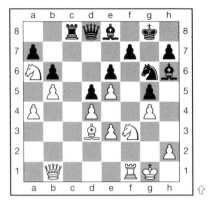

26. ♗×g6!

Excellent: White exchanges the last enemy piece displaying any signs of life!

26...h×g6 27. ♖c1 ♗f8 28. ♖c2

Winning the struggle for the open file.

28...♗e7 29. ♕c1 ♖×c2 30. ♕×c2 ♗d7 31. ♔f2 ♔f8 32. ♔e2 ♕c8 33. ♕×c8+ ♗×c8 34. ♘b8 ♔e8?

More stubborn was 34...♗b7 35. ♘d7+ ♔g7 (35...♔e8? 36. ♘f6+).

35. ♘c6 a6 36. ♘×e7 ♔×e7 37. b×a6 ♗×a6+ 38. ♔d2 ♗c4

38...f6 39. e×f6+ ♔×f6 40. ♘e5 ♗c8 41. ♔c3+−.

39. ♘×g5 ♗b3

Black wins back the pawn, but White has calculated a move further.

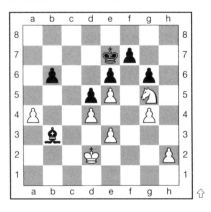

40. ♘h7!

Now the black king is cut off from the passed pawn that White will obtain on the h-file. The bishop is also unable to intervene, since the white king controls all the key squares.

40...♗×a4 41. h4 ♗b5 42. h5 g×h5 43. g×h5 ♗d7 44. ♔c3 ♗c8 45. h6 ♗a6

Black has been condemned to the role of spectator as his opponent has built up his position. White now has all his forces ready for the decisive manoeuvre.

46. ♘g5 ♔f8 47. h7 ♔g7 48. ♘×f7 ♔×h7 49. ♘g5+ ♔g6 50. ♘×e6 ♔f5 51. ♘g7+ ♔g6

51...♔e4 52. ♔d2+−.

52. ♘e8 ♔f7 53. ♘c7 ♗b7 54. ♘b5 ♔e6 55. ♔b4 ♗c6 56. ♘c3 ♔f5 57. ♘a4 ♔e4 58. ♘×b6 ♔×e3 59. ♔c5

Black resigned.

Notice how White was able to use his space advantage to play on both wings.

Space advantage; attack on the dark squares

Game 25
Lastin – S. Ivanov
Aeroflot Open, Moscow 2004

1. e4 e6 2. d4 d5 3. e5 c5 4. c3 ♕b6 5. ♘f3 ♘c6 6. a3 ♘h6 7. b4 c×d4 8. c×d4 ♘f5 9. ♗b2 ♗e7 10. ♗d3 a5

(see next diagram)

10...♗d7, Khalifman–Dolmatov, 19th EU-Cup, Rethymnon 2003 (Volume 2, game 20 on page 22).

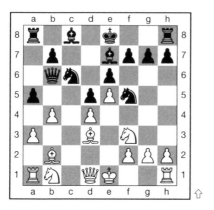

11. ♕a4

11. ♗×f5 e×f5 12. ♘c3 ♗e6 13. b5 a4
14. ♕d3 (14. ♖a2 ♘b8 15. 0–0 ♘d7 16. ♘×a4
♕×b5 17. ♘c3 ♕c4 18. ♕b1 0–0 19. ♖c1↑,
Grosar – Tabernig, Montecatini Terme 1997;
14. b×c6 ♕×b2 15. 0–0 b×c6 16. ♘×a4
♕b5 17. ♘c3 ♕c4 18. ♘e2 0–0 19. ♖c1
♕a6 20. ♖c3 ♖fc8. Draw, Shirov – Khalifman,
Linares 2000) 14...♘b8 15. ♗c1 h6 16. ♘g1?!
(16. 0–0±) 16...♘d7 17. ♘ge2 ♕c7 18. ♗d2
♘b6 19. ♖c1 ♕d7 20. ♘a2 0–0 21. ♗b4
♖fc8 22. ♖×c8+ ♖×c8 23. 0–0 ♗g5 24. f4
♗e7 25. ♗×e7 ♕×e7 26. ♘b4 ♕d7 27. ♖c1?
(27. ♘c3⇄) 27...♖×c1+ 28. ♘×c1 ♘c4∓,
Sveshnikov – Moskalenko, Norilsk 1987.

11...0–0 12. b5 f6

12...♗d7 13. g4?! (13. 0–0 ♘h4? 14. ♘×h4
♗×h4 15. ♕c2!±, Mukhametov – Rechel,
Berlin 1997) 13...♘h4 14. ♘×h4 ♗×h4
15. 0–0 f6↑, Malysheva – S. Ivanov, Rilton
Cup, Stockholm 2003.

13. ♗×f5

After f7–f6, the exchange on f5 is very unpleasant for Black, since he no longer has
e6 as a secure base and the e-file is open.
Using his space advantage and strongpoint
at e5, White should be able to gain the advantage.

13...e×f5

13...f×e5 14. ♗h3 (White misses the strong
14. ♗×h7+! ♔×h7 15. ♕c2+ e4 16. b×c6+–

but still keeps the advantage.) 14...e4
15. ♘fd2 ♘e5 16. d×e5 ♕×f2+ 17. ♔d1
e3 18. ♕g4 ♗d7 19. a4 e×d2 20. ♗d4 h5
21. ♕×e6+ ♗×e6 22. ♗×e6+ ♔h8 23. ♗×f2
♖×f2 24. ♖a2 ♗b4 25. ♘×d2±, Vysochin –
Sambuev, St. Petersburg 2003.

14. 0–0

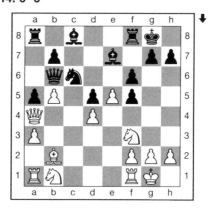

14...♗e6

14...f×e5 should be considered: 15. d×e5
♗e6 16. ♘bd2 ♘b8 17. ♗d4 ♕d8 18. ♘b3
♘d7 19. ♖ac1 ♘b6 20. ♗×b6 ♕×b6 21. ♘bd4
♖fc8

A) 22. ♘×e6 ♕×e6 23. ♖×c8+ ♕×c8
(23...♖×c8 24. ♕×a5±) 24. b6 ♕e6 25. ♖c1
♕×b6 26. ♕d7 ♗×a3 27. ♘g5 h6 (27...♖d8?
28. ♕f7+ ♔h8 29. e6 ♕b2 30. ♖f1 ♖f8 31. e7
♗×e7 32. ♕×e7 ♕f6 33. ♕a3±) 28. ♘e6 ♗f8
29. ♕×d5 ♔h8 30. ♘×f8 ♖×f8 31. e6 ♖e8
32. ♖e1 ⯬;

B) 22. ♖×c8+ ♖×c8 23. ♕b3 ♖c4 24. ♕d3
g6 25. ♖d1 a4 26. h4 ♗c8 27. ♘e2 ♕c5
28. g3 ♔f8 29. ♔g2 ♕×b5 30. ♘f4 ♖c5
31. ♕e3 ♔e8 32. ♘d4 ♕a6 33. e6 ⯬, Rainfray – Drosdovsky, Cannes 1997.

15. ♘c3 ♘a7 16. ♕b3 ♖fd8

16...♖ad8 17. ♖ad1 f×e5 18. ♘×e5 f4
19. ♖fe1 ±.

17. ♖fe1 f×e5 18. ♘×e5 ♗f6

18...♕×d4?? 19. b6 ♘c8 20. ♘f3 ♕f6
21. ♘b5+–.

19. a4 ♕×d4?!

Now the bishop slumbering on b2 wakes up. Instead 19...Bac8 20. Wd1 Bc7 21. Ne2!?± would have been more prudent.

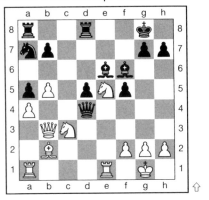

20. Ne4!± Wxe4□ 21. Bxe4 fxe4

With the disappearance of the black queen the game becomes a matter of technique. White pushes home his advantage efficiently.

22. f3! Be8

22...exf3 23. Nxf3 Bxb2 24. Wxb2±.

23. fxe4 dxe4 24. Wg3 Bd5

24...Bad8 25. Bf1 Bf8 26. Ba3+-.

25. Bd1 Bad8 26. Bf1

26. Nc6! Bxb2 27. Nxd8 Bxd8 28. Bxd5 Bxd5 29. Wb3+-.

26...Bxe5 27. Bxe5 Bd7 28. Bd1 Bee7

Or 28...g6

A) 29. Bb2 e3 30. We1 e2 31. Bd2 (31. Bc1 Bb3-+) 31...Bde7 32. Bxd5 Bf7 33. Bc3 b6 34. Bd4 Bf1+ 35. Wxf1 exf1W+ 36. Kxf1 Nc8 37. Bd7±;

B) 29. Be1 Nc8 30. Bb2 Bde7 31. Wg5+-.

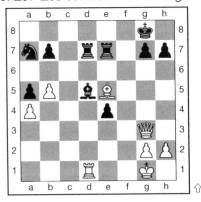

29. Bxg7! Bxg7 30. Wb8+ Kf7 31. Bxd5 Bxd5 32. Wxb7+ Ke6 33. Wxg7 e3 34. Wh6+

Black resigned.

Space advantage

Game 26
Korchnoi – Kotsur
34th Olympiad, Istanbul 2000

1. d4 e6 2. e4 d5 3. e5 c5 4. c3 Wb6 5. Nf3 Bd7 6. a3 Nc6 7. b4 cxd4 8. cxd4 Bc8 9. Bb2 Nh6!?

Black strives to complete his development. He fails to equalise with 9...Na5, e.g. 10. Nbd2 Nc4 11. Bxc4 (11. Nxc4 dxc4 12. Bc1±) 11...dxc4 12. Bc1 c3 13. Bxc3 (13. Bxc3 Bxc3 14. Bxc3 Wa6 15. Ne4 Bc6 16. Nfd2∞ or 15. d5 Ne7!) 13...Be7 14. 0-0 Nd5 15. Ne4 Be7 16. Bd2 0-0 17. Nc5 Bc6 18. Bg5 Wd8 19. Wd2 Nc7 20. We3 b6 21. Ne4±, Sax – Nogueiras, Lucerne 1989.

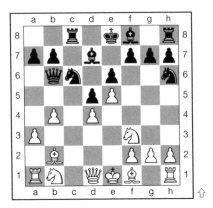

10. Bd3

Another important variation is 10. Nc3 Na5 11. Na4 Wc6

A) 12. Bc1 Nc4 13. Bxc4 dxc4 14. Nc3 Be7 15. 0-0 0-0 16. d5 exd5 17. Nd4 Wg6 18. Nxd5 Bg5 19. f4±, Dür – Damjanović, Graz 1979 (Volume 2, game 30 on page 29);

B) 12. ♘c5 ♘c4 13. ♗xc4 dxc4 14. 0–0 ♕d5 15. ♕e2 ♘c6 16. ♖fe1 ♗e7 17. ♖ac1 0–0 18. ♘e4 (18. a4 b6 19. b5 ♗a8 20. ♘a6 ♘f5∓) 18...♘f5∓, Korchnoi – Iruzubieta Villaluenga, Oviedo 1992 (Volume 2, game 37 on page 33).

10...♘a5 11. 0–0 ♘c4 12. ♗xc4 ♖xc4 13. ♘c3 ♕a6

Black strengthens his grip on the light squares and in particular the a4 square, to impede the transfer of the c3 knight to c5.

14. ♖c1

The advantages of the queen's position on a6 can be seen in the variation 14. ♕d3?! (to be able to expel the rook from c4 by ♘d2) 14...♘f5 15. g4? ♖xd4 16. ♕xa6 ♖xg4+.

14...♗e7 15. ♘d2!?

White insists on playing this manoeuvre, even though it now involves a pawn sacrifice. However this sacrifice is as good as forced, since otherwise White would find it difficult to get any play.

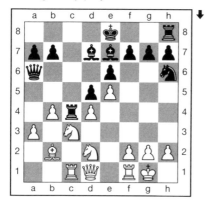

15...♖c8

Black trusts his opponent, although taking the pawn would have led to very interesting complications, e. g. 15...♖xd4!? 16. ♘e2 (16. ♘b5 ♗xb5 17. ♗xd4 ♘f5 18. ♖c8+ ♗d8 19. ♘b3±) 16...♖h4 17. g3 (17. ♘d4?! 0–0 18. ♖c7 ♗a4 19. ♕e2 ♗d8 20. ♕xa6 bxa6 21. ♖xa7 ♗b6 22. ♘2f3 ♗xa7 23. ♘xh4= g5! 24. ♘hf3 g4 25. ♘d2 ♖c8∓) 17...♗a4!?

(17...♖g4!?) 18. ♕e1 ♗b5 19. ♖c8+ ♗d8 20. gxh4 ♗xe2 21. ♕c1 0–0⇄. In all these variations it is White who is struggling for equality. However, after the retreat of the black rook to c8 Black remains under pressure.

16. ♘b3

White now has a clear plan – transfer the knight to c5.

16...b6

16...0–0 17. ♘c5 ♕c6 18. a4!?±.

17. b5! ♗xb5?!

Black enters complications needlessly. He should have just retreated with 17...♕b7, after which it would not have been easy for White to turn his space advantage into something substantial.

18. ♘xb5 ♖xc1 19. ♘d6+!

Possibly Black underestimated this move.

19...♗xd6 20. ♕xc1 ♗b8

20...♗e7 21. ♕c6+ ♔d8 (21...♔f8? 22. ♕a8+) 22. ♖c1 +–.

21. ♕c6+ ♔e7 22. ♖c1±

White controls the only open file, whilst Black's king is stuck in the centre and his pieces are scattered all over the board.

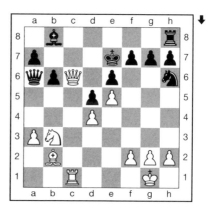

22...♖d8?

The decisive error. 22...♘f5 would have been more stubborn, e. g.

23. g4!? (23. ♘c5? ♕c8−+; 23. ♗c3? ♖c8 24. ♗b4+ ♔d8∓) 23...♘h4 24. a4 f6 25. ♖c3! (25. ♗a3+ ♔f7 26. ♕d7+ ♔g6 27. exf6 gxf6 28. ♕xe6 ♕d3 29. ♕xd5 ♗f4∓) 25...♖d8 26. g5!? ♘f5! (26...♔f7? 27. g6+! ♔xg6 28. ♖g3+ ♔f7 29. ♘c5 ♕c8 30. ♘xe6 ♖g8 31. ♕xd5 ♕xe6 32. ♕b7+ ♕e7 33. e6+ ♔xe6 34. ♖e3+ ♗e5 35. ♕e4+−) 27. ♘c5 ♕c8 28. ♕xc8 ♖xc8 29. ♘a6 ♖g8 30. ♘xb8 ♖xb8 31. gxf6+ (31. ♖c7+ ♔d8 32. ♖xa7 fxg5∓) 31...♔d7 32. ♗a3 gxf6 33. exf6 ♘d6 34. ♖g3 (34. ♖h3 ♖h8 35. f4⇄) 34...♖f8 35. ♖g7+ ♔c6 36. ♖xa7 ♖xf6 37. ♗xd6 ♔xd6=;

23. a4!? (Psakhis) 23...f6□ 24. ♗a3+ ♔f7 25. ♕d7+ ♔g6 26. exf6 gxf6 27. ♕xe6 ♕xa4 (27...♕d3 28. ♕xd5±) 28. ♖c6 ♗d6 29. g4 ♕xc6 30. gxf5+ ♔g7 31. ♗xd6 ♖g8! 32. ♔h1±.

23. a4!+− f6 24. ♗a3+ ♔f7 25. ♘c5 ♕c8 26. ♘b7!

Black resigned, since he loses his rook.

Space advantage

Game 27
Svidler – Volkov
Russian Championship,
Krasnoyarsk 2003

1. e4 e6 2. d4 d5 3. e5

"I don't consider myself to be an expert in the 3. e5 system, but in the 3. ♘c3 or 3. ♘d2 variations I would have had to begin my preparation somewhere around move 15, so secure is Volkov in the variations that he plays. The impulse to play 3. e5 was provided by one of Sergey's own games played in the Russian Club Championship in Togliatti, and which I witnessed." (Peter Svidler).

3...c5 4. c3 ♕b6 5. ♘f3 ♗d7 6. a3 a5 7. b3

After 7. ♗e2 a4 Black has good counterplay.

7...♘a6

7...♘e7 8. dxc5 (8. ♗e2 cxd4 9. cxd4 ♗b5 10. ♗xb5+ ♕xb5 11. ♘c3 ♕a6 12. a4 ♘ec6 13. ♘b5 ♕b6=, Zviagintsev – Volkov, St. Petersburg 1999) 8...♕xc5 9. c4 ♕c7 10. ♘c3 ♗c6 11. ♗b2 ♘d7 12. cxd5 ♘xd5 13. ♘b5 ♕b6∞, Delchev – Volkov, 3rd European Championship, Batumi 2002 (see also exercise 34 on page 139, solution page 150); 7...♘c6 8. ♗e3 ♘h6 9. ♗d3 ♘f5 10. ♗xf5 exf5 11. 0−0 cxd4 12. cxd4 h6 13. ♘c3 ♗e6 14. ♘a4 ♕b5 15. ♘e1 ♗e7 16. ♘d3±, Vorobiov – Volkov, Aeroflot Open, Moscow 2004 (see also exercise 52 on page 142, solution page 153).

8. ♗e3 ♖c8 9. ♗d3

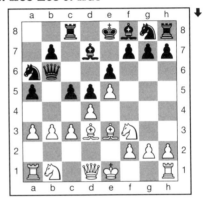

"So far just as in the game Sveshnikov – Volkov, Togliatti 2003. I played on the same team as Sergey in this event and I was worried about his position ... This feeling did not lessen after the further moves 9...♘h6 10. ♗xh6 gxh6. However he went on to win this game and later in his annotations he showed that his position was fine throughout." (Svidler).

This game continued: 11. 0−0 ♗g7 12. ♖a2 cxd4 13. cxd4 ♗b5 14. ♖d2?! 0−0 15. ♗xb5 ♕xb5=. A stronger line for White was: 14. ♗xb5+ ♕xb5 15. ♖c2 (15. ♖e2 0−0 16. ♖e3±) 15...0−0 16. ♕c1± ♖c6 17. ♖xc6 bxc6 18. ♕e3 c5 19. ♖c1 ♖c8 20. ♘bd2± or 14. ♖e2!? ♗xd3 15. ♕xd3 0−0 16. h3±.

9...♘e7

Volkov is the first to vary.

10. 0–0

10. dxc5 ♘xc5 11. ♗c2 ♕a6∞ (Svidler).

10...♘f5 (10...♗b5 11. c4±) **11. ♗xf5 exf5 12. ♖e1**

Here 12. ♘bd2!? is better: 12...♗e7 13. c4 ♗e6 14. cxd5 ♗xd5 15. ♘c4 ♕g6 16. ♖c1 0–0 17. dxc5 ♗xc4 18. ♖xc4 ♘xc5 19. b4 (19. ♗xc5 ♖xc5 20. ♕d7 ♖xc4 21. bxc4 ♗xa3 22. ♕xb7±) 19...axb4 20. axb4 ♖cd8 21. ♕b1 ♘e6 22. b5 ♖d5 23. ♖fc1 ♖fd8 24. ♕b3± or 24. h3±.

12...c4?!

A very ambitious move. Instead, 12...♗e6 13. ♘bd2 ♗e7, was a quieter continuation, after which White could hardly count on a serious advantage.

13. bxc4 ♖xc4

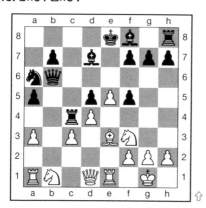

14. e6

A tempting pawn sacrifice. But it is difficult to see how else White could develop his initiative, e. g. 14. ♘fd2 ♖c8 15. ♖a2 (15. c4? ♕b2) 15...♗e7 16. ♕h5 ♕g6±.

14...♗xe6 (14...fxe6? 15. ♘e5) **15. ♘e5 ♖c7 16. ♕a4 ♔d8 17. c4**

This move is also very tempting, although it involves a rook sacrifice. However, White has a more restrained yet stronger continuation:

17. ♘d2! f6! 18. ♖ab1 ♕d6 19. ♘d3 ♕xa3 20. ♕b5!±

A) 20...♗d7 21. ♕xd5 ♕xc3 22. ♖b3 ♕c6 23. ♕xa5 ♕a4 24. ♕b6 ♕c6 25. d5 ♕xb6 (25...♕xd5 26. ♗f4±) 26. ♗xb6±;

B) 20...♕xc3 21. ♖b3 ♕c6 22. ♕xa5 g5 23. ♖c1 ♕d6 24. ♖xb7 ♕a3 25. ♖b8+ ♗c8 26. ♕xd5+ ♕d6 27. ♖xc8+ ♖xc8 (27...♔xc8 28. ♕xf5+ ♔d8 29. ♘c4 ♕e7 30. d5) 28. ♖xc8+ ♔xc8 29. ♕xf5+ ♔c7 30. d5 with a decisive attack.

17...f6 18. c5

18. cxd5 ♗xd5 19. ♘c3 ♗b3 (19...♖xc3?? 20. ♕d7#) 20. d5 ♘c5!? ⇄ or 20...♕xe3!? ⇄.

18...♕b2 19. ♘d3 ♕xa1 20. ♕xa5

The crisis of the game: Black has an extra rook, but he is behind in development and his queen is stranded in enemy territory.

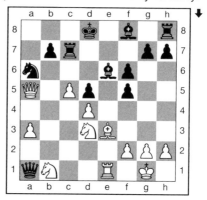

20...♕a2?!

It appears that Black is in serious trouble, e. g. 20...g5 21. ♘c3 b6!? 22. ♕xa6 ♕xc3 23. cxb6 ♖c6 24. ♕a8+ ♖c8 25. b7, but Svidler discovered a fantastic defence for Black – 20...♗c8! (protecting the a6 knight in advance) 21. ♘d2! (21. ♘c3 b6! 22. cxb6 ♕xc3 23. bxc7+ ♕xc7 24. ♕xd5+ ♕d7 −+) 21...b6! (21...♕a2 22. ♗f4!+−) 22. cxb6 ♕xa3 23. bxc7+ ♘xc7 24. ♕b6 ⯊, and it is not clear whether White has anything more than simply compensation for the pawn.

21. ♗f4 ♕c4 22. ♘b4! ♔e8

22...♕xd4 23. ♘xa6 ♕xf4 24. g3!+−.

23. ♗xc7 ♔f7 (23...♘xc7 24. ♕xc7+–)
24. ♕b6± ♗c8

24...♘xc7 25. ♕xc7+ ♔g6!? 26. ♕g3+ ♔f7
27. ♕e3 ♗d7 28. ♘d2 ♕b5 29. ♘xd5+–.

25. ♘xa6 ♕xa6 (25...bxa6 26. ♕b2±)
26. ♕xa6 bxa6

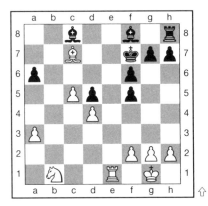

The endgame is very difficult, probably lost for Black. The material is equal but White has better development and the dangerous passed pawn on c5. Furthermore Black has to worry about the d5 pawn.

27. ♘c3 ♗e6 28. ♖b1 ♗e7 29. ♖b7 ♖e8 30. f3 g5 31. ♖a7 f4 32. ♗d6 ♔f8 33. ♖xa6 ♗xd6 34. ♖xd6 ♗f7 35. ♘xd5 ♖e1+

35...♗xd5 36. ♖xd5 ♖e1+ 37. ♔f2 ♖a1
38. c6! ♖c1 39. ♖c5+–.

36. ♔f2 ♖c1 37. ♔e2 (37. ♘xf6+–)
37...♖c2+ 38. ♔d1

38. ♔e1+–; 38. ♔d3?? ♗g6#.

38...♖xg2 39. c6 ♗h5!

Volkov defends very resourcefully.

40. c7 ♗xf3+ 41. ♔c1 ♖g1+ 42. ♔d2

(see next diagram)

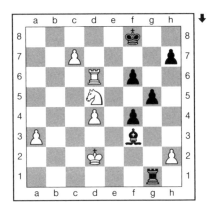

42...♖g2+ 43. ♔e1

Here 43. ♔c3 would have settled it more quickly: 43...♗g4 44. ♘xf6 ♗f5 45. ♖d5!? ♗e6 46.♖d7!.

43...♖e2+ 44. ♔f1 ♖c2 45. ♖d8+ ♔f7 46. c8♕ ♖xc8 47. ♖xc8 ♗xd5 48. a4 ♔e6 49. a5 ♔d7 50. ♖c3 ♗b7 51. ♖b3 ♗a6+ 52. ♔f2 f5 53. ♖b6 ♗c8 54. d5

Black resigned.

Pawn sacrifice for the initiative

Game 28
Sveshnikov – Komarov
Yugoslav League,
Vrnjačka Banja 1999

During my preparation for this game I realised that my opponent was an expert in the French Defence and well versed in its theoretical subtleties, so I decided to surprise him. I remembered Nimzowitsch and his 4. ♕g4 move.

1. e4 e6 2. d4 d5 3. e5 c5 4. ♕g4?!

There is another possibility to complicate the game by means of a more reasonable pawn sacrifice: 4. ♘f3!? ♘c6 5. ♗d3 cxd4 6. 0–0 ♘ge7 (6...f5!?) 7. ♗f4 ♘g6 8. ♗g3 ♗e7 (8...♕b6?! 9. ♘bd2 ♕xb2 10. ♘b3⩲; 8...f5∞) 9. ♘bd2
A) 9...0–0 10. h4 (10. ♘b3 ♗d7 11. ♘bxd4 ♘xd4 12. ♘xd4 ♕b6 13. ♗xg6 fxg6 14. ♕d2 g5!=) 10...f5∞;

B) 9...f5 10. exf6 gxf6 11. ♘h4 ♘xh4 (11...
♔f7 12. ♕h5 f5∞; 11...f5 12. ♘xg6 hxg6
13. ♘f3 ♗f6 14. ♖e1 ⩲) 12. ♕h5+ ♔d7
13. ♕xh4 e5 14. c4 dxc3 15. bxc3 ♔c7 ∓.

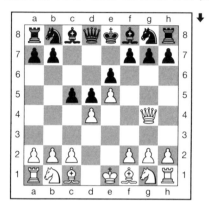

4...cxd4! 5. ♘f3 ♘c6 6. ♗d3 ♘ge7!

6...♕c7!? 7. 0–0 ♘xe5 9. ♘xe5 ♕xe5 9. ♗f4
♘f6 10. ♕g3 (10. ♗b5+ ♗d7 11. ♗xd7+
♔xd7 12. ♕g3 ♕f5∓) 10...♕h5∞ 11. ♗e5
♗e7 12. ♘d2 0–0 13. ♗xd4 ♕g4 14. ♕e3
♗d6 15. f4 ♕h4 16. g3 ♕h6 17. ♘f3 ♘g4
18. ♕e2 ♗e7 19. c3 ♗d7 20. ♖ae1 b6∓.

7. 0–0 ♘g6 8. ♖e1 ♗e7

8...♕c7

A) 9. ♕h5∞;

B) 9. ♗g5?! ♘gxe5 (9...a6) 10. ♘xe5
♘xe5∓;

C) 9. ♕g3 ♘b4 (9...♗d7 10. h4 ♖c8 11. h5
♘ge7 12. ♘bd2 f6 13. ♘b3 fxe5 14. ♘xe5
♘xe5 15. ♖xe5 ♘c6 16. ♗f4→) 10. ♘xd4
♘xd3 11. cxd3⇄.

9. c3

Black has played the opening simply and
well. White cannot regain the d4 pawn, so
the plan of c2–c3 is practically forced, although it was more precise to play 9. a3!?
first:

A) 9...0–0 10. h4 ♕c7 (10...♘xh4? 11. ♗xh7+
♔xh7 12. ♘g5+ ♗xg5 13. ♗xg5 ♕c7
14. ♕xh4+ ♔g8 15. ♗f6+–) 11. ♗g5

(11. ♗xg6 fxg6 12. ♘bd2 ♖f5∓) 11...♗xg5
12. hxg5⇄;

B) 9...♗d7! 10. b4 ♕c7 11. b5 h5 13. ♕g3 h4
13. ♕g4 ♘cxe5 14. ♘xe5 ♘xe5 15. ♕xg7
♖h5!∓.

The further pawn sacrifice 9. h4 ♗xh4∓ is
dubious.

9...dxc3

9...♗d7 10. cxd4 ♘b4 11. ♖d1 h5 12. ♕h3
♘xd3 13. ♖xd3 ♗a4 14. b3 ♗b5∓.

10. ♘xc3 ♗d7! 11. ♗d2 (11. a3!?)
11...♘b4 12. ♗b1 ♖c8 13. a3 ♘c6

13...♘a6 14. ♗d3 ♘c5 15. ♗c2 ⩲.

14. ♗d3 0–0

Black was right to delay castling, and now
14...♘a5!?∓ could be considered.

15. h4 f5!?

15...♕c7 16. ♘b5 ♕b6 (better is 16...♕b8
17. ♗c3 ⩲) 17. h5 ♘gxe5 18. ♘xe5 ♘xe5
19. ♖xe5 ♗xb5 20. ♗h6 g6 (20...♗f6
21. ♗xg7+–) 21. hxg6 fxg6 22. ♗xf8
♖xf8 23. ♕xe6+ ♕xe6 24. ♖xe6 ♗xd3
25. ♖xe7+–.

16. exf6 ♖xf6

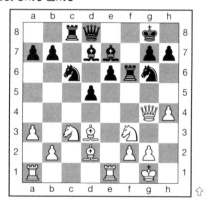

17. ♗g5

17. ♘g5 ♘f8!∓ (17...♘ce5 18. ♖xe5 ♘xe5
19. ♗xh7+ ♔h8 20. ♕e2 ♗d6 21. f4 ±);
17. h5!?

A) 17...♘f8 18. h6 ♖f7 19. ♘g5 ♗xg5
20. ♗xg5 ♕c7 21. ♖ac1 (21. ♘b5 ♕b8∞)
21...♘e5 22. ♕h3 ♘xd3 23. ♕xd3 ♕b6
24. ♕d2 ⩲;

B) 17...♖×f3?! 18. ♕×f3 ♘ge5 19. ♕h3 ♕b6 20. ♗f4 ♘×d3 21. ♕×d3 ♖f8 22. ♗g3±;

C) 17...♘f4 18. ♗×f4 (18. h6 ♕f8∓) 18...e5□ 19. ♕g3 ♖×f4 (19...e×f4) 20. ♘×e5 ♘×e5 21. ♖×e5 ♖f7 22. ♖f1 (22. ♗×h7+ ♔×h7 23. ♕g6+ ♔g8 24. h6 ♕f8∓) 22...♗d6 23. ♗×h7+ ♔h8 24. ♗d3 ♗×e5 (24...♗f5 25. ♖×f5 ♗×g3 26. ♖×f7 ♗b8∞) 25. ♕×e5 ♕f6 26. ♕×f6 ♖×f6 27. ♘×d5 ♖d6 28. ♘f4 ♔g8 29. ♖e1⇄.

17...♖×f3! 18. ♕×f3

18. ♗×g6? ♖×c3!−+.

18...♗×g5

An important moment; here 18...♘×h4!? 19. ♗×h4 ♗×h4 deserved serious consideration.

A) 20. ♘×d5 e×d5 21. ♕×d5+ ♔h8 22. ♕h5

A1) 22...g6 23. ♗×g6 ♗×f2+ 24. ♔×f2 (24. ♔h1 ♕h4+ 25. ♕×h4 ♗×h4−+);

A2) 22...♗×f2+! 23. ♔×f2 ♕b6+ 24. ♔g3 ♕c7+ 25. ♔f2 ♕b6+=;

B) 20. ♖ad1 ♕f6 21. ♕×f6 ♗×f6, and the two pawns are sufficient compensation for the exchange.

19. ♗×g6 ♗×h4?!

Black cannot stand the tension and makes an error. Stronger was 19...♗f6! 20. ♗d3 ♗×h4 21. ♕h5 g6 (21...h6) 22. ♗×g6 h×g6 (22...♗×f2+ 23. ♔×f2 ♕f6+ 24. ♗f5 e×f5 25. ♖ad1 ±) 23. ♕×g6+ ♔h8 24. ♕h6+ ♔g8 25. ♕g6+ ♔f8 26. ♕h6+ ♔f7 27. ♕h7+= with perpetual check.

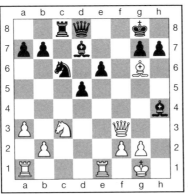

20. ♗f7+! ♔h8 21. ♖ad1!±

White has outplayed his opponent; now he has to convert his advantage.

21...♕b6

21...♗f6 22. ♕h5 ♘d4 23. ♘e2 ♘×e2+ 24. ♖×e2±.

22. ♗×e6 ♗×e6 23. ♖×e6 ♘d4 24. ♖×d4 ♕×d4 25. g3! ♗g5

25...♗f6 26. ♘×d5 ♗e5± 27. ♘e7

A) 27...♖d8 28. ♘f5 ♕c5 (28...♕×b2 29. ♕d5+−) 29. ♕e4+−;

B) 27...♖b8 28. ♕e2+−;

C) 27...♖a8 28. ♘f5 ♕×b2 29. ♕e4 g6□ 30. ♖×e5 g×f5 31. ♕×f5 (31. ♖×f5 ♕c1+ 32. ♔g2 ♕c6±) 31...♕c1+ 32. ♔g2 ♕c6+ 33. f3±.

26. ♘b5!?±

Even stronger was 26. ♕f5!±.

26...♕d2

26...♕×b2 27. ♘d6 ♖b8 28. ♘f7+ ♔g8 29. ♕×d5+−.

27. ♘d6 ♖b8 28. ♖e2! ♕c1+ 29. ♔h2!+−

An important finesse; 29. ♔g2 ♗f6 30. ♕×d5 ♕c6± would be weaker.

29...h6 30. ♘e8! ♕c5□ 31. ♕f7 ♕d4□ 32. f4! ♗d8

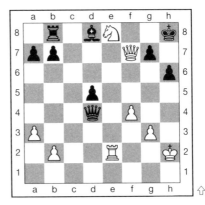

33. ♕f8+?!

This move does not jeopardise the win but it would have been better to play 33. ♔h3!+− (Prophylaxis!). Also good was 33. ♘×g7 ♕×g7 34. ♖e8+ ♔h7 35. ♕f5+ ♕g6 36. ♖h8+ ♔×h8 37. ♕×g6+−.

33...♔h7 34. ♕f5+ ♔h8

34...♔g8 35. ♘×g7 ♗b6 36. ♘e6+−; 35...♔×g7 36. ♕d7+ ♔g6 37. ♕d6++−.

35. ♕f8+ ♔h7 36. ♔h3! b5 37. ♕f5+

37. ♖d2! ♗e7 38. ♕f7+−.

37...♔g8 38. ♕e6+ ♔h7 39. ♕f5+ ♔g8 40. ♕g6 ♗f6 41. ♖e6!

Black resigned.

After this game we can draw some theoretical conclusions. The 4. ♕g4 variation is not dangerous for Black; furthermore, the onus is on White to show that he has sufficient compensation for the sacrificed pawn.

Advantage in space and development

Game 29
Sveshnikov – Timman
Tilburg 1992

This was the decisive game in our match, the first being drawn. At this time Timman was a candidate for the World Championship and was soon to play a match against Karpov. It is interesting that a few months before I had also beaten another pretender to the title (PCA version), Nigel Short, in a mini-match. Both Short and Timman had problems in the opening against me.

1. e4 e6 2. d4 d5 3. e5 c5 4. c3 ♘c6 5. ♘f3 ♕b6 6. a3 c4 7. ♘bd2 ♗d7?!

(see next diagram)

Up till this game, Black's move order in this line was not considered important, but now it is clear that it is disadvantageous for him to allow 8. b3. So 7...♘a5! is better.

8. b3! c×b3 9. ♘×b3 ♘a5 10. ♘×a5 ♕×a5 11. ♗d2 ♕a4 12. ♕b1 ♗c6

12...♕c6 13. ♗d3 h6 14. 0−0 ♘e7 15. ♖c1±, Sveshnikov – M. Kislov, Moscow 1994;

12...b5?! 13. ♗d3 h6 (13...♘e7 14. 0−0 ♘c8 15. ♗×h7 g6 16. ♗×g6+−) 14. 0−0 ♘e7 15. ♕b4 ♘c6 16. ♕×a4 b×a4 17. c4±.

13. ♗d3 ♘e7 14. 0−0 h6

After 14...♘c8 15. ♗×h7± White's big lead in development makes itself felt.

15. ♖c1 ♘c8

After this, a forcing variation leads straight into a lost ending for Black, so 15...b5 16. ♖c2 ♖b8 17. ♖b2± was better.

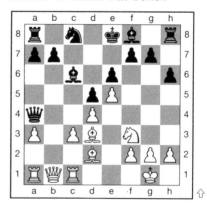

16. c4 d×c4

The line 16...♘b6 17. c×d5 e×d5 (17...♘×d5 18. ♖c4 ♕a6 19. ♖×c6+−) 18. e6 f×e6 19. ♗g6+ ♔d8 20. ♘e5+− brings no relief.

17. ♖xc4 ♕b5 18. ♕xb5 ♗xb5 19. ♖xc8+ ♖xc8 20. ♗xb5++− ♔d8 21. ♘f1 ♔c7 22. ♖c1+ ♔b8 23. ♖xc8+ ♔xc8 24. ♗e8 f6 25. a4 ♗e7 26. ♗f7 ♔d7 27. d5 e×d5 28. e6+

Black resigned, in view of 28...♔c7 29. ♘h4 ♗c5 30. ♘f5. The result of the game was decided right in the opening!

Advantage in space and development

Game 30
Praznik – Yakimenko
Correspondence 1994/96

1. e4 e6 2. d4 d5 3. e5 c5 4. c3 ♘c6 5. ♘f3 ♕b6 6. a3 c4 7. ♘bd2 ♗d7 8. b3 c×b3 9. ♘×b3 ♘a5 10. ♘×a5 ♕×a5 11. ♗d2 ♗a4 (11...♕a4, Timman) 12. ♕b1 ♕c7 13. ♗d3 ♘e7 14. 0–0 h6 15. ♖c1 ♕d7 16. ♖a2 ♘c8? 17. c4 d×c4 18. ♖×c4 ♗c6

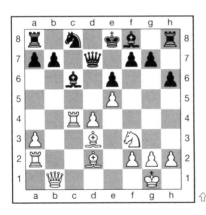

19. ♖xc6! b×c6 20. d5! ♕×d5 21. ♗e4 ♕d7 22. ♖c2! ♘e7 23. ♖b2 ♘d5 24. ♖b7 ♕d8 25. ♘d4 ♗c5 26. ♘xe6 f×e6 27. ♗×d5 0–0 28. ♕g6

Black resigned in view of 28...♗e7 29. ♗e4 ♕×d2 30. ♕h7+ ♔f7 31. ♗g6#. An attractive and energetic game by White!

Space advantage, play on both wings, typical piece sacrifice

Game 31
Sveshnikov – Eingorn
52nd USSR Championship, Riga 1985

1. e4 e6 2. d4 d5 3. e5 c5 4. c3 ♘c6 5. ♘f3 ♕b6 6. a3 c4 7. ♗e2 (7. ♘bd2!) 7...♗d7 8. 0–0 ♘a5 9. ♘bd2 ♘e7 10. ♖b1 h6 11. ♖e1 ♗c6 12. ♘f1 ♕b3 13. ♗f4 ♗a4?!

Here 13...♕×d1 14. ♗×d1 ± is better.

14. ♕c1 ♕b6

14...♕c2? 15. ♗d1 ♕×c1 16. ♗×a4++−.

15. ♘3d2 ♘g6 16. ♗e3 ♘h4 17. f4 (17. ♘g3±) 17...h5

17...♘f5 18. ♗f2 0–0–0 19. g4 ♘e7 20. ♘e3±.

18. ♗f2 ♘f5 19. ♘g3 ♘×g3 20. ♗×g3±

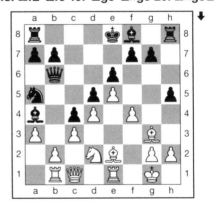

20...♘b3?!

20...h4 21. ♗f2 h3 22. ♗g4 h×g2 23. ♘f3 0–0–0 24. ♗h4 ♖e8 25. ♕d2 ♘b3 26. ♕×g2±.

21. ♘×b3 ♗×b3 22. ♗h4↑ ♕c7 23. f5!?

The quiet 23. ♗f3± is not bad either, building up the attacking potential of the white pieces.

23...e×f5 24. ♗f3 ♕d7 25. ♖e2⯹

25. e6 f×e6 26. ♕g5 ♔f7 27. ♗×h5+ ♔g8⇄, and there is no mate in sight.

25...♛e6 26. ♛g5 ♚d7

What now?

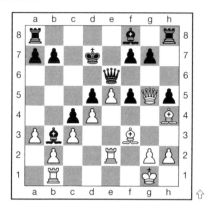

27. ♗×d5!?

A bold decision in time pressure, although 27. ♖f1 is better.

27...♛×d5 28. ♛×f5+ ♚e8

28...♛e6!? 29. ♛e4 ♚c7 30. d5 ♛g4 31. ♖f1 ♗c5+ 32. ♚h1 f5!?∓.

29. ♖f1 ♗a4 30. ♖ef2 ♗c6 31. ♛×f7+

White could just strengthen his position with 31. h3!?.

31...♛×f7 32. ♖×f7 ♖g8 33. e6
(33. ♗g5!?) **33...♗d6?!**

Instead, 33...g5! would have drawn: 34. ♗×g5 ♖×g5 35. ♖×f8+ ♚e7 36. ♖1f7+ ♚×e6 37. ♖f6+ ♚e7 38. ♖6f7+ ♚d6 39. ♖f6+=.

34. ♗g5 ♖c8□ 35. ♖1f5!? ♗e4

35...g6 36. ♖5f6 ♗e7 37. ♖h7 ♗×f6 38. ♗×f6=.

36. ♖a5 a6 37. ♖d7 ♗f8□ 38. ♖e5

38. d5 b6 (38...♗c5+? 39. ♖×c5 ♖×c5 40. ♖d8#) 39. ♖×a6 ♗c5+ 40. ♚f1 ♖f8+ 41. ♚e1 ♗×g2 42. d6 ♖f1+ 43. ♚e2 ♖f2+ 44. ♚e1=; 38. ♚f1!?±.

38...♗c6 39. ♖f7 ♗d6 40. d5□ ♖c7?!

40...♗×e5 41. ♖e7+ ♚f8 42. ♖f7+=.

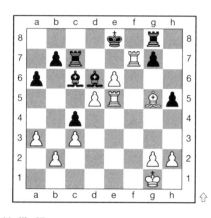

41. ♖ef5

The sealed move, forcing a draw. Instead, I could have played 41. d×c6!? ♗×e5 42. ♖d7! (I missed this.) 42...♖c8□ 43. c×b7 ♖b8 44. ♖e7+ ♚f8 45. ♚f2, although here too there is no win in sight.

Draw.

Space advantage, play on both wings, blockade of one wing

Game 32
Sveshnikov – Eingorn
Sochi 1986

1. e4 c5 2. c3 e6 3. d4 d5 4. e5 ♘c6 5. ♘f3 ♛b6 6. a3 c4 7. g3 ♗d7 8. h4

White decides to take space on the king-side and secure an active post on h3 for his bishop.

8...♘a5 9. ♘bd2 ♛c6 10. ♘g5

Clearing f3 for the queen and planning to route the knight to f4.

10...h6 11. ♘h3 ♛a4 12. ♛f3 ♛c2 13. ♘f4 ♘e7 14. ♘g2!?

In closed positions such manoeuvres are fully justified. The important thing is to form a plan and bring the pieces to good squares.

14...♛h7?!

(see next diagram)

This move is much too optimistic; better was 14...♘b3 15. ♘×b3 ♛×b3 16. ♘e3±.

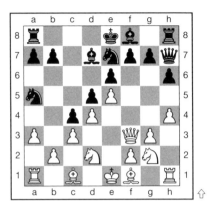

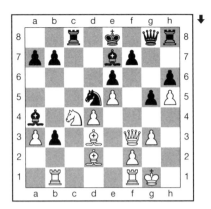

15. b4!

Apparently my opponent missed this reply.

15...c×b3□ 16. ♗d3 ♕g8

Black's last two moves were forced. Now White gains a lasting initiative for the sacrificed pawn – in this the poor position of the black queen is an important factor.

17. ♖b1 ♗a4 18. ♘e3 ♖c8 19. c4 d×c4 20. ♘d×c4 ♘×c4 21. ♘×c4 ♘d5

The most logical: since Black is behind in development, he should try to block the position. In reply to 21...♘c6 White could choose between the violent 22. d5 and the logical 22. ♗e3!? building up the dynamic potential of his position, e. g. 22. ♗e3 ♘d8 (22...b5?! 23. ♘b2! ♗×a3 24. ♘×a4 b×a4 25. ♗b5+−)

A) 23. d5!? e×d5 24. ♘d6+ ♗×d6 25. e×d6 ♗c6 (25...♕f8 26. ♕×d5→) 26. ♗×a7 ♘e6 27. 0-0 ♕f8 28. ♖fe1 ♕×d6 29. ♗d4⩲;

B) 23. 0-0! ♗c6 24. ♕e2 g5 25. h5± with later doubling of the rooks on the b-file.

22. ♗d2 ♗e7 23. 0-0 g5 24. h5!

(see next diagram)

An echo of Nimzowitsch – blockade of the wing!

24...♕g7 25. ♘e3 ♗c6 26. ♘×d5?!

Here 26. ♗e4!? would have been stronger, e. g. 26...♘×e3 27. ♗×c6+ b×c6 (27...♖×c6 28. ♗×e3±) 28. ♗×e3 g4 29. ♕e4 ♕h7 30. ♕×h7 ♖×h7 31. ♖×b3±.

26...♗×d5 27. ♗e4 g4 28. ♕e2 ♗c4 29. ♗d3 ♗d5

Or 29...b5 30. ♖fc1 ♗g5 31. ♖×b3 0-0 32. ♗×c4 b×c4 33. ♖bc3±.

30. ♗b5+ ♖c6?!

Now Black errs in turn. 30...♔d8 31. ♖fc1 ♖×c1+ 32. ♗×c1 would have been better, when White would still have difficulty demonstrating an advantage.

31. ♗×c6+ b×c6

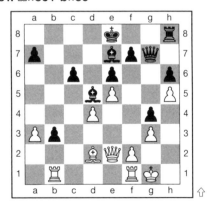

32. ♖×b3!?

I could not resist this tempting move, although I saw that the simple 32. ♕d3± kept the advantage.

32...♗×b3 33. ♖b1 0–0?

The decisive error in time pressure. Instead, 33...♗d5! 34. ♖b8+ would have led to a draw:

A) 34...♗d8 35. ♗a5 0–0 36. ♗×d8 ♖e8 (36...♗f3 37. ♕b2 ♕h7 38. ♗f6±) 37. ♕d1 ♗f3 38. ♕b3 ♕f8 39. ♗c7±;

B) 34...♔d7!, and White must give perpetual check with 35. ♖b7+ ♔e8 36. ♖b8+, since 36. ♕a6?! f6! 37. ♕×a7 c5 38. ♖b7 f×e5 39. d×c5 ♕h7!∓ does not work.

34. ♖×b3 ♖d8 35. ♗a5± (35. ♖b7±) 35...♖e8 36. ♕e4 ♖c8 37. ♗d2!

Not letting the queen out of jail.

37...♗d8 (37...♗g5 38. ♗b4+−) 38. ♖b7 ♗b6 39. ♗e3+− ♖d8 40. a4

Black has no defence against a4–a5.

40...♔h8 41. ♕×c6 ♕h7 42. a5 ♗×a5 43. ♖×a7

Black resigned.

Space advantage, converting a material advantage

Game 33
Sveshnikov – Bareev
Moscow 1991

This game was very important. A win would enable our team Poliot Cheliabinsk to qualify for the European Champions Cup.

1. e4 e6 2. d4 d5 3. e5 c5 4. c3 ♘c6 5. ♘f3 ♘h6?! 6. d×c5! ♘g4?

A serious error. Instead, 6...♗×c5 was better, as Bareev played later, e.g.: 7. b4! (7. ♗×h6 g×h6 8. b4 ♗f8!=, Sveshnikov–Glek, Moscow 1991) 9...♗b6

A) 8. ♗×h6 g×h6 9. b5!? (9. ♗d3) 9...♘e7 10. ♗d3±, Sveshnikov–Dukhov, Moscow 1992 (game 59 on page 116);

B) 8. b5 ♘e7

B1) 9. ♗×h6 g×h6 10. ♗d3± (10. ♕d2 ♕c7 11. ♕×h6 ♘g6 12. ♕g5 ♕c5⇄);

B2) 9. ♗d3 ♘g4 10. 0–0 ♕c7 11. ♕e2 ♘g6 12. ♗×g6 h×g6 13. h3 (13. ♗a3!? ♗d7 14. ♗d6 ♕c8∞) 13...♘h6 14. ♗e3 ♗×e3 15. ♕×e3⇄.

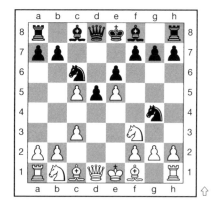

7. ♕a4!± h5□ 8. h3 ♘h6 9. ♗e3

A solid move, but 9. b4!?± was even better.

9...♘f5 10. ♗d4 ♗d7 11. ♗b5 g5 12. ♘bd2 ♖h6

With the threat 13...g4.

13. 0–0–0 g4 14. ♘e1

To exchange on g4 at an appropriate moment.

14...a6 15. ♗×c6 ♗×c6 16. ♕c2 ♕c7 17. ♘d3 ♗b5 18. ♘f4 0–0–0 19. g3! ♔b8

Better was 19...♗×c5 20. ♗×c5 ♕×c5 21. h×g4 h×g4 22. ♖×h6 ♘×h6 23. ♕h7± ♕f8□.

20. ♘b3 ♗e7 21. h×g4

Now that the bishop has left f8, the h-file can be opened.

21...h×g4 22. ♖×h6 ♘×h6 23. ♔b1 ♘f5 24. ♖h1 ♗g5

Instead, 24...a5 25. ♖h7 a4 26. ♘c1± would have been more tenacious.

25. ♘g2! ♕c8

(see next diagram)

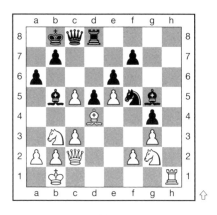

26. ♖h5! ♖g8 27. ♕d1

Not letting Black get counterplay on the h-file.

27...♗e7 28. ♘e3 ♘xe3 29. ♗xe3 ♗e8 30. ♔a1 ♔a8 31. ♕d4

Not forgetting about the opposing king.

31...♗d8 32. ♖h7 +−

The game is practically over.

32...♕c6 33. ♘c1 a5 34. ♘d3 ♗e7 35. b3 ♔b8 36. ♔b2 ♕a6 37. a4 ♔c8 38. ♔c2 ♗d8 39. ♔d2 f6

Instead, 39...♗c7 40. ♕f4 ♗d8 41. ♕h6 +− does not help.

40. exf6 ♗g6 41. ♖g7

Black resigned.

Space advantage, converting a material advantage

Game 34
Sveshnikov – Bareev
Russian Championship, Elista 1996

1. e4 e6 2. d4 d5 3. e5 c5 4. c3 ♘c6 5. ♘f3 ♕b6

After his unfortunate experience with 5...♘h6 Bareev plays the standard theoretical move.

6. a3

Other possibilities are 6. ♗e2 and 6. ♗d3?!.

6...♘h6

If 6...♗d7 7. b4 cxd4 8. cxd4 ♖c8±; or 6...a5 7. b3!?, and the a5 pawn causes Black nothing but difficulties.

7. b4 cxd4 8. cxd4 ♘f5 9. ♗b2

In my opinion 9. ♗e3?! f6!? gives Black good counter-chances.

9...♗e7

The alternative is 9...♗d7 10. g4!? ♘h6 (10...♘fe7 11. ♘c3±) 11. ♖g1!?±.

10. h4!?

A rarely played move. The idea is to control g5 or seize the initiative after 10...0–0 11. g4 ♘h6 12. ♖g1.

Also playable is 10. ♗d3 a5!∞, for which see the game Khalifman – Dolmatov, 19th EU-Cup, Rethymnon 2003 (Volume 2, game 20 on page 22).

10...h5

Here Black could consider 10...♗d7 11. g4 ♘h6 12. ♖g1±, as in Sveshnikov – Doroshkevich, Chigorin Memorial, St. Petersburg 2000.

10...0–0 11. g4 ♘h6 12. ♖g1

A) 12...f6 13. exf6 ♖xf6 14. g5 ♖xf3 15. gxh6 ♖f7 16. ♗d3 (16. ♖xg7+ ♖xg7 17. hxg7±) 16...g6 17. ♗xg6 hxg6 18. ♕h5 ♗f6 19. ♕xg6+ ♔f8 20. h7±;

B) 12...♗d7 13. ♘c3± f6 14. ♘a4 ♕d8 15. b5± ♘a5 16. exf6 gxf6 (16...♖xf6 17. g5 ♖xf3 18. ♕xf3 ♘f5 19. ♘c5 ♖c8 20. ♖c1 b6 21. ♘xd7 ♕xd7 22. ♖g4± ♖xc1+ 23. ♗xc1±) 17. g5 fxg5 18. ♘xg5 ♗xg5 19. ♘c5 ♘f5 20. ♗c1± (20. ♕h5±).

11. ♗d3! a5

11...♗d7 12. ♗xf5 exf5 13. ♘c3 ♗e6±.

12. ♗xf5 exf5 13. ♘c3

(see next diagram)

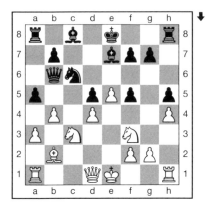

13...a×b4?!

Better is 13...♗e6! 14. b5 a4, e.g.:

A) 15. ♗c1 ♘a5

A1) 16. ♕×a4 0–0⩱ 17. ♗g5 (17. ♕c2 ♖fc8∓) 17...♘c4 18. ♕b3 ♗×a3⇄;

A2) 16. ♗g5 ♗×g5 (16...♘b3!⇄) 17. ♘×a4 ♕×b5 18. ♖b1 ♘b3 19. ♕×b3 ♕×b3 20. ♖×b3 ♗e7 21. ♘c5 ♗c8 (21...♗×c5 22. d×c5 d4 23. ♖×b7 ♗d5 24. ♖b4 ♗×f3 25. g×f3 ♔e7 26. ♖×d4) 22. ♔d2±;

B) 15. ♕d3!? ♘a7 (15...♘a5 16. ♘×a4±) 16. 0–0 ♖c8 17. ♗c1 ♖c4 18. ♘e2 ♕×b5 (18...0–0!?⇄ 19. ♗g5 ♗×g5 20. ♘×g5 ♖fc8 21. ♕f3 g6 22. ♘f4 ♕×d4 23. ♘g×e6 f×e6 24. ♕g3 ♕×f4 25. ♕×g6+=) 19. ♗g5!? ♕b3 20. ♕×b3 a×b3 21. ♗×e7 ♔×e7 22. ♖fb1 ♖hc8 23. ♖×b3 b5 24. ♘f4±;

C) 15. b×c6 ♕×b2 16. ♘×a4 ♖×a4 17. c×b7 ♕c3+ (17...0–0 18. 0–0+–; 17...♗b4+ 18. a×b4 ♕×b4+ 19. ♘d2 ♖×a1 20. ♕×a1 ♕×b7 21. ♕a3±) 18. ♘d2 0–0 19. ♖b1

C1) 19...♖×d4 20. b8♕ ♖×b8 21. ♖×b8+ ♗f8 22. ♖h3 ♕c7 23. ♖a8± ♕×e5+ (23...♕c6) 24. ♕e2 ♕c7⇄ 25. ♕×h5 (25. ♖b3 ♖×h4∓) 25...♖g4 26. ♔d1 ♖×g2 (26...d4 27. ♖g3) 27. ♖g3 ♖×g3 28. f×g3 ♕c6 29. ♖×f8+ ♔×f8 30. ♕h8+ ♔e7 31. ♕×g7 ♕a4+ 32. ♔e2=;

C2) 19...♗b4 20. ♖×b4 ♖×b4 21. a×b4 ♕×d4 22. 0–0 ♖b8 23. ♕a1 ♕×b4 24. ♖b1±.

14. ♘×d5 ♕a5

14...♕d8 15. ♘×e7 ♘×e7 (15...♕×e7 16. d5 b×a3 17. 0–0+–) 16. 0–0 ♗e6 17. a×b4 ♖×a1 18. ♕×a1±.

15. ♘×e7

15. a×b4?! ♗×b4+ 16. ♔e2□ (16. ♔f1? ♕b5+ 17. ♔g1 ♖×a1 18. ♗×a1 ♕×d5–+) 16...♕×d5 (16...♕b5+ 17. ♕d3 ♕×d3 18. ♔×d3 ♖×a1 19. ♖×a1±) 17. ♖×a8 0–0∞.

15...b3+

15...b×a3+ 16. ♘d2+–; 15...♔×e7 16. 0–0 ♕d5 17. ♕d2 ♖h6 18. a×b4±.

16. ♘d2 ♘×e7 17. ♕×b3

Simpler and stronger is 17. 0–0! ♗e6 18. ♖c1±.

17...♖h6!? 18. ♗c3 ♕d5?

An error; 18...♕a6! was necessary, with the following sample variations:

A) 19. ♖b1 ♕×a3 20. ♕×a3 ♖×a3 21. ♗b4 ♖a4±;

B) 19. ♘c4 ♗e6 20. ♕b5+ (20. ♘d6+ ♕×d6 21. e×d6 ♗×b3 22. d×e7 ♔×e7 =) 20...♕×b5 21. ♘d6+ ♔d7 22. ♘×b5±;

C) 19. d5!? ♖b6 20. ♕c4 ♕×c4 21. ♘×c4 ♖b3 22. ♗b2 (22. ♔d2 ♘×d5 23. ♗b4 ♘×b4 24. a×b4 ♖×a1 25. ♖×a1 ♗e6⇄) 22...♘×d5 23. 0–0–0 ♘c3 (23...♗e6 24. ♔c2±) 24. ♖d3 ♘e2+ 25. ♔c2 ♖×d3 26. ♔×d3 ♘f4+ 27. ♔e3 ♘d5+ 28. ♔f3 ♗e6⇄.

19. 0–0 ♕×b3 20. ♘×b3± ♖c6?!

Better is 20...♗e6 21. ♘c5 ♗d5 22. ♘d3±.

21. ♗b4 ♘d5 22. ♘a5!±

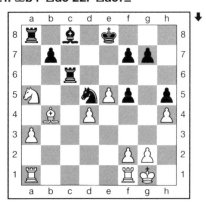

Now the position has stabilised. White is in effect a pawn and a half up, for which the control of the d5 square is not sufficient compensation for Black.

22...♖c2 23. ♖fc1 ♖xc1+ 24. ♖xc1 b6 25. ♘c4 ♗e6 26. ♘d6+ ♔d7 27. ♔h2 ♖a4 28. ♖b1 g6

28...f6!? 29. ♘c4 f4 30. exf6 gxf6±.

29. f3 f4?! 30. ♘e4 ♗f5 31. ♖b3 ♔c6 32. ♖b2 ♘e3 33. ♘c3 ♖a7 34. ♗f8 ♖a8 35. ♗e7 ♖a7 36. ♗d8 ♖a6

36...♖xa3 37. ♖xb6+ ♔d7 38. ♖d6+ ♔c8 39. ♘d5±.

37. a4 ♘d5 38. ♘xd5 ♔xd5 39. ♖xb6 ♖xa4 40. ♖d6+ ♔c4 41. d5± ♖a8?!

41...♖a2 42. e6 fxe6 43. dxe6 ♖e2 44. e7 ♔c5 45. ♖f6 ♔d5 46. ♖f8 ♗d7 47. ♖xf4±.

42. e6 fxe6 43. dxe6 ♗xe6 44. ♖xe6 ♖xd8 45. ♖xg6 ♔d5 46. ♖g5+ ♔e6 47. ♖xh5±

(see next diagram)

47...♖g8 48. ♔g1 ♔f6 49. ♔h2 ♔e6 50. ♔h1 ♔f6 51. ♔g1 ♖g7

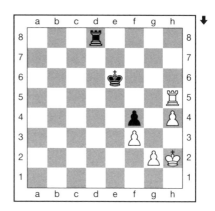

51...♔e6 52. ♖g5 ♖xg5 53. hxg5 ♔f5 54. ♔f2 ♔xg5 55. ♔e2 +−.

52. ♖h8 ♔f5 53. ♔h2 ♖g6 54. h5 ♖f6

54...♖g5! 55. ♔h3 (55. ♔g1!+−) 55...♖g3+ 56. ♔h4 ♖xg2 57. ♖f8+ ♔e5 58. h6 ♖h2+ 59. ♔g5 ♖g2+ 60. ♔h5 ♖h2+ 61. ♔g6 ♖g2+ 62. ♔f7 ♖h2 63. ♔g7 ♖g2+ 64. ♔h8 ♖g3 65. h7 ♖xf3 66. ♔g7 ♖h3 67. h8♕ ♖xh8 68. ♔xh8 (68. ♖xh8 f3 69. ♖f8 ♔e4 70. ♔g6 ♔e3 71. ♔g5 f2 72. ♔g4 ♔e2=) 68...♔e4 69. ♔g7 f3 70. ♔g6 ♔e3 71. ♔g5 f2 72. ♔g4 ♔e2=.

55. ♖a8 ♖f7 56. ♔h3

Black resigned, in view of 56...♖g7 57. ♖a5+ ♔f6 58. ♖a6+ ♔g5 59. ♖g6+.

2.3 For and against the blockade, weak colour complex

Pawn sacrifice to create a blockade

Game 35
Nimzowitsch – Leonhardt
San Sebastian 1912

1. e4 e6 2. d4 d5 3. e5 c5 4. ♘f3 ♛b6 5. ♗d3 cxd4 6. 0–0 ♘c6 7. a3 ♘ge7 8. b4 ♘g6 9. ♖e1 ♗e7 10. ♗b2 a5 11. b5 a4 12. ♘bd2 ♘a7 13. ♗xd4 ♗c5 14. ♗xc5! ♛xc5

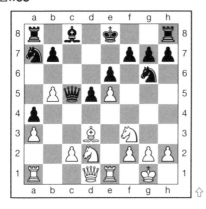

15. c4 dxc4 16. ♘e4 ♛d5 17. ♘d6+ ♚e7 18. ♘xc4 ♛c5 19. ♗xg6! hxg6 20. ♛d6+ ♛xd6 21. exd6+

Black resigned.

Weakness of the dark (and the light) squares

Game 36
Réti – Spielmann
Vienna 1928

1. e4 e6 2. d4 d5 3. e5 c5 4. c3 ♘c6 5. ♘f3 cxd4?!

Of course, this exchange is premature, since White is now able to develop his knight at c3.

6. cxd4 ♛b6 7. ♘c3± ♗d7 8. ♗e2 ♘ge7 9. 0–0 ♘f5 10. ♘a4 ♛a5 11. ♗d2

(see next diagram)

Note that here 11. g4? loses to 11...♘fxd4 12. ♘xd4 ♘xd4∓.

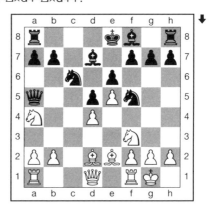

11...♗b4?!

The exchange of the dark-squared bishops is unfavourable for Black. The queen must retreat with 11...♛d8!. Then 12. ♘c5 ♘cxd4 13. ♘xd7 ♛xd7 14. ♘xd4 ♘xd4 15. ♗d3⩲ gives White compensation for the pawn, of course, but no more. And in the variation 12. ♗g5!? ♛a5! 13. ♖c1 ♘cxd4 14. ♘xd4 ♘xd4 15. ♛xd4 ♛xa4 16. ♛xa4 ♗xa4 17. ♖c7 h6 Black equalises, e.g.: 18. ♗d2 ♗c6 19. ♖xb7 ♗xb7 20. ♗b5+ ♚d8 21. ♗a5+ ♚e7 22. ♗b4+ ♚d8 23. ♗a5+.

In this line, 13. b3 (instead of 13. ♖c1) deserves attention: 13...♖c8 14. g4⩲.

12. ♗xb4 ♛xb4 13. a3 ♛e7 14. ♖c1 0–0 15. ♘c5 b6?

Better was 15...♖fc8, although here too after 16. g4 ♘h6 17. h3⩲ or 16. b4 ♖c7 17. ♛d2⩲ White has a stable advantage.

16. ♘xd7 ♛xd7 17. ♗b5 ♘fe7?

More stubborn was 17...♖fc8 18. ♛d3⩲.

18. ♛d3 h6 19. ♖c3 a5 20. ♖fc1 ♖fc8 21. ♛c2

Black resigned.

Blockade, attack on the kingside and on both wings

Game 37
Sveshnikov – Lputian
GMA, Moscow 1989

1. e4 e6 2. d4 d5 3. e5 c5 4. c3 ♘e7 5. ♘f3 ♘ec6 6. ♗d3

Against V. Kovačević (Belgrade 1988) I continued with 6. h4, but gained no advantage:

6. h4 ♘d7 7. h5 f6 8. exf6 ♘xf6 9. h6 g6 10. ♗g5 ⇄; perhaps 6. ♗e3!?.

6...b6 7. ♗g5 ♛d7

7...♗e7 8. ♗xe7 ♛xe7 ±.

8. 0–0 ♗a6 9. dxc5 bxc5

9...♗xd3 10. ♛xd3 ♗xc5 11. ♘bd2 ±.

10. ♗xa6 ♘xa6 11. c4!?

White plays to restrict the opposing minor pieces.

11...h6

11...dxc4?! 12. ♛xd7+ ♔xd7 13. ♘a3 ±.

12. ♗h4

I had reached this position on my board at home and I considered it appropriate for a principled struggle.

12...♘c7 13. ♘c3 ♗e7 14. ♗xe7 ♘xe7

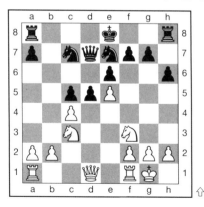

White has a marked advantage, since each of his pieces is better posted than its black

counterpart. Furthermore White has a specific target – the c5 pawn. Black's main problem is the poorly placed knight at c7. If he plays dxc4, the c5-pawn becomes very weak. Sooner or later Black will have to play d5–d4, and then White will transfer a knight to d3, with a clear plan of attacking the kingside. These are the dynamic features of the position.

15. ♖c1

To be able to respond to 15...0–0 with 16. ♘e4 followed by ♘d6.

15...♖c8 (obviously the only move) **16. ♛e2**

Here and on the previous move, ♘a4 was not dangerous for Black thanks to the reply ♘a6.

Fritz suggests 16. ♖e1!?.

16...0–0 17. ♖fd1

Renewing the threat of ♘e4 and ♘d6. If 17...♘a6 then 18. ♘b5 is possible.

17...♛c6

The move is justified tactically: 18. b4 cxb4 19. cxd5 ♛a6, e. g. 20. d6 bxc3 21. ♛xa6 ♘xa6 22. dxe7 ♖fe8 with a draw.

18. b3!

With the threat 19. ♘a4 ♘a6 20. cxd5 exd5 21. ♘xc5 ♘xc5 22. b4.

18...♖fd8 19. ♖d2 ♖d7 20. ♘a4

If 20. cxd5 exd5 21. b4 c4 22. ♘d4 ♛b6 Black can hold the position. But now he has to commit himself in the centre.

20...d4 (forced) **21. ♘e1 a5**

Played in anticipation of the necessity to play ♘c7–a6. Black establishes a lasting grip on the b4 square.

22. ♘d3 ♘a6 23. ♖e1 ♖dc7?

Not concrete enough. The immediate 23…♖e8 (or 23…♖f8) was more accurate, planning ♘e7–c8–b6. In the absence of direct threats Black has relaxed his attention …

24. h4!

As Alekhine taught, when you have a pawn on e5 you must attack the enemy king.

24…♖e8 25. ♕g4 ♔h7

If 25…♘c8, then 26. ♘f4 ♔h7 27. ♘h5 ♖g8 28. ♖d3, and the rook enters play. White seems to have a decisive attack.

26. ♖e4 ♘c8 27. ♕f3 ♘b6 28. ♘×b6 ♕×b6

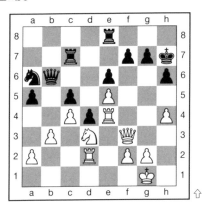

29. ♖g4 ♖g8

If 29…♘b4 there follows 30. ♘f4 ♖g8 31. ♘h5 ♕b7 32. ♕f6 or simply 32. ♕g3.

30. ♘f4 ♕b4

Now 30…♘b4 is pointless. White would drive the knight back with a2–a3 and the second rook would come into the attack via d3. The queen raid distracts White to a considerable extent and almost proves successful.

31. ♖d1 ♕c3 32. ♕e4+ ♔h8

(see next diagram)

32…g6 33. h5+−.

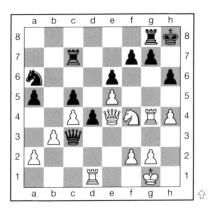

Here I used up nearly all my remaining time (not much, I have to say) but I still went astray. Stronger is 33. ♖d3! ♕c2 34. a3 (threatening 34…♘b4) 34…♘b8 35. ♘h5 ♘d7 (c6), and now comes the "Karpovian" move (as Razuvaev termed it) 36. ♔h2!, threatening to capture on g7 without allowing Black to check on c1.

33. ♖g3

Now the pace of the white attack slows, although it should still be winning.

33…♕b2 34. ♘h5 ♘b4 35. ♕g4

Now the threat is 36. ♘f6, but there is a simple defence. Here 35. ♕f4? would fail to 35…♕e2. But 35. ♕f3! instead was winning, e.g. 35…♖cc8 (35…♕c2 36. ♘×g7 ♖×g7 37. ♕f6 ♕h7 38. ♖×g7 ♕×g7 39. ♕d8++−) 36. ♘×g7! ♖×g7 37. ♕f6 ♖cg8 38. ♕×h6+ ♖h7 39. ♕f6+ ♖hg7 40. ♖g5+−.

35…♖cc8

35…♘×a2 36. ♘f6 ♘c3 37. ♖e1 ♖cc8⇄.

36. ♕f3 ♕c2

(see next diagram)

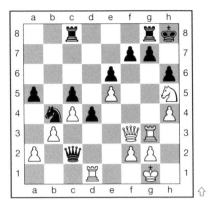

37. ♘f6!?

Seeing that my attack was going nowhere and with my flag hanging, I was prepared to force a draw. After 37...g×f6! White would have no more than a perpetual check. However, as he told me after the game, Lputian thought that he could play for a win, and so he avoided the draw, underestimating the strength of my next move.

37...♘c6?

37...g×f6 38. ♕×f6+ ♔h7 39. ♕×f7+=.

38. ♖e1! ♖gd8?

Now it is too late to capture on f6: 38...g×f6 39. ♕×f6+ ♔h7 40. ♕×f7+ ♔h8 41. ♕×e6 ♕d2 42. ♖ee3! So Black saves the exchange.

Instead 38...d3!? was worth consideration: 39. ♘×g8 d2 40. ♖f1 ♖×g8 41. ♕d1 (41. ♕×c6 d1♕ 42. ♖×d1 ♕×d1+ 43. ♔h2 ♕d4±) 41...♕×a2 42. ♖d3 a4 43. b×a4 ♕×c4 44. ♖×d2 ♕×h4 45. f4 ♘d4± 46. ♕e1 ♕e7 47. a5 ♖a8 48. ♖a2±.

39. ♕g4 ♕g6 40. ♕d1

I managed to play this move with seconds to spare. And then something unexpected happened – Lputian resigned. He thought that he was losing his queen after 40...♕f5 41. ♖f3. In fact the winning move was 41. ♖g5! and if 41...♕f4 then 42. ♖×g7. To be frank I only saw this later, when I was able to consider the position calmly and at leisure.

For and against the blockade; the f7–f6 break

Game 38
Sveshnikov – Razuvaev
GMA, Palma de Mallorca 1989

Yuri Razuvaev and I have been battling each other in the French Defence for many years now. In December 1988 I managed to win quite a good game against him, and now came a new encounter.

1. e4 c5

A little finesse. If immediately 1...e6 2. d4 d5 3. e5 c5 White has the extra possibility of 4. ♘f3 ♘c6 5. ♗d3.

2. c3

Objectively stronger is 2. ♘f3 or 2. f4, but I wanted to stick to my guns.

2...e6 3. d4 d5 4. e5

The starting point. The rest of the proof was a more difficult matter.

4...♘c6 5. ♘f3 ♕b6

If you want to play this position with Black, then I recommend you consider the immediate attack on the e5 pawn with 5...f6!?. Although White gained an advantage in the game Nimzowitsch – Levenfish, Carlsbad 1911 with 6. ♗b5 ♗d7 7. 0–0 ♕b6 8. ♗×c6 b×c6 9. e×f6 ♘×f6 10. ♘e5 ♗d6 11. d×c5 ♗×c5 12. ♗g5 (game 56 on page 112) I think that Levenfish went wrong on move 6; the immediate 6...♕b6 is better, with a complicated game.

6. a3

The move 6. ♗d3 was tried in our previous encounter. As well as this and the move played in the game, there is 6. ♗e2, which Victor Kupreichik has helped develop.

6...♗d7

Another more radical possibility was 6...c4. In that case the character of the position changes but that's another story, one played out in my four duels with grandmaster Viacheslav Eingorn.

7. ♗e2

White should fight for advantage with 7. b4!? c×d4 (I doubt we need dwell for long on 7...c4?!, since after 8. a4! White's space advantage on the kingside can prove decisive in the future) 8. c×d4 ♖c8 and now:

9. ♗b2 ♘a5 10. ♘bd2 ♘c4 11. ♘×c4 (11. ♗×c4?! d×c4 12. ♖c1 c3!?) 11...d×c4 12. ♖c1 ♕a6 13. d5 e×d5 14. ♕×d5 with a complicated game.

The simple 9. ♗e3 deserves consideration, e.g. 9...♘h6 10. ♗d3 ♘f5 11. 0–0 ♗e7 12. ♗×f5 e×f5 13. ♘c3 ♗e6 14. ♘a4 ♕d8 15. ♖c1 0–0 16. ♘c5 with a slight edge to White, as in the game Kontić – Ulibin, Titograd 1987.

Those were early days in the development of the theory of this line. Of course, today you can find out the correct way to play this line just by looking at the latest games of first category players. But we should show how all this developed.

7...♘h6!

In Romanishin – Foisor (Tbilisi 1986) Black obtained a comfortable game after 7...♘ge7 8. d×c5 ♕c7! 9. 0–0 ♘×e5 10. ♘×e5 ♕×e5 11. ♘d2 ♕c7 12. b4 g6!. Instead of 11. ♘d2 the immediate 11. b4 is interesting.

8. b4 c×d4 9. ♗×h6?!

It would have been better to play 9. c×d4 ♘f5 10. ♗b2 (10. ♗e3 ♗e7 11. 0–0 0–0∓) 10...♘a5! 11. ♘bd2 ♘c4∓.

9...d3!?

An interesting idea: Black deprives the e5 pawn of support, although he loses a tempo and the white bishop comes to a more active position. The natural 9...g×h6 10. c×d4 ♗g7 11. ♘c3 0–0 12. ♘a4 ♕d8 13. ♘c5 allows White to take the initiative.

10. ♗×d3

Confronted by something unexpected, my resolve weakened and I offered a draw. I think this was my first serious error of the game. It is not difficult to explain my offer: at that point we were both on two out of two. However, my opponent showed his character and decided to fight on.

10...g×h6 11. 0–0

White is unable to defend the pawn after 11. ♖a2 ♗g7 12. ♖e2 ♕c7.

11...♗g7 12. ♖e1

12. ♕e2 0–0 13. b5 ♘e7!∓.

12...0–0

The complications arising after 12...f6?! 13. e×f6 ♗×f6 14. b5!? (14. ♕c2 0–0–0! ↑) 14...♘e7 15. ♘e5± are rather in White's favour. Instead, 12...♕c7!? 13. ♕e2± deserved attention.

13. ♘bd2

13. ♕c2 ♕c7! attacking the e5 pawn.

13...f6

Black's play is understandable: it is necessary to open the f-file, double the rooks on it, and transfer the bishop from d7 to g6 or h5 via e8. White meanwhile will try to open the game with c2–c4.

14. e×f6 ♗×f6

If 14...♖×f6 then 15. c4! would disturb the enemy pawn centre. There are two good alternatives in 15. ♕c2 e5 16. ♗×h7+ ♔h8 17. b5!± and 15. ♘b3 e5 16. ♗c2 ♘e7 17. ♖×e5 ♖×f3 18. ♖×e7 ♕×f2+ 19. ♔h1 ♖f7 20. ♕×d5±.

15. ♖a2!

(see next diagram)

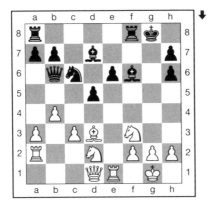

A flexible move that has a tactical justification. If 15. ♕c2 ♖f7 (15...e5⇄) 16. b5 ♘e7∓.

15...♔h8?!

More critical was 15...e5!? 16. c4 e4 17. cxd5 exd3 18. dxc6 ♗xc6 19. ♕b3+ ♔h8 20. ♕xd3 ♖ad8 with compensation for the sacrificed pawn. Instead, 15...♗xc3?! fails to 16. ♗xh7+ ♔xh7 (16...♔h8 17. ♗b1!→ with multiple threats.) 17. ♕c2+ ♔g8 18. ♕xc3 e5? 19. ♕d3 and Black is in a bad way.

16. c4!

Now it is not easy for Black to mobilise his centre pawns. Also playable was 16. ♘b3 ♗xc3 17. ♘c5 ♕c7 18. ♘xe6 ♗xe6 19. ♖xe6±.

16...a5?!

Provoking a crisis. Instead 16...♖ae8 was to be considered, although the position arising after 17. ♕b1 ♖e7 18. ♘b3 ♗c3 (or 18...dxc4 19. ♗xc4) 19. ♖e3 is also better for White.

17. b5 ♘d4

It would be better to play 17...♘e7 18. ♕e2± but Razuvaev decided to simplify the position.

18. ♘xd4

Or 18. ♘e5!? ♗e8 19. ♕g4±.

18...♕xd4 19. ♘f3 ♕f4 20. ♖e3?

A blunder, I simply missed that after 20...dxc4 21. ♖e4 ♕d6! it is not possible

to recapture on c4, since 22. ♗xc4 is impossible and if 22. ♖xc4 then 22...♗xb5. The simple 20. ♖ae2!? followed by 21. ♕b1 or 21. ♕c2 would have kept the advantage; for example 20...♖ae8 21. ♕c2± or 20...♗c3 21. ♖f1±. The alternative 20. ♖c2± also keeps a stable advantage, since Black has great difficulties with the defence of the e6 pawn. But now White loses control of the blockading squares e5 and d4 and Black gets good counterplay.

20...dxc4!

Seizing his opportunity.

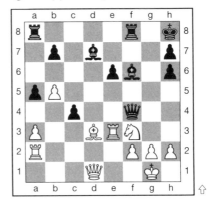

21. ♗xh7

White has no good moves here, so I decided at least to weaken the black king's protection. If 21. ♕a4 ♖ac8 22. ♗f1 ♖c5∓.

21...♗xb5 22. ♗b1

If 22. ♗e4 the resolute 22...c3! 23. ♗xb7 ♖ad8 is unpleasant, since the c3 pawn is very threatening.

22...♖ad8 23. ♖d2

I wanted to exchange the inactive rook, but it is possible that 23. ♕c2 was stronger, although after 23...♖f7 Black's position is clearly better.

23...c3 24. ♕c2

If 24. ♖xd8 ♖xd8 25. ♕c1 ♗d4∓.

24...♕f5 25. ♖xd8 ♖xd8 26. ♕c1 (The only move.) **26...♕d5.**

After 26…♗d3?!, anticipating 27. ♖×d3 ♖×d3 28. ♘e1 ♗g5! 29. ♗×d3 ♗×c1 30. ♗×f5 e×f5 with a depressing endgame for White, or 28. ♗×d3 ♕×d3 29. ♕×h6+ ♔g8∓, White can turn the tables completely with 28. ♗c2!!±, e. g. 28…♕d5 29. ♕×h6+ ♔g8 30. ♕g6+ ♗g7 31. ♗×d3+−.

27. ♗c2!

Razuvaev missed this. He was expecting to win prettily after the natural 27. ♖e1? ♕d2!! 28. ♘×d2 c×d2 29. ♕d1 d×e1♕+! (29…♗a4 30. ♖f1 ∓) 30. ♕×e1 ♗a4−+. Now the struggle flares up again with renewed intensity.

27…♖d7?!

Not seeing any concrete threats, Black plays a prophylactic move. 27…♔g7∓ was better.

28. h4!?

Creating an escape square for the king and at the same time controlling g5. The alternative was 28. ♖e1∓.

28…♔g7 29. ♖e4 ♗d3

It is understandable that Black seeks to ensure his king's safety by exchanging bishops.

30. ♖g4+ ♔h7?

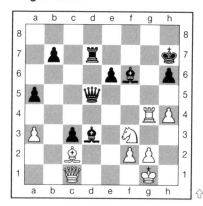

This natural move played in time trouble actually brings my opponent to the edge of defeat. The correct 30…♔f7! 31. ♗×d3 ♕×d3 32. ♕×h6 c2 33. ♕h5+ ♔f8! (33…♔e7? 34. ♕c5+ und ♖c4) 34. ♕c5+ ♗e7 35. ♕c8+ ♖d8 would still have won.

31. ♖d4?

The last and decisive mistake. The idea was a good one, but badly carried out. I was rushing, since Black was very short of time. Instead, with his flag hanging I doubt very much whether Black would have been able to find the correct reply to 31. ♘d4!. After the game Razuvaev said that he had seen this and intended to reply 31…♕c4?!, based on the variation 32. ♕b1 ♖×d4 33. ♖×d4 ♕×d4 34. ♗×d3+ ♔h8 and White has to fight for the draw. But 32. ♗b3! is a different story:

a) 32…♖×d4 33. ♗×c4 ♗×c4 34. ♕b1+ ♔h8 35. ♕g6 ♖×g4 36. ♕×f6+ and 37. ♕×c3 with good winning chances for White.

b) 32…♕a6 33. ♘×e6 ♕d6 34. ♕f4! ♕e7 (34…c2? 35. ♕×d6 c1♕+ 36. ♔h2 ♖×d6 37. ♘f8+ ♔h8 38. ♖g8#) 35. ♕b8 and Black is lost.

If instead 31…♗f5 White can play 32. ♘×f5 e×f5 33. ♕f4.

So Black should play 31…♗×c2! 32. ♕×c2+ ♔h8 33. ♕g6 ♗g7 34. ♘×e6 and now:

a) 34…♕d1+? 35. ♔h2 c2 36. ♕e8+ ♔h7 37. ♘f8+! ♗×f8 (or 37…♔g8 38. ♘g6+ ♔h7 39. ♕h8+! ♗×h8 40. ♘f8#!) 38. ♕g6+ ♔h8 39. ♕g8#.

b) 34…c2! and White has to take perpetual check with 35. ♕e8+ ♔h7 36. ♕g6+. But Black would have had to find this variation in time trouble! This would have been the logical conclusion to the game.

31…♗×d4 (The only move.) 32. ♗×d3+ ♔g7 33. ♕f4 ♗×f2+! (The most precise.) 34. ♔×f2 ♕×d3 35. ♕e5+ ♔h7 36. ♕×e6 c2 37. ♘e5 c1♕

Or 37…♕d2+ 38. ♔g3 ♖g7+.

38. ♘×d3 ♕d2+

White resigned.

The f7–f6 break

Game 39
Casper – Uhlmann
DSV Tournament, East Berlin 1982

For many years the German grandmaster Wolfgang Uhlmann was one of the top specialists in the French Defence. In this game he faced a young and talented compatriot, who carried out a splendid attack.

1. e4 e6 2. d4 d5 3. e5 c5 4. c3 ♘c6 5. ♘f3 ♕b6 6. a3 c4 7. ♘bd2

Here is an example from modern practice: 7. ♗e2 ♗d7 8. ♘bd2 ♘a5 9. ♖b1 ♘e7 10. 0–0 ♕c7 11. ♖e1 ♘c8 12. ♘f1 ♘b6 13. ♗f4 ♘b3 14. ♘3d2 ♘a5 15. ♘g3 ♗a4 16. ♕c1 0–0–0= (Ni Hua – Bareev, Peking 2003).

7...f6

Uhlmann's trademark. He has closed the centre with c5–c4 and now begins to undermine it. White has a space advantage but his pieces are not placed very harmoniously.

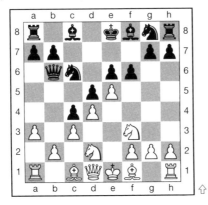

8. ♗e2

White develops quickly and prepares to attack in the centre with b3 und c4. Less dangerous for Black would be 8. exf6 ♘xf6 9. b3 cxb3 10. ♖b1 ♗d6 11. ♗d3 0–0 12. 0–0 e5↑ or 8. g3 fxe5 9. ♘xe5 ♘xe5 10. dxe5 ♗c5 11. ♕h5+ g6 12. ♕e2 ♘e7 13. ♗g2 ♗d7 14. 0–0 0–0–0 15. ♘f3 ⇄ (Honfi – Uhlmann, Solingen 1974).

8...♕c7 !?

A) 8...♗d7 9. 0–0 0–0–0 10. b3 cxb3 11. ♘xb3 ♕c7 12. ♖b1 ♗e8 13. ♗f4 h6 14. c4 g5 15. ♗d2 ♗g6 16. cxd5 ♖xd5 17. ♗c4 ♗xb1 18. ♗xd5 exd5 19. ♕xb1± (Sveshnikov – Meshkov, Podolsk 1990);

B) 8...fxe5 9. ♘xe5

B1) 9...♘f6 !? 10. f4! (10. 0–0 ♗d6 11. ♘df3 0–0 12. ♕c2 ♕c7 13. ♗f4 ♘h5 14. ♘xc6 ♘xf4 15. ♘ce5 ♗d7 16. ♖fe1 ♖f5 17. ♗f1 ♘g6± (Teske – Uhlmann, GDR Championship, Nordhausen 1986) 10...♗d6 11. ♗h5+! (11. ♘df3± planning 0–0, ♕c2, ♔h1, ♗e3) 11...g6 12. ♗f3 0–0 13. ♕e2 ♕c7 14. g3 ♗d7 15. ♘xd7!± (Th. Pähtz – Uhlmann, GDR Championship, Nordhausen 1986);

B2) 9...♘xe5 10. dxe5 ♘h6 11. ♘xc4! dxc4 12. ♗xh6 ♗d7□ 13. ♗g5 ♕xb2 14. 0–0 ♕xc3 15. ♗h5+ g6 16. ♕b1!!± (Th. Pähtz – Uhlmann, Erfurt 1985, exercise 11 on page 136).

9. 0–0 !? fxe5 10. ♘xe5 ♘xe5 11. dxe5 ♘e7

11...♕xe5 12. ♖e1 ♕d6 13. b3 cxb3 14. c4 ♘f6 15. ♕xb3 ♗e7 16. cxd5 exd5 17. ♗b5+± (Casper – Knaak, GDR Championship, Fürstenwalde 1981).

12. b3! cxb3 13. c4!

The signal for the attack. White sacrifices two pawns, after which all his pieces spring to life. The d2 knight suddenly has access to a lot of squares, the bishops have dangerous fields of fire and the queen's rook comes into action. Meanwhile, Black requires two tempi to evacuate his king to safety away from the centre.

13...♕xe5 14. ♖b1→ ♘g6

If 14...♗d7 15. ♗b2± with the idea of ♗h5+.

15. cxd5±

(see next diagram)

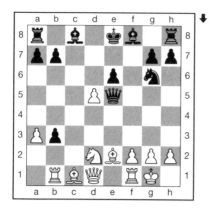

15...♕×d5?!

Instead of this, the tempo-gaining 15...♗d6!? was much better, after which in the variation 16. ♘f3 (an unclear position arises from 16. ♗b5+ ♔f7 17. ♘f3 ♕×d5 18. ♖×b3 ⯗ or 18. ♘g5+ ♔e7 ⇄) 16...♕×d5 17. ♖×b3 ♕×d1 18. ♖×d1 White must accept an exchange of queens. But even without out the queens he has a strong initiative, e.g. 18...♗c7 19. ♗b5+ ♔e7 20. a4 a6 21. ♗d3 ⯗. If Black chooses 17...♘f4 (instead of 17...♕×d1) then 18. ♗b5+ ♔f7 (18...♔e7) 19. ♕c2± (19. g3!? ⯗) 19...♕f5, and White gains a strong attack with both 20. ♗d3, e.g.: 20...♘×d3 21. ♖×d3 ♖e8 22. ♕e2 ♗c7 23. ♖c3 ♗b8□ 24. ♖d1 e5 25. ♘g5+ ♔g8 (25...♔g6 26. h4+−) 26. ♕b5 ♕f8 27. ♕d5+ ♔h8 28. ♘f7+ ♔g8 29. ♘d8++− or 24...♔g8 25. ♕c4 b6 26. ♕c6 ♕f7 27. ♕a4 ⯗ (but not 27. ♘g5? ♕h5−+), and 20. ♕×f5+ e×f5 21. ♖d1, for instance 21...♗c7 22. ♖c3 ♗b8 23. ♗c4+ ♔g6 24. g3 ♘h3+ 25. ♔g2 f4 26. ♗d3++−.

After the move in the game, however, White is able to keep the queens on and his attack grows rapidly.

16. ♗c4 ♕d6 17. ♕×b3 ♗e7 18. ♗b5+ ♗d7

18...♔f7!? 19. ♖e1 (19. ♘e4?! ♕d5 20. ♕f3+ ♕f5 21. ♖b3 ♖d8±) 19...♖f8 20. ♘e4↑.

19. ♘e4 ♕d5

19...♕c7 20. ♕×e6±.

20. ♗×d7+ ♕×d7 21. ♖d1 ♕c6 22. ♕×b7 ♕×b7 23. ♖×b7±

Black has managed to reach an endgame after all, but although the material is equal White's pieces are much more active.

23...0−0 24. ♗g5!? ♗×g5

24...♗×a3?? 25. ♖dd7+−; 24...♖fd8!?.

25. ♘×g5 ♖fb8

25...h6? 26. ♖dd7+−.

26. ♖dd7 ♖×b7 27. ♖×b7 ♘f8

27...♘f4!? 28. g3 ♘e2+ 29. ♔g2 ♘d4 30. ♖d7 e5 31. f4+−.

28. g3 h6

28...e5 29. ♔g2!? a6 30. ♔f3±; 28...a5!?.

29. ♘f3 a5

29...♘g6 30. ♔g2! with the idea of h4−h5 (30. h4 ♖f8! 31. ♘d4 ♖f7; 30. ♘d4!?).

30. ♘e5 a4 31. f4 g5?!

31...♘h7 32. ♔g2!? ♘f6 33. ♖b6 ♖c8 (33...♖d8 34. ♖a6 ♖d2+ 35. ♔h3 ♖d4 36. ♖×e6±) 34. ♖a6 ♖c2+ 35. ♔h3±.

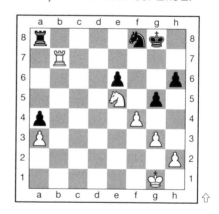

32. ♘g4!+− g×f4 33. ♘f6+!

33. ♘×h6+? ♔h8 34. g×f4 ♘g6⇄.

33...♔h8 34. g×f4 ♖c8 35. ♖f7! ♖d8

35...♖c3 36. ♖×f8+ ♔g7 37. ♘d7 ♖×a3 38. ♖a8+–.

36. ♔f2 ♖d3 37. ♔e2 ♖×a3

37...♖d8 38. ♔f3 ♖d3+ 39. ♔g4 ♖×a3 (39...♖d8 40. ♔h5) 40. ♖×f8+ ♔g7 41. ♘d7 ♖d3 42. ♖f7+! ♔×f7 43. ♘e5+ ♔e7 44. ♘×d3.

38. ♖×f8+ ♔g7 39. ♘d7 ♖a2+ 40. ♔e3 ♖×h2 41. ♖a8 a3 42. ♘e5 a2 43. ♖a7+ ♔f8 44. ♘f3 ♖b2 45. ♘d4 ♔e8 46. ♘×e6 h5 47. f5 ♖b7 48. ♖×a2 ♔e7 49. ♘d4 ♔f6 50. ♔f4

Black resigned.

The f7–f6 break and counterplay against the d4 pawn

Game 40
Potkin – Filippov
Russian League, Togliatti 2003

This is a model game from Black's point of view, since it shows how to deal with the move 9. ♗e3. If White wants to fight for an advantage, the bishop must be developed at b2 in this line.

1. e4 e6 2. d4 d5 3. e5 c5 4. c3 ♘c6 5. ♘f3 ♕b6 6. a3 ♘h6 7. b4 c×d4 8. c×d4 ♘f5 9. ♗e3

9. ♗b2 ♗d7 (9...♗e7, Lastin – S. Ivanov, Moscow 2004, game 25 on page 51) 10. g4, Sveshnikov – Radjabov, Tallinn 2004 (Volume 2, game 61 on page 53).

9...f6!

(see next diagram)

Immediately attacking the e5 pawn! I think this equalises for Black. Instead, 9...♗d7 10. ♗d3 g6 11. 0–0 ♗e7 12. ♘c3 ♕d8 13. ♖c1 ♖c8 14. ♘a4 b6 15. ♗a6 ♖b8 16. ♘c3±, Vlassov – Einarsson, Reykjavík (Rapidplay) 2003 is weaker.

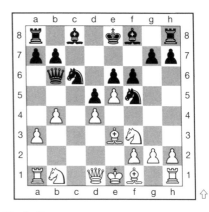

10. ♗d3

10. e×f6 g×f6

A) 11. ♕d2? is bad in view of 11...♘×b4 12. ♘c3□ (12. a×b4?! ♗×b4 13. ♘c3 ♗d7 14. ♖c1 ♖c8∓) 12...♕a5∓, Sveshnikov – Doroshkevich, Anapa 1991 (exercise 33 on page 139, solution page 150);

B) 11. ♗d3, Morozevich – Bareev, Monte Carlo 2002 (Volume 2, game 42 on page 36);

10. b5 ♘×e5 11. d×e5 ♘×e3 12. f×e3 ♕×e3+ 13. ♕e2 ♕c1+ 14. ♕d1. Draw, Romanishin – Lputian, Yerevan 1988.

10...♘×e3 11. f×e3 f×e5 12. b5

12. 0–0 e4 13. ♗×e4 d×e4 14. ♘g5 ♗e7 15. ♘×e4 e5 16. ♘bc3 e×d4 17. ♘d5 ♕d8∓.

12...♘×d4!

This temporary piece sacrifice gives Black adequate counter-chances.

13. e×d4 e4 14. ♗×e4

14. 0–0 e×f3 15. ♕×f3 ♕×d4+ 16. ♔h1 ♗d7 17. ♘c3 ♗d6 18. b6 a6 19. ♖ae1 0–0–0∓, Otero – Nogueiras, Guillermo García Memorial, Santa Clara 1999.

14...d×e4 15. ♘e5 ♗d7

15...♕a5+

A) 16. ♕d2 ♕×d2+ (16...♕×b5 17. ♘c3 ♕a6 18. ♘×e4∞ ♗d7 19. ♘×d7 ♔×d7 20. d5 ♖d8 21. d6!?±) 17. ♘×d2 ♗d7 18. ♘×d7 ♔×d7 19. ♖f1 =;

B) 16. ♘d2?! ♕c3 17. 0–0? (17. ♖f1 ♕e3+ 18. ♕e2 ♕×d4–+; 17. ♖c1□ ♕e3+ 18. ♕e2 ♕×d4 19. ♘dc4 ♗×a3 20. ♘×a3 ♕×e5

21. 0-0 ♗d7 22. ♘c4 ⩲) 17...♕xd4+ 18. ♔h1
♕xe5–+, Saldano Dayer–Del Rio Angelis,
Málaga 2004;

15...g6 16. 0-0 ♗g7 17. ♔h1 ♗xe5 18. dxe5
♕xb5 19. ♘c3 ♕xe5 20. ♕b3 b6∓, Hurley–
Clarke, Irish Championship, Dublin 1996.

16. 0-0

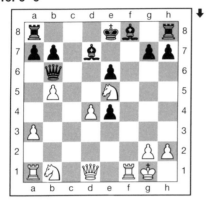

16...0-0-0

16...♗c5!? 17. ♘c3 (17. ♘xd7 ♗xd4+
18. ♔h1 ♕xb5!–+) 17...♗xd4+ 18. ♔h1
A) 18...♕c5 (18...♗xc3?? 19. ♕xd7#;
18...♗xe5 19. ♕h5+ ♔d8 20. ♕xe5±)
19. ♘xd7 ♕xc3 20. ♖c1 ♕d3 21. ♕h5+
♔xd7 (21...g6 22. ♕h4+–) 22. ♕f7+ ♔d8
23. ♕c7+ ♔e8 24. ♕xb7 ♗f6 (24...♖d8
25. ♕f7#) 25. ♕xa8++–;
B) 18...0-0-0 19. ♘a4 ♕d6□ (19...♕xb5
20. ♕xd4 ♕xa4 21. ♖ac1+ ♔b8 22. ♕d6+
♔a8 23. ♖fd1±) 20. ♘f7 ♕d5 21. ♘xh8
transposes to the game.
16...♗xb5 17. ♘c3 ♗xf1 18. ♕a4+ ♗b5
19. ♘xb5 0-0-0 20. ♘c4 ♕a6 21. ♘xa7+
♔c7! 22. ♘b5+ ♔b8 23. ♕b3 ♖d5 24. ♖b1 ⩲.

17. ♘c3 ♗c5

17...♗e8!? 18. ♘e2 ♔b8 19. ♖b1 ♖d5
20. ♘c4 ♕c7±. Instead, 18...♗xb5?! is
weaker because of 19. ♖b1 ♗xa3 (19...♗xe2
20. ♕c2+ ♕c7 21. ♕xc7+ ♔xc7 22. ♖fc1+
♔b8 23. ♘c6+ ♔c8 24. ♘xd8+ ♔xd8
25. ♖xb7) 20. ♘c4 ♕a6 21. ♘xa3 ♗xe2
22. ♕c2+ ♔b8 23. ♖f7 b6 24. ♕c7+ ♔a8
25. ♕c6+ ♔b8 26. ♘c2 ♖c8 27. ♕d6+ ♔a8
28. ♘b4 ♕c4 29. ♕d7+–.

18. ♘a4 ♗xd4+ 19. ♔h1 ♕d6 20. ♘f7 ♕d5

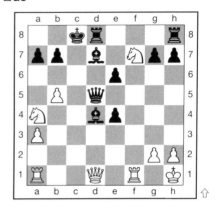

21. ♘xh8

21. ♖c1+ ♔b8 22. ♘xh8 ♗xb5 (22...♖xh8)
23. ♕c2 ♕d7 (23...♕c6 24. ♕d2±) 24. ♘f7
♗xa4 25. ♕xe4 ♕d5 26. ♕xh7±.

Instead, 23. ♘f7 leads to interesting complications favouring White: 23...♗xf1 24. ♘xd8
♗d3 25. ♘f7 (25. ♘xe6!?) 25...♗e3 26. ♖c3
♗d4 27. ♕c1 ♗xc3 28. ♘xc3 ♕c5 29. ♕f4+
♔c8 30. ♘d6+ (30. ♕d6 ♕xd6 31. ♘xd6+
♔d7 32. ♘dxe4 ♔c6 33. ♘g5±) 30...♔d7
31. ♘dxe4 ♗xe4 32. ♘xe4 ♕xa3 33. ♕f7+
♔d8 (33...♕e7 34. ♘c5+ ♔d6 35. ♘xb7+
♔d7 36. ♘c5+ ♔d6 37. ♕f2±) 34. g3±
or 23...♖d7 24. ♕c2 a6 25. ♕c8+ ♔a7
26. ♘c3 ♗xc3 27. ♕xc3 ♗xf1 28. ♖xf1 ♕b5
(28...♕d4 29. ♕xd4+ ♖xd4 30. ♔g1 e3
31. ♘g5±) 29. ♕c1 ♖d3 30. ♖e1 ♕f5 31. ♘g5
e3 32. ♘h3±.

21...♖xh8

21...♗xa1 22. ♕xa1 ♖xh8 23. b6 a6
(23...♗xa4? 24. ♕xg7+–) 24. ♖c1+ ♔b8
25. ♕xg7 ♖d8 26. ♘c5 ⩲.

22. ♘c3

22. ♖c1+ ♔b8 23. ♕d2 e3 24. ♕b4 b6⇄
(24...♖c8).

22...♗xc3 23. ♕c2 ♕d2 24. ♖ac1 ♕xc2 25. ♖xc2 ♗xb5 26. ♖f7 ♖d8 27. ♖xc3+ ♗c6 28. ♔g1 ♖d1+ 29. ♔f2 ♖d2+ 30. ♔e1

30. ♔g3 g5 31. ♖xh7?! e3! 32. ♖xc6+ (32. ♖xe3 ♖xg2+ 33. ♔h3 g4+ 34. ♔h4 ♖xh2+ 35. ♔xg4 ♖xh7 –+) 32...bxc6 33. ♖g7 ♖d5∓;

30. ♔f1 =.

30...♖xg2 31. ♖g3! ♗e8

31...♖xg3 32. hxg3 ♗e8 33. ♖xg7 ♗g6 34. ♔d2 ♔b8! 35. ♔e3 a6 36. ♖e7 ♗f5 37. ♔f4 h5 =.

32. ♖c3+

32. ♖fxg7! ♖xg3 (32...♖xh2? 33. ♖g8±) 33. hxg3 ♗g6 34. g4 ♔b8!? 35. ♔d2 a6 36. ♔e3 ♔a7 37. ♖e7 ♔b6 =.

32...♗c6 33. ♖g3 ♗e8

Draw.

Giving up the pawn centre, playing for blockade of the squares e5 and d4

Game 41
Grischuk – Radjabov
FIDE Grand Prix, Dubai 2002

1. e4 e6 2. d4 d5 3. e5 c5 4. c3 ♘c6 5. ♘f3 ♗d7 6. ♗e2 ♖c8 7. 0–0 a6

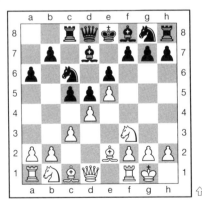

A very crafty plan by Black: he delays committing the g8 knight, and meanwhile White lacks any point of attack. Also Black has made provision against the move 8. dxc5 with the useful moves ♖c8 and a6. Nevertheless White has many interesting possibilities.

8. ♔h1 !?

The plan chosen by Grischuk is very interesting, although I prefer Oll's idea 8. dxc5!? ♗xc5 9. ♗f4 ♘ge7 10. ♗d3 f5 11. exf6 gxf6 12. ♘h4 0–0 13. ♕g4+ ♔h8 14. ♕h5 f5 15. b4 ♗b6 16. ♘d2 ♗c7 ∞ (Oll – Ivanchuk, Polanica Zdrój 1998). The moves 6...♖c8 and 7...a6 were a waste of time after all, and the plan of giving up the pawn centre and playing for a blockade was very logical.

8. ♔h1 !? is Grischuk's trademark move, of which he is very fond. The move keeps open many possibilities: White prepares g2–g4 and avoids a *zwischenzug* knight check on f3 in various lines where Black captures on d4 or e5 with a knight. However, moving the king into the corner consumes time; I think that White should choose a more concrete plan. In this respect he has very many possibilities available, for instance:

A) 8. a3 cxd4 9. cxd4 ♘ge7 10. ♘c3 ♘f5 11. g4 (11. ♗e3 ♗e7 12. ♗d3 ♘xe3 13. fxe3 0–0 14. ♖f2 f6 15. ♕c2 f5 =, Ivanović – Bareev, Moscow (Blitz) 1993) 11...♘h4 12. ♘xh4 ♕xh4 13. ♗e3 g5 14. ♘a4 h5 ⇄, Xie Jun – Karpov, Guangzhou (Rapidplay) 2000;

B) 8. b3 ♘ge7 9. ♗b2 ♘f5 10. ♗d3 cxd4 11. ♗xf5 exf5 12. ♘xd4 ♗e7 13. ♖e1 0–0 14. ♕d3 ♘xd4 15. cxd4 ♕a5 16. ♘c3 ♖c6 17. a3 ♗e6 18. b4 ♕c7 19. f4 ♖c8 20. ♖ec1 g6 21. ♘d1 ♕b6 22. ♖xc6 ♖xc6 23. ♘e3±, Sveshnikov – Epishin, Moscow 1992;

C) 8. ♘a3!? ♘ge7 9. ♘c2 ♘g6 10. ♗d3 ♗e7 11. g3 c4 12. ♗e2 f6 13. exf6 ♗xf6 14. h4 h6 15. h5 ♘ge7 16. ♗f4 0–0 17. ♕d2±, Sveshnikov – Razuvaev, Moscow (Rapidplay) 1992;

D) 8. g3 h6 9. h4 ♕c7 10. h5 ♘ge7 11. ♖e1 cxd4 12. cxd4 ♕b6 13. g4 g6 14. hxg6 ♘xg6 15. ♘c3 ♖g8 16. ♔h1 ♗e7 17. ♖g1 ♗g5 18. ♖b1 ♕d8 19. ♗e3 f6 ⇄, Grischuk – Bareev, Chalkidiki 2002.

I would recommend choosing 8. dxc5 or 8. ♘a3. Also 8. ♗e3 deserves attention.

8...♘ge7 ?!

In the next game of their tie-breaker, Radjabov chose another, more logical, plan: 8...c×d4!?, with which he showed the quiet 8. ♔h1 to be unnecessary and at the same time pre-empted White's possible d×c5 (see Volume 2, Chapter 1 "Theoretically important games for independent analysis", game 39, page 34).

9. d×c5!

If White gives up his pawn centre like this, Black usually gets sufficient counterplay in the middle of the board. Here however Black has lost time with the unnecessary moves a6 and ♖c8, which should allow White to count on some advantage.

9...♘g6 10. ♗e3 ♘c×e5 11. ♘×e5 ♘×e5 12. b4 ♗e7 13. ♘d2 ♘c6 14. f4

Obviously White must not allow e6–e5.

14...♗f6 15. ♖c1 0-0 16. ♘f3

Black must remain on the defensive. The only possibility of counterplay lies in advancing with e6–e5, but this is not easy to achieve.

16...♖e8

16...♘e7!? 17. ♗d3!?±.

17. a4 ♕c7 18. ♗d3

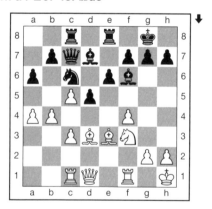

18...g6

Black had to play 18...e5!? 19. f×e5 ♘×e5 20. ♘×e5 ♗×e5 21. ♗d4± with chances of salvation. Now he is almost stifled.

19. b5 a×b5 20. a×b5 ♘e7

20...♘a5 21. ♗d4 ♗g7 22. ♕a4 ♖a8 23. ♖a1 f6 24. ♕b4 ♕d8 25. ♖fe1 ±.

21. ♗d4 ♗g7

21...♗×d4 2. c×d4 ♖a8 23. ♘e5 ♘f5 24. c6 ♗c8 25. ♗×f5 e×f5 26. ♕b3±.

22. ♕d2 f6

22...♖a8 23. ♖a1 ♘f5 24. ♗×f5 g×f5 25. b6±.

23. c4

White immediately tries to take advantage of the weakening of the e6 pawn.

23...d×c4

23...e5?! 24. c×d5 e×d4 25. d6±;

23...♖a8 24. ♖fe1 ♗h6 25. ♗e3 ♖f8 26. ♘d4±.

24. ♗×c4 ♘f5

24...♗h6 25. g3!?±.

25. ♗g1

25. ♗c3!? ♖a8 (25...♕×c5? 26. ♗b4 ♕c7 27. ♖fd1 ♖cd8 28. ♗×e6+ ♗×e6 29. ♖×c7 ♖×d2 30. ♖×d2+−) 26. g4 ♘e7 27. g5±.

25...♖cd8 26. ♕a2 ♕×f4?!

26...♔h8 27. ♘d4!? e5 28. f×e5 ♕×e5 29. ♖cd1±.

27. ♘d4 ♕g4

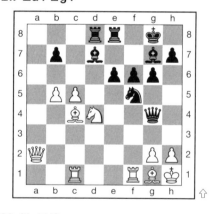

28. ♖×f5!?

28. ♘×f5! g×f5 29. c6 b×c6 30. b×c6 ♗c8 31. c7 ♖d6 32. ♗c5 ♗f8 33. ♗b5+−.

28...g×f5?

28...♖a8□ 29. ♕b3 (29. h3 ♕xd4 30. ♗xd4 ♖xa2 31. c6 bxc6 32. bxc6 ♗c8 33. ♖fd1 ♖a5 34. ♗xf6 ♗xf6 35. ♖xf6 ♔g7 36. ♖ff1 ±) 29...gxf5 30. c6 bxc6 31. bxc6 ♗c8 32. ♘xe6 ♔h8 33. ♘c7 ♕f4 34. ♘xe8 ♕xc1 35. ♕g3 ♕g5 36. ♕d6±.

29. c6+− bxc6 30. bxc6 ♗xc6

30...♗c8 31. ♘xe6 ♗xe6 32. ♗xe6+ ♔h8 33. c7 +−.

**31. ♗xe6+ ♔h8 32. ♘xc6+− ♖d1?!
33. h3 ♕h5 34. ♗f7**

Black resigned.

2.4 Play on both wings

Play on both wings is the highest form of mastery in chess. It is another matter that it is not a simple task to watch over both wings and the centre at the same time; every single move acquires great importance and a single mistake can ruin all your previous efforts. But White's plan is clear: first, create weaknesses in the enemy kingside (or threaten to attack the king) so as to hinder kingside castling, and then start some activity on the queenside. If Black manages to castle kingside after all, then play switches back from the queenside to the kingside.

The game Paulsen – Schwarz, Leipzig 1879 (game 2 on page 13), which the reader will have seen in Chapter 1, is a classical model of play on both wings. Now let us analyse examples from the play of modern grandmasters.

Play on both wings

Game 42
Sveshnikov – Vaganian
Moscow 1985

1. e4 e6 2. d4 d5 3. e5

Since one of Black's main problems in this system is his bad light-squared bishop, he can try to exchange it as soon as possible. This is the plan that Vaganian chooses here.

3...♘e7 4. ♘f3 b6 5. c3 ♕d7

All according to Black's plan to exchange the light-squared bishops. Of course the immediate 5...♗a6? fails to 6. ♗xa6 ♘xa6 7. ♕a4+.

6. a4

In the game Kupreichik – Vaganian (Russian Cup, Kiev 1984, game 16 on page 32) White continued 6. ♘bd2 a5 7. h4!? and gained a fine victory after a sharp struggle. But the move 6. ♘bd2 seems imprecise to me: the

c1 bishop is blocked and the d4 pawn can become a target. After the move in the game the white pieces develop more harmoniously.

6...a5?!

A consistent but dubious decision, since now Black will find it more difficult to break with c7–c5, and queenside castling will be very risky. 6...c5 is better.

7. ♘a3!

Here the knight is well placed, taking part in the action on the queenside yet having easy access to the kingside (♘c2–e3–g4).

7...♗a6 8. ♗xa6 ♘xa6 9. 0–0

More energetic is 9. h4!?, to take space and begin to play against the e7 knight. If this knight goes to c6, the kingside will be weakened. The reply to 9...h5 will be 10. ♗g5, delaying a decision about where to develop the queen's knight and the queen. If Black does not play 9...h5, then White increases the pressure with 10. h5.

9...c6

Such moves are not made willingly, and if the pawn had to be advanced, it would have been better to move it to c5. 9...♘f5 also deserved consideration.

10. ♕d3

Here 10. b3 or 10. ♘c2 was possible.

10...♘c7 11. ♘c2

Here 11. b3 was stronger, to answer 11...c5 with 12. c4, planning ♘b5, ♖d1 and ♗a3. Opening the position favours White, since he is ahead in development.

11...c5

(see next diagram)

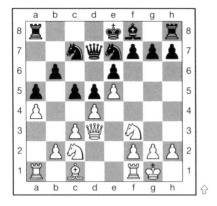

We can now assess the results of the opening: White has a big advantage in space and a lead in development, as well as the more active pieces. The only virtue of Black's position is the absence of pawn weaknesses. White's task is to create some such weaknesses.

12. h4! c4

A big decision, since it gives White the possibility of a b2–b3 break, whilst Black is forced to wait passively. Better was 12...♘c6 13. h5 h6 with some defensive chances.

13. ♕e2 h5

This is to secure a base for the knight at g6 or f5, but now there is a weakness on h5. It was preferable to play 13...b5 14. a×b5 ♕×b5 15. ♗g5 ♘c6, seeking counterplay on the queenside.

14. ♗g5 ♘g6

After 14...♘f5 15. ♘e3 ♘×e3 16. f×e3 Black might begin to have problems with his f7 pawn. The c7 knight is very badly placed, and any further piece exchanges will just highlight this.

15. ♖fb1! ♗e7 16. ♗×e7

The simplest; if 16. b3 f6 17. e×f6 g×f6 18. ♗e3 ♕c6 Black gains counterplay.

16...♘×e7

If 16...♕×e7, then 17. g3! is unpleasant.

17. ♘e3 ♖b8

Another drawback of 13...h5 becomes apparent – kingside castling will walk into a mating attack: 17...0–0 18. ♘g5! g6 (18...f6 19. e×f6 g×f6 20. ♘h3) 19. g4 etc. And the knight cannot establish itself at f5.

18. b3

White's play is very logical: with 12. h4 he forced Black to weaken his kingside, and now Black has problems with castling. Taking advantage of the disconnected black rooks and the bad knight on c7, White starts an attack on the queenside. If Black connects his rooks by castling on the kingside, White will switch to the other plan: attacking the king. It is all quite simple; many of my games with this system have followed this pattern.

18...c×b3 19. ♖×b3 ♘f5

Trying to change the situation on the board somehow, Black voluntarily takes on new weaknesses. Instead, 19...♕c6 offered poor prospects in view of 20. ♖ab1, with the idea of ♕b2.

20. ♘×f5 e×f5 21. ♘g5 ♖h6

So the black king has been left in the middle, and its fate seems unenviable. Black would also have a difficult position after 21...g6 22. ♕b2 ♕c6 23. ♖b1 0–0 24. ♖×b6 ♖×b6 25. ♕×b6 ♕×c3 26. e6!. And if 21...♘e6 then 22. ♘×e6 ♕×e6 (22...f×e6 23. ♕a6, and the b-pawn is lost) 23. ♕b5+ preventing castling, since after 23...♕d7 24. ♕×a5 the two rooks win easily against the queen.

22. ♘h3

The knight transfers to the blockading square f4. The computer's suggestion of 22. e6! is also good.

22...♕c6

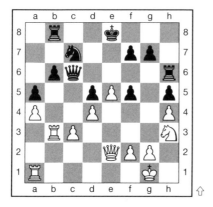

23. ♕f3!

White takes aim at the weak black pawns. Since the opponents's king is insecure, it suits White to keep the queens on.

23...♕c4 24. ♖ba3!

The most difficult move of the game, effectively depriving Black of all counterplay. White could probably also win by 24. ♖ab1 ♕xa4 25. ♕xf5 ♕d7 or 24. ♖bb1 ♖c6, but Black would have some counter-chances. Now he is forced to give up a pawn or acknowledge the futility of the manoeuvre ♖h8–h6.

24...g6 25. ♘f4 ♔d7 26. ♖b1 ♔c6 27. ♖ab3 b5

Here 27...♕xa4 fails to 28. c4! with a quick win. Neither does 27...♖hh8 help – after 28. e6! ♘xe6 29. ♘xd5 ♕xd5 30. ♖xb6+ White wins the queen.

28. ♕g3!

The is more accurate than 28. axb5+ ♔b6!, granting Black a breathing space, whereas now the curtain can be brought down. Note: in this game several different white plans are woven together: blockade, exploitation of a weak dark-square complex and even an attack on the king. But one main theme runs throughout the game: play on both wings.

28...♖h7 29. ♕g5

Having planned to play this if Black played 28...♖hh8, I missed that here I could have finished the game more quickly with 29. ♘xg6!.

29...♔d7 30. ♕f6 ♕c6 31. e6+ ♘xe6 32. ♘d3 ♔c8 33. ♘e5 ♕c7 34. ♘xg6 ♖b7

Or 34...fxg6 35. ♕xe6+ ♕d7 36. ♕xg6 etc. Note that all six black pawns are very weak. Now the harvest begins.

35. ♕xf5 ♖g7 36. ♖xb5 ♖xb5 37. ♖xb5 ♕d7 38. ♕xd5

Black resigned (38...♕xd5 39. ♘e7+).

Play on both wings

Game 43
Sveshnikov – Nevednichy
Bled Open 1991

1. e4 e6 2. d4 d5 3. e5 c5 4. c3 ♘c6 5. ♘f3 ♕b6 6. a3 ♗d7 7. b4 cxd4 8. cxd4 ♖c8

One of the problematic positions of this opening. If 8...♘ge7 then 9. ♘c3 followed by ♘c3–a4–c5.

9. ♗b2

After 9. ♗e2? a5! 10. b5 ♘xd4! 11. ♘xd4 ♖xc1 12. ♕xc1 ♕xd4 13. ♕c7! (in a game against Hoàng, Cheliabinsk 1990, page 42, I stood worse after 13. ♕c3 ♗c5 but I had to play for a win, so I avoided the perpetual check), or 9. ♗e3 ♘h6 10. ♗d3 ♘g4 11. 0–0 ♗e7 the chances are equal.

9...♘a5

Here 9...♘xb4?! 10. axb4 ♕xb4+ 11. ♕d2 ♖c2 does not work: 12. ♗a3! (stronger than 12. ♗c3 ♕b3 13. ♕e3 ♘h6 14. ♗d3 ♖xc3 15. ♘xc3 ♕xc3+ 16. ♔e2 ♕b2+ 17. ♕d2 ♕xd2+ 18. ♘xd2 a6±) 12...♕a4 13. ♗xf8+−.

10. ♘bd2

If 10. ♗c3?! ♘c4 11. ♗d3 ♗e7 12. 0–0 ♘h6 13. ♕e2 ♘f5 14. g4 ♘h4 15. ♘xh4 ♗xh4 Black seizes the initiative (Klinger – Arencibia, World Championship U20, Gausdal 1986).

10...♘c4 11. ♘xc4!

Instead, 11. ♗xc4?! dxc4 12. ♖c1 c3! 13. ♖xc3 ♖xc3 14. ♗xc3 ♕a6 (Subit – Vilela, Tunis 1987) leads to a complicated position with equal chances. The less known continuation 11. ♘xc4 appeared in the games of T. Prokhorovich in the 1950s and was analysed by me and the students in my chess school.

11...dxc4 12. ♖c1 a5

Here 12...♕a6 (with the idea of 13. ♘d2 b5 14. ♘e4 ♗c6 with counterplay) is weaker because of 13. d5! exd5 14. ♕xd5 ♘e7 15. ♕e4 b5 16. ♘d4±.

13. ♘d2!

13. ♗xc4!? axb4 14. ♕b3 ♕a5! with an unclear position.

13...axb4 14. ♘xc4

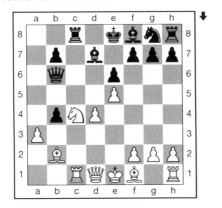

14...♕a7?!

An interesting exchange sacrifice was played in the game Mark Tseitlin – Yusupov (Riga 1984): 14...♖xc4!? 15. ♗xc4 bxa3 16. ♗c3 ♕c6 17. ♗e2 ♘e7 18. 0–0. Here Black blundered his queen with 18...♘d5? (18...♕b6

was necessary) and soon lost after 19. ♗a5 ♗e7 20. ♖xc6 ♗xc6 21. ♕b3 0–0 22. ♗b5.

Lputian demonstrated another plan against me in a later game (Moscow 1991): 14...♕d8 15. axb4 b5! (weaker is 15...♗xb4+ 16. ♗c3 ♗xc3+ 17. ♖xc3 or 16...♗e7? 17. ♗a5) 16. ♘d6+ ♗xd6 17. exd6 ♘f6 18. ♖c5 (18. ♗d3 0–0 19. ♖c5↑) 18...♘d5 19. ♗d3 0–0 20. 0–0 ♕b6! 21. ♕h5 f5 22. ♖fc1 ♖a8!?.

15. axb4 ♗xb4+ 16. ♗c3 ♗xc3+?!

Now White has a stable advantage. Instead, 16...♗e7 17. ♕b3 b5 was worth considering, to gain compensation for the pawn after 18. ♘d6+ ♗xd6 19. exd6 ♘f6 20. ♗xb5 0–0.

17. ♖xc3 ♔f8 (the only move) **18. ♖a3 ♕b8 19. ♘d6 ♖d8 20. ♕f3 ♘h6**

Here 20...♗e8 would fail to 21. ♗c4 (21. ♗b5 also retains the advantage) 21...♕c7 22. 0–0 ♖xd6 23. exd6 ♕xc4 24. ♖a8 ♕b5 (24...♕xd4 25. ♖d1 +−) 25. ♕a3! ♕d7 26. ♖c1, whilst 20...♘f6 would be answered by 21. ♗e2 ♗c6 22. ♕f4±.

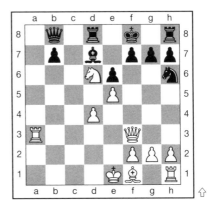

21. ♗d3 (It is necessary to control the f5 square.) **21...f5**

An attempt to activate the bishop with 21...♗c6 would fail miserably after 22. ♕f4 ♗xg2 23. ♖g1 ♗d5 24. ♖xg7.

22. ♕×b7 ♔e7

Here 22...♘f7 is no better: 23. ♕×b8 ♖×b8 24. ♖a7 ♘×d6 25. ♖×d7.

23. ♔e2 ♘f7 24. ♕×b8 ♖×b8 25. ♘×f7 ♖b2+ 26. ♔e3 ♔×f7 27. ♖a7 ♖d8 28. ♖c1

There are no saving chances in an endgame, and with a few precise blows I was able to force my opponent to capitulate.

28...g5 29. ♖cc7 ♔e7

29...♔e8 30. d5 e×d5 31. e6+−.

30. d5 f4+ 31. ♔d4

Black resigned.

Play on both wings

Game 44
Sveshnikov – Fominikh
Russian Championship, Elista 1996

1. e4 c5 2. ♘f3!

In my preparation I established that my opponent generally answered 2. c3 with 2...d5 3. e×d5 ♕×d5 4. d4 ♘f6 5. ♘f3 ♗g4 whilst after 2. ♘f3 he played only 2...e6 or 2...♘c6. So it was clear to me that I should play 2. ♘f3! first.

2...♘c6

Black was obviously not attracted by the sharp line 2...e6 2. c3 d5 4. e5 d4, which entails a pawn sacrifice.

3. c3!

The exclamation mark is not for the objective strength of the move, but for its psychological subtlety: the strongest reply is 3...♘f6!, but my opponent does not play this! Furthermore, Black's second-strongest line 3...d5 4. e×d5 ♕×d5 5. d4 can lead to complications because Black has played ...♘c6 so early, and Alexander was probably not prepared for these. On the other hand, based on my great experience with it, I am happy to play any line of the c3 Sicilian.

3...e6?!

In my opinion this is a serious concession in the opening: now instead of a Sicilian it will be a French.

4. d4 d5 5. e5!

The is definitely stronger than the anaemic 5. e×d5 e×d5!, after which White's advantage is merely symbolic.

5...♗d7 6. ♗e2 ♘ge7 7. ♘a3 ♘f5

The main line is considered to be 7...c×d4 8. c×d4 ♘f5 9. ♘c2 ♘b4 10. 0–0 ♘×c2 11. ♕×c2 ♖c8 12. ♕d3 ♕b6, but in this variation too I think I have been able to pose some problems for Black.

8. ♘c2 ♗e7 9. 0–0

9. ♗d3!? c×d4 10. ♗×f5 e×f5 11. ♘c×d4±.

9...c×d4 10. c×d4 h5?!

Fortifying the knight's position at f5 like this is not without some drawbacks.

11. b4!

The only danger for White is if the opponent is able to castle queenside and then launch a counter-attack on the kingside (g5–g4 etc.), so it is important to seize the initiative on the opposite wing.

11...♖c8

This move looks natural but it does not interfere with my plan. Instead 11...g5!?± came into consideration.

12. ♖b1 a6 13. a4 ♕b6

After 13...♘a7 14. ♘e3 White is the more active on both wings.

14. b5 a×b5 15. ♗×b5

The opposition of queen and rook is uncomfortable for Black; furthermore a new target has appeared – the b7 pawn.

15...♕c7 16. ♘e3!

A thematic move: it threatens to exchange on f5, which would considerably weaken Black's kingside.

16...♘×e3 17. ♗×e3 ♘a5

The only source of counterplay.

18. ♗g5!

Taking advantage of the first opportunity to exchange the bishops and take control of the g5 square.

18...♗xb5 19. ♖xb5 ♘c4 20. h4 b6 21. ♗xe7

Here 21. ♕e2 ♖a8 22. ♖a1 would also be good; it is very hard for Black to gain any counterplay.

21...♕xe7 22. ♘g5 ♖a8

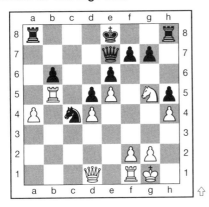

The critical position. White has achieved a lot, but Black has also been able to create some counterplay against the a4 pawn. All in all though, my space advantage and the insecure position of the black king allow me to play for a win by playing on both wings.

23. ♖b3!

Beginning an attack on the f7 pawn.

23...♖a7 24. ♕c2

Here 24. ♕e2!? to bring the other rook into play was also good.

24...g6

The best chance lay in 24...f6! 25. exf6 gxf6, so as to answer 26. ♕g6+ with 26...♔d8!. I did not see this during the game and I would have had to be content with 26. ♘h3±.

25. ♖f3 ♖f8

But not 25...0–0 26. ♖f6 ♖fa8?! 27. ♘xe6 fxe6 28. ♕xg6+ ♕g7 29. ♕xh5±.

26. ♖b1

The last reserves are brought up.

26...♕d7 27. ♖b4

The good knight on g5 is no weaker than the f8 rook, and the a4 pawn will have its say.

27...♖c7 28. ♖c3

Now Black is unable to castle, so White can switch his attack to another target. This is where the space advantage comes in useful!

28...♔d8

Seeking refuge on the queenside.

29. ♘h7 ♖h8 30. ♘f6 ♕e7

Despite the reduced material, Black's pieces are cramped.

31. ♕b3 ♖c6 32. ♖b5 ♕c7

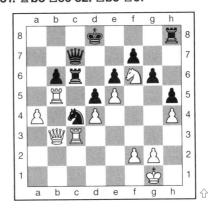

33. a5!

The decisive breakthrough.

33...♔c8

Obviously 33...bxa4? fails to 34. ♖b8+, but there is no salvation for Black, either in 33...♘xa5? 34. ♖xa5! ♖xc3 35. ♖a8+ ♔e7 36. ♕b4+ or 34...bxa5 35. ♖xc6 ♕xc6 36. ♕b8+ ♔e7 (36...♕c8 37. ♕d6+) 37. ♕xh8 ♕c1+ 38. ♔h2 ♕f4+ 39. ♔h3 ♕f5+ 40. ♔g3 ♕d3+ 41. f3 ♕b5 42. ♕c8 and 43. ♘g8#.

34. axb6 ♕b7 35. ♘e4! dxe4 36. ♖xc4 ♖xc4 37. ♕xc4+ ♔d7 38. ♖a5! ♖c8

38...♕xb6 39. ♕a4+. The rest is quite simple.

39. ♕b5+ ♕c6 40. ♖a7+ ♔d8 41. ♕xc6 ♖xc6 42. ♖a8+

Black resigned. In my opinion this game is extremely instructive:

1) To counter the threat to his f5 knight, Black weakened g5 by h7–h5;

2) By starting activity on the queenside, White discouraged Black from castling on that side;

3) The attack on the h5 and f7 pawns also discouraged kingside castling.

4) Making use of his space advantage and the disconnection of the black rooks, White switched the attack back to the queenside, where he landed the decisive blow.

Play on both wings

Game 45
Sveshnikov – Dreev
Zonal Tournament, St. Petersburg 1993

This game was played towards the end of the Zonal and was influential in the fight for qualification for the Interzonal. At such an important moment it is never a good idea to play a weak opening, but at that time Dreev played nothing but the French. These days he also plays the Caro-Kann, although 1…c6 is not the best move either. Incidentally, Bareev is in a similar position; both grandmasters err on the very first move. Thus their prospects in the fight for the world championship are zero. If a player has neither 1…e5 nor 1…c5 in his repertoire, sooner or later he ends up in an impasse.

Any player who aspires to the highest level should answer 1. e4 with 1…c5. It is said that it is impossible to become world champion without a mastery of the Ruy Lopez; I would add that it is equally impossible without the Sicilian. You should play the Lopez with White and the Sicilian with Black! I think

that one of the reasons why Keres never became world champion was that Paul Petrovich mainly played 1…e5, which is not an adequate solution to the problems of the opening.

1. e4 e6 2. d4 d5 3. e5 c5 4. c3 ♘c6

In my preparation I studied the variation with 4…♕b6 and 5…♗d7, as Dreev played against Igor Zaitsev in Protvino 1990. Black has problems in this line, e. g.: 4…♕b6 5. ♘f3 ♗d7 6. a3 cxd4 (or 6…♗b5 7. c4!) 7. cxd4 ♗b5 8. ♗xb5+ ♕xb5 9. ♘c3 ♕a6 10. ♘e2 followed by castling kingside and play on both wings (Sveshnikov – Gurgenidze, Volgodonsk 1981).

5. ♘f3 ♗d7

Many play this, but 5…♕b6 is better, and if 6. a3 – 6…c4! with complex play; but positions with pawn chains are not to everybody's taste.

6. ♗e2 ♘ge7

The alternative is 6…f6, attacking the e5 pawn.

7. ♘a3 cxd4 8. cxd4 ♘f5 9. ♘c2 ♘b4

Here 9…♕a5+ does not equalise after 10. ♗d2 ♕b6 11. ♗c3 (Sveshnikov – Psakhis, Sochi 1987).

10. 0–0

This move is clearly stronger than 10. ♘e3, as Spassky played in his match against Korchnoi (Belgrade 1977, Volume 2, game 15 on page 19).

10…♘xc2 11. ♕xc2 h5?!

A novelty, but not a good one. Normally 11…♕b6 12. ♕d3 is played, with a small but stable advantage for White (Sveshnikov – Zlotnik, Moscow 1991), or 11…♖c8 12. ♕d3 ♕b6 (12…a6 13. ♕b3±) 13. a4± (13. g4!?).

12. ♗d2!

A multi-purpose move which keeps open the possibility of developing activity on both wings.

12…♗e7 13. ♗d3!

White must stay alert, since if 13. ♖fc1 Black can be first to seize the initiative with 13...g5!.

13...♕b6?

This is already a clear error. Instead, 13...g5 was better, with a sharp game in which White, in my opinion, retains the better chances, e. g.: 14. ♗xf5 exf5 15. ♕b3 ♗c6 (15...g4 16. e6 ♗xe6 17. ♘e5 ⇄) 16. e6±. The alternative 14. ♗c3 is not bad either: 14...g4 15. ♘e1 ♕b6 (15...♘h4 16. g3 ♘f5 17. ♘g2 h4 18. ♕e2±) 16. ♗xf5 exf5 17. ♗d3±.

The combination of the moves 11...h5, 12...♗e7 and 13...♕b6 cannot be recommended, since the g5 square is weakened.

14. ♗xf5 exf5 15. ♗g5

Obviously White grasps the opportunity to exchange the dark-squared bishops.

15...♗xg5

After thinking for over half an hour, Dreev makes what is probably the best decision – at least to have an extra pawn as compensation for his bad position.

16. ♘xg5 ♕xd4

Otherwise Black is just worse.

17. ♖fd1

Also possible is 17. ♖ad1, but I wanted to use this rook on the c-file in the variation 17...♕a4 18. b3 ♕c6.

17...♕h4

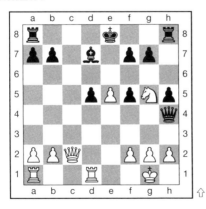

A dubious decision; it was better to return the pawn with 17...♕b6, although after 18. ♖xd5 ♗c6 19. ♖d6 with the idea of ♕e2, White is clearly better.

18. ♕d2!

My opponent apparently missed this very strong move.

18...♕c4

Faced with the unpleasant threat of 19. f4!, the queen must go back.

19. ♖ac1 ♕b5

The only move. 19...♕xa2 fails to 20. ♖c7 ♖d8 21. e6! fxe6 22. ♘xe6! ♗xe6 23. ♕g5 and White wins.

20. a4!

The computer quickly finds this move, but at the board I had to spend time calculating the variations.

20...♕b3

If 20...♕xa4 or 20...♕b6 White wins with the simple 21. ♕xd5.

21. ♖c3 ♕b6

21...♕a2 22. ♖c7±.

22. ♕xd5 0–0!

There will not be another opportunity.

23. a5

Here 23. ♕xd7 is not possible because of 23...♖ad8, since the rook on d1 is unprotected.

23...♕xb2?

In time pressure (he had to conduct a difficult defence for the whole game) Dreev makes a fatal error. Of course, in the variation 23...♕g6 24. ♕xd7 ♕xg5 25. ♕xb7 White has an extra pawn, but he would need to overcome some technical difficulties to convert his advantage.

24. ♕f3!

This move wins the game (this is where the weakness of the h5 pawn tells!) – apparently Black overlooked it.

24...g6 25. ♖×d7 ♖ac8 26. ♖×c8 ♖×c8 27. ♖d1 ♖c1 28. ♕d5 ♖×d1+

The mate threat forces Black to exchange rooks.

29. ♕×d1 ♕×e5 30. ♕d8+ ♔g7 31. ♕h8+!

This exchanging combination in the style of Petrosian is the simplest way to win.

31...♔×h8 32. ♘×f7+ ♔g7 33. ♘×e5 ♔f6 34. f4 g5 35. ♘f2 g×f4 36. ♘d3 b5 37. ♘×f4 h4 38. ♔e3 ♔e5 39. ♘g6+

Black resigned.

Play on both wings

Game 46
Sveshnikov – M. Gurevich
Ekaterinburg 2002

1. e4 e6 2. d4 d5 3. e5

Mikhail Gurevich is regarded as one of the foremost specialists in the French Defence for Black. Not long ago he played a "thematic match" against Sasha Grischuk with the 3. e5 variation. Many other grandmasters are influenced by Mikhail's play, so it was particularly interesting for me to play against an expert like him.

3...c5 4. c3 ♘c6

This was already a surprise. In the most recent games of his that I was familiar with, Mikhail had employed the variation with ♕b6 and ♗d7 etc. However, this was only relatively surprising, since Gurevich had also used 4...♘c6 quite often. At the Dubai 2002 tournament I managed to gain an advantage in the opening against grandmaster Sergey Volkov after 4...♕b6 5. ♘f3 ♗d7 6. a3 a5 (the latest fashion, although White has not yet been able to demonstrate a clear advantage against 6...♗b5!?) 7. ♗e2 a4 8. 0–0 ♘c6 9. ♗d3 ♘a5 10. ♗c2 ♘c4 11. ♘g5!? c×d4 (11...♗e7 was to be considered) 12. c×d4 ♘×b2 13. ♕f3 ♘h6 14. ♘c3

♘c4 (14...♕×d4!? 15. ♗×b2 ♕d2 16. ♗×a4 ♗×a4 17. ♘×a4 ♕×g5 18. ♕b3 ♗e7 19. ♕b5+ ♔f8 20. ♕×b7±) 15. ♖d1. Mikhail avoids these variations.

5. ♘f3 ♗d7 6. ♗e2

For the present I am not trying to show anything new in my system, since I am happy with the current theory. It is from Black that I am expecting to see something new …

6...♘ge7

Another possibility is 6...f6, as Gulko, Psakhis, Vaisser and others have played against me, although I have usually managed to gain an advantage.

7. ♘a3 c×d4 8. c×d4 ♘f5 9. ♘c2

Here 9. 0–0 is interesting, not fearing the doubling of the a-pawns, since in return White acquires some important trumps: two bishops and the half-open b-file.

9...♘b4

All this has been known since the game Spassky – Korchnoi (Belgrade 1977), which continued 10. ♘e3 ♘×e3 11. f×e3 ♗e7 12. a3 ♘c6 with complicated play (Volume 2, game 15 on page 19).

10. 0–0

It seems to me that in 10. 0–0 ♘×c2 11. ♕×c2 ♕b6 13. ♕d3 I have hit upon a good new set-up for White, which has given me good results. However, my opponent had prepared something new …

10...♗a4?!

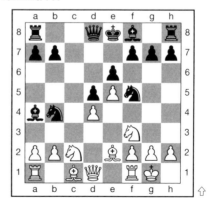

The advantage of this move is obvious: White is forced to play b2–b3, after which the b3 square is unavailable to the white queen and in addition the c3 square is weakened, so that in the future White will have to worry about its defence. But the disadvantages are also clear: Black loses at least one tempo and, although in the French Advance the play does not develop very quickly, a tempo is definitely worth something!

11. b3

Before I made this forced move I thought for about ten minutes, since I wanted to understand what my opponent had in mind.

11...♗d7 12. ♘e3 a5 13. a3

Otherwise 13...a4 is unpleasant.

13...♘c6 14. ♗b2

Of course I really wanted to keep this bishop on its "natural" operating diagonal, c1–h6, but in order to be able to transfer the other bishop to an active post at d3 I first have to defend the d4 pawn.

14...♗e7 15. ♗d3 g6?

A typical error! Even Botvinnik himself once made a similar mistake. The simple 15...♘xe3 16. fxe3 0–0 was to be considered, when the white position is slightly better but Black has equalising chances. Now White achieves more.

16. ♕d2 ♕b6

Now the capture 16...♘xe3 is unconvincing, since White replies 17. ♕xe3, and the weakness of the kingside dark squares will be felt.

17. ♗c2!

It was not easy to decide on this move, since it loses time, but g7–g6 has created strategic weaknesses in Black's position, so White does not need to hurry, especially since Black has difficulty deciding what to do with his king.

17...h5

A thematic move, preventing g2–g4, but in reality it just creates another weakness.

18. ♗c3!

Emphasising that the black king will not be able to find a safe haven on the queenside.

18...♔f8

It is hard to suggest another plan. But now that Black has committed his king White abruptly alters the pattern of play.

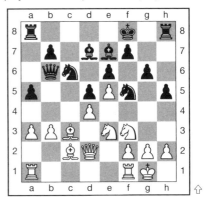

19. ♗xf5!

A typical exchange in this kind of structure. On this theme, see also the game Sveshnikov – Ortega, Sochi 1987 in the chapter on Blockade (game 64 on page 122).

19...gxf5 20. g3!

I am awarding my moves a lot of exclamation marks, but I just want to emphasise that White's last few moves are links in the same chain.

20...♔g8

If 20...h4!? White had the choice between 21. ♔g2 and 21. gxh4. I would probably have chosen the latter, followed by ♔h1 and an attack on the g-file.

21. ♘g2 ♕d8 22. ♖fb1

The immediate 22. b4 came into consideration, but I was interested to find out what Black was going to do if I bided my time. I could see no play for my opponent.

22...♕f8 23. b4 axb4 24. axb4 ♘a7

If 24...♖xa1 25. ♖xa1 ♘xb4, White can choose between 26. ♗xb4 ♗xb4 27. ♕g5+ ♔h7 (here 27...♕g7 28. ♕d8+ ♔h7 29. ♕xd7 is bad) 28. ♕xh5+ ♔g8 29. ♕g5+ ♔h7 30. ♕e3± and the simple 26. ♖b1! ♘c6 27. ♖xb7 ♕c8 28. ♖b1 with a clear advantage.

25. ♕d1

Reminding Black about the weakness of his h5 pawn and also preparing to transfer the bishop to its operational diagonal. White's task is clear: exchange the dark-squared bishops, even if this involves the loss of a pawn.

25...♗b5 26. ♗d2 ♘c6

Here 26...♗d3 fails to 27. ♖b3 ♗e4 28. ♖ba3, when the only way to defend the knight is the awkward 28...♕b8. Now it appears that Black has managed to activate his pieces a little, but after …

27. ♗g5 ♖xa1 28. ♖xa1 ♗xg5 29. ♘xg5

White has succeeded in carrying out his strategic plan, and a great many weaknesses have been created in Black's position.

29...h4

Not a move that Black will have enjoyed playing, but he is trying – at the cost of a pawn – to create at least some basis for counterplay. Instead 29...♕xb4 30. ♖a8+ ♔g7 31. ♖xh8 ♔xh8 fails to 32. ♕xh5+, mating, whilst 29...♘xb4 30. ♘f4 leaves the black king completely unprotected.

30. ♘xh4 ♔g7

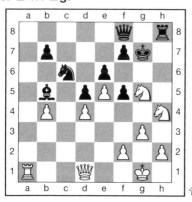

But here I went wrong. I had forty minutes left to my opponent's twenty, and with an extra pawn and a big positional advantage, thinking that the game was effectively over, I relaxed.

31. ♘g2?!

The accurate move 31. ♕d2 would have brought Black to the edge of defeat. The simple 31. ♖b1 was not bad either.

31...♕xb4 32. ♘f4 ♗a6 33. h4

Obviously stronger was 33. ♖b1 ♕c3 34. ♘f3 with a small advantage to White.

33...♖h6

The best defence! Now a knight manoeuvring to f6 is less dangerous; also the e6 pawn is defended.

34. ♘f3

White's misfortune is not so much that he has lost the b4 pawn, as that now Black is able to attack the d4 pawn.

34...♖h8! 35. ♖b1 ♕c3 36. ♖b3 ♕c4 37. ♖a3

Here 37. ♖b6!? came into consideration.

37...♖c8 38. ♖a1

White played the last few moves up to the time control planlessly; I was annoyed at the missed opportunities. Gurevich, meanwhile, consolidated his position.

38...♘d8 39. ♘g5 ♕c3 40. ♔g2 ♖c4?

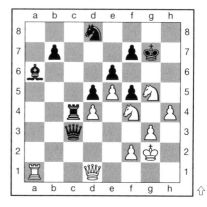

41. ♘e2?

The time control has been reached. I thought that I had let the win slip and my attention was focused on defence. Later the computer indicated a forced win beginning 41. ♘h5+!! ♚f8 42. ♘f6, and now neither 42...♚e7 nor 42...♛xd4 43. ♛h5 saves Black. The strange thing is that this simple solution just did not occur to me during the game, yet it would have been the logical culmination of all my previous play! Of course, 40...♖c4 was a blunder, but if White still had such a possibility it shows that my position still held the promise of a big advantage.

In the game, after

41...♛b2 42. ♖b1 ♛a2 43. ♖a1 ♛b2 44. ♖b1 ♛a2

a draw was agreed. I did not play 45. ♖c1, since now White can play for a win only at great risk.

Conclusions: a convincing advantage for White in the opening, good play in the middlegame (note the typical exchange 19. ♗xf5!) and very slack play in the fourth hour. It is a pity that I did not take advantage of my opponent's blunder with 40...♖c4?. I think that I was affected by tiredness after seven tough games against strong players in the previous rounds of the Russian Team Championship.

Play on both wings

Game 47
Grischuk – M. Gurevich
North Sea Cup, Esbjerg 2000

1. e4 e6 2. d4 d5 3. e5 c5 4. c3 ♘c6 5. ♘f3 ♗d7 6. ♗e2 ♘ge7 7. ♘a3 cxd4 8. cxd4 ♘f5 9. ♘c2 ♛b6

Mikhail Gurevich's pet line.

10. 0–0

10. h4 f6 11. g4 ♘fxd4 12. ♘cxd4 ♘xe5 13. g5 ♗c5 14. 0–0 ♘xf3+ 15. ♗xf3 ♛b4

16. ♘e1 ♛xh4 17. ♘g2 ♛b4 ⇄, Movsesian – Gurevich, Sarajevo 2000;

10. g4, Wemmers – Gurevich, Belgium 2004 (see page 98).

10...a5

10...♘a5 11. g4 ♘e7 12. ♘fe1 h5 13. gxh5 ♗b5 14. ♘d3 ♘f5 15. b4 ♘c6 16. a4 ♗c4 17. a5 ♛d8 18. ♗e3 ♛h4 (Grosar – Dizdar, Nova Gorica 1997) 19. ♘f4 ♗xe2 20. ♛xe2 g5∓;

10...♖c8!? 11. ♗d3 (11. ♛d3!?) 11...a5 (11...♘b4 12. ♘xb4 ♗xb4 13. a3 ♗e7 14. ♗xf5 exf5 15. ♗g5!? ♗xg5 16. ♘xg5⇄) 12. a3 a4 13. ♗xf5 exf5 14. ♘e3⇄.

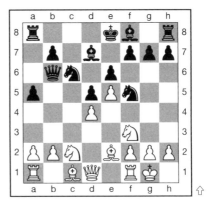

11. ♔h1

11. b3, Timman – Jóhannesson, Reykjavík 2004 (see page 97).

11...♘b4

11...h5!? 12. ♗g5 ♖c8 13. ♛d2 ♗e7 14. ♖ab1 ♗xg5 15. ♛xg5 ♘ce7 16. ♗d3 ♗b5 17. ♗xb5+ ♛xb5 18. ♘e3 ♛e2 19. ♘xf5 ♘xf5 20. ♚g1 ♖c2. Draw, Peng Xiaomin – Zhang Zhong, Shenyang 1999.

12. ♘e3

If 12. ♘xb4 axb4!? 13. ♛d3 ♖a5 Black gets counterplay on the a-file.

12...♖c8

12...♗b5 13. ♘xf5 exf5 14. ♖e1!?±;

12...♘xe3 13. fxe3 (13. ♗xe3 ♗e7 14. ♛d2 ♖c8!?=) 13...♗e7 14. a3 ♘c6 15. b3!?±;

12...♗e7!? 13. ♘×f5 e×f5 14. ♗d2 0–0 15. a3 ♘c6 16. ♗c3 ♖fb8⇄, Cherniaev–Dzhakaev, 4th European Championship, Istanbul 2003.

13. ♘×f5 e×f5 14. ♗d2

The bishop heads for c3, where it will defend the weak pawns and impede Black's counterplay on the queenside.

14...♗e7

14...♘c2 15. ♖b1 ♘×d4? 16. ♗e3+−.

15. a3 ♘c6 16. ♗c3

Gurevich recommends 16. b4!, and now 16...a×b4 17. a×b4↑ ♗×b4? (17...♘×b4 18. ♕b3+−) fails to 18. ♖b1 ♕a5 19. ♖×b4! ♘×b4 20. ♕b3±. But White has another plan: to fortify his queenside and launch an offensive on the opposite wing.

16...0–0 17. ♕d2 ♖a8!

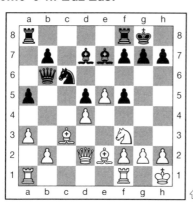

A very interesting and original idea. Black wants to transfer his king's rook to the queenside to b8 and then prepare the pawn advance b7–b5–b4.

18. ♘e1

Meanwhile White begins to transfer his knight to e3.

18...♖fb8 19. ♘c2 g6 20. ♘e3

Here again Gurevich suggests 20. b4!?, but, as previously mentioned, Grischuk has something else in mind.

20...♗e6 21. f4

White now plans the g2–g4 break, and Black hinders this.

21...h5!?

21...♕d8 22. g4 f×g4 23. f5 g×f5 24. ♘×f5 ♗g5∞ 25. ♕d3 h5 26. ♘g3⩱ (26. h3!?).

22. ♕d1

White is preparing a combination involving the sacrifice of a piece, but Gurevich finds an elegant refutation. The straightforward 22. g3 ♕d8 23. h3 b5⇄ leads to a position with chances for both sides. Gurevich recommends 22. ♗f3!? ♖d8 (22...♕d8 23. ♕d1!±) 23. g3±.

22...♔g7 23. ♗×h5? (23. ♗f3 ♖d8 24. ♖c1±) 23...g×h5 24. ♕×h5 ♖h8 25. ♘×f5+ ♗×f5 26. ♕×f5

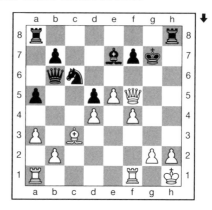

26...♘×d4!

This move looks extremely risky, since now the c3 bishop is poised to enter the attack at any moment, but Gurevich has calculated everything accurately.

27. ♕d3

White cannot save the game with either 27. e6 f×e6 28. ♕g4+ ♔f7 29. f5 ♖×h2+! 30. ♔×h2 ♖h8+ 31. ♔g3 ♗h4+! 32. ♕×h4 ♕c7+ 33. ♕f4 ♘e2+− +, or 27. ♕g4+ ♔f8 28. f5 ♖h4! 29. ♕d1 (29. ♕g3 ♘e2) 29...♘b3 30. f6 ♗c5−+.

27...♖×h2+!

An elegant although not difficult combination.

28. ♔xh2 ♖h8+ 29. ♔g3 (29. ♔g1 ♘f3#) **29...♗h4+ 30. ♔g4** (30. ♔h2 ♗f2+) **30...♕h6!**

White resigned in view of 31. g3 (31. ♗xd4 ♕h5+ 32. ♔h3 ♗f2#) 31...♕h5+ 32. ♔h3 ♗g5+ 33. ♔g2 ♕h2#.

Play on both wings

Game 48
Shirov – Kramnik
6th Amber (blind), Monte Carlo 1997

1. e4 e6 2. d4 d5 3. e5 c5 4. c3 ♘c6 5. ♘f3 ♕b6 6. a3 ♘h6 7. b4 cxd4 8. cxd4 ♘f5 9. ♗b2 ♗d7

9...♗e7 10. ♗d3 a5 11. ♕a4 0–0 12. b5 ♘h4 13. ♘xh4 ♗xh4 14. g3 ♗d8 15. 0–0 ♗d7 16. ♖a2 ♘a7 17. ♘c3 f6 18. ♗a1 f5 19. f4±, Kiik – Korchnoi, Rilton Cup, Stockholm 2003.

10. g4 ♘fe7

10...♘h6 occurred in the game Short – Lputian, Batumi 1999 (game 52 on page 103).

11. ♘c3

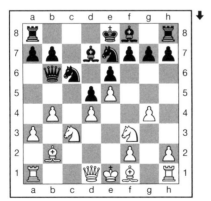

11...h5

It also looks logical to play 11...♕d8 12. h4 h5 13. ♘b5 ♘c8 (13...♘g6 14. ♘g5!? ♘xh4 15. f4!? f6 16. ♖xh4→ or 14...hxg4

15. ♕xg4±) 14. ♘g5 hxg4 15. ♕xg4 ♗e7 16. ♗c1 (better is 16. ♖g1 ± ♗xg5 17. ♕xg5) 16...a6 17. ♖g1 f5 18. exf6 ♗xf6 17. ♘h7 axb5 20. ♕g6+ ♔e7 21. ♘xf6 gxf6 22. ♕g7+ ♔d6 23. ♗f4+ e5 24. dxe5+ and here Lastin – Malakhatko (St. Petersburg 2003) ended in a draw after 24...♘xe5 25. ♖g6 ♖f8 26. 0–0–0 ♘b6 etc. But 24...fxe5! would have led to an advantage for Black after 25. ♖g6+ ♗e6 26. ♗h3 ♖e8 27. ♕xb7 ♘8a7 28. 0–0–0 exf4 29. ♗xe6 ♖xe6 30. ♖g5 (30. ♖xe6+ ♔xe6–+) 30...♕xg5 (30...♖e5 31. ♖g6+ ♖e6 32. ♖g5 ♖e5 33. ♖g6+=) 31. hxg5 ♖g8 32. ♕f7 ♖xg5 33. ♕xf4+ ♖ge5∓.

So far it has not been possible to crack Black's position after 11...♘a5!? e. g.: 12. ♕c2!? ♘c4 13. ♗xc4 dxc4 14. ♘d2 ♕c6 15. ♘ce4 ♘d5 (15...c3, Sveshnikov – Radjabov, Tallinn 2004, Volume 2, game 61 on page 53) 16. ♘xc4 ♘b6 17. ♘cd6+ ♗xd6 18. ♘xd6+ ♔e7 19. ♕xc6 ♗xc6 20. ♖g1 ♘c8 21. b5 ♗d5∓, Sveshnikov – Potkin, Russian Championship, Krasnoyarsk 2003. All the same, I do not really trust 11...♘a5!?.

12. g5

12. ♘a4!? ♕d8 (12...♕c7 13. g5±) 13. ♘c5 ♗c8 (13...♘g6 14. gxh5 ♖xh5 15. ♘xb7 ♕c7 16. ♘c5±) 14. g5 b6 15. ♘a6 ♘b8 16. ♖c1, Flores – Vallejo Pons, World Championship U18, Oropesa del Mar 1999; 16. ♘xb8 ♖xb8 17. ♗d3±.

12...♘f5

On f5 the knight is not very secure. In my opinion 12...♘g6 13. ♘a4 ♕d8 is more interesting, with the following continuations:

14. h4 a5 15. b5 ♘a7 16. ♖c1 (16. ♕b3 ♗e7 17. ♖c1 or 17. b6 ♗xa4 18. ♕xa4+ ♘c6∓) 16...♗e7 17. ♕b3 0–0 18. ♘d2 ♖c8 19. ♖xc8 ♕xc8 20. ♖h3 ♕e8 21. ♘c3⇄;

14. ♖c1 ♗e7 15. ♖g1 0–0 16. h4 a5 17. b5 ♘a7 18. ♕b3 ♘c8 19. ♗c3 ♘xh4 20. ♘xh4 ♗xg5 21. ♕d1 (21. ♖c2 ♗xh4 22. ♗d2 ♘e7∓) 21...♗xc1 22. ♕xh5∓ ♗e8 23. ♗d3 f5=, Peng Xiaomin – Korchnoi, Calcutta 2000.

In recent years Victor Lvovich Korchnoi has become one of the most important specialists in the French with 3. e5. He fought against this system for many years with the black pieces and then began playing it with White as well. Still, I dare say Peng Xiaomin's play can be improved upon. Thus instead of 15. ♖g1 White could consider 15. h4!? a5 16. b5 ♘a7 17. ♕b3± ♖c8 18. ♗d3 or 18...♖×c8 ♘×c8 19. ♘c5 ♕c7 20. ♘×d7 ♔×d7±. I think that theory will develop in this direction.

13. ♘a4 ♕d8

13...♕c7 14. ♖c1 a6 15. ♗d3±.

14. ♗d3

14. ♘c5 a5 15. ♘×d7 ♕×d7 16. b5±.

14...h4

Possibly forced; in any case it is hard to come up with anything else. Thus 14...b6 is very unpleasant for Black after 15. ♗×f5!? (15. ♖g1 ♘ce7 16. ♘c3 a5 17. b5 ♘g6⇄; 15. ♖c1 a5 16. b5 ♘ce7 17. ♘c3 ♖c8 18. ♕d2 ♘g6 19. 0-0±) 15...e×f5 16. g6→ or 16. ♘c3 ♗e6 17. g6→. And if 14...g6, then 15. ♘c5 ♗×c5 16. d×c5±.

15. ♖c1 ♗e7 16. ♖g1

16. ♘c5!? ♗c8 17. ♖g1± was better.

16...g6 17. ♗×f5

Exchanging the opponent's only active piece. Yet 17. ♘c5!? seems even more logical.

17...e×f5 18. ♘c5 ♖b8

18...b6? 19. e6! f×e6 (19...b×c5 20. d×c5 0-0 21. e×d7+−) 20. ♘×d7 ♕×d7 21. ♕c2 ♘d8 22. ♘e5±.

19. ♕e2 (19. e6!?) **19...♗e6 20. ♕e3 ♕b6 21. ♕d3**

To be able to answer ...a5 with b4−b5.

21...♔f8 22. ♗c3 ♔g7 23. ♘d2 a5

Black tries to create counterplay.

24. b5 ♘a7 25. a4 ♗×c5 26. d×c5 ♕×c5 27. ♔e2!

(see next diagram)

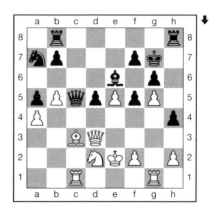

White connects the rooks. His king is quite comfortable in the centre.

27...♘c8

27...♕a3!? 28. ♗d4 ♕×d3+ 29. ♔×d3 ♘c8 30. ♖c7± (30. b6!?; 30. f4!?±).

28. ♗×a5 ♕a7

28...♕e7 29. ♖c7 ♕e8 30. ♕d4±.

29. ♗c7 ♖a8 30. a5±

It is surprising how White has managed to create two distinct "boxes" in which to hem in the enemy forces, one on the queenside and the other on the kingside!

30...d4

Black seeks to activate his bishop, but for this it was probably better to play 30...f4.

31. ♘c4! ♘e7 32. ♗b6 ♕b8 33. ♕×d4 ♘d5 34. ♘d6 h3 35. ♖gd1 ♖h5 36. ♕c5 ♘×b6 37. ♕×b6 ♖×g5 38. ♖c7

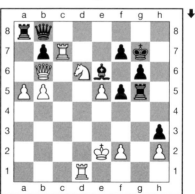

Total domination. White threatens 39. ♘xf7 as well as the simple capture on b7, after which his pawns would promote.

38...♕h8 (38...f4 39. ♘xf7 +−) **39. ♘xf7 ♕h5+ 40. ♔d2! ♗xf7 41. ♖xf7+!**

41. ♕f6+ ♔h6 42. ♖xf7 would transpose (but not 42. ♕xf7 ♖d8+ 43. ♖d7 ♖xd7+ 44. ♕xd7 ♕h4⇄) 42...♖g2 43. ♕g7+ ♔g5 44. ♔e3! etc.

41...♔h6

41...♔xf7 42. ♕xb7+ ♔e6 43. ♕xa8 +−.

42. ♕f6 ♖g2 43. ♕g7+ ♔g5 44. ♔e3! ♕g4

44...♕xd1 45. f4+ ♔h4 46. ♕f6+ g5 47. ♖h7+ ♕h5 48. ♖xh5+ ♔xh5 49. ♕xf5 ♖g1 50. ♔f2 +−.

45. ♖d4

Black resigned.

Play on both wings

Game 49
Shirov – van Wely
Corus, Wijk aan Zee 2001

1. e4 e6 2. d4 d5 3. e5 c5 4. c3 ♘c6 5. ♘f3 ♗d7 6. ♗e2

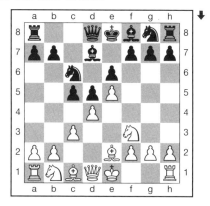

6...♘ge7

An alternative to this developing move is the immediate attack on the white centre with 6...f6, e.g.: 7. 0–0 fxe5 8. ♘xe5

(8. dxe5 ♕c7 9. ♖e1 0-0-0 10. ♗d3 ♘h6 11. ♘a3 a6 12. ♗g5 ♖e8 13. ♗f4 ♗e7 14. ♕d2 ♖ef8⇄, Movsesian–Shirov, Bundesliga 1999/2000) 8...♘xe5 9. dxe5 ♕c7 10. ♖e1 0-0-0 11. c4 ♕xe5 12. ♗f3 ♕d6 13. cxd5 exd5 14. ♘c3 ♘f6 15. ♘xd5 ♘xd5 16. ♕xd5 ♕xd5 17. ♗xd5 ♗f5 18. ♗f3 ♗d6 19. ♗e3 Draw. Movsesian–Shirov, 34th Olympiad, Istanbul 2000.

7. ♘a3 cxd4 8. cxd4 ♘f5 9. ♘c2 ♕b6

The continuation 9...♘b4 10. 0–0 ♘xc2 11. ♕xc2 ♕b6 12. ♕d3± is also critical, when White has a small but stable advantage.

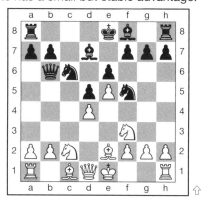

10. g4?!

The result of the game and the players' names tend to exert a great influence over the way we award exclamation and question marks. Yet though Shirov won the game after 10. g4, it is my view that the main continuation 10. 0–0 is stronger for White, e.g.:

A) 10...♖c8 11. ♔h1 ♘a5 12. g4 ♘e7 13. ♘fe1 h5 14. gxh5 ♘f5 15. ♗g4 ♘h6 16. ♗h3 ♘c6 17. b3 ♔d8 18. ♘g2 ♔c7 19. ♘f4 ♖d8 20. ♖g1 ♔b8 21. ♗b2 ♘e7 22. ♘e3 ♘ef5 (Charbonneau–Barsov, Montréal 2003) and here 23. ♘xf5 ♘xf5 24. ♗xf5 exf5 25. ♕f3± would have given White a small advantage.

B) 10...a5 11. b3 ♖c8 12. ♗b2 ♘b4 13. ♘xb4 axb4 14. ♖e1 ♗b5 15. ♖c1 ♖xc1 16. ♕xc1 ♗e7 17. g4 ♘h6 18. ♕c8+ ♗d8 19. h3 ♗c6 20. ♕b8 0–0 21. ♕d6 ♖e8 22. ♕c5 ♕xc5 23. dxc5 ♗e7 24. a4!? ♗xc5 25. ♘d4 ⩲, Timman–Jóhannesson, Reykjavík 2004.

10...♘fe7

10...♘h6 11. ♖g1↑.

11. 0–0

11. ♘h4 ♘b4 12. ♘a3 ♘ec6 13. ♗e3 ♗e7 14. ♘g2 f6 15. ♘b5 fxe5 16. 0–0 0–0 17. dxe5 ♗c5⇄, Wemmers–Gurevich, Belgium 2004.

11...h5

The moves 11...♖c8, 11...a5 and 11...♘g6 also come into consideration.

12. h3!?

The essence of White's plan here is to keep control of the square f5. Of course Black can open the h-file, but how can he attack with just his rook?! It is quite unclear who will benefit from the opening of the file. My judgement is that White's chances are better.

12...hxg4 13. hxg4 f6

If 13...f5!? then 14. ♘g5! is unpleasant for Black (but not 14. g5?! ♘g6, when he is in good shape – his king will be comfortable in the centre) e. g. 14...fxg4 (14...♖h4!?) 15. ♗xg4 ♘d8 16. ♔g2±. Van Wely thinks Black can equalise with 13...♘g6 14. ♗e3 ♗e7, but in fact he has a stronger move in 14...♖c8 15. ♗d3 ♘h4∓. Also if 14. ♔g2 (instead of 14. ♗e3) 14...♗e7 15. ♖h1 0–0–0∓ Black's chances are better.

14. ♗d3! 0–0–0

14...fxe5 15. dxe5!? (15. ♘xe5 ♘xe5 16. dxe5 ♕c7 17. ♕e2±) 15...♕c7 16. ♗f4±; 14...a5!? (van Wely).

15. b4

Thanks to his space advantage, White can easily transfer pieces to the queenside, so his attack will have a good chance of success. After the opening of the h-file Shirov induced his opponent to castle queenside in order to start an attack on the kingside, but this plan is too slow.

15...♘xd4?

This attractive blow has a serious snag. Once the white pawn centre disappears, the dark squares in the opposing camp become extremely weak.

15...f5!? 16. ♘g5!? ♖h4 17. ♗e2 ♖e8! 18. ♗f4 (18. ♘f7 ♘g6⇄) 18...fxg4 19. b5 ♘a5 20. ♘e3!?↑;

15...♗e8 (Shirov, Ftáčnik) 16. a4 ♘g6 17. a5→.

16. ♘cxd4 fxe5 17. ♕e2! e4

If 17...exd4 18. ♗f4! ♘c6 (18...a6 19. ♖ac1+ ♘c6 20. ♕e5+−) 19. b5± the black king is soon in trouble.

18. ♗f4

Preventing the black king from fleeing to the corner.

18...♘g6

Black cannot regain the piece: 18...exd3 19. ♖ac1+ ♘c6 20. ♕e5 ♗e8 21. ♕b8+ ♔d7 22. ♖xc6! bxc6 23. ♘e5+ ♔e7 24. ♗g5#!; 18...♘c6 19. ♘xc6 ♗xc6 20.b5→.

19. ♖ac1+ ♗c6 20. ♗g3 ♗d6

Neither 20...exf3 21. ♕xe6+ ♖d7 22. ♕e8+ ♕d8 23. ♖xc6+! bxc6 24. ♗a6+ ♖b7 25. ♗xb7+ ♔xb7 26. ♕xc6# nor 20...♗xb4 21. ♘xc6 bxc6 22. ♖xc6+! ♕xc6 23. ♗a6+ ♔d7 24. ♗b5+− enable Black to save the game.

21. b5?!

An inaccuracy, after which Black could have put up a protracted resistance. The computer immediately finds the right solution: 21. ♗xe4!? dxe4 22. ♘xc6 bxc6 23. ♕xe4 ♘e7 24. ♕xe6+, and White wins.

21...♗xg3 22. fxg3 exf3?

Black misses his chance: 22...♘e5! 23. ♘xe5 ♕xd4+ 24. ♔g2 exd3 (24...♕xe5 25. bxc6+–) 25. ♘xd3 ♕e4+ 26. ♕f3! ♖hf8 27. ♕xe4 dxe4 28. ♘f4 ♖d2+ 29. ♔g1 e5 30. ♘g2 (30. ♘e6 ♖xf1+ 31. ♔xf1 ♖xa2 32. bxc6 bxc6 33. ♘xg7 ±) 30...♖f3 31. bxc6 ♖xa2 32. cxb7+ ♔xb7 ±.

23. ♕e3!

Control over the dark squares is re-established, after which Black's position immediately becomes hopeless.

23...♕c7 24. ♖xf3+– ♘e5

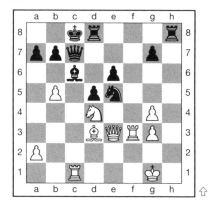

25. bxc6! ♘xf3+ 26. ♕xf3 ♕e5

26...b6 27. ♘xe6 ♕d6 28. ♗a6+ ♔b8 29. c7+.

27. cxb7+ ♔xb7 28. ♘c6

Black resigned.

Play on both wings

Game 50
Grischuk – Graf
35th Olympiad, Bled 2002

1. e4 e6 2. d4 d5 3. e5 c5 4. c3 ♘c6 5. ♘f3 ♗d7 6. ♗e2 ♘ge7 7. ♘a3 ♘g6 8. h4!?

A quite aggressive move. White provokes the exchange on a3, when he will have a damaged queenside pawn structure but can hope to exploit Black's weak dark squares.

8...cxd4 9. cxd4

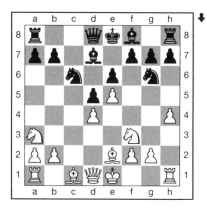

9...♗xa3

Black accepts the challenge. The quieter 9...♗b4+ 10. ♔f1 h6 11. ♘c2 ♗e7 12. h5 ♘f8 followed by the transfer of the knight to g5 was played in Movsesian – Nikolić, 34th Olympiad, Istanbul 2000.

10. bxa3 h6 11. h5 ♘ge7 12. 0–0 ♘a5 13. ♖b1 ♗c6 14. ♗d3 ♘c4

One of the disadvantages for White of the exchange on a3 is revealed: the knight cannot be ejected from c4 and exchanging it is unfavourable, since then the c6 bishop would be activated, and the d5 square would become available to Black's knight or queen. However, for the moment the c4 knight is not causing White any particular problems.

15. ♘h4!

White prepares an attack on the kingside (f2–f4–f5, ♕g4) and at the same time prevents the other black knight from taking up a good position at f5.

15...♕a5

Of course, castling kingside, as suggested by various computer programs, would be to commit hara-kiri.

16. ♕g4

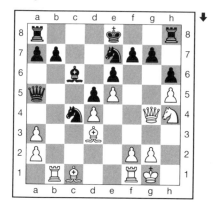

16...♔d7

Queenside castling is not possible because the king needs to protect the e7 knight (see the note to White's 17th). If 16...♘d2!? White reaches a promising position with 17. ♕×g7 ♖g8 18. ♕×h6! (18. ♗×d2 ♕×d2 19. ♕h7 ♕f4⇄) 18...♘×b1 19. ♗×b1 (Notkin). And it will rarely be good for Black to capture on a3; the pawn will not play an important role for a long time to come, whereas the square a3 might well become useful for the white bishop.

19...♗b5 20. ♗d2

A) 20...♕×a3 21. ♖e1

A1) 21...♘c6 22. ♕f6

A1a) 22...♕e7 23. ♕f4 ♗c4 24. h6 ♘b4 25. h7 ♖h8 26. ♕g3 ♘×a2 (26...♗×a2 27. ♕g7 ♔d7 28. ♗×b4 ♕×b4 29. ♕×f7++−) 27. ♘f3 ♖c8 28. ♗g5+−;

A1b) 22...♘×d4 23. h6 ♖f8 24. h7 ♔d7 25. ♔h2 ♖ac8 26. ♗h6±;

A2) 21...♖c8 22. ♕f6±;

B) 20...♕a4 21. ♖c1

B1) 21...♖c8 22. ♗b4 ♖×c1+ (22...♖c4 23. ♕d2±) 23. ♕×c1 ♔d7 (23...♘c6 24. h6±) 24. ♗c2 ♖c8 25. ♕g5±;

B2) 21...♕×d4 22. ♗g5 ♕×e5 23. ♗f6 ♕d6 24. ♘f3 =̄.

17. ♖b4

White prevents counterplay with ♘d2 and ♕c3 and attacks the knight c4 one more time, just in case. Now he is threatening to capture on g7, which is not so strong immediately because of 17. ♕×g7 ♖ag8 18. ♕f6 (18. ♕×f7 ♖f8 19. ♕g7 ♖fg8=) 18...♕c3⇄.

17...♖ag8

17...♘×a3? 18. ♗d2! (18. ♖b3!?).

18. f4 (18. ♕d1) **18...f5 19. e×f6 g×f6 20. ♕e2**

A pawn weakness has appeared in the black position at e6 and White immediately takes aim at it.

20...♘d6

Black does not have time to play 20...f5 (with the plan of transferring a knight to e4) because of 21. ♖e1.

21. f5!±

It is important not to let Black set up the defensive structure mentioned in the previous note.

21...e×f5

Notkin's suggestion 21...♘e4!? can be met by the very unpleasant 22. f×e6+ ♔×e6 23. ♘g6! e.g.: 23...♘×g6 24. h×g6 ♕d8 (24...♖×g6 25. ♕h5+−) 25. ♗×e4 d×e4 26. ♕g4+ ♔e7 27. ♕f5 ♔e8 28. d5 ♕×d5 29. ♕×f6 e3 30. ♕f7+ ♔d8 31. ♕×d5+ ♗×d5 32. ♖d1+−.

22. ♘×f5 ♘e×f5 (22...♘e4 23. ♕f3) **23. ♗×f5+ ♘×f5 24. ♖×f5**

Black's position leaves a lot to be desired: he has an unsafe king, a bad bishop and weak pawns. Furthermore there are bishops of opposite colours, which will make White's attack all the stronger.

24...♕d8 25. ♖b3

White brings into play his only inactive piece.

25...♖h7

25...♖e8 26. ♕g4! (26. ♕f2!?) 26...♖e6 27. ♗×h6!.

26. ♕f3

Here White could have played conceptually with 26. ♕f1, so as to arrange his heavy pieces by the book: the rooks in front, the queen behind. Grischuk probably decided that it would be good to target the d5 pawn; it might become possible to sacrifice the exchange and shatter Black's position.

26...♖e8?

White's calculation is justified – this move makes an elegant finish possible. More stubborn would be 26...♖hg7 27. ♖b2 ♕a5 (Notkin), but here too White would have good winning chances with 28. ♖e2 or 28. ♗×h6!?.

27. ♖×f6!

It becomes clear that the check on e1 can be ignored.

27...♔c8

27...♖e1+ 28. ♔f2 ♖×c1 29. ♕f5+ ♔c7 30. ♕×h7+ ♔b8 31. ♕g7+–.

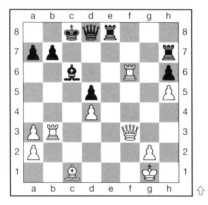

28. ♖×c6+! b×c6 29. ♕g4+ ♕d7

29...♖d7 30. ♗f4, and Black must give up his queen to fend off mate.

30. ♕g3 ♔d8 (30...♕c7 31. ♗f4) **31. ♗×h6!**

The computer reckons that the white position so good that it is winning even after 31. a4. But the move played allows White to achieve his goal more quickly.

31...♖×h6

31...♕c7 32. ♖b8+ ♔d7 33. ♕×c7+ ♔×c7 34. ♗f4+ ♔d7 35. ♖b7+ ♔e6 36. ♖×h7+–; 31...♖e1+ 32. ♕×e1 ♖×h6 33. ♕g3+–.

32. ♖b8+ ♔e7 33. ♕g7+ ♔d6 34. ♕×h6+

Black resigned, in view of 34...♔e6 (34...♔c7 35. ♕f4+; 34...♔e7 35. ♖b7! ♕×b7 36. ♕g7+) 35. ♕f4+ ♔e7 36. ♕f8#!

Play on both wings

Game 51
Grischuk – Lputian
35th Olympiad, Bled 2002

In this game the young Russian grandmaster missed the moment when he needed to switch to defence.

1. e4 e6 2. d4 d5 3. e5 c5 4. c3 ♘c6 5. ♘f3 ♕b6 6. a3 ♘h6 7. b4 c×d4 8. c×d4 ♘f5 9. ♗b2

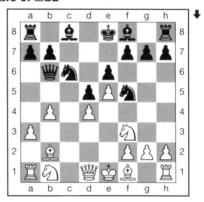

9...♗e7!?

9...♗d7, Sveshnikov – Lputian, Tilburg 1992 (Volume 2, page 50), Sveshnikov – Dvoiris, Cheliabinsk 2004 (Volume 2, game 59 on page 52); 9...a5, Sveshnikov – Bareev, Moscow (Rapidplay) 1995 (Volume 2, game [1] on page 116).

10. h4

10. ♗d3!?, Khalifman – Dolmatov, 19th EU-Cup, Rethymnon 2003 (Volume 2, game 20 on page 22).

10...a5!? 11. b5 (11. ♕a4!? 0–0 12. b5±) 11...♘c×d4 12. ♘×d4 ♘×d4 13. ♕g4 ♘×b5 14. ♕×g7 ♖f8∞;

10...0–0 11. 0–0 f6?! 12. ♗×f5 e×f5 13. ♘c3 ♗e6 14. ♘a4 ♕d8 15. ♘c5 ♗×c5 16. d×c5 f×e5, Sveshnikov–Paramos Dominguez, Oviedo (Rapidplay) 1993.

10...h5

10...a5!?

A) 11. g4 ♘h6 12. g5 ♘f5 13. b5 h6↑ (13...0–0⇄);

B) 11. b5 a4 12. g4 ♘h6 13. ♖g1 ♘a5 14. ♘c3 ♘b3 15. ♖a2 ♕a5 16. ♗d3 ♗d7 17. ♘d2 ♘×d4 18. ♘×d5 ♗×b5 19. ♗c3 ♕d8 20. ♘×e7 ♗×d3 21. ♗b4 ♘g8 22. ♘×g8 ♕d5 23. ♖g3 ♕h1+. White resigned (Yemelin–Dolmatov, Russian Championship, Krasnoyarsk 2003).

11. ♗d3

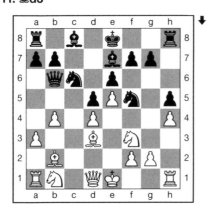

11...a5

11...g6 12. ♗×f5 g×f5 13. ♘c3 ♖g8

A) 14. 0–0 ♖g4 15. ♘e2 ♗d7 16. g3 0–0–0 17. ♗c1 ♖dg8 18. ♔h1 ♔b8 19. ♗f4 ♔a8 20. ♕d2 f6 21. e×f6 ♗×f6 22. ♖fc1 e5? (22...♖c8 23. ♖c5±) 23. d×e5±, Grischuk–Zhang Pengxiang, Shanghai 2001;

B) 14. g3?! ♖g4 15. ♘h2 ♖g8 16. ♕×h5 a5!∞;

C) 14. ♘g5 ♕×d4 15. ♕×d4 ♘×d4 16. ♘×d5 ♘c2+ 17. ♔d2 e×d5 18. ♔×c2 ♗×g5 19. h×g5 ♖×g5 20. ♗d4 ♗e6 21. g3∞, Grischuk–Sakaev, Tomsk 2001.

12. ♗×f5 e×f5 13. ♘c3 ♗e6

13...a×b4 14. ♘×d5 ♕a5 15. ♘×e7 b3+ 16. ♘d2 ♕×e7 17. ♕×b3 ♖h6 18. ♗c3 ♕d5 19. 0–0 ♕×b3 20. ♘×b3 ♖c6 21. ♗b4±, Sveshnikov–Bareev, Russian Championship, Elista 1996 (game 34 on page 65).

14. b5

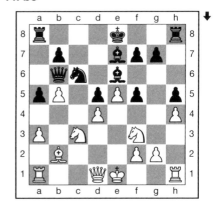

14...a4!

14...♘a7 15. a4 ♘c8 16. 0–0 ♕d8 17. g3 ♘b6 18. ♗a3 ♖c8 19. ♘e2 ♘c4 20. ♗×e7 ♕×e7 21. ♘f4 g6 22. ♘g5 ♖g8 23. ♘h7!±, Shirov–Taddei, Neuilly-sur-Seine (simul) 2001.

15. ♕d3 ♘a7 16. 0–0 ♖c8 17. ♗c1 ♖c4 18. ♖d1?!

From the opening theory point of view, 18. ♘e2 comes into consideration here. A later game continued 18...♕×b5 19. ♗g5 ♕b3 20. ♕×b3 a×b3 21. ♗×e7 ♔×e7 22. ♖fb1 ♖hc8 23. ♖×b3 b5 24. ♘f4 g6± 25. g3 ♖c3 (25...♖8c6 26. ♔g2 ♖a6 27. ♖d1 ♖aa4±) 26. ♖ab1 ♖8c4 27. ♔g2 ♔e8 28. ♘g5 ♗d7 29. e6 (29. ♖×c3 ♖×c3 30. ♔h2±), Vysochin–Polivanov, Chigorin Memorial, St. Petersburg 2002.

18...♘×b5 19. ♘e2 ♕c6 20. ♗g5

White's position looks active enough, but he is a pawn down. In what follows he has drawing chances, but nothing more.

20...♗×g5 21. ♘×g5 ♘c3 22. ♘×c3 ♖×c3 23. ♕e2

23. ♕d2 ♖c2 (23...0–0 24. ♘h3!∞) 24. ♕f4 (24. ♕b4!?) 24...0–0 25. ♘h3!?.

23...g6 24. ♖d3 0-0 25. ♖ad1 ♖c8 26. ♖×c3∓

26. ♘×e6 ♕×e6 27. ♕b2 ♖3c7 28. ♕b5 ♕d7 29. ♖b1 ♖c1+ 30. ♔h2∓.

26...♕×c3 27. ♕b5

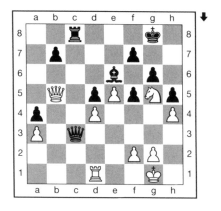

27...♕b3

27...♕×a3? 28. ♘×e6 f×e6 29. ♕d7 ♖c6 30. ♕e8+ ♔g7 31. ♕d7+=.

28. ♖b1 ♖c1+ 29. ♔h2 ♕×b5

29...♖×b1? 30. ♕e8+ ♔g7 31. ♘×e6+ f×e6 32. ♕e7+=.

30. ♖×b5 ♖c4 31. ♖×b7 ♖×d4 32. ♘×e6 f×e6 33. ♖e7

33. g3 ♖d3 34. ♖e7 ♖×a3 35. ♖×e6 ♔f7∓.

33...♖×h4+ 34. ♔g3 ♖e4 35. ♖×e6 ♔f7 36. ♖f6+ ♔e7 (36...♔g7 37. ♖a6!?) **37. ♖×g6 ♖g4+ 38. ♖×g4 f×g4 39. ♔f4**

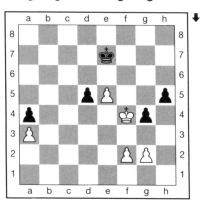

39...♔f7!

39...♔e6 40. g3 d4 41. ♔e4 d3 42. ♔×d3 ♔×e5 43. ♔e3=.

40. f3

40. g3 ♔e6−+.

40...g×f3 41. ♔×f3 ♔e6 42. ♔f4 h4 43. ♔g4 ♔×e5 44. ♔×h4 ♔f4 45. g3+ ♔e4

White resigned.

A fine win by Lputian and one of Grischuk's rare defeats with this system.

How could Lputian win with Black against someone who is currently an objectively stronger player? My friend Smbat and I played more than ten training games with the 3. e5 French, of which he won the majority. We have also played countless blitz games, so Lputian has enormous experience with and a good feel for these positions. Hence Grischuk did not manage to gain any advantage out of the opening. Through inertia, he continued playing for a win and missed the moment when he had to try to make a drew.

Play on both wings

Game 52
Short – Lputian
3rd European Championship, Batumi 1999

1. e4 e6 2. d4 d5 3. e5 c5 4. c3 ♘c6 5. ♘f3 ♕b6 6. a3 ♘h6 7. b4 c×d4 8. c×d4 ♘f5 9. ♗b2 ♗d7 10. g4

I always look with special interest at Lputian's games, since I do not know of any other player who handles so well with Black the positions in the 3. e5 system where White plays the bayonet attack g2–g4. Short is a fine attacking player with a good feeling for the initiative. So here we have a game between two real experts; it is a very interesting one, full of tactical and strategic finesses.

Clearly weaker is 10. ♘c3 ♘f×d4 11. ♘×d4 ♕×d4 12. ♕×d4 ♘×d4 13. ♘×d5 ♘c2+ 14. ♔d2 ♖c8 15. ♖c1 ♘×a3! 16. ♘c7+ ♔d8

17. ♘xe6+ ♗xe6 18. ♗xa3 ♖xc1 19. ♔xc1 a5 with excellent play for Black (Donev – Gärtner, Austria (Vorarlberg) 1997/98).

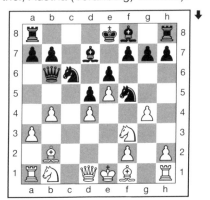

10...♘h6

10...♘fe7 is also worth considering, e.g.: 11. ♘c3 h5 12. ♘a4 ♕d8 13. ♘c5 ♗c8 14. g5 b6 15. ♘a6 ♘b8 16. ♖c1 ♗xa6 17. ♗xa6 ♘xa6 18. ♕a4+ ♕d7 19. ♕xa6 ♘g6 20. ♖c3 ♗e7 21. 0–0 0–0 (Flores – Vallejo Pons, World Championship U18, Oropesa del Mar 1999, see page 95).

11. ♖g1

11. h3 f6 12. ♘c3 fxe5 13. dxe5 ♗e7 14. ♘a4 ♕d8 15. ♖c1 0–0 16. ♘c5 ♗xc5 17. ♖xc5 ♘f7 18. ♗g2 b6 19. ♖c1 ♘e7 20. ♕d2 ♘g6 21. h4 ♘h6 22. g5 ♘g4⇄ (Sveshnikov – Lputian, Sochi 1993).

11...f6 12. exf6 gxf6 13. ♘c3 ♘f7 14. ♘a4 ♕c7!?

A novelty. 14...♕d8 15. ♘c5 b6 16. ♘xd7 ♕xd7 17. ♖c1 ♘cd8 18. h4! ♗d6 19. ♖c3 b5 20. g5 fxg5 21. ♘xg5 a6 22. ♕c2 ♘xg5 23. ♖xg5 ♕e7 (Vasyukov – Bukhman, St. Petersburg 1994).

15. ♖c1 ♕f4

(see next diagram)

A critical position, in which White stands better, in my judgement.

15...♕d6 – see Sveshnikov – Dvoiris (Cheliabinsk 2004, Volume 2, game 59 on page 52).

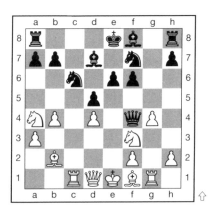

16. ♘c5

16. b5?! ♘a5 17. ♘c5 ♗xc5 18. ♖xc5 ♕e4+⇄.

16...♗xc5 17. dxc5

A logical move which opens the way for the bishop, but 17. ♖xc5!? is also interesting, e.g. 17...e5 18. dxe5 (18. ♖xd5?? ♕e4+–+) 18...♗xg4 19. ♗e2 fxe5 20. ♕xd5 ♖d8 21. ♕c4± or 17...♘d6 18. ♗c1 ♕e4+ 19. ♗e3 ♕g6 20. ♗d3 ♕f7±.

17...♘ce5 18. ♘xe5 ♘xe5 19. ♖g3!

Now it is clear that White has held on to his opening advantage.

19...a6

19...h5!? 20. gxh5 (20. g5 h4∓) 20...0–0–0⇄.

20. ♗e2 ♗b5 21. ♕d4! ♕xd4 22. ♗xd4 ♖f8 23. g5± ♗xe2 24. ♔xe2 ♘d7 25. gxf6

25. c6!? bxc6 26. ♖xc6 e5 27. ♗c5 ♘xc5 28. bxc5+–.

25...e5 26. ♗b2

It is hard to believe that Black could have saved the game after the simple 26. ♗xe5! ♘xe5 27. ♖e3 ♔d7 28. ♖xe5 ♖ae8 29. f4 e.g.: 29...♖xe5+ 30. fxe5 ♔e6 (30...♖e8 31. ♖f1 ♖xe5+ 32. ♔d3+–) 31. c6+– or 29...♖xf6 30. ♖xe8 ♔xe8 31. ♔e3+–.

26...♖xf6 27. ♖g8+ ♖f8 28. ♖xf8+ ♔xf8 29. ♖d1 d4 30. f4! a5! 31. fxe5 axb4

32. a×b4 ♖a2 33. ♖d2 ♘×e5 34. ♗×d4 ♖×d2+ 35. ♔×d2 ♘f3+ 36. ♔c3

36. ♔e3 ♘×h2 37. b5 ♔e7 38. c6 b×c6 39. b6 ♔d8 40. ♗e5? ♘g4+.

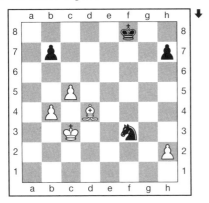

36...♔e7

The h2 pawn is poisoned – 36...♘×h2? 37. b5 ♔e8 38. c6 b6 (38...b×c6 39. b6 ♔d7 40. ♗e5! ♔c8 41. ♗×h2+–) 39. ♗×b6+–. Lputian puts up maximum resistance and is rewarded with a draw.

37. h3

37. b5 ♔d7 38. h3.

37...♘g5 38. h4 ♘f3 39. h5 ♘h4 40. ♔d3 (40. ♔c4!?) **40...♘f5 41. ♗e5 ♔e6 42. ♔e4 ♘e7 43. b5 ♘c8 44. ♗b8**

44. c6 b×c6 (44...b6!?) 45. b×c6 ♘e7 46. c7 ♔d7 47. ♗h2.

44...♘e7 45. c6 (45. ♗g3+–) **45...b×c6 46. b6 ♘d5 47. b7 ♘f6+ 48. ♔f3**

48. ♔f4 ♘×h5+ 49. ♔f3 ♘f6=.

48...♘d7 49. ♗c7

49. ♗f4 ♔f5 50. ♔g3 c5=.

49...♔f5= 50. ♗f4 c5 51. ♗d6 c4 52. ♔e3 ♔e6!

52...♔g5 53. ♔d4 ♔×h5 54. ♔×c4+–.

53. ♗g3

53. b8♕ ♘×b8 54. ♗×b8 ♔f5 55. h6 c3 56. ♗d6 c2 57. ♔d2 ♔e6 58. ♗a3 ♔f7 59. ♔×c2 ♔g8=.

53...c3! 54. ♗e1 c2 55. ♔d2 ♔d5 56. ♗g3 (56. ♔×c2 ♔c6=) **56...♔c6 57. b8♕ ♘×b8 58. ♗×b8 ♔d5= 59. ♔×c2 ♔e4 60. h6 ♔f5 61. ♗a7 ♔g6 62. ♗e3 ♔f7 63. ♔d3 ♔g8 64. ♔e4 ♔f8 65. ♔f5 ♔f7 66. ♗d4 ♔g8 67. ♔f6 ♔f8 68. ♗c5+ ♔g8 69. ♔e7 ♔h8 70. ♔f8**

Draw.

Play on both wings, attack on the king on the queenside

Game 53
I. Zaitsev – Faragó
Szolnok 1975

This encounter is reminiscent of the game Zaitsev–Pokojowczyk in the first chapter (game 11 on page 22).

1. e4 e6 2. d4 d5 3. e5 c5 4. c3 ♘c6 5. ♘f3 ♕b6 6. a3 c4 7. ♘bd2 ♘a5!

7...♗d7 8. b3! c×b3 9. ♘×b3±.

8. ♗e2 ♗d7 9. 0–0 h6 10. ♖b1 ♘e7 11. g3 0–0–0 12. ♘h4

12. b4 c×b3 13. c4 ♗a4 14. ♗b2⇄.

12...f5 13. e×f6 g×f6 14. ♗g4 e5 15. b3!∞

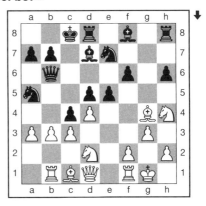

15...c×b3 16. ♘×b3 f5

16...♘×b3 17. ♖×b3 ♕c7 18. ♗×d7+ ♕×d7 19. ♕h5±.

17. ♗h3!± ♗a4 18. ♘×a5

18. ♕e2!? e4 19. ♘c5 ♕×b1

A) 20. ♗f4+− ♕b6 21. ♘xa4 ♕c6 22. ♘xf5 ♘xf5 23. ♗xf5+ ♖d7 24. ♕h5 ♗xa3 25. ♗xd7+ ♔xd7 (25...♕xd7 26. ♕e5+−) 26. ♖a1 ♘c4 27. ♘c5+ ♗xc5 28. ♕g4+ ♔d8 29. dxc5+−.

B) 20. ♘xf5 ♘xf5 21. ♗xf5+ ♗d7 22. ♘xd7 ♖xd7 23. ♗xd7+ ♔xd7 24. ♕g4+ ♔c6 25. ♕e6+ ♔b5 26. ♕e5 ♖h7 27. ♕xd5+ ♔a4 28. ♕g8+−.

18...♗xd1

18...♕xa5 19. ♕h5 (19. ♕e2 e4 20. ♘xf5 ♘xf5 21. ♗xf5+ ♔b8 22. ♗f4+ ♗d6 23. ♗xd6+ ♖xd6±) 19...♗e8 (19...♗c2 20. ♖b2 ♗d3 21. ♖d1 e4 22. ♗f4+−) 20. ♕e2 e4 21. ♘xf5 ♘xf5 22. ♗xf5+ ♗d7 23. ♖b5 ♕a6 24. ♗xd7+ ♖xd7 25. f3+−.

19. ♖xb6 axb6 20. ♖xd1 bxa5 21. dxe5

21. ♘xf5 ♔c7 22. dxe5 ♘xf5 23. ♗xf5±.

21...♔c7 22. f4

22. ♗xf5!? ♘xf5 23. ♘xf5 a4 24. e6 ♖e8 25. ♖e1 ♖h7 26. g4±.

22...b5 23. ♘xf5 ♘xf5 24. ♗xf5 ♗c5+ 25. ♔g2 d4 26. ♖d3 dxc3 27. ♖xc3 ♔b6 28. ♗e3! ♗xe3 29. ♖xe3± ♔c5 30. ♗g6 ♖hg8 31. ♗f7 ♖g7 32. e6 ♖f8 33. ♖e5+ ♔c6 34. ♖f5+− ♖b8 35. e7 ♖xf7 36. ♖xf7 ♔d7 37. ♖f8 ♖e8 38. ♖f5 ♖b8 39. ♖f8 ♖e8 40. ♖f5 ♖b8 41. a4 b4 42. ♖xa5 b3 43. ♖e5 ♔e8 44. ♖e1 b2 45. ♖b1 ♔xe7 46. a5

Black resigned.

An excellent game by Igor Arkadevich!

Play on both wings

Game 54
Bronstein – Mestel
England – USSR, London 1976

A very instructive game. I admire the purity with which Bronstein carries out his strategic ideas. White has two methods of playing on both wings. We have already discussed the first method, when White creates weaknesses in the enemy's kingside and then later shifts the weight of the struggle to the queenside. In this game Bronstein demonstrates another method of playing on both wings: on the queenside, where White is weaker, he is content to defend (with the minimum of forces), he deprives the opponent of counterplay and then he takes the offensive with f4–f5, opening the f-file.

Generally, such model games arise between players of widely differing strength. In the mid-seventies Mestel was one of the strongest English grandmasters. David Ionovich's creative achievement is therefore all the more praiseworthy.

1. e4 c5 2. c3 e6 3. d4 d5 4. e5 ♘c6 5. ♘f3 ♕b6 6. a3 c4 7. ♘bd2 ♘a5 8. h4 ♗d7 9. h5

Taking space on the kingside.

9...h6 10. g3 ♘e7 11. ♗h3 ♘b3 12. ♘xb3 ♗a4 13. ♘fd2 ♘c6 14. 0–0± ♘a5 15. f4 ♘xb3 16. ♘xb3 ♗xb3

The b3 bishop is actually out of the game, so that White is practically playing with an extra piece. Now any exchange on the f-file is advantageous for White. The only requirement is to control the c2 square, to prevent the bishop transferring to its operational diagonal (b1–h7).

17. ♕e2 0–0–0 18. f5±

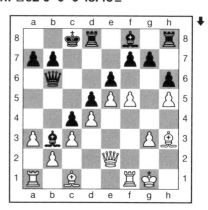

18...♖e8 19. ♗e3 ♗a4 20. f×e6 f×e6 21. ♖f7 ♖e7 22. ♖f2 ♖e8 23. ♖af1 ♗e7 24. ♕g4 ♗d8 25. ♕g6 ♖e7 26. ♖f7 ♗e8?

26...♖he8 27. ♗c1 ♖×f7 28. ♖×f7 ♔b8 29. ♕×g7 +−.

27. ♖×e7

Black resigned.

A crystal-clear illustrative game: White defended on the queenside and attacked on the kingside.

In Chapter 1 "Theoretically important games for independent analysis", on page 11 in Volume 2, special attention should be given to the encounters Sveshnikov – Brumen, Bled 2000 (Volume 2, game 56 on page 48) and Sveshnikov – Dizdar, Bled 2002 (Volume 2, game 57 on page 49).

Conclusions: we can say that when the play is on both wings, the advantage is more often than not with White, since, thanks to his space advantage, it is easier for him to regroup his pieces.

Chapter 3

The many facets of the blockade

3.1 Aaron Nimzowitsch: theoretician, practical player and romantic

Having worked with children for quite a long time, I am constantly thinking about new lessons. For many years I have wanted to write an article about blockade, since this theme is important to me, and has cropped up in dozens of my games. But it is not possible to discuss blockade without mentioning the man who was the first to give it a theoretical basis and to explain it – Aaron Nimzowitsch.

The future great chess player was born in Riga in the same year, 1886, as that in which Wilhelm Steinitz became the first official world champion in history. Eight year old Aaron was introduced to chess by his father. In 1902 the young man set off to study in Germany and it was there that childhood enthusiasm grew into a real love. Nimzowitsch played constantly in all sorts of competitions, first of all in club events and then in international tournaments. By 1906 he had already achieved his first major success by winning first prize in a strong tournament in Munich (ahead of Rudolf Spielmann!).

The years of the First World War and the Russian Revolution undoubtedly influenced Nimzowitsch's fate. It is not known for certain what he did between 1914 and 1920. Only when he left Riga in the spring of 1920, first for Sweden, and then for Copenhagen, did he return to active chess playing. The peak of Nimzowitsch's sporting career falls in the 20s

and the beginning of the 30s. Here are some of his results: 1923 Copenhagen 1st place; 1925 Marienbad sharing 1st and 2nd place; 1926 Dresden 1st, Hannover 1st; 1927 London 1st; 1928 Berlin 1st; 1929 Carlsbad 1st; 1930 Frankfurt am Main 1st; 1933 Copenhagen sharing 1st and 2nd. After his victory in Carlsbad and 2nd place in the tournament in San Remo (1930) the chess world began to talk about organising a match for the crown between Nimzowitsch and Alexander Alekhine. Alas, in the path of the pretender there rose "a golden barrier" – a prize fund of $10,000 – which he was not able to overcome.

What a pity! … At that stage Nimzowitsch's results could have been the envy even of a world champion. In games against Efim Bogoljubow, who played two matches for the world championship with Alekhine, he scored 4/5. In games with the future world champion Max Euwe – 1½/2, with Salo Flohr – 2½/3.

In the meantime we remember Aaron Nimzowitsch not only because of his sporting results but also for his scientific and creative contribution, and for his selfless love and devotion to chess.

This is what the Swedish grandmaster Gideon Ståhlberg wrote in his memoirs (Chess and Chessmasters): "… Few masters

– perhaps none – were so fond of the game of chess as Nimzowitsch. … Chess was the great interest of his life, not because it became his profession, but because from his childhood onwards he cherished it more than anything else". The famous English master and chess author Harry Golombek included Nimzowitsch among the chess romantics. Innovative ideas were his principal bequest to the chess world.

While Alekhine possessed colossal practical strength and absorbed ideas from other chess players like a sponge, basing whole systems and variations on these ideas (in this respect Garry Kasparov is similar to him), Nimzowitsch thought for himself. From his pen issued such remarkable textbooks as *Blockade*, *My System*, *My System in Practice*, and *How I became a Grandmaster*.

No less important is Nimzowitsch's contribution to chess opening theory. "It is difficult to name another chess player who had a comparable influence on our contemporaries", – Harry Golombek.

Here are the most important of them: the Nimzo-Indian Defence – **1. d4 ♘f6 2. c4 e6 3. ♘c3 ♗b4**; in the Queen's Indian Defence, after **1. d4 ♘f6 2. c4 e6 3. ♘f3 b6 4. g3** the move **4...♗a6**; in the French Defence, **1. e4 e6 2. d4 d5 3. ♘c3 ♗b4** for Black and **1. e4 e6 2. d4 d5 3. e5!** for White. In addition there is the variation **1. e4 c5 2. ♘f3 ♘c6 3. ♗b5!** (Nimzowitsch's punctuation!) in the Sicilian defence, a line which is gaining ever more attention from contemporary grandmasters. For Black **1. e4 c5 2. ♘f3 ♘f6?!** (my punctuation, E. S.). In the Caro-Kann Defence: **1. e4 c6 2. d4 d5 3. e×d5 c×d5 4. c4** – this variation was played by Alekhine and Botvinnik. There were also some dubious opening ideas for example **1. e4 ♘c6** or the Nimzowitsch opening **1. b3**.

I don't think I have a right to change anything of what Nimzowitsch wrote about the blockade, if only because it is impossible to put it better!

"I have succeeded in finding the theoretical basis of the rule which explains why it is necessary to block passed pawns.

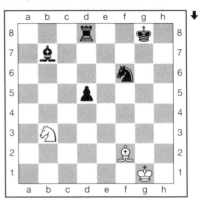

"The important question is this: is it sufficient to impede the advance of the d5 pawn with the arrangement of pieces shown in the diagram (♘b3 and ♗f2), or should it be physically restrained by placing the knight on d4? Answer: in view of the tremendous mobility of the passed pawn, mild measures such as impeding its advance through the influence of pieces posted at a distance are inadequate, because the pawn could move forward anyway, even at the cost of its life.

"**1...d4 2. ♗×d4** (or 2. ♘×d4). Now the black pieces standing behind the pawn suddenly come to life: the bishop commands a diagonal pointing towards the enemy king, the rook gets an open file and the knight a new central square. Accordingly the blockade is logically justified by the fact that the passed pawn is (as I jokingly put it) like a criminal, one who is so dangerous that placing it under police surveillance (by the knight on b3 and the bishop on f2) is inadequate; no, it must be put in jail, completely deprived of its liberty by means of a blockade by the knight on d4.

"It might be thought that blockading the pawn has a purely "local" significance, and is thus a spatially limited exception: a pawn which wanted to advance is immobilised; so only the pawn suffers, nothing else. However, such an understanding is superficial. In reality, a whole complex of enemy pieces suffers, whole areas of the board are barred to manoeuvres and sometimes the entire enemy position can find itself constricted; in other words, the paralysis of the blockaded pawn spreads to the forces in the rear".

In order to paint a fuller picture of Nimzowitsch I shall cite what several of his colleagues (famous chess players) had to say about him.

"Nimzowitsch is an eternal thinker and an engine of chess history. His restless mind will never make peace with the statement that the truth has been found … He is an individualist and so it is easy for him to find himself in opposition to Réti, just as he was once in opposition to the conservative methods of the German school (Tarrasch). He cannot be considered a man of his time. His task is to reflect the future …" (Pyotr Romanovsky, 1925).

"Bent Larsen and Tigran Petrosian, chess players moving in opposite creative directions, both present themselves as followers of Nimzowitsch … After all there was a time when such concepts as centralisation, prophylaxis, overprotection, blockade and others were only the recipes of the eccentric Nimzowitsch. Today general acceptance of these ideas has made them seem almost banal. Previously these recipes were thought of only as quirks of Nimzowitsch's individual approach to chess; now they are being taught. And they are nothing special – they are even very simple. Revelations, flashes of illumination, discoveries, which are only accessible to brilliant individuals, are precious - precisely because they become public property. And they allow the next genius to begin from a new level". (Mikhail Tal, 1974)

Everybody accepts the fact that Tal, Fischer, Karpov and Kasparov are geniuses, but only Tal dared to say that Nimzowitsch was a genius. That is how much he valued Nimzowitsch's contribution to chess!

* * *

3.2 The classical blockade

Many games by Aaron Nimzowitsch have rightly entered the treasury of chess art. In my view the game with Salwe beautifully demonstrates the plan of giving up a pawn centre and then blockading the vacated central squares with one's own pieces.

Game 55
Nimzowitsch – Salwe
Carlsbad 1911

French Defence C02

1. e4 e6 2. d4 d5 3. e5(!)

Creating the famous "pawn chain".

3...c5 4. c3

In the 1920s Nimzowitsch thought up and successfully adopted the plan with 4. ♕g4?!.

4...♘c6 5. ♘f3 ♕b6 6. ♗d3 ♗d7?

A serious opening mistake. More accurate is 6...cxd4! 7. cxd4 and only now 7...♗d7.

7. dxc5!

Today this move is considered normal and natural, but at that time, almost a hundred years ago, it was a revelation: to give up the centre, and for what – for an ephemeral opportunity to occupy the liberated square d4 with one's own pieces! This is what grandmaster Milan Vidmar wrote about this move: "After 6...♗d7 even the artificial 7. dxc5 is possible, which, however, gives White a good game".

In general, Nimzowitsch's play in this game was so revolutionary that at first it attracted very little praise. Very few critics could appreciate the beauty of his ideas at their true value. For the move 7. dxc5, one of the deepest ever made on the chess board, Nimzowitsch was universally condemned!

7...♗xc5 8. 0–0 f6?

8...a5 came into consideration.

9. b4! ♗e7 10. ♗f4 fxe5?

Here 10...♘h6 would have been better.

11. ♘xe5 ♘xe5 12. ♗xe5 ♘f6

If 12...♗f6, then 13. ♕h5+ g6 14. ♗xg6+ hxg6 15. ♕xg6+ ♔e7 16. ♗xf6+ ♘xf6 17. ♕g7+ and ♕xf6 (Nimzowitsch).

13. ♘d2 0–0 14. ♘f3

The knight, the e5 bishop, and the c3 pawn all participate in an immediate blockade of the central points d4 and e5. Now it is the turn of other white pieces – queen and rook.

14...♗d6

On 14...♗b5 Nimzowitsch gives the variation 15. ♗d4 ♕a6 16. ♗xb5 ♕xb5 17. ♘g5 ♕c6 18. ♖e1 with an advantage. But slightly better is 14...♘g4 15. ♗g3 (if 15. ♗d4, then 15...♕c7 16. h3 – against the threat of 16...♖xf3 – 16...♖xf3 17. hxg4 ♖f7; of course White has an advantage but Black can defend) 15...♗f6 (15...♗d6? 16. ♗xh7+! ♔xh7 17. ♘g5+) 16. h3 ♘h6 17. ♗e5 ♘f7 18. ♗xf6 gxf6 19. c4! – Black's position is difficult.

15. ♕e2! ♖ac8 16. ♗d4! ♕c7 17. ♘e5!

Notice how elegantly the bishop on e5 gave way to the knight. The blockade is consolidated and the two squares are already occupied by white pieces. Everything is so clear that is hardly necessary to add any exclamation marks.

17...♗e8 18. ♖ae1!

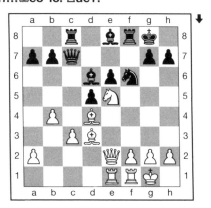

This is in full accordance with the principles formulated by Nimzowitsch: "first restrain, then blockade, and finally, destroy". The position is begging to be given a diagram in order to show more clearly Black's suffocation – or blockade!

18...♗xe5

This is tantamount to resignation, but what else is there? On 18...♗h5 it is possible to play the calm 19. f3 with g2–g4 to follow.

**19. ♗xe5 ♕c6 20. ♗d4 ♗d7 21. ♕c2 ♖f7
22. ♖e3 b6 23. ♖g3 ♔h8 24. ♗xh7! e5
25. ♗g6 ♖e7 26. ♖e1 ♕d6 27. ♗e3 d4
28. ♗g5 ♖xc3 29. ♖xc3 dxc3 30. ♕xc3
♔g8 31. a3 ♔f8 32. ♗h4 ♗e8 33. ♗f5
♕d4 34. ♕xd4 exd4 35. ♖xe7 ♔xe7
36. ♗d3 ♔d6 37. ♗xf6 gxf6 38. ♔f1 ♗c6
39. h4**

Black resigned.

"This game is instructive from beginning to end; furthermore I consider it to be the first in which my new philosophy of the centre was exhibited." (Nimzowitsch)

Game 56
Nimzowitsch – Levenfish
Carlsbad 1911

French Defence C02

**1. e4 e6 2. d4 d5 3. e5 c5 4. c3 ♘c6
5. ♘f3 f6 6. ♗b5 ♗d7 7. 0-0 ♕b6
8. ♗xc6 bxc6 9. exf6 ♘xf6 10. ♘e5 ♗d6
11. dxc5!! ♗xc5**

"After the completion of the game Levenfish told me that he found my total disregard for the centre completely incomprehensible" (Nimzowitsch).

12. ♗g5 ♕d8 13. ♗xf6 ♕xf6

Not 13...gxf6 14. ♕h5+ ♔e7 15. ♕f7+ ♔d6
16. ♘xd7 ♕xd7 17. ♕xf6.

14. ♕h5+!

It is useful to provoke the move g7–g6, which weakens the dark squares and, more importantly, closes the e8–h5 diagonal for the light-squared bishop.

**14...g6 15. ♕e2 ♖d8 16. ♘d2 0-0
17. ♖ae1 ♖fe8 18. ♔h1 ♗d6**

19. f4!

Strengthening control over the e5 square. Now playing b2–b4 and ♘d2–b3 would be enough for a complete blockade. Levenfish of course does not allow this.

19...c5 20. c4! ♗f8

Losing a pawn, but 20...d4 21. ♘e4 ♕e7
22. ♘xd6 ♕xd6 leaves White with an even greater positional advantage.

21. cxd5 ♗c8

21...exd5 fails to 22. ♘xd7.

22. ♘e4 ♕g7 23. dxe6

A pity: 23. d6! would have made the game more complete. Of course the move chosen also wins.

**23...♗xe6 24. ♕a6 ♔h8 25. ♖d1 ♗g8
26. b3 ♖d4 27. ♖xd4 cxd4 28. ♕a5 ♖c8
29. ♖d1 ♖c2 30. h3 ♕b7 31. ♖xd4 ♗c5
32. ♕d8!! ♗e7**

32...♗xd4 fails to 33. ♕xd4 ♕g7 34. ♘d6!
with the threat 35. ♘e8.

**33. ♕d7 ♕a6 34. ♖d3 ♗f8 35. ♘f7+ ♗xf7
36. ♕xf7 ♖c8 37. ♖d7**

Black resigned.

These two games are beautiful examples of blockade, which I propose to call "classical". Of course the blockade existed even before Nimzowitsch and, for example, the move d×c5 in the French Defence was used by Steinitz. Many people have intuitively used this method even without reading books about blockade. For example, I have found some decent games of my own in which I made use of blockade, played when I was just a second category player. But when I was preparing to teach some children I read Nimzowitsch again and reflected upon this theme, and my own tournament results improved.

Game 57
Sveshnikov – Razuvaev
Belgrade 1988

French Defence C02

Yuri Razuvaev and I have been facing each other over the chessboard for many years. When I am Black it is usually a Catalan or some sort of Queen's Gambit; when I am White, it is invariably a 3. e5 French. Our adherence to our opening principles develops the theory. At the same time interesting psychological situations arise, like in a match.

1. e4 c5 2. c3 e6 3. d4 d5 4. e5 ♘c6

Since the f6 square is unavailable, Black sometimes chooses the setup with 4...♘e7 and 5...♘ec6. For examples see the games Sveshnikov–Kovačević, Belgrade 1988 (game [1] on page 118), Sveshnikov–Lputian, Moscow 1989 (game 37 on page 69) and Kupreichik–Kovačević, Ljubljana/Portorož 1989 (game [2] on page 118). Black can also exchange the light-squared bishops with 4...♕b6, 5...♗d7 and 6...♗b5 – see Sveshnikov–Ehlvest, Leningrad 1984 (game [3] on page 118), as well as games by Igor Zaitsev.

5. ♘f3 ♗d7

Our previous games went the same way. Although I often obtained promising positions,

I did not manage to win a single game, and in Sochi 1986 I even lost one. So for this game I prepared long and hard. I noticed that in a game against Kaidanov (Dubna 1979), Razuvaev had answered

6. ♗d3!?

… with 6...f6?!. That meant that he was not prepared to win the pawn. Furthermore, he had no taste for defence, preferring positions with clear counterplay. Without doubt the strongest line for Black here is 6...c×d4 7. c×d4 ♕b6 8. ♘c3 ♘×d4, but this requires an excellent knowledge of concrete variations. I studied this line in 1987/88 and also played a few tournament games with it in minor competitions to gain a good grasp of the position. White can also play 6. ♗e2, 6. a3 or 6. d×c5.

6...c×d4

This is more accurate than 6...♕b6?!, since then White has another possibility – 7. d×c5 ♗×c5 8. 0–0 (8. b4!? ♗×f2+ 9. ♔e2 is unclear) 8...a5 9. a4, followed by ♘a3.

7. c×d4 ♕b6

7...♘b4 8. ♗e2 ±.

8. ♘c3 ♘×d4 9. ♘×d4 ♕×d4 10. 0–0

If White does not wish to offer the second pawn, he can play 10. ♕e2!?.

10...a6

I can honestly say that I had no doubt that my opponent would limit himself to one pawn, even though the variations 10...♕×e5!? 11. ♖e1 ♕d6 (or 11...♕b8 12. ♘×d5 ♗d6) 12. ♘b5 ♕b6 13. ♗e3 ♕a5 14. ♗d2 ♕b6 come into consideration for Black.

11. ♕e2 ♘e7

11...g6!? and 11...♕a7 have also been played.

12. ♔h1

A necessary move, since White cannot get by without f2–f4.

12...♘c6 13. f4 ♘b4

13...♗c5.

14. ♖d1!

14. ♗b1 ♛c4 is better for Black.

14...♘xd3 15. ♖xd3 ♛c4?!

Some preliminary conclusions can already be drawn, even though I was still in my preparation. White had used ten minutes to Black's one hour and ten minutes; the time limit was forty moves in two hours each. Furthermore, I think Black has already made his first mistake; he should have played 15...♛b6 16. ♗e3 ♗c5! 17. ♗xc5 ♛xc5 18. f5!? when White has enough initiative for the pawn, but not more.

16. b3!

16. ♗e3 ♗b4! or 16...♗c5.

16...♛c7 17. ♗b2 ♗c6

This was the first new move as far as I was concerned. In a game of Glek's there occurred 17...♖c8 18. f5!, and White developed a dangerous attack.

18. ♖c1 ♖d8

If 18...♗e7 then 19. f5! is unpleasant, whilst now 19. f5 would be answered by 19...d4.

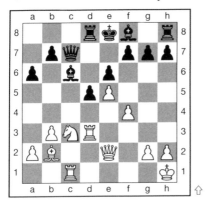

19. ♛f2!

A typical manoeuvre in such positions, already seen in my games. Not only does it prepare to transfer the queen to the kingside, but it also vacates the e2 square so that the knight can go to d4.

19...♗e7

After 19...d4 20. ♘e2! ♛b6 (20...♛a5 21. ♖xd4) 21. ♖xd4 White keep the advantage.

20. ♘e2 0–0 21. ♘d4

The development of the pieces is thus completed; for the pawn, White has the strong d4 square. As well as the possibility of regaining the pawn on c6 and later conquering the c-file, White has an even stronger plan available: a kingside attack by f4–f5.

21...♛d7 22. f5 exf5

22...♗g5? fails to 23. f6 ♗xc1 24. ♗xc1, and Black has no pieces capable of defending his king.

23. ♖g3!

A strong move instead of the small-minded 23. ♘xf5, when by 23...d4! (returning the pawn to open lines for the bishop and rook) 24. ♖xd4 ♛e6 Black would gain counterplay.

23...g6

23...♗h4 obviously fails to 24. ♖xg7+ ♔xg7 25. ♛xh4 with a winning attack on the dark squares.

24. ♛f4!

Once again 24. ♘xf5 is answered by 24...d4.

24...♖fe8

There is no other defence against the threat of 25. ♛h6 and 26. ♖h3.

25. ♘xf5 ♗f8

Now 25...d4 fails to 26. ♘h6+ ♔g7 27. ♛xf7+ ♔xh6 28. e6.

26. ♗d4!

A beautiful move: blockade à la Nimzo-witsch! The knight has joined the attack, now the bishop takes its place on the blockading square, and Black's light-squared bishop is reduced to the role of a large pawn.

26...♖e6

Black's clock was down to a few minutes, and so it was naturally hard for Yuri to de-cide on 26...f6!? which seems to be the best chance, although after 27. e×f6 ♖e4 28. ♕f2 ♔f7 29. ♘e7 the material is equal but White retains an attack.

28. ♘e7+ also comes into considera-tion, e. g.: 28...♔f7 29. ♕g5!? (29. ♕f2±) 29...♖×d4 30. ♘×g6 ♗d6 31. ♘e5+ ♗×e5 32. ♕×e5 ♖g8 33. ♕h5+ ♔f8 34. ♕h6+ win-ning.

27. ♘h6+ ♗×h6

If 27...♔g7 28. ♖f1 ♗b5 29. ♕×f7+ ♕×f7 30. ♖×f7+ ♔h8! (but not 30...♔×h6 31. ♖h3+ ♔g5 32. ♗e3+ ♔g4 33. ♖g3+ ♔h5 34. ♖×h7+ ♗h6 35. ♖×h6#) no clear win is apparent, but 28. a4, followed by ♖f1 and ♘×f7, is better.

28. ♕×h6 ♖de8 29. ♖f1 ♕c7?

There is no salvation in 29...♖×e5 30. ♗e3 f6 31. ♗×e5 f×e5 32. ♖×e5, or even 31. ♖×f6! ♖×e3 32. ♖×g6+ h×g6 33. ♕h8+ ♔f7 34. ♕g7+ ♔e6 35. ♕f6#. However, Black can defend more stubbornly with 29...♗b5 30. ♖f5! (30. ♖f4 ♖×e5 31. h3±) 30...f6 31. ♖×f6 ♖×f6 32. e×f6 ♖e1+ 33. ♗g1 ♖f1 34. ♖f3 ♖×f3 35. g×f3±.

30. ♖h3 f5 31. e×f6 ♕f7

Or 31...♖e1 32. ♕×h7+! ♕×h7 33. f7+ ♕×f7 34. ♖h8#.

32. ♕×h7+!

Black resigned.

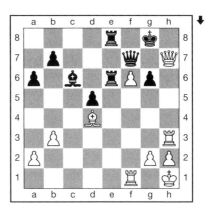

After the game my opponent congratulated me and mentioned Nimzowitsch. I think the famous teacher would have been pleased with one of his many pupils!

Game 58
Sveshnikov – J. Ivanov
Cheliabinsk 1989

Sicilian Defence B22

1. e4 c5 2. c3 ♘f6 3. e5 ♘d5 4. ♘f3 e6 5. ♗c4 ♘b6 6. ♗b3 d5 7. d4 ♘c6 8. ♗g5 ♗e7 9. h4 h6 10. ♗×e7 ♕×e7 11. d×c5

Giving up the centre to play for blockade: with this move White secures the d4 square for his knight.

11...♘d7 12. ♕e2 ♘×c5 13. ♗c2 ♕c7 14. 0–0 0–0?! 15. ♖e1

Anticipating any undermining of the e5 pawn.

15...f5 16. e×f6

White obtains another central square. The future struggle will rage around the d4 and e5 squares.

16...♖×f6 17. ♘bd2 b6 18. b4 ♘d7 19. ♘b3 ♘f8?

An error. 19...a6 was better, although the white advantage would not be in doubt.

20. ♖ac1 ♕f4

This inappropriate activity proves to be a waste of time.

21. b5 ♘d8

In the hope of bringing the knight to f7.

22. ♘bd4 ♗d7 23. g3 ♕d6 24. ♘e5

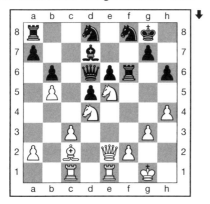

The goal is achieved. The rest is basic technique.

24...♖c8 25. ♗b3

Preparation for c3–c4. Restrict, blockade and now destroy. All according to Nimzowitsch!

25...♗e8 26. ♕e3 ♘f7 27. f4

A very picturesque position: almost all the white pieces are posted on dark squares but they are exerting pressure on the light squares!

27...♕c5 28. c4 ♕a3 29. c×d5 ♖×c1 30. ♕×c1 ♕d6 31. ♘ec6 ♗d7 32. ♕c4 e×d5 33. ♕×d5 ♕a3 34. ♘d8 ♕b4 35. ♕e4 ♕c3 36. ♕e3

Black resigned.

Game 59
Sveshnikov – Dukhov
Tal Memorial, Moscow 1992

French Defence C02

1. e4 e6 2. d4 d5 3. e5 c5 4. c3 ♘c6 5. ♘f3 ♘h6 6. d×c5 ♗×c5

6...♘g4? 7. ♕a4! h5 8. h3 ♘h6 9. ♗e3 ♘f5 10. ♗d4 ♗d7 11. ♗b5 with advantage for White, Sveshnikov–Bareev, Moscow 1991 (game 33 on page 64).

7. b4!

Fighting for the d4 and e5 squares!.

7...♗b6 8. ♗×h6

If the bishop were still at f8, capturing on h6 would be a mistake. In any case, 8. ♗d3! first was stronger.

8...g×h6 9. b5 ♘e7 10. ♗d3 ♘g6 11. 0–0 f6?

11...♕e7 was better.

12. ♗×g6+!

This improves the opposing pawn structure but secures the squares d4 and e5.

12...h×g6 13. ♕d3 ♔f7

13...f5 was slightly better.

14. e×f6 ♕×f6 15. ♘bd2 ♖d8 16. ♖ae1 a6

The counterplay is clearly arriving too late.

17. ♘e5+ ♔g7 18. ♘df3 ♗d7 19. ♘d4!

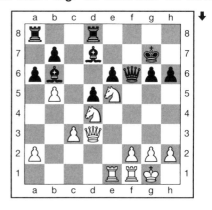

Every time I manage to post my knights like this I remember Nimzowitsch.

19...♗×d4 20. ♕×d4 a×b5

Or 20...♗×b5 21. ♖e3 ♗×f1 22. ♖f3 and wins.

21. ♖e3 ♖a4 22. ♕b6 ♖f4 23. ♕c7 g5 24. ♘×d7 ♕e7 25. ♘c5

About such positions the American grandmaster Reuben Fine used to say that a combination is as natural as a baby's smile. Black resigned.

Game 60
Kupreichik – Huzman
Sverdlovsk 1987

French Defence C02

1. e4 e6 2. d4 d5 3. e5 c5 4. c3 ♘c6
5. ♗e2 ♛b6 6. ♘f3 ♘h6 7. ♗xh6 gxh6
8. ♛d2 ♗g7 9. 0–0 0–0 10. ♘a3 f6
11. exf6 ♖xf6 12. dxc5 ♛xc5 13. b4 ♛f8
14. ♘c2 ♗d7 15. b5 ♘e7 16. ♘e5 ♖d8
17. ♘d4 Blockade!

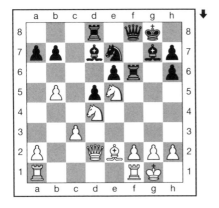

17...♘g6 18. ♘xd7 ♖xd7 19. ♗g4
♖d6 20. ♘xe6!? ♖fxe6 21. ♗xe6+
♖xe6 22. ♛xd5 ♛f7 (22...♘f4!?⇄)
23. f4! ♖e7 24. ♛f3 ♘h4 25. ♛h3 ♘f5
26. ♖ad1 ♘e3? (26...♛e6) 27. ♖d8+
♖e8 28. ♖xe8+ ♛xe8 29. ♖e1+− ♗xc3
30. ♖xe3 ♗d4 31. ♔f2 ♛f7 32. ♔f3
♗xe3 33. ♛c8+ ♔g7 34. ♔xe3 ♛xa2
35. ♛xb7+ ♔g8 36. h3 h5 37. ♛c8+ ♔g7

38. ♛d7+ ♔g6 39. ♛e8+ ♔h6 40. ♛e5
♛xg2 41. ♛f6+ ♛g6 42. ♛f8+ Black resigned.

Nimzowitsch devised the following position to demonstrate the advantages of the blockade and its real worth.

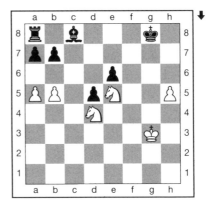

White is the exchange and a pawn down in the endgame (!) but White is better according to Nimzowitsch. I recommend that you analyse this position for yourself and if you have a chess program I suggest that you use this position to test its "understanding" of chess.

You have now become familiar with examples of "classical blockade" (giving up the pawn centre in order to occupy it with pieces). But there are also other types of blockade.

* * *

117

The following three games are especially recommended for personal study (see page 113) and are included at this point in the German and English editions.

Game [1]
Sveshnikov – Kovačević
GMA, Belgrade 1988

1. e4 e6 2. d4 d5 3. e5 c5 4. c3 ♘e7 5. ♘f3 ♘ec6 6. h4 ♘d7 7. h5 f6 8. exf6 ♘xf6 9. h6 g6 10. ♗g5 ♗d6 11. ♗e2 0-0 12. 0-0 cxd4 13. ♘xd4 ♗d7 14. ♘d2 ♘xd4 15. cxd4 ♕b6 16. ♘f3 ♘e4 17. ♗e3 ♕xb2 18. ♖b1 ♕xa2 19. ♖xb7 ♖f7 20. ♗d3 ♖b8 21. ♖xb8+ ♗xb8 22. ♘e5 ♗xe5 23. dxe5 ♘c3 24. ♕g4 ♕a4 25. ♕g5 ♗e8 26. ♕d8 ♕d7 27. ♕b8 ♕c6 28. ♖a1 ♖b7 29. ♕d8 ♕d7 30. ♕xd7 ♗xd7 31. ♗xa7 ♗b5 32. ♗c5 ♖b8 33. ♖c1 ♗xd3 34. ♖xc3 ♖c8 35. ♖xd3 ♖xc5 36. ♖a3 g5 37. ♖g3 d4 38. ♖xg5+ ♔f8 39. ♔f1 d3 40. ♔e1 ♖c2 41. f4 ♖e2+ 42. ♔d1 ♖f2 43. ♖g4 ♖f1+ 44. ♔d2 ♖h1 45. g3 ♖xh6 46. ♖h4 ♖g6 47. g4 ♖g7 48. ♔xd3 ♖a7 49. ♖h6 ♖a4 50. ♔e3 ♖a3+ 51. ♔f2 ♖a4 52. ♔g3 1-0

Game [2]
Kupreichik – Kovačević
Vidmar Memorial, Ljubljana/Portorož 1989

1. e4 e6 2. d4 d5 3. e5 c5 4. c3 ♘e7 5. ♘f3 ♘ec6 6. ♗e3 ♘d7 7. ♗d3 a5 8. ♘bd2 cxd4

9. cxd4 a4 10. a3 ♗e7 11. h4 h6 12. h5 ♘b6 13. ♘h2 ♘a5 14. ♕g4 ♗f8 15. ♖c1 ♗d7 16. 0-0 ♘bc4 17. ♘xc4 ♘xc4 18. ♕e2 b5 19. f4 ♗e7 20. f5 exf5 21. ♗xf5 ♘xe3 22. ♕xe3 ♗g5 23. ♕g3 ♗xf5 24. ♖xf5 ♖c8 25. ♖cf1 0-0 26. e6 ♕c7 27. ♕e1 ♕e7 28. ♖xf7 ♖xf7 29. ♖xf7 ♖c1 30. ♕xc1 ♕xe6 31. ♖f4 1-0

Game [3]
Sveshnikov – Ehlvest
Kotov Memorial, Leningrad 1984

1. e4 e6 2. d4 d5 3. e5 c5 4. c3 ♕b6 5. ♘f3 ♗d7 6. a3 ♗b5 7. c4 ♗xc4 8. ♗xc4 dxc4 9. ♘bd2 ♕a6 10. ♕e2 cxd4 11. ♘xd4 ♗c5 12. ♘4f3 c3 13. ♘e4 ♕xe2+ 14. ♔xe2 cxb2 15. ♗xb2 ♘a6 16. ♖hd1 ♘e7 17. ♖ac1 b6 18. ♘d6+ ♔f8 19. ♘g5 h6 20. ♘gxf7 ♖h7 21. ♖c3 g6 22. ♖f3 ♔g8 23. ♗c1 ♔g7 24. ♘xh6 ♖f8 25. ♖xf8 ♔xf8 26. ♖d3 ♘c6 27. ♘g4 ♘d4+ 28. ♔f1 ♘f5 29. ♘b5 ♖b7 30. ♖d8+ ♔e7 31. ♗g5+ ♔f7 32. ♖h8 ♗f8 33. ♗f6 ♖d7 34. ♖h7+ ♔e8 35. ♗g5 ♗g7 36. ♔e2 ♖d5 37. ♖xg7 ♖xb5 38. ♖xa7 ♖b2+ 39. ♔f3 ♖b3+ 40. ♔f4 ♖xa3 41. ♘f6+ ♔f8 1-0

3.3 The modern view of Nimzowitsch's theory

Since blockade ideas come up very often (every fourth or fifth game I would say), for the convenience of the reader we will try to separate out the various themes and even create a sort of classification.

The blockading knight

This is the most commonly encountered theme. There are innumerable games featuring a white knight at d4 blockading a black isolated pawn at d5. The strategic picture is very unfavourable for Black, whose hopes reside in active piece play and tactical finesses. Positions of this type can arise from the Tarrasch Defence to the Queen's Gambit, a very difficult opening for Black. I shall examine just one example drawn from the classics.

Game 61
Flohr – Capablanca
Nottingham 1936

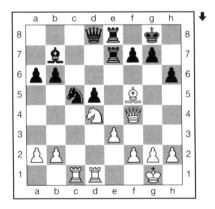

21...a5?!

This fortifies the position of the knight at c5, but at the same time weakens another square – b5.

22. &d3 Ee5 23. &b5 E8e7 24. Wf3 Eg5 25. We2 Eg6 26. &d3 Ef6 27. &b1 &a6 28. Wh5 &b7 29. a3 a4 30. Wg4 Ee5

31. ♘f3 Ee7 32. ♘d4 Ee5 33. ♘f3 Ee7 34. Wg3 &a6 35. ♘d4 Ed7 36. &f5 Ec7 37. &b1 Wc8?

Flohr plays in his usual patient manner and Capablanca, exhausted by a long defence, commits an error. It was essential to play 37...&c8, but even then Black's position would remain difficult.

38. ♘f5! Eg6 39. ♘d6! Exg3 40. ♘xc8 Exg2+ 41. ♔xg2 Exc8 42. &a2 Ec6 43. &xd5 Eg6+ 44. ♔h1 ♘d3 45. Ec2 Ed6 46. &f3 Ef6 47. &e4! Ed6 48. &xd3 &xd3 49. f3

and Black resigned on move 64. Even Capablanca found it difficult to fight against the blockading knight at d4!

It is less common to come across the blockade of a pawn on other squares. Under the cover of a knight blockading the enemy's centre or opposite wing, an attack can be launched against the enemy king. This was the plan carried out in the game Sveshnikov – Lputian (Moscow 1989, game 37 on page 69). A knight at f4 can also be very active and aggressive. Here are two examples.

Game 62
Sveshnikov – Korchnoi
Interzonal, Biel 1993

Sicilian Defence B22

1. e4 c5

Victor Lvovich plays the French Defence more frequently, but apparently he did not want to face the variation 2. d4 d5 3. e5!? that I always play. And perhaps the move 2. c3 against the Sicilian did not seem to him to be very dangerous.

2. c3

From the strictly mathematical or scientific point of view, I consider that this move is insufficient to play for a win, but in order to prove this Black has to play 2…♘f6!. All other moves are weaker. At any event, in the Biel Interzonal neither Judit Polgár nor Victor Korchnoi was able to equalise in the opening.

2…d5 3. e×d5 ♕×d5 4. ♘f3 ♘c6 5. d4 ♘f6 6. ♗e2 e6 7. 0-0 c×d4 8. c×d4 ♗e7 9. ♘c3 ♕d6 10. ♘b5 ♕d8 11. ♗f4 ♘d5 12. ♗g3 0-0 13. ♗c4 a6 14. ♗×d5 a×b5!?

The theoretical main line is 14…e×d5 15. ♘c7 ♖b8 (15…♖a7 is answered by 16. ♕b3 with the idea of ♕b6) 16. ♘e5, when Black faces a tough struggle to draw. The move in the game has been much less investigated.

15. ♗e4! ♖a6?!

15…b4 was played previously, with a slight advantage to White.

16. ♕e2 f5?!

More critical is 16…♘×d4 17. ♘×d4 ♕×d4 18. ♖fd1 ♕b6.

17. ♗d3

Played in order to keep options in the centre. However, it would have been simpler (perhaps also better) to play 17. ♗×c6 b×c6 18. ♗e5 ♕d5 19. b3, and White retains a small but stable advantage.

17…♖a5

Naturally it would have been bad to play 17…f4? 18. ♕e4 f×g3 19. ♕×h7+ ♔f7 20. ♕h5+ or 17…♘×d4? 18. ♘×d4 ♕×d4 19. ♗e5 and 20. ♗×b5, followed by 21. a4. But 17…♘b4!? deserved attention, e.g.: 18. ♗×b5!? f4 19. ♗×a6 b×a6 20. ♗×f4 ♖×f4 21. ♖ac1 with a very unclear position. However, this variation did not appeal to Korchnoi.

18. ♖fd1 ♘b4 19. ♗e5 ♘×d3 20. ♖×d3 ♕d5

(see next diagram)

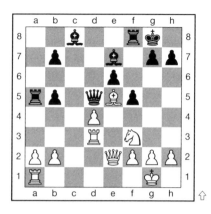

21. ♘e1!

The knight heads for f4 – the best square for this piece.

21…♗d7

White would have a clear advantage after 21…♖×a2 22. ♖g3 ♗f6 23. ♗×f6 ♖×f6 24. ♖×a2 ♕×a2 25. ♕×b5.

22. ♖g3 ♖f7

If 22…♗f6 then 23. ♘d3 ♖×a2 24. ♖×a2 ♕×a2 25. h3 and the white initiative is even more dangerous.

23. ♘d3!?

During the game I remembered that I was playing against Korchnoi, who likes to take pawns. But I would not have been able to forgive myself after the game if I had chosen the small-minded 23. b3.

23…♖×a2

Played almost without thinking.

24. ♖c1

I was very pleased with my position and could not see a decent move for Black. For instance the natural 24…♗c6 would be answered by 25. ♘f4 with the idea of 25…♕c4 26. ♕e3 ♕a4 27. ♗×g7.

24…♖a6! 25. ♘f4

Mission accomplished; the knight has reached the desired destination.

25…♖c6!

120

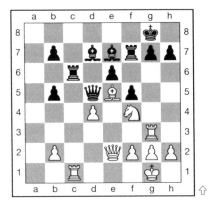

26. ♕d2

At this moment I thought I was winning. But if I had seen Black's 27th move then I would have chosen 26. ♖f1 ♕e4 27. ♕h5 instead. White's position is clearly better, but it is difficult to demonstrate a win, e. g.: 27...♗f6! 28. ♖e3 ♕c2 29. ♗xf6 (29. d5 exd5 30. ♘xd5 ♗xe5 31. ♖xe5 ♖e6 does not work) 29...♖xf6 30. d5 ♖a6 (but not 30...♖d6? 31. dxe6 ♗xe6 32. ♕e8+ ♖f8 33. ♕e7) 31. dxe6 ♗xe6 32. ♕e8+ ♖f8 33. ♕xb5 ♗c4 34. ♕xb7 ♗xf1 35. ♖e7 ♔h8 36. ♖xg7 ♖h6 37. ♕e7 ♕c8 38. ♖g3!, and White wins; but Black can play more strongly with 30...♖b6!. During and even after the game I could not help feeling that there should be a forced win for White somewhere, but demonstrating it with concrete variations proved impossible – in every case Black has a defence.

26...♖xc1+ 27. ♕xc1 ♕c4! 28. ♖c3 ♕a2 29. h3 ♗c6 30. ♖xc6!?

This move was chosen for practical reasons. White is now insured against losing, whereas after 30. b3 ♗g5 all three results are still possible.

30...bxc6 31. ♕xc6 h6

31...♗f6? loses to 32. ♗d6! ♗e7 33. ♕e8+ ♗f8 34. ♘xe6.

32. ♕xb5

32. ♕e8+ does not work after 32...♗f8 33. ♘xe6 ♕a7!, and the worst is over for Black: 34. ♗d6 ♕d7 35. ♕xd7 ♖xd7 36. ♗xf8 ♔f7.

32...♗f6 33. ♕e8+ ♖f8 34. ♕c6 ♗xe5 35. dxe5 ♕xb2! 36. ♕xe6+ ♔h7 37. ♘g6 ♕b1+ 38. ♔h2 ♖d8?

With his flag hanging, Black makes an error. He could have kept the balance with 38...♖b8!.

39. ♕f7! ♕c2

Here 39...♕e4 failed to 40. f3. Now 40. ♘f8+ misfires: 40...♖xf8 41. ♕xf8 ♕xf2 with a draw.

40. f4?

On the last move before the time control, for which I had two minutes left, I let the victory slip. I failed to grasp the opportunity offered by 40. ♘f4!. Then 40...♕xf2 would fail to 41. ♘h5 ♖g8 42. ♘f6+ ♔h8 43. ♕xg8#, or 40...♕e4 41. ♘e6 ♖g8 (41...♕xe5+? 42. f4 ♕f6 43. ♕xf6 gxf6 44. ♘xd8) 42. ♘g5+ hxg5 43. ♕h5#. There remains just 40...♖g8 41. e6 ♕xf2 (or 41...♕e4 42. ♘g6! ♕c2 43. e7 ♕c7+ 44. f4) 42. ♕xf5+ g6 43. ♕f6, and the e-pawn is unstoppable.

40...♕e4 41. e6 ♖d2 42. ♘f8+ ♔h8 43. ♘g6+

Draw. A tense but interesting game, not without its mistakes, in which Black had to conduct a difficult defence (and White, according to Korchnoi, a difficult attack).

Game 63
Sveshnikov – Agrinsky
Moscow Open 1998

French Defence C02

1. e4 e6 2. d4 d5 3. e5 c5 4. c3 ♘e7 5. ♘f3 ♘f5 6. h4 ♗e7 7. ♗d3 (7. h5∞) 7...cxd4 8. cxd4 ♘c6 9. ♗xf5!? exf5 10. ♗g5!? ♗e6

10...♗b4+ 11. ♘c3 ♕a5 12. ♗d2 ♗e6 13. a3 ♗xc3 14. ♗xc3±.

11. ♘c3 h6 12. ♗xe7 ♕xe7 13. ♕d2 ♕b4 14. 0–0 0–0 15. ♖fc1 ♖fc8 16. a3 ♕b3 17. ♘e2 ♘e7 18. ♖c5 (18. ♘f4±) **18...b6! 19. ♖c3 ♕a4?!** (19...♖xc3±) **20. b3 ♕e8 21. ♖d3!**

The rook is preserved for the attack!

21...♖c6 22. ♘f4!

The first blockading knight.

21...♖ac8 23. ♘e1 ♘g6! 24.♖g3! ♕e7?

If 24...♘xh4?! 25. ♖xg7+! ♔xg7 26. ♘h5+ ♔g6 27. ♘f6 ♕f8 28. ♕f4 ♔g7 29. ♕xh4 ♖c1 30. ♖xc1 ♖xc1 31. ♕g3+ (31. f3⩱) 31...♔h8 32. ♕e3 ♖a1 33. a4 White has a slight advantage, but 24...♘xf4! 25. ♕xf4 ♔h7! is unclear.

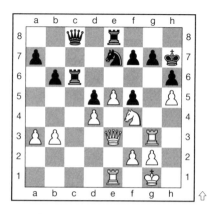

31. e6 ♘g8 32. ♕e5 fxe6? 33. ♕xg7#.

Exploiting a weak colour complex

This theme is closely linked to that of blockade, since weak squares are in fact a prerequisite for establishing a blockade.

Game 64
Sveshnikov – L. Ortega
Sochi 1987

French Defence C02

1. e4 e6 2. d4 d5 3. e5 c5 4. c3 ♘c6 5. ♘f3 ♘ge7 6. ♘a3 cxd4 7. cxd4 ♘f5 8. ♘c2 ♕a5+ 9. ♗d2 ♕b6 10. ♗c3 ♗e7 11. ♗d3 a5 12. ♘e3 g6 13. 0–0 ♗d7 14. ♗c2 h5 15. ♕d2 ♔f8 16. g3 ♘b4 17. ♗xf5! (White has the advantage) **17...gxf5 18. h4 ♗b5 19. ♖fd1 ♕a6 20. ♘g5 ♖c8 21. a3 ♘c6**

Or 21...♘d3 22. a4 ♗c4 23. b3.

22. ♘g2 ♔g7 23. ♖e1 ♗c4 24. ♘f4

(see next diagram)

Everything on dark squares, just as in draughts! I suddenly remembered my childhood passion for that game.

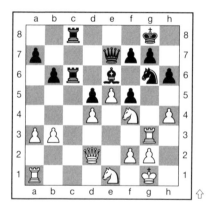

25. ♘xe6!± ♕xe6 26. h5 ♘e7 27. ♘d3 ♔h7 28. ♖e1 ♖g8?

Better is 28...♖c2! 29. ♕d1 ♖8c3 30. ♘f4 ♕c8 31. e6 fxe6 (31...♖c1? 32. ♖xc3 ♖xd1 33. ♖xd1 ♕xc3 24. exf7 ♕c8 35. ♘e6+−) 32. ♖xc3 ♕xc3 33. ♘xe6±.

29. ♘f4

The second blockading knight!

29...♕c8 30. ♕e3 ♖e8

(see next diagram)

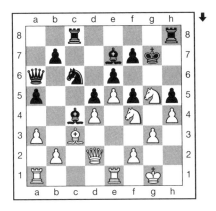

24...♗b3 25. ♕e3 ♕b5 26. ♖ac1

No need to rush – now Black cannot even play ♗c2.

26...♗c4 27. ♔g2 ♖cg8 28. ♕f3 ♔f8 29. ♘fxe6+

The infant smiles once again!

Black resigned.

Game 65
Sveshnikov – Bjerke
Gausdal 1992

Two Knights Defence C55

1. e4 e5 2. ♘f3 ♘c6 3. ♗c4 ♘f6 4. d4 exd4 5. e5 d5 6. ♗b5 ♘e4 7. ♘xd4 ♗c5 8. ♗e3 ♗d7 9. ♗xc6 bxc6 10. 0-0 ♕e7 11. f3 ♘d6 12. ♗f2 ♘f5 13. c3 0-0 14. ♖e1 ♗b6 15. ♕c2 ♕g5 16. ♕d2 ♕g6 17. ♘a3 ♖ad8 18. b4 ♖fe8 19. ♘ac2 a5 20. bxa5 ♗xa5 21. ♘b3

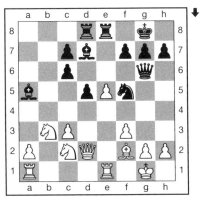

Blockade on the dark squares and a passed pawn on the a-file – the white advantage is beyond dispute.

21...♗b6 22. ♗c5! f6 23. exf6 gxf6 24. ♘cd4 ♖e5 25. a4 ♘d6 26. a5 ♘c4 27. ♕f2 ♖de8 28. ♖xe5

28. axb6 cxb6 29. ♗b4 c5.

28...fxe5 29. ♘c2 ♗f5 30. ♘e1 ♗xc5 31. ♘xc5 e4 32. fxe4 dxe4 33. ♕d4! ♕f7 34. a6 e3 35. ♕f4 ♕d5 36. a7 ♘b6 37. ♖a5 ♕d2 38. ♕g3+ ♗g6 39. ♘cd3 ♕xc3 40. ♖g5 ♕f6 41. h4

Under the cover of the a-pawn, White has been able to shift the play to the kingside.

41...♔h8

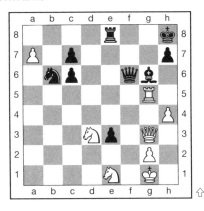

42. ♖e5! ♖a8 43. ♘f4 ♖xa7 44. ♖e6 ♕d4 45. ♘f3 ♖a1+ 46. ♔h2 ♕d1 47. ♘xg6+ hxg6 48. ♕e5+

Black resigned.

Blockade of a wing

Nimzowitsch pointed out that a blockade can be applied not just to a few weak squares but to an entire wing.

Game 66
Nimzowitsch – Duhme
Hanover 1926

English Opening A34

1. c4 e6 2. e4 c5?! 3. ♘c3 ♘c6 4. f4 d6 5. ♘f3 g6 6. d4 ♗g7? 7. d×c5 d×c5 8. ♕×d8+ ♔×d8 9. e5 h5?! 10. ♗e3 b6 11. 0-0-0+ ♔e7 12. ♗f2 ♘h6 13. ♗h4+ ♔f8 14. ♗d3 ♗b7 15. ♗e4 ♘a5 16. ♗×b7 ♘×b7 17. ♖d7 ♖b8 18. ♖hd1 ♔g8 19. ♗e7 ♘f5 20. ♘g5 ♖e8

Black has played correctly from the positional point of view but without considering the dynamics of the position, whereas Nimzowitsch paid attention to both factors.

21. ♗f6 ♗×f6 22. e×f6 ♘a5 23. ♖d8 ♔f8 24. ♖1d7 ♘h6 25. ♘ce4! ♘c6 26. ♖×f7+! ♘×f7 27. ♘×e6+ ♔g8 28. ♖×e8+ ♔h7 29. ♘4g5+

Black resigned.

Game 67
Sveshnikov – Kupreichik
Russian Cup, Kiev 1984

Sicilian Defence B22

1. e4 c5 2. c3 ♕a5?!

It is curious that it was Dr. Tarrasch, widely considered to be a dogmatist, who introduced this "lateral" queen attack into practice. In any case, this move violates various opening principles and is inadequate for fighting for equality.

3. ♘f3

White has a wide choice of attractive continuations, for instance 3. ♘a3 or 3. g3.

3...♘c6 4. a3!?

The inventor of the 2. c3 variation, Semyon Alapin, handled the opening rather uncertainly in the afore-mentioned game against Tarrasch: 4. ♘a3 e6 5. ♘c4 ♕c7 6. d4 c×d4 7. ♘×d4?! a6 8. ♗d3 b5 9. ♘e3 ♘f6 10. 0-0 ♗b7 11. ♘f3 ♗d6 ⇄ (Alapin – Tarrasch, Vienna 1898). Instead 4. ♗c4 is interesting: 4...e6 5. 0-0 ♗e7 6. ♖e1 ♘f6 7. e5 ♘d5 8. d4 c×d4 9. c×d4 d6 10. ♗×d5 ♕×d5 11. ♘c3 ♕a5 12. e×d6 ♗f6 13. d5+− (Mukhametov – Moor, Baden 1997).

4...e6 5. d4 ♘×d4! 6. ♘×d4 c×d4 7. b4 ♕c7

7...♕e5 8. ♕×d4 ♕c7 9. ♘d2 ♘e7 10. ♘f3 ♘c6 11. ♕e3 a5 12. ♗b2± (Kharlov – Camara, São Paulo 1991).

8. c×d4 ♘f6 9. ♗d3 d5 10. e5 ♘d7

(see next diagram)

This position resembles a French Defence with 3. e5 but in a form highly favourable for White. First he gains control of the c-file, and then he switches play to the kingside.

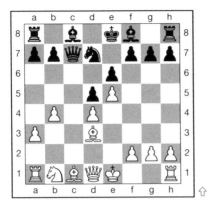

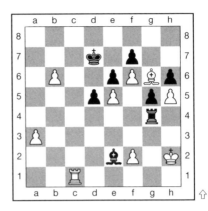

11. ☐a2 ♘b6 12. ☐c2 ♛d8 13. ♛g4! g6 14. ♗g5 ♗e7 15. ♗h6 ♗d7 16. 0-0 ♗a4? 17. ☐c3 a6 18. ☐fc1 ☐c8 19. ☐×c8 ♘×c8 20. ♘d2 ♘a7 21. ♘f3 ♗f8 22. ♛f4 ♘c6 23. ♗×f8 ♔×f8 24. ♛h6+ ♔g8 25. h4 ♛f8 26. ♛f4 h6 27. h5 g5 28. ♛f6! ♛g7

If 40...f×g6 41. h×g6 the white pawns are unstoppable.

41. f4 ♗c4 42. ♗×f7 ☐×f4 43. ☐b1 ♔c8 44. ♗×e6+ ♔b8 45. ☐b4 ♔b7 46. f7

Black resigned.

Sacrifice of one or two pawns to establish a blockade

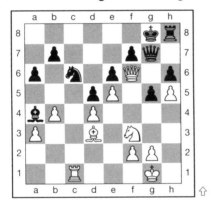

29. g4!

The black kingside is blockaded!

29...♛×f6 30. e×f6 ♔f8 31. ♘e5 ♔e8

31...♘×d4? 32. ☐c8+ ♗e8 33. ♘d7+.

32. ♗×a6 ♘×e5 33. d×e5 ♔d7 34. ♗×b7 ☐b8 35. ♗a6 ♗b3 36. ♗d3 ☐a8 37. b5 ☐a4

37...☐×a3 38. b6 ♗c4 39. ♗×c4 d×c4 40. ☐×c4 ☐b3 41. ☐c7+ ♔d8 42. ☐×f7 +–.

38. b6 ☐×g4+ 39. ♔h2 ♗c4 40. ♗g6! ♗e2

(see next diagram)

Game 68
Brinckmann – Nimzowitsch
Kolding 1922/23

Nimzo-Indian Defence E43

1. d4 e6 2. c4 ♘f6 3. ♘c3 ♗b4 4. ♗d2 0-0 5. ♘f3 d6 6. e3 b6 7. ♗d3 ♗b7 8. ♛c2 ♗×f3 9. g×f3 ♘bd7 10. a3 ♗×c3 11. ♗×c3 c6 12. 0-0-0 d5 13. e4 g6 14. c×d5 c×d5 15. e5 ♘h5 16. h4 a5 17. ☐dg1 ♛e7 18. ♛d2 ☐fe8 19. f4

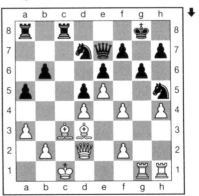

19...b5!

"Black gives up a pawn to be able to exchange the opponent's light-squared bishop; after that White must lose because of the weakness of his light squares." (Nimzowitsch)

20. ♗xb5 ♖ab8 21. ♗e2 ♘b6 22. ♔d1 ♘c4 23. ♗xc4 dxc4 24. ♖g5 ♘g7 25. h5 ♘f5 26. hxg6 fxg6 27. ♖xf5 exf5 28. ♗xa5 ♖b3 29. ♔e2 ♕b7 30. ♗b4 ♕a6

White resigned.

Game 69
Doghri – Matsuo
Olympiad, Yerevan 1996

Two Knights Defence C55

1. e4 e5 2. ♘f3 ♘c6 3. ♗c4 ♘f6 4. d4 exd4 5. e5 d5 6. ♗b5 ♘e4 7. ♘xd4 ♗c5 8. ♗e3 ♗d7 9. ♗xc6 bxc6 10. ♘d2 ♕h4 11. ♘xe4 ♕xe4 12. 0-0 ♗b6 13. ♖e1 ♕g6 14. ♘b3 0-0 15. ♗c5 ♖fe8 16. a4 ♗f5 17. ♖c1 ♖ab8 18. ♖e3!? ♗xc5 19. ♘xc5 ♖xb2 20. ♕d4!? ♖xc2 21. ♖xc2 ♗xc2

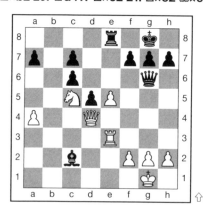

This position is a clear illustration of the advantages of the blockade. White is two pawns down and has no real threats, but Black's lack of counterplay makes the position very difficult for him.

22. h3 a5 23. ♔h2 ♗f5 24. ♖g3 ♕h6 25. f4 g6 26. ♘b3 ♖a8 27. ♖c3 ♕h4

28. ♖xc6 ♖b8 29. ♘xa5 ♕e1 30. ♖c5 ♗e4 31. e6 c6 32. ♘xc6 ♖e8 33. ♘e7+ ♔f8 34. ♖c8

Black resigned.

Exchange sacrifice to establish a blockade

Game 70
Reshevsky – Petrosian
Candidates Tournament, Zürich 1953

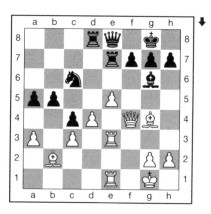

*"The exchange sacrifice **25...♖e6!** made by Petrosian deeply impressed me. It is a purely positional sacrifice with a quiet move, without any checks or visible threats! Simply to secure d5 for the knight!"* (Tal)

Now White could have played 26. h4! with the idea of h5 and ♖g3, attacking g7 (Bronstein) but the game went otherwise:

26. a4 ♘e7 27. ♗xe6 fxe6 28. ♕f1 ♘d5 29. ♖f3 ♗d3 30. ♖xd3 cxd3 31. ♕xd3 b4 32. cxb4 axb4 33. a5 ♖a8 34. ♖a1 ♕c6 35. ♗c1 ♕c7 36. a6 ♕b6 37. ♗d2 b3 38. ♕c4 h6 39. h3 b2 40. ♖b1 ♔h8 41. ♗e1

Draw.

Game 71
Tal – Petrosian
25th USSR Championship, Riga 1958

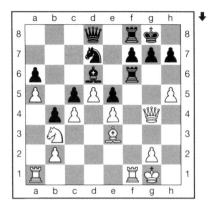

31...罩f4!

Here is an opportunity to recall Nimzowitsch and his theory of blockade.

32. 奧×f4?

Better is 32. 罩×f4! e×f4 33. 奧×f4.

32...e×f4 33. 包d2 包e5 34. 豐×f4 包×c4 35. e5 包×e5 36. 包e4 h6 37. 罩ae1 奧b8 38. 罩d1 c4 39. d6 包d3 40. 豐g4 奧a7+ 41. 含h1 f5 42. 包f6+ 含h8 43. 豐×c4 包×b2 44. 豐×a6 包×d1 45. 豐×a7 豐×d6 46. 豐d7 豐×f6 47. 豐×d1 罩b8 48. 罩f3 罩a8 49. 豐e1 罩×a5 50. 豐×b4 罩e5,

and the game was drawn in 73.moves.

In the following game the exchange sacrifice never actually happened, but the idea was in the air all the time.

Game 72
Krizsány – Sveshnikov
Nova Gorica 1997

Queen's Gambit D31

1. d4 d5 2. c4 e6 3. 包c3 c6 4. 包f3 d×c4 5. e3 b5 6. a4 奧b4 7. 奧d2 a5 8. a×b5 奧×c3 9. 奧×c3 c×b5 10. b3 奧b7 11. b×c4 b4 12. 奧b2 包f6 13. 奧d3 包bd7 14. 豐c2 豐c7 15. 0–0 0–0 16. e4 e5 17. c5! e×d4 18. 奧×d4 h6! 19. 罩fe1 罩fe8 20. e5 包d5

21. 奧b5 罩e6 22. 豐f5 包e7 23. 豐g4 包f8 24. 奧c4 罩g6 25. 豐h3 包e6 26. 奧e3 包d5

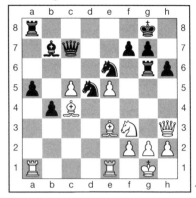

27. 包h4 包×e3 28. 罩×e3 包g5 29. 豐f5 罩c6 30. f4 罩×c5 31. 奧b3 罩c1+ 32. 罩×c1 豐×c1+ 33. 含f2 包e4+ 34. 罩×e4 豐b2+, and Black won.

Piece sacrifice to establish a blockade

This idea also occurs occasionally in practice. I invite the reader himself to select some examples.

Blockade in the endgame
a) the advantage of a blockading knight against a bishop

Let us examine another classical example.

Game 73
Flohr – Capablanca
Moscow 1935

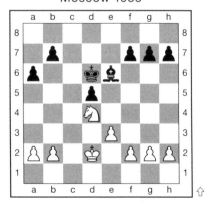

White has a solid advantage. The study of such endgames is a separate subject, so we shall just note this position and observe the course of the struggle.

**25. ♔c3 b6 26. f4 ♗d7 27. ♘f3 f6!
28. ♔d4 a5 29. ♘d2 ♗c8 30. ♘b1 ♗e6
31. ♘c3 ♔c6 32. a3 h6 33. g3 h5 34. b4
a×b4 35. a×b4 ♔d6 36. b5 g6 37. ♘a4
♔c7 38. ♘c3 ♔d6 39. f5 g×f5 40. ♘e2
♗d7 41. ♘f4**

It is interesting to note how the knight has transferred from one strong blockading square (d4) to another (f4), taking aim at the d5 and h5 pawns.

**41...♗e8 42. ♘×d5 ♗×b5 43. ♘×b6
♗c6 44. ♘c4+ ♔e6 45. ♘b2 ♗b5
46. ♘d1 ♗e2 47. ♘f2 ♗f1 48. ♘d3 ♗×d3
49. ♔×d3 ♔e5 50. ♔e2 ♔e4 51. h3**
(51. ♔f2 h4!) **51...♔d5 52. ♔f3 ♔e5**

Draw.

Only a master of Capablanca's stature is capable of saving such a difficult endgame, but even he needed to apply enormous effort.

b) Blockade with opposite-coloured Bishops

Game 74
Sveshnikov – Gligorić
Yugoslav Cup, Herceg-Novi 1999

Two Knights Defence C55

**1. e4 e5 2. ♘f3 ♘c6 3. ♗c4 ♘f6 4. d4
e×d4 5. e5 d5 6. ♗b5 ♘e4 7. ♘×d4 ♗c5
8. ♗e3 ♗×d4** (8...0–0!?) **9. ♕×d4 0–0
10. ♗×c6 b×c6 11. ♘c3 ♗f5** (11...♘g5)
12. ♘×e4 ♗×e4

12...d×e4 13. 0–0–0 is better for White.

13. 0–0–0 ♕e7

13...♗×g2?! allows 14. ♖hg1 ♗e4 15. e6 ♗g6 16. h4 with an attack.

14. f3 ♗g6 15. ♖he1 (15. ♕c3)

(see next diagram)

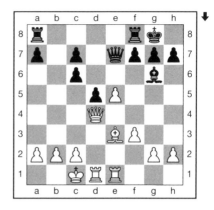

The blockade on the dark squares gives White a clear advantage. It is very difficult for Black to defend, since he lacks counterplay. It is well worth studying this type of endgame. Sometimes Black escapes thanks to some tactical nuances, as happens here, but most of the time he does not.

15...♖fe8 16. a3 a5

Bad is 16...♕×e5? 17. ♕×e5 ♖×e5 18. ♗×a7 ♖ae8 19. ♗f2 ♖e2 20. ♖×e2 ♖×e2 21. ♖d2.

**17. ♕c3 ♕×e5 18. ♕×e5 ♖×e5 19. ♗f4
♖×e1 20. ♖×e1 c5 21. ♗×c7 f6 22. ♖e7 a4
23. ♖d7** (23. ♗b6) **23...♖c8 24. ♗b6 d4!
25. ♖d5 d3 26. c×d3 c4 27. d4 c3 28. ♖c5
c×b2+ 29. ♔×b2 ♖×c5! 30. ♗×c5 ♗f7!,**

with a draw on the 49th move.

Game 75
Sveshnikov – Volzhin
Moscow (Rapidplay) 1996

Two Knights Defence C56

**1. e4 e5 2. ♘f3 ♘c6 3. ♗c4 ♘f6 4. d4
e×d4 5. e5 d5 6. ♗b5 ♘e4 7. ♘×d4
♗c5 8. ♗e3 ♗d7** (8...0–0) **9. ♗×c6 b×c6
10. ♘d2!? ♕e7?!** (10...♘h4, 10...♘×d2)
11. ♘×e4 d×e4 12. e6! f×e6 13. ♕h5+

13. ♘×c6!? comes into consideration: if 13...♗×c6 14. ♕h5+ g6 15. ♕×c5 with advantage.

**13...g6 14. ♕e5 0–0 15. ♘×c6 ♗×c6
16. ♗×c5 ♕f6 17. ♕×f6 ♖×f6 18. c4 ♖f5
19. ♗e3 a6 20. 0–0–0**

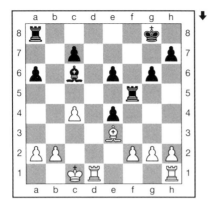

A typical endgame has arisen, in which the weakness of the dark squares and the disrupted black pawns guarantee a very solid advantage for White.

20...♖ff8 21. ♔c2

Better was 21. ♖d2 ♖fd8 22. ♖hd1 ♖×d2 23. ♖×d2, when Black has a difficult position.

21...♖ad8 22. ♖×d8 ♖×d8 23. ♖d1 ♖×d1 24. ♔×d1 e5 25. ♗g5 e3 26. f3 ♗d7 27. ♗d8 c6 28. ♔e2 ♔f7 29. ♔×e3 ♗f5 30. ♔d2 ♔e6 31. ♔c3 c5! 32. g4 ♗b1 33. b3

and in time trouble Black was unable to save the ending, although obviously the play of both sides could be improved.

Game 76
Sveshnikov – Yakovenko
Ekaterinburg 2002

Two Knights Defence C55

This game was played in the Russian Team Championship. My opponent was helped in his preparation by his team-mate Alexander Potapov, who had easily made a draw with me in the Two Knights Defence a few years earlier. He advised Dmitry Yakovenko to play the same variation.

1. e4 e5 2. ♘f3 ♘c6 3. ♗c4 ♘f6 4. d4 e×d4 5. e5 d5 6. ♗b5 ♘e4 7. ♘×d4 ♗c5

8. ♗e3 ♗d7 9. ♗×c6 b×c6 10. ♘d2 ♘×d2 11. ♕×d2 0–0

11...♕e7 !?

13. ♘b3 ♗b6 13. 0–0!

13. 0–0–0?! is weaker in view of 13...♕e7!, e.g.: 14. ♖he1 a5 15. a3 a4 16. ♗g5 ♕e6 17. ♘d4 ♕g6 18. f4 ♗a5 19. c3 c5∞, Sveshnikov – Zaja, Slovenian League, Bled 2001.

13...f6 14. e×f6!

The afore-mentioned game continued: 14. f4 f×e5 15. f×e5 ♖×f1+ 16. ♖×f1 ♕g5 17. ♖e1 draw (Sveshnikov – Potapov, St. Petersburg 1998) but that very evening I found the right plan for White and saved it on my computer. The idea waited four years to appear in practice!

14...♕×f6 15. ♘c5 ♗f5 16. c3 ♕g6 17. f3!

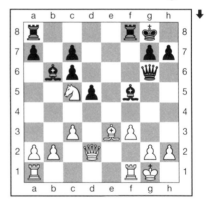

An important move: the scope of the opposing light-squared bishop must be restricted. A very interesting position now arises. Normally White strives to achieve an advantage in development and to start an attack, but here the picture is quite different. The plan is to restrict the activity of Black's light-squared bishop and enter an endgame with bishops of opposite colour. You would think that White would not have very much advantage, but in fact the black position is very difficult, almost hopeless, as Yakovenko could testify. White's advantage is based on a blockade. The playing strength of the black player has nothing to do with it - there is simply no opportunity for him to demonstrate it. I won this game very easily.

17...♖ae8 18. ♗d4 ♖e7 19. ♖ae1 ♖fe8 20. ♖xe7 ♖xe7 21. b4± h6 22. a4 a6

22...a5?! 23. bxa5 ♗xa5 24. ♘b3 ♗b6 25. a5 ♗xd4+ 26. cxd4±.

23. a5 ♗xc5 24. ♗xc5 ♖e6 25. ♖e1 ♔h7 26. ♗d4 ♕e8 27. ♖xe6 ♕xe6 28. ♕f2

28. ♕d1 ♕e7 29. ♕f1 ♗c8.

28...♗d3 29. ♕h4 g5

29...♗b5 30. h3 ♕f7 31. ♕g3 ♗d3 32. ♗e5 ♕g6 33. ♕f4 ♕f5 34. ♕d4±.

30. ♕g3 ♔g6

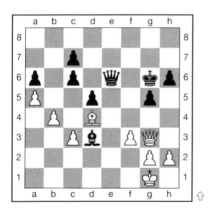

31. h3! ♕e7 32. ♗c5! ♕f6

32...♕g7 33. ♕e1!±.

33. ♕xc7 ♕xc3 34. ♕xc6+ ♔h7

34...♔h5 35. g4+ ♔h4 36. ♗f2+ ♔xh3 37. ♕xh6#.

35. ♕d7+ ♔g6 36. ♕e8+ ♔h7 37. ♕e3+− ♕c2 38. ♕e7+ ♔g6 39. ♕e8+ ♔f5 40. ♗d6

Black resigned.

Game 77
Nisipeanu – Azmaiparashvili
Pune 2004

Sicilian Defence B54

1. e4 d6 2. d4 ♘f6 3. f3 c5 4. ♘e2

Azmaiparashvili is known to be a great expert in the Pirc-Ufimtsev Defence. Perhaps that is why his opponent invites transposition to the Sicilian.

4...cxd4 5. ♘xd4 e5!?

The most critical move.

6. ♘b3 d5 7. ♗g5 ♗e6 8. ♗xf6 gxf6 9. exd5 ♗xd5

9...♕xd5!? 10. ♕xd5 ♗xd5 11. ♘c3 ♗e6 12. 0-0-0 ♘d7 13. ♗b5 0-0-0 14. ♘e4 ♗e7 =, Czebe – Nakamura, Budapest 2002.

10. ♘c3 ♗b4 11. ♕d2 ♗e6

11...♘c6 12. 0-0-0 ♗xb3 13. ♕xd8+ ♖xd8 14. ♖xd8+ ♔xd8 15. axb3 ♗xc3 16. bxc3 ♔e7 17. ♗d3 h5 18. ♗f5±, Nevednichy – Tugui, Târgoviște 2001.

12. ♕xd8+ ♔xd8 13. 0-0-0+ ♔c7 14. ♘d5+ ♗xd5 15. ♖xd5 ♘d7 16. ♗d3

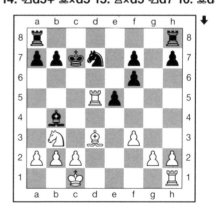

At first sight it seems we have a dead-drawn ending with opposite-coloured bishops. But White has a range of small advantages, the most important being that he can blockade Black's centre pawns with his bishop. Furthermore the h7 and f7 pawns are weak, and

White has a pawn majority on the queenside. Thus in fact Black faces a difficult defence.

16...♖ag8 17. g3 h5?!

Black should definitely have limited himself to the more modest 17...h6!?, since now White can quite easily create a passed pawn on the h-file. Also interesting is 17...♘b6 18. ♖b5 ♗d6, and White will lose time bringing the rook back into play.

18. ♗e4 b6

18...h4 19. g4.

19. ♖hd1 ♖d8 20. c3 ♗e7 21. ♗f5 ♘b8 22. ♖xd8!

Just as in the previous example, White is happy to exchange all the rooks. He will be even happier if the knights also come off, after which the "pure" endgame of opposite-coloured bishops will be very difficult (perhaps even lost) for Black.

22...♖xd8 23. ♖xd8 ♔xd8 24. h4!

The h-pawn is fixed, and soon White will set up his first passed pawn.

24...♘a6 25. g4 ♗f8

Here 25...hxg4 26. fxg4 would be even worse for Black, since his centre pawns are immobilised, and White would have a protected passed pawn.

26. gxh5 ♘c7 27. ♘d2 ♗h6 28. ♔c2 ♘d5 29. ♘f1 ♘f4 30. ♘g3 ♘g2 31. ♗e4 ♘xh4 32. ♘f5! ♘xf5 33. ♗xf5 ♔e7 34. b4 ♗f8 35. c4 ♔e7 36. ♔b3 ♔d6 37. ♔a4 ♗e3 38. ♔b5

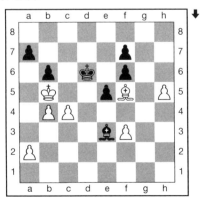

Zugzwang. White creates a second passed pawn on the other wing.

38...♔c7 39. c5 bxc5 40. bxc5 ♗h6 41. ♔c4 ♔c6 42. ♗e4+ ♔c7 43. ♔d5 ♔d7 44. ♗d3 ♗f4 45. ♗b5+ ♔e7 46. ♔e4 ♔e6 47. ♗c4+ ♔e7 48. ♔f5 ♗g5 49. c6 ♔d6 50. ♗xf7 ♔xc6 51. ♔g6

Black resigned.

c) Blockade of the king or an entire wing

Often the side with the advantage uses his better development to pass directly into an endgame in which, thanks to the blockade, he shuts the enemy king (and sometimes even the whole wing) out of the game.

Game 78
Sveshnikov – Tarasov
Rostov on Don 1970

Sicilian Defence B22

1. e4 c5 2. c3 ♘f6 3. e5 ♘d5 4. d4 cxd4 5. cxd4 d6 6. ♘f3 ♘c6 7. ♗c4 e6 8. 0–0 ♗e7 9. ♕e2 0–0 10. ♘c3 (10. ♖e1!?) 10...♘xc3 11. bxc3 dxe5 12. dxe5 ♕c7 (12...♕a5) 13. ♗d3 g6? 14. h4 b6 15. ♗g5 ♗b7 16. ♕e3 ♖fd8 17. ♗f6

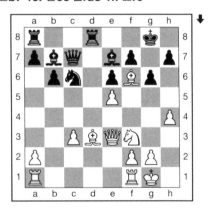

17...♗xf6 18. exf6 ♕d6 19. ♖fd1 ♕c5?!

Black does not sense the danger; 19...♕f8 is better.

20. ♕xc5! bxc5 21. ♗e4

Now it becomes clear that, thanks to the strong pawn on f6 and the possession of the e5 square, the endgame is winning for White.

21...♘a5 22. ♖xd8+ ♖xd8 23. ♗xb7 ♘xb7 24. ♖b1 ♘d6 25. ♖d1 ♘b7 26. ♖xd8+ ♘xd8 27. ♘e5 ♘b7 28. ♘d7 c4 29. f3 ♘d6 30. a4! ♘f5 31. ♔f2 ♘xh4 32. ♘e5 g5 33. ♘c6! a6 34. ♘b4 ♔f8 35. ♘xa6 ♔e8 36. ♘c5 ♔d8 37. ♘e4 ♘f5 38. ♘xg5 ♘d6 39. ♘xh7 ♔c7 40. ♔e3 e5 41. g4 ♔d7 42. ♘g5

Black resigned.

This was one of my first experiences with the 2. c3 Sicilian. Twenty-five years later (!) I was able to play a similar game against a grandmaster.

Game 79
Sveshnikov – Rausis
Latvia 1995

(First 13 moves as in the previous game.)

13...♗d7 14. ♗g5 ♖fd8 15. ♕e4 g6 16. ♕h4 ♗e8 17. ♗e4 ♗xg5 18. ♕xg5 ♕e7 19. ♕h6 ♕f8 20. ♕f4 ♖ab8 21. ♖fe1 ♘e7 22. h4 ♖bc8 23. ♗xb7 ♖xc3 24. ♖ac1 ♖xc1 25. ♖xc1 ♘f5 26. ♗e4 ♕b4 27. ♕g5 ♕e7 28. ♕f6!

And there it is, my favourite endgame!

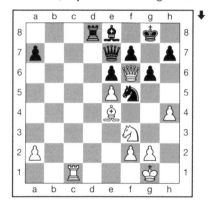

28...♕xf6 29. exf6 ♘d6 30. ♖d1 ♔f8 31. ♘e5 ♗b5 32. ♗c6 a6 33. a4 ♗xc6 34. ♘xc6 ♖d7 35. ♘b8 ♖d8 36. ♘xa6

♘b7 37. ♖xd8+ ♘xd8 38. ♘c7 ♘c6 39. g4,

and White won. The similarity between the two games is amazing, wouldn't you agree?

On the way to assimilating a particular topic, chess students are usually expected to memorise a lot of different ideas, but when the time comes for them to put their knowledge into practice, it is not so easy. And this is understandable, given the wide variety of ideas and especially positions. To help my students gain a better grasp of a particular topic, I always try to link the ideas to a particular opening scheme with a particular pawn structure. In my view, this type of lesson gives more tangible results: it becomes much easier to recall and apply an idea.

Let us return to our topic. I suggest the following classification by opening:

Typical openings for mastering the subject of "Blockade".

For White:

1) French Defence with 3. e5;

2) Two Knights Defence with 4. d4 exd4 5. e5;

3) Sicilian Defence with 4...e5 or 5...e5 (the blockading knight).

For Black:

1) Abrahams-Noteboom Variation of the Queen's Gambit Semi-Slav – 1. d4 d5 2. c4 e6 3. ♘c3 c6 4. ♘f3 dxc4 5. a4 ♗b4 6. e3 b5 7. ♗d2 a5;

2) King's Indian Defence;

3) Ragozin System in the Queen's Gambit Declined – 1. d4 d5 2. c4 e6 3. ♘c3 ♘f6 4. ♘f3 ♗b4!?;

4) Sicilian Defence with 5...e5 6. ♘db5 d6 7. ♘d5 ♘xd5 8. exd5;

5) Nimzo-Indian Defence.

I am sure that the theme of blockade is not confined to these openings. I hope that in this respect readers and chess trainers will share their experiences and observations. In conclusion, I should like to present an example from one of my own games as a junior.

Game 80
Araslanov – Sveshnikov
Cheliabinsk 1965

Sicilian Defence B33

1. e4 c5 2. ♘f3 ♘c6 3. d4 c×d4 4. ♘×d4 ♘f6 5. ♘c3 e5 6. ♘db6 d6 7. ♘d5 ♘×d5 8. e×d5 ♘e7 9. c4 ♘g6 10. ♗d3 ♗e7 11. 0–0 0–0 12. ♗e3 a6 13. ♘c3 f5 (13...♗g5!?) **14. f3** (14. ♕b3) **14...♗f6 15. ♖c1 ♗d7 16. ♕d2 ♕e7 17. b4**

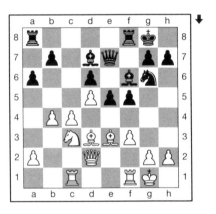

The diagram position is typical of both the King's Indian and the Sicilian Defence with 4...e5 or 5...e5.

17...e4 18. f×e4 f4 19. ♗f2 ♗e5 20. ♗e2 ♘h4 21. ♗d4 ♗×d4+ (21...f3!) **22. ♕×d4 f3! 23. g×f3 ♗h3 24. ♕e3 ♘g2 25. ♕f2 ♘f4 26. ♖fd1 ♖f6 27. ♗f1 ♖g6+ 28. ♔h1 ♗g2+ 29. ♗×g2 ♖×g2 30. ♕e1**

Now 30...♕e5! would have given Black the advantage, but I played something else and the game ended in a draw. I found the double pawn sacrifice for the blockade (the manoeuvre ♗f6–e5, followed by f3, ♘g2, ♘f4) on my own, but at that time I had not even heard of blockade, I just played chess. In that tournament I gained the norm for first category. I have included this game to encourage you not to be afraid of experimenting, to have confidence in your own powers. If a first category player is able to play in that way, without any special knowledge, then after studying this chapter you the reader should be able to manage even better.

To consolidate what you have learnt in this chapter, I suggest some homework. Find examples of blockade in your own games and try to classify them according to themes. If you think your own playing standard is too low for this, use games by modern grandmasters. Good luck!

Chapter 4

What would you play?

In the following examples taken from real games, try on your own to find the strongest continuation, whether it be combinational or positional. Check your solutions on pages 146–156.

1

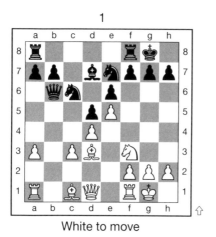

White to move

3

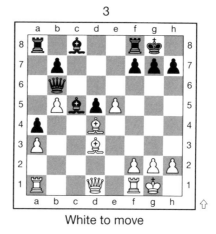

White to move

2

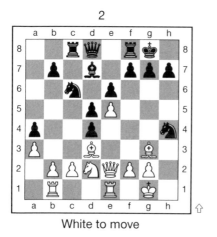

White to move

4

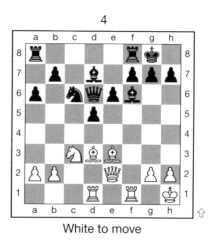

White to move

5

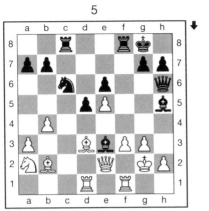

Evaluate the consequences of 24...♗×f3+.

8

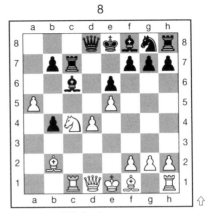

White to move

6

White to move

9

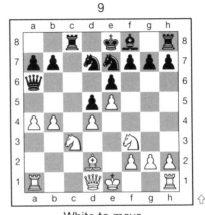

White to move

7

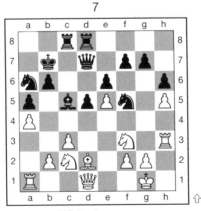

White to move

10

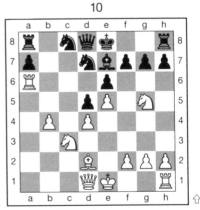

White to move

11

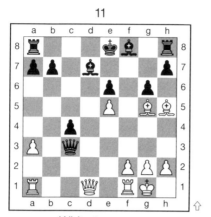

White to move

12

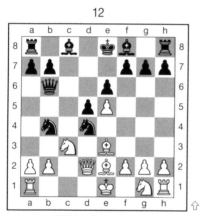

White to move

13

White to move

14

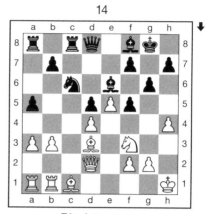

Black to move

15

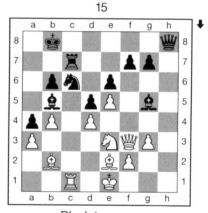

Black to move

16

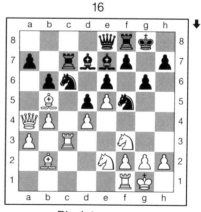

Black to move

17

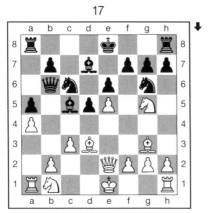

Black to move

18

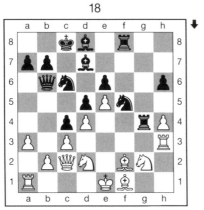

Black to move

19

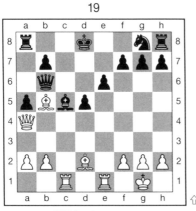

White to move

20

White to move

21

White to move

22

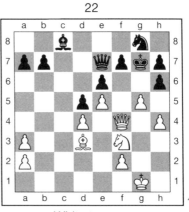

White to move

23

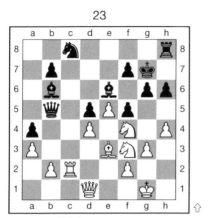

White to move

24

White to move

25

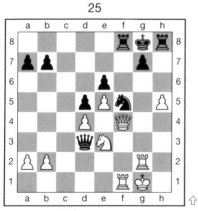

White to move

26

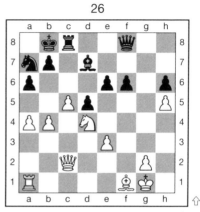

Evaluate the consequences of 36. ♗b5.

27

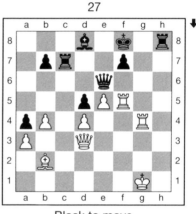

Black to move

28

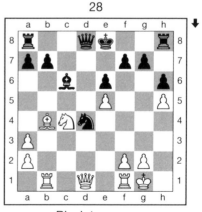

Black to move

29

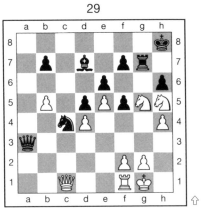

White to move

30

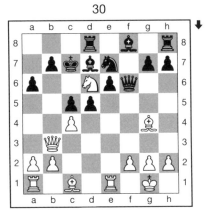

Black to move

31

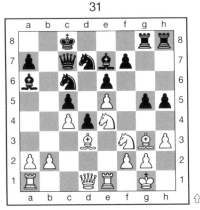

White to move

32

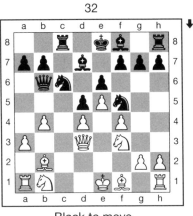

Black to move

33

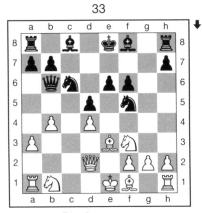

Black to move

34

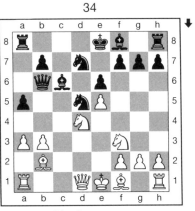

Black to move

35

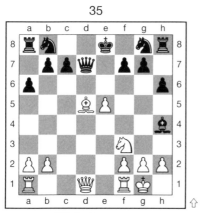

White to move

38

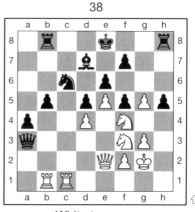

White to move

36

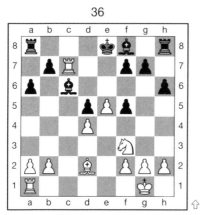

White to move

39

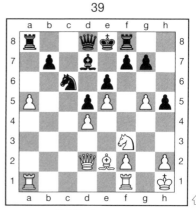

White to move

37

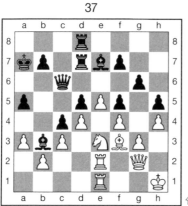

White to move

40

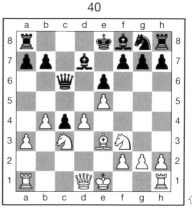

White to move

41

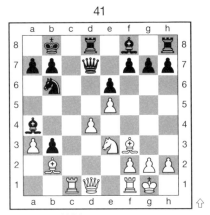

White to move

44

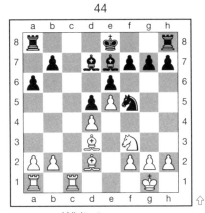

White to move

42

White to move

45

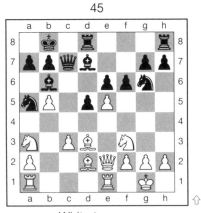

White to move

43

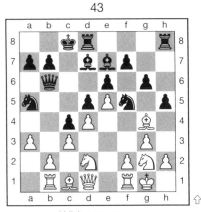

White to move

46

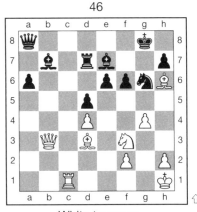

White to move

47

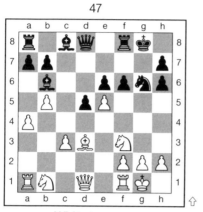

White to move

50

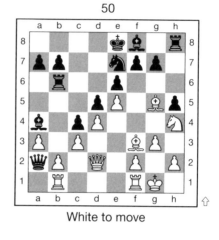

White to move

48

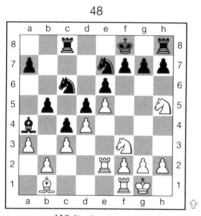

White to move

51

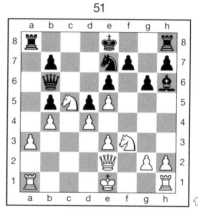

White to move

49

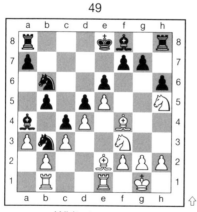

White to move

52

White to move

53

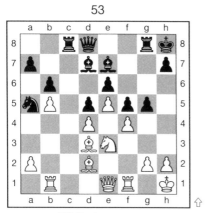

White to move

54

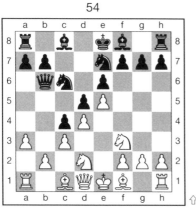

White to move

55

White to move

56

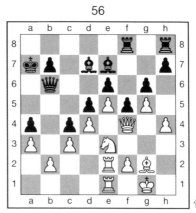

White to move

57

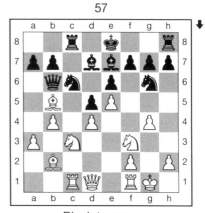

Black to move

58

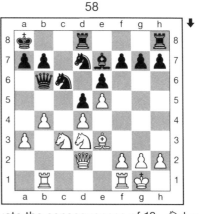

Evaluate the consequences of 18...♘d×e5.

59

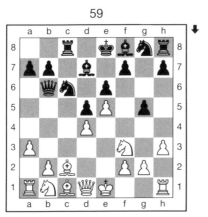

Evaluate the consequences of 10...♘×d4.

60

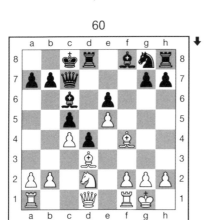

Black to move

61

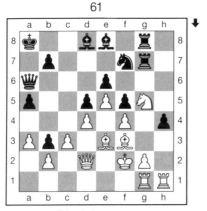

Black to move

62

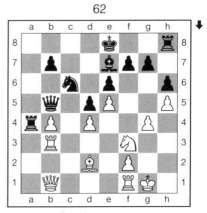

Black to move

63

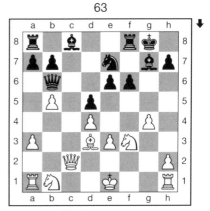

Black to move

64

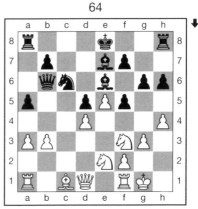

Black to move

65

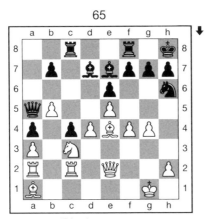

Black to move

66

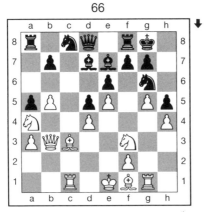

Evaluate the consequences of 19...♘xh4.

67

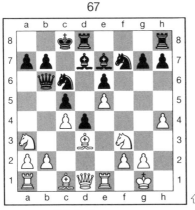

White to move

68

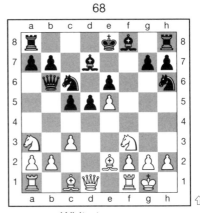

White to move

69

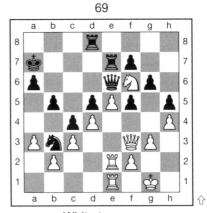

White to move

70

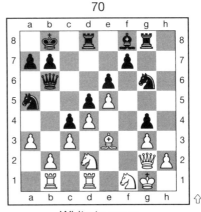

White to move

Check your solutions

1

Bellucco – Longo, *Italy 1979*

12. ♗xh7+! ♔xh7 13. ♘g5+ ♔g6 (13...♔g8
14. ♕h5 ♖fb8 15. ♕xf7+ ♔h8 16. ♕h5+ ♔g8
17. a4! ♗e8 18. ♕h7+ ♔f8 19. ♘xe6+ ♔f7
20. ♘g5+ ♔f8 21. ♕h8+ ♘g8 22. e6+−)
14. ♕g4 f5 15. ♕g3 ♖h8? (15...♖g8! 16. a4
♕a5 17. ♗a3 with an attack) **16. ♘xe6+ ♔f7
17. ♕xg7+ 1−0**

2

Sanguinetti – Albert, *Mar del Plata 1957*

**16. ♗xh7+! ♔xh7 17. ♕h5+ ♔g8 18. ♗xh4
f6** (18...♕e8 19.♗f6! ♘e7 20. ♘f3 ♘f5
21. g4+−) **19. exf6 ♖xf6** (19...♕e8 20. ♕g4
♕f7 21. ♘f3 e5 22. ♕g3 e4 23. ♘g5 ♕xf6
24. ♘xe4±) **20. ♗xf6 ♕xf6 21. ♘f3± ♖f8
22. ♕h2 ♕g6 23. ♘e5 ♘xe5 24. ♕xe5
♕xc2 25. ♕xd4 ♕f5 26. ♖bc1 ♗c6 27. ♖e5
♕g6 28. ♖e3 ♖f6 29. ♖ce1 ♔f7 30. ♕e5
♕f5 31. ♕xf5 exf5 32. ♖e7+ ♔g6 33. f4
d4 34. ♖1e6 d3 35. ♔f2 d2 36. ♔e2 ♗xg2
37. ♔xd2 ♗c6 38. ♔c3 ♖xe6 39. ♖xe6+
♔h5 40. ♔d4 ♔g4 41. ♔e5 ♔h5 42. ♖d6 g6
43. ♖d1 ♗e8 44. ♖g1 1−0**

3

Prié – Walton, *West Bromwich 2004*

**17. ♗xh7+! ♔xh7 18. ♕c2+ ♕g6 19. ♕xg6+
♔xg6 20. ♗xc5 ♖e8 21. ♗d6 ♖a5 22. b6
♖b5 23. ♖ab1 ♗d7 24. ♖xb5 ♗xb5 25. ♖d1
♖c8 26. ♗c7 ♗c4 27. ♖d4 ♖a8 28. g4
♖a5 29. f4 ♖b5 30. f5+ ♔h7 31. e6 fxe6
32. fxe6 ♖b1+ 33. ♔f2 ♖f1+ 34. ♔e3 ♖e1+
35. ♔d2 ♖xe6 36. ♔c3 ♖e3+ 37. ♔b4 ♖b3+
38. ♔xa4 ♖b2 39. h4 ♔g6 40. h5+ ♔f7
41. g5 ♖g2 42. ♗f4 ♖b2 43. ♗e3 ♗b5+
44. ♔a5 ♗c6 45. a4 ♖c2 46. ♔b4 ♖a2
47. ♖f4+ ♔e6 48. ♗d4 ♗e8 49. h6 gxh6**

**50. gxh6 ♖h2 51. a5 ♗c6 52. ♖f6+ ♔d7
53. ♖f7+ ♔e8 54. ♖h7 1−0**

4

Lemmers – Visser, *Hengelo 1992*

**18. ♗xh7+! ♔xh7 19. ♕h5+ ♔g8 20. ♘e4!
♕e5 21. ♘xf6+ gxf6 22. ♕g4+ ♔h8 23. ♖f3
♕e4 24. ♖h3+ ♕h7 25. ♖xh7+ ♔xh7
26. ♕h5+ ♔g8 27. ♗h6 ♘e5 28. ♖d3 ♗e8
29. ♕h4 ♖c8 30. ♖g3+ ♘g6 31. ♕xf6 1−0**

5

Illescas Cordoba – Speelman, *Linares 1992*

24...♗xf3+?

The quiet 24...a6 would have retained
Black's advantage.

**25. ♖xf3 ♖xf3 26. ♕xf3 ♖f8 27. ♗xh7+!
♕xh7**

27...♔xh7 28. ♕xf8+−.

**28. ♕xe3 ♕c2+ 29. ♕d2 ♕e4+ 30. ♔g1+−
d4 31. ♖e1 ♕d5 32. ♘c1 ♘xe5 33. ♖xe5
♕xe5 34. ♗xd4 ♕e4 35. ♗b2 ♖f3 36. ♕d8+
♖f8 37. ♕d2 ♖f3 38. ♘e2 e5 39. ♘c3
♕d4+ 40. ♕xd4 exd4 41. ♘b5 d3 42. ♗c1
a6 43. ♘c3 ♖f6 44. h4 ♔f7 45. ♗f4 ♖c6
46. ♗d2 ♔e6 47. ♔f2 ♔e5 48. ♔e3 ♖g6
49. ♗e1 ♔f5 50. ♔xd3 ♖d6+ 51. ♔e3 ♔g4
52. ♘e2 ♖e6+ 53. ♔d3 ♖e8 54. ♗c3 ♔f3
55. ♘d4+ ♔xg3 56. ♘f5+ ♔g4 57. ♘xg7
♖d8+ 58. ♔c2 ♖c8 59. h5 ♔g5 60. ♔d3
♔h6 61. ♗e5 b5 62. ♗c3 ♖c6 63. ♗e5 ♖c4
64. ♘e6 a5 1−0**

6

Hansen – Lovik, *Copenhagen 2004*

Black's last move was 11...♘e7?? and after
12. b4+− the bishop is lost. This is one of
the most common traps in the French Defence, taking the lives of a multitude of bishops through many generations.

☑ 7

Ivanović – Levitt, *Saint John 1988*

17. g4! ♘e7 18. b4 d4 19. bxc5 dxc3 20. ♕b1+– cxd2 21. ♕xb6+ ♔a8 22. ♕xa6+ ♕a7 23. ♕xa7+ ♔xa7 24. ♘e3 ♖xc5 25. ♖d1 ♖c1 26. ♔g2 ♖xd1 27. ♘xd1 ♘d5 28. ♔f1 ♘f4 29. ♖g3 ♖d5 30. g5 ♘xh5 31. ♖g1 hxg5 32. ♖xg5 g6 33. ♖g4 ♔b6 34. ♔e2 f6 35. exf6 ♖f5 36. ♘xd2 ♖xf6 37. ♘c4+ ♔a6 38. ♘c3 ♖f5 39. ♔e3 g5 40. ♘e4 ♘f4 41. ♖xg5 ♘d5+ 42. ♔d4 1–0

☑ 8

Fressinet – Shirov, *Bordeaux 1999*

17. ♕b3? (not 17. ♘b6? as in Milliet – Zakurdjaeva, Baku 2002, but White missed 17. ♘d6+! ♗xd6 18. exd6 ♕xd6 19. d5 exd5 20. ♗xg7 ♖e7+ 21. ♗e2 ♗b5 22. ♖c2 ♕g6 [22...b3 23. 0–0 bxc2 24. ♗xb5+] 23. ♗xh8 ♕xg2 24. ♖f1+–) **17...♕d5 18. f3 ♘h6 19. ♗d3 ♘f5 20. ♗e4 ♕d8 21. ♗xf5 exf5 22. ♘b6 ♕h4+ 23. g3 ♕h3 24. ♔f2 f4 25. a6 bxa6 26. ♖xc6 ♖xc6 27. ♕a4 ♕h6 28. ♔g2 fxg3 29. d5 ♕d2+ 30. ♘h3 ♕h6+ 31. ♔g4 ♕g6+ 32. ♔f4 ♕h6+ 33. ♔e4 ♕g6+ 34. ♔e3 ♗c5+ 35. ♗d4 ♕h6+ 36. ♔d3 ♕g6+ 37. ♔c4 ♗xb6+ 38. dxc6 ♗c7 0–1**

☑ 9

Fingerov – Vysochin, *Sebastopol 2000*

13. ♘b5! ♘c6 (13...♘f5 14. g4 ♘h6 15. ♖c1 ♖xc1 16. ♕xc1 ♕c6 17. ♕xc6 bxc6 18. ♘xa7 ♘b8 19. h3+–; 13...♘g6 14. ♖c1+–) **14. ♘d6+ ♗xd6 15. b5 ♕b6 16. bxc6 ♕xc6 17. exd6 ♕xd6 18. ♕b3+– b6 19. ♗b4 ♕f4 20. 0–0 f6 21. a5 ♔f7 22. axb6 axb6 23. ♖a7 ♖hd8 24. ♕a4 ♔e8 25. ♕a3 ♖c7 26. ♖e1 ♖c6 27. ♗f8 ♘c5 28. dxc5 ♔xf8 29. cxb6+ ♕d6 30. ♕xd6+ ♖cxd6 31. b7 ♖b6 32. ♘d4 e5 33. ♖a8 ♔e8 34. ♖xd8+ ♔xd8 35. b8♕+ 1–0**

☑ 10

Belov – Lisy, *Vladimir 2002*

17. ♖xe6! 0–0 (17...fxe6 18. ♘xe6 ♕b6 19. ♘xd5+–) **18. ♕g4± h5 19. ♕xh5 ♗xg5 20. ♗xg5 ♕c7 21. ♘xd5 ♕c4 22. ♖d6 a5 23. ♖xd7 axb4 24. ♕d1 b3 25. ♖c7 ♕xd5 26. 0–0 b2 27. ♕c2 ♕xd4 28. ♖b7 ♕xe5 29. ♗e3 ♘d6 30. ♕xb2 ♕xb2 31. ♖xb2 ♘c4 32. ♖b3 ♘xe3 33. ♖xe3 ♖fe8 34. ♖f3 ♖e2 35. g3 ♖ea2 36. h4 g6 37. ♔g2 ♖a1 38. ♖xa1 ♖xa1 39. g4 ♔g7 40. ♖b3 ♖a4 41. ♔g3 ♖c4 42. ♖b7 ♖a4 43. f3 ♖c4 44. ♖e7 ♖a4 45. ♖e4 ♖a5 46. ♖b4 ♖c5 47. ♔f4 ♖a5 48. ♔e4 f5+ 49. ♔f4 fxg4 50. fxg4 g5+ 51. hxg5 ♔g6 52. ♖b6+ ♔g7 53. ♖e6 ♖a1 54. g6 ♖a5 55. ♖b6 ♖c5 56. ♖e6 ♖a5 57. ♔g3 ♖g5 ½–½**

☑ 11

Th. Pähtz – Uhlmann, *Erfurt 1985*

16. ♕b1! ♗g7 (16...gxh5 17. ♕xb7 ♖d8 [17... ♖c8 18. ♖ad1+–] 18. ♗xd8+–; 16...♗c6 17. ♗xg6+ hxg6 18. ♕xg6+ ♔d7 19. ♕f7+ ♔c8 20. ♗f6+–; 16...♕d3 17. ♕xb7 ♕d5 18. ♕xd5 exd5 19. ♗f3±) **17. ♕xb7 0–0 18. ♗e7 ♖fe8 19. ♗f3± ♗a4 20. ♗f6 ♗xf6 21. exf6 ♕xf6 22. ♕a6 ♗b3 23. ♗xa8 ♖xa8 24. ♖ac1 ♕e7 25. ♖fe1 ♖e8 26. ♖e3 ♕d7 27. ♕a5 ♖e7 28. h4 ♕d4 29. ♕g5 ♖f7 30. ♕g3 ♕f4 31. ♕xf4 ♖xf4 32. ♖xe6 a5 33. ♖e7 a4 34. ♖c7 ♖xh4 35. ♖e1 ♔f8 36. ♖e5 h5 37. ♖a5 ♖e4 38. ♖aa7 h4 39. ♔h2 g5 40. f3 ♖e3 41. ♔h3 1–0**

☑ 12

Kupreichik – Charochkin, *Schwäbisch Gmünd 2002*

11. ♗d1! ♘bc6 12. ♘ge2 ♗c5 13. ♘a4+– ♘f3+ 14. gxf3 ♘xe5 15. ♘d4 ♗b4 16. ♘xb6 ♗xd2+ 17. ♔xd2 axb6 18. ♗e2 ♗d7 19. ♖hc1 0–0 20. ♖c7 ♗c8 21. ♘b5 ♖d8 22. ♗xb6 ♘d7 23. ♗a7 b6 24. ♘d6 1–0

☑ 13

Euwe – Kramer, *Zaanstreek 1946*

10. ♕d4!± ♘7g6 11. ♕xc5 ♗xc5 12. ♘c7+ ♔e7 13. ♘xa8 ♗d6 14. ♗e3 (14. h4! h5 15. ♘a3 ♗d7 16. ♘b6 axb6 17. ♘b5 ♗xb5 18. ♗xb5±) 14...♗d7 15. ♗xa7 ♖xa8 16. ♗e3 f5 17. f3 ♘c4 18. ♗xc4 dxc4 19. ♘d2 b5 20. ♔e2± ♘f4+ 21. ♗xf4 ♗xf4 22. g3 ♗e5 23. a3 ♗c6 24. ♖hd1 g5 25. ♖f1 ♗f6 26. g4 h5 27. gxf5 exf5 28. ♔f2 ♔f7 29. h3 ♖d8 30. ♖ad1 ♖d3 31. ♔e2 g4 32. hxg4 hxg4 33. fxg4 fxg4 34. ♖f4 g3 35. ♘e4 ♗xe4 36. ♖xe4 g2 37. ♖g4 ♖xd1 38. ♔xd1 ♔e6 39. ♖xg2 ♔d5 40. ♖g6 ♗e7 41. ♔e2 ♔c5 42. ♔e3 ♗d8 43. ♔e4 ♗c7 44. ♖f6 1–0

☑ 14

Cherniaev – Dzhakaev, *Istanbul 2003*

24...♘xd4! 25. ♘g5 h6 26. ♕b2 ♗c5 27. b4 axb4 28. axb4 ♖xa1 29. ♖xa1 ♗b6 30. ♘h3 ♕xh4 31. ♗e3 f4 32. ♗xd4 f3 33. ♗xb6 ♗xh3 34. gxf3 ♗g4+ 0–1

☑ 15

Csom – Portisch, *Budapest 1964*

28...♘xd4! 29. ♗xd4 ♖xc1+ 30. ♔d2 ♕c8 31. ♗d1 ♕c4 32. ♗b2 ♖b1 0–1

☑ 16

Portisch – Milić, *12th Olympiad, Moscow 1956*

20...♘xe5! 21. ♖xc7 (21. ♗xd7 ♘xf3+) 21...♘xf3+ 22. gxf3 ♗xb5 23. ♕c2 ♗d6 24. ♖xa7 ♕b8–+ 25. ♖a4 ♖c8 26. ♕d1 ♗xh2+ 27. ♔h1 ♗d6 28. ♖g1 ♕b7 29. ♘c3 ♗xa4 30. ♘xa4 ♖c4 31. ♘c3 ♖xd4 32. ♕a4 ♖h4+ 33. ♔g2 ♕c8 34. ♖c1 ♕d8 35. ♘e2 ♖h2+ 36. ♔g1 ♖h5 37. ♕a6 ♗f8 38. ♖c8 ♕e7 39. ♕xb6 d4 40. ♗xd4 ♕g5+ 41. ♘g3 ♘xg3 42. ♖xf8+ ♔xf8 43. ♕d6+ ♔e8 44. ♕c6+ ½–½

☑ 17

Brumm – Teloudis, *Regional League (Germany) 1981*

12...♘cxe5! 13. ♗xe5 ♘xe5 14. ♕xe5 ♕xb2 15. ♕xg7 0–0–0 16. ♘xf7 ♖hg8 17. ♕xh7 ♖xg2 18. ♖f1 ♖f8 19. ♕h3 ♖xf2 0–1

☑ 18

Smolensky – Rubinchik, *Ukraine 1979*

21...♘xe5! 22. ♘e3 (22. dxe5 ♕xf2+ 23. ♔xf2 ♘d4+ 24. ♖f3 [24. ♔g1 ♘xc2–+] 24...♖xf3+ 25. ♘xf3 ♘xc2 26. ♖c1 ♗b6+ 27. ♔e2 ♗a4–+; 22. ♕d1 ♖xg2 23. ♗xg2 ♘d3+ 24. ♖xd3 cxd3–+) 22...♖f4 23. ♘xf5 ♖4xf5 24. ♗e3 ♗a4! 25. ♕b1 (25. ♕xa4 ♕xb2 26. ♖d1 ♗xh4+! 27. ♖xh4 ♕xc3–+) 25...♘g4 26. ♗g1 ♕c7 0–1

☑ 19

Sveshnikov – Genov, *Bulgaria 1988*

17. ♖xc5! ♕xc5 18. ♖c1 ♕b6 19. ♗e3 ♕d6 20. ♗c5 ♕b8 21. ♕a3! b6 22. ♗xb6+ 1–0

☑ 20

Grosar – Raičević, *Yugoslav Championship, Kladovo 1991*

30. ♘g5+ ♔g8 31. ♘xf7 ♔xf7 32. ♕f4+ ♔g8 33. ♗xg6 ♖h7 34. ♖d1 ♗e8 35. ♗xh7+ ♔xh7 36. ♖d3 ♗g6 37. ♖h3 ♔g8 38. ♘e2 ♗f5 39. ♖g3+ ♔f7 40. ♖g7+ 1–0

☑ 21

Sveshnikov – Atalik, *Slovenian Championship, Bled 1999*

21. ♕xf5! exf5 22. ♘xd5 ♔f7 23. ♘xb6 axb6 24. ♗f3 ♖he8 25. ♗xb7 ♖c2 26. a4! ♖ee2 27. ♗f3 ♖f2 28. ♗xf2 ♖xf2 29. ♗d5+ ♗e6 30. ♔g1 ♖c2 31. ♗f3 ♖c4 32. ♗e3 ♖b4 33. a5 bxa5 34. ♖xa5 ♖xb2 35. ♖a6 ♗e7 36. ♖a7 ♖a2?? (36...♗c8±) 37. d5 1–0

☑ 22

Shabalov – Nogueiras, *34th Olympiad, Istanbul 2000*

21. ♕g4 (21. ♕f6+! ♕xf6 22. exf6+ ♔f8 23. ♗xh7+–) **21...♔h8 22. gxh6 ♘xh6 23. ♕f4 ♔g7 24. ♖c1 ♗d7 25. ♘g5 ♘f5 26. ♗xf5 exf5 27. ♕c7 h6 28. e6 hxg5** (28...fxe6 29. ♘f3∞) **29. exd7 ♕e1+ 30. ♔g2 ♕e4+ 31. ♔h2 ♕xd4 32. ♕g3 f4 33. ♕xg5+ ♔h7 34. d8♕ 1–0**

☑ 23

Prokhorov – Griezne, *Open, Swidnica 2000*

28. ♘xe6+ fxe6 29. ♗xh6+ ♔xh6 30. ♕c1+ ♔g7 31. ♖xc8 ♕d7 32. ♖xh8 ♔xh8 33. h5 ♔g7 34. ♕g5 ♕f7 35. hxg6 ♕xg6 36. ♕e7+ ♕f7 37. ♕b4 ♕c7 38. ♔g2 ♔g6 39. ♕xa4 f4 40. ♕e8+ ♔f5 41. ♕h5+ 1–0

☑ 24

Grosar – Furlan, *Slovenian League, Bled 2000*

24. ♘e5! fxe5 25. ♕xe5 ♘f5 26. ♗xf5 exf5 27. ♕g3+ ♔h8 28. ♖xe8+ ♗xe8 29. ♗f4 1–0

☑ 25

Shirov – Gurevich, *French League, Belfort 2004*

35. ♖xg7+ ♔xg7 36. ♕g5+ ♔f7 37. ♘xf5 exf5 38. ♖xf5+ ♔e8 39. ♕g6+ ♔e7 40. ♕d6+ ♔e8 41. ♕e6+ ♔d8 42. ♕xd5+ ♔e8 43. ♕e6+ ♔d8 44. ♕d6+ ♔e8 45. ♕b8+ ♔e7 46. ♕xb7+ ♔e8 47. ♕c6+ ♔e7 48. ♕d6+ ♔e8 49. ♕g6+ ♔e7 50. ♖f7+ ♖xf7 51. ♕xd3+ ♖xh5 52. ♕a3+ ♔e8 53. ♕a4+ ♔f8 54. ♕b4+ ♔g8 55. ♕b8+? (55. ♕c4) **55...♔h7 = 56. ♕b3 ♖g5+ 57. ♔h2 ♔g6 58. ♕e6+ ♔g7 59. d5 ♖g6 60. ♕e8 ♖h6+ 61. ♔g3 ♖g6+ 62. ♔h2 ½–½**

☑ 26

Iuldachev – Kotronias, *Mumbai 2003*

36. ♗b5 axb5 37. axb5 ♘xb5 (37...♗xb5

38. ♖xa7 ♗a6 39. ♖xa6 bxa6 40. ♕a4±) **38. ♕a4 ♘xd4?** (38...♕e8 39. ♕a8+ ♔c7 40. ♕a5+ ♔b8 41. ♕a8+ ♔c7 42. ♘xb5+ ♗xb5 43. ♕a5+ ♔b8=) **39. ♕a7+ ♔c7 40. ♕b6+ ♔b8 41. ♖a7 1–0**

☑ 27

Delchev – Gurevich, *3rd European Championship, Batumi 2002*

33...♖h5! 34. ♖ff4 ♗g5! 35. ♕g3 ♗xf4 36. ♖g8+ ♔e7 37. ♕xf4 ♕h6 0–1

☑ 28

Stević – Nikolić, *Čelje 2003*

18...♘f3+! 19. gxf3 ♕g5+ 20. ♔h2 ♕h4+ 21. ♔g1 ♕xc4∓ 22. ♗d6 ♕h4 23. ♖e1 ♕g5+ 24. ♔f1 ♕xh5 25. ♖b3 ♖d8 26. ♕d3 ♖d7 27. ♔e2 f6 28. ♕c4 ♔f7 29. ♕g4 ♕g5 30. ♖g1 ♖c8 31. f4 ♕xg4+ 32. ♖xg4 ♗e4 33. ♖b2 ♖c4 34. f3 ♗c6 35. ♔f2 f5 36. ♖h4 ♖d8 37. ♔g3 ♖c3 38. ♖b3 ♖xb3 39. axb3 ♗d5 40. ♖h2 ♖c8 41. ♗b4 ♗xb3 42. ♖d2 ♗d5 43. ♖d3 b6 44. ♖c3 ♖xc3 45. ♗xc3 ♔e8 46. ♗b4 g6 47. ♗d6 ♔d7 48. ♔f2 ♔c6 49. ♔e3 ♔b5 50. ♔d4 ♗xf3 51. ♔c3 g5 52. ♗f8 g4 0–1

☑ 29

Vallejo Pons – Hernandez, *Dos Hermanas 2002*

31. ♘xf7+!+– ♖xf7 32. ♕xh6+ ♔g8 33. ♘f6+ ♖xf6 34. exf6 ♕f8 35. ♕g6+ ♔h8 36. ♖a1 ♗e8 37. ♕g5 ♘b6 38. ♖a7 ♘d7 39. ♖xb7 ♕xf6 40. ♕xf6+ ♘xf6 41. b6 1–0

☑ 30

Dvoiris – Naumkin, *Cappelle la Grande 2001*

16...♔xd6?

Now Black is exposed to a devastating attack. Instead 16...♘c6! was correct: 17. cxd5

(17. ♘×b7 d×c4 18. ♕×c4 ♔×b7 −+) 17…e×d5 18. ♘×b7 c4! −+.

17. ♕b6+ ♘c6 18. c×d5 ♔×d5

Or 18…e×d5 19. b4! +− (19. g3 g5 20. b4 c×b4 21. ♗e3 d4 22. ♗×d4 ♕×d4 23. ♖ad1 ♗g7 ⇄) 19…c×b4 20. ♗e3 d4 (20…♗×g4 21. ♗c5+ ♔d7 22. ♕×b7#) 21. ♗×d4 ♗×g4 (21…♕×d4 22. ♖ad1 ♕×d1 23. ♖×d1+ ♔e7 24. ♕e3+) 22. ♗×f6 g×f6 23. f3 ♗e6 24. ♖ad1+ ♗d5 25. ♕×b7 +−.

19. ♗g5! ♕×g5 20. ♖ad1+ ♘d4 21. ♗×e6+ 1−0

☑ **31**

Shirov – Bern, *Bergen (simul) 2001*

17. ♘d6+! ♗×d6 18. e×d6 ♕b8 19. b4! **♕×b4** (19…♘×b4 20. ♘e5 h4 21. ♘×d7 ♔×d7 22. ♗e5 ♘×d3 23. ♕×d3 ♖h6 24. ♖ab1 ♕a8 ⇄; 21. ♖h2! ♘×e5 [21…g4 22. h×g4 h3 23. ♕a4; 21…♘×d3 22. ♕×d3 g4 23. h×g4 h3 24. g×h3±] 22. ♗×e5) **20. ♖b1** **♕a3 21. ♗e4** (21. ♖b3 ♕a5 22. ♗e4±) **21…♘b4 22. ♘×d4! h4 23. ♗h2 ♗×c4** **24. ♘c2** (24. ♘c6 +−; 24. ♖e3 +−) **24…♘×c2** **25. ♕×c2 ♗a6 26. ♖e3 ♕a5 27. ♕b2 g4** **28. ♖a3 ♕b4 29. ♖×a6 ♕×e4 30. ♖×a7 g3** **31. ♖c7+ 1−0**

☑ **32**

McConnell – Morphy, *New Orleans 1850*

11…♗×b4+! 12. a×b4? (12. ♘bd2□ ♗a5 ∓) **12…♘×b4 13. ♕d2 ♖c2 14. ♕d1 ♘e3 0−1**

☑ **33**

Sveshnikov – Doroshkevich, *Anapa 1991*

11…♘×b4! 12. ♘c3 (12. a×b4 ♗×b4 13. ♘c3 ♗d7 14. ♘g1 [14. ♖c1 ♖c8] 14…e5 −+) **12…♕a5** (12…♘c6 13. ♗d3 ⯒) **13. ♗b5+** **♗d7?!** (13…♘c6 ∓) **14. 0−0! ♗×b5 15. a×b5** **♕b6 16. ♘×b5 ♕×b5 17. ♖a5! ⯒ ♕b6**

18. ♕e2 ♗×b4 (18…a6!? ∓) **19. ♖b5 ♕a6** **20. ♖b1 ♗e7 21. ♗f4! ♖d8** (21…♘d6 22. ♗×d6 ♖×d6 23. ♘e5! →) **22. ♔f1 ♖d7** (22…0−0 23. g4!?; 22…♔f7?! 23. ♘e5+! →) **23. ♖×b7! ♖×b7!** (23…♕×b7? 24. ♖×b7 ♖×b7 25. ♕×e6±) **24. ♕×a6 ♖×b1+ 25. ♔e2** **♖b2+!** (25…♔f7 26. g4! ♘g7 [26…♘d6 27. ♕×a7 ♖d8 28. g5±] 27. ♕×a7±) **26. ♔f1!** (26. ♔d3? ♔f7 27. g4 ♖×f2 ∓) **26…♖b1+** **27. ♔e2 ♖b2+ 28. ♔f1 ½−½**

☑ **34**

Delchev – Volkov, *3rd European Championship, Batumi 2002* **14…a4! 15. ♗c4** (15. b4 ♘×b4!? 16. a×b4 ♗×b4+ ⯒ 17. ♔e2 a3! 18. ♘×c6 b×c6 →) **15…a×b3 16. 0−0 ♘c5 17. ♘×b3 ♗a4** **18. ♘fd2 ♘×b3 19. ♘×b3 ♖c8 20. ♗×d5** **e×d5 21. e6 ♕×b3 22. ♕g4 f×e6 23. ♖ab1** **d4 24. ♗×d4 ♕d5 25. ♖fe1 ♗d7 26. ♖e5** **♕c4 27. ♖be1 ♖c6 28. ♖5e4 ♕d5 29. ♖e5** **♕d6 30. h4 ♔f7 31. ♗a1 h6 32. h5 ♕×a3** **33. ♖5e3 ♕b4 34. ♕g6+ ♔g8 35. ♖d1 e5** **36. ♕d3 ♖d6 37. ♕e2 ♗b5 38. ♕f3 ♕f4** **39. ♖×d6 ♕×f3 0−1**

☑ **35**

Grosar – Sulava, *Croatian League, Pula 1992* **14. e6!**

Also very strong is 14. ♘×h4 ♘e7 (14…c6 15. ♗×f7+ ♕×f7 16. e6 +−) 15. ♗×b7 ♖a7 16. ♗e4 +−.

14…f×e6 15. ♘e5 ♕d5 16. ♕h5+ ♔e7 (16…g6 17. ♕×g6+ ♔e7 18. ♕g7+) **17. ♖ad1** **♘f6 18. ♕f7+ ♔d6 19. ♘g6** (19. ♖×d5+ e×d5 20. ♘g6 ♖e8 21. ♘×h4 +−) **19…♘c6** **20. ♖×d5+ ♘×d5 21. ♘×h4 +− ♘e5 22. ♕h5** **♖hf8 23. ♖d1 ♖f6 24. f4 ♖×f4 25. ♘g6** **♖f5 26. ♖×d5+ ♔×d5 27. ♘e7+ ♔e4** **28. ♕e2+ ♔d4 29. ♕d2+ ♔c5 30. ♕c3+** **♔d6 31. ♕b4+ ♔d7 32. ♘×f5 e×f5 33. ♕×b7** **♖e8 34. ♕d5+ ♔c8 35. ♕a8+ ♔d7 36. ♕×a6** **♖e6 37. ♕b5+ ♔d6 38. a4 ♘g4 39. ♕b4+** **c5 40. ♕d2+ ♔c6 41. h3 ♘e3 42. ♕d8 ♘d5** **43. ♕a8+ ♔d6 44. ♕f8+ ♖e7 45. a5 ♘b4** **46. ♕×f5 ♖a7 47. ♕f8+ ♔d5 48. ♕d8+ ♔c4**

49. ♕g8+ ♘d5 50. ♕e6 ♖e7 51. b3+ ♔d4 52. ♕d6 ♖b7 53. a6 ♖b6 54. ♕d7 ♖xa6 55. ♕g4+ ♔e3 56. ♕f3+ ♔d4 57. ♕d1+ 1–0

☑ **36**

Sveshnikov – Totsky, *Cheliabinsk 1990*

20. e6 fxe6 21. ♖e1 ♗d7 (21...♔d8 22. ♗a5 [22. ♖f7 ♔e8 23. ♖xf5 ♗e7±] 22...♗b4□ 23. ♗b6 ♗xe1 24. ♖xc6+ ♔e7 25. ♖c7+ ♔f6 26. ♘xe1 ♖hc8 27. ♗d7 ♖c1 28. ♔f1±) **22. ♘e5 ♗d6 23. ♖xd7 ♗xe5 24. ♖xb7 0–0–0 25. ♖b4 ♗d6 26. ♖c1+ ♔d7 27. ♖b7+ ♔e8 28. ♗a5 ♖a8 29. ♖c6+– ♗f4 30. g3 ♗g5 31. ♖xe6+ ♔f8 32. ♖e5 ♗f6 33. ♖xf5 ♗g8 34. ♖xd5 ♔h7 35. ♖d6 ♖hb8 36. ♖xb8 ♖xb8 37. ♗c3 1–0**

☑ **37**

Motylev – Balashov, *Russian League, Ekaterinburg 2002*

39. e6! fxe6 40. ♘xd5 exd5 41. ♖xe7± ♗a4 42. ♖1e6 ♖xe7 43. ♖xe7 ♕f6 44. ♖e5 ♗c6 45. ♕e2 ♖d6 46. ♖e7 a4 47. ♕e5 ♔b8 48. ♔g1 ♔a7 49. ♔f2 ♔b6 50. ♔e3 ♔a6 51. ♔d2 ♔b6 52. ♔c1 ♔a6 53. ♔c2 ♔b6 54. ♔d1 ♔a6 55. ♔d2 ♔b6 56. ♖h7 ♕d8 57. ♖e7 ♔a7 58. ♖e6 ♖xe6 59. ♕xe6 1–0

☑ **38**

Shabalov – Akobian, *US Championship, Seattle 2003*

31. g6 fxg6 32. ♘xe6 ♗xe6 33. ♖xc6 ♕e7 34. ♖xb5 ♔f7 35. ♘g5+ ♕xg5 36. ♖c7+ ♕e7 37. ♖xe7+ ♔xe7 38. ♖c5 ♖hc8 39. ♕a6 ♖xc5 40. ♕a7+ ♔e8 41. dxc5 ♖c8 42. ♕xa4+ ♗d7 43. ♕d4 ♗e6 44. f4 ♔e7 45. ♕b4 ♖c6 46. ♔h3 ♗d7 47. ♔h4 ♔f7 48. ♔g5 ♔e7 49. ♕b3 ♖e6 50. ♕xd5 ♗c6 51. ♕a2 ♗d7 52. ♔h6 ♗e8 53. ♔g7 ♗d7 54. ♕h2 ♖c6 55. ♕h4+ ♔e8 56. ♕f6 ♖xf6 57. exf6 ♗e6 58. c6 g5 59. fxg5 f4 60. g6 fxg3 61. f7+ 1–0

☑ **39**

Degraeve – Barsov, *Montréal 2002*

22. a6 bxa6 23. ♗xa6 ♖b8 24. ♗d3± ♕e7 25. ♕e3 ♔d8 26. ♖fc1 ♔c7 27. ♖a7+ ♖b7 28. ♖xb7+ ♔xb7 29. ♗b5 ♘a7 30. ♗e2 ♔a8 31. ♖a1 ♖b8 32. ♘e1 g6 33. ♘d3 ♗b5 34. ♘c5 ♗xe2 35. ♕xe2 ♖b6 36. ♕a2 ♕c7 37. h4 ♖b5 38. ♕a6 ♖b6 39. ♕a4 ♕e7 40. ♔g2 ♕c7 41. ♕e8+ ♖b8 42. ♘a6 ♕c8 43. ♕xf7 1–0

☑ **40**

Antoshin – Kasparian, *USSR 1955*

12. d5 exd5 13. ♘d4!

With a typical pawn sacrifice White gains the d4 square for his knight and then begins a pawn storm in the centre.

13...♕c8 14. 0–0 ♘e7 15. f4 ♘f5 16. ♘xd5 ♘xe3 17. ♘xe3 a5 18. ♖c1 b5 19. e6 fxe6 20. ♕h5+ ♔d8 21. ♖fd1 ♕a6 22. ♕f7 ♔c8 23. ♘xb5 ♗xb5 24. ♘xc4 ♗xc4 25. ♕d7+ ♔b8 26. ♕d8+ 1–0

☑ **41**

Delchev – Moreno Carnero, *Andorra la Vella 2002*

20. d5! (To vacate the d4 square.) **20...exd5 21. ♕d4±** (Blockade) **21...h5 22. ♖fd1 ♗c6 23. ♖d3 ♗e7 24. ♖xb3 ♖h6 25. ♕f4** (25. ♗e2±) **25...♕e6 26. h4 g5 27. hxg5 ♖g6 28. ♗d4?!** (28. ♗xh5) **28...♗xg5 29. ♕h2 ♘c4 30. ♖d3 ♖dg8∓ 31. ♖cd1 ♗xe3 32. fxe3 ♖g5 33. ♗c3? d4 34. exd4 ♗xf3 35. ♖xf3 ♖xg2+ 36. ♕xg2 ♖xg2+ 37. ♔xg2 ♘e3+ 38. ♖xe3 ♕g4+ 39. ♖g3 ♕xd1 40. ♗b4 ♕xd4 41. ♗d6+ ♔c8 0–1**

☑ **42**

Fressinet – Soćko, *German League 2002/03*

18. d5

White sacrifices a pawn to establish a blockade and complete his development.

18...e×d5 19. ♗d3 ♗g5 20. ♖c2 ♘e7
21. 0-0 ♗h6 22. ♗d4 (Blockade) 22...0-0
23. ♕b1 ♖e8 24. f4 g6 25. ♕×b4 ♗f8
26. ♕e1 ♘c8 27. ♕g3 ♗g7 28. f5 ♘×b6
29. a×b6 ♖c8 30. ♖cf2 ♗d7 31. ♖f4 ♖c4
32. f×g6 f×g6 33. ♗×c4 d×c4 34. ♕f3 ♗e6
35. ♕f2 ♕d5 36. ♗c3 ♕c6 37. h3 ♗h6
38. ♖f3 ♖d8 39. ♔h2 ♗g7 40. ♖e1 ♖d5
41. ♗b4 h5 42. ♕g3 ♕e8 43. ♗d6 ♔h7
44. ♖ef1 ♖b5 45. ♖f8 ♕c6 46. ♖1f6 ♗×f6
47. ♖×f6 ♕e8 48. ♖f8 ♕d7 49. ♕g5 ♖×b6
50. ♖d8 ♖×d6 51. e×d6 ♕f7 52. ♕e5 1-0

☑ 43

Sveshnikov – Naumkin, *Leningrad 1991*

15. ♗×f5 g×f5 16. ♘f3 ♖dg8 17. h4 ♗×a3
18. ♘g5⩲ ♗e8 19. ♘f4 ♗e7 20. ♘×h5 ♕d8
21. ♔g2 ♘b3 22. ♗f4 ♖g6 23. ♘f6! ♗×f6
24. e×f6 ♖×f6 25. ♕e2 ♖fh6 26. ♕e5 ♕b6
27. ♖fe1 ♘a5 28. ♕b8+ ♔d7 29. ♖a1 ♘c6
30. ♕d6+ ♔c8 31. ♖×a7!+–.

☑ 44

Sveshnikov – Totsky, *Cheliabinsk 1990*

16. ♗×f5 e×f5 17. ♗g5! ♗f8?! (17...♗c6)
18. ♖c7 h6 19. ♗d2 ♗c6 and for the continuation see No. 36.

☑ 45

Sveshnikov – Shabalov, *Riga 1990*

15. ♗×g6 h×g6 16. ♗f4 ♗c5 17. ♘c2 ♘c4
18. a4 ♖hf8 19. ♗g3 f5 20. ♗f4 ♕a5
21. ♖ec1± ♖c8 22. ♘cd4 ♔a8 23. ♘b3
♕d8 24. h4 ♗e7 25. g3 ♘a5 (25...♗a3!?)
26. ♘bd4 ♖c4 27. ♗g5 ♗×g5 28. ♘×g5 ♕e7
29. ♕e3 ♖fc8 30. ♘gf3 ♕c5 31. ♘g5 ♕b6
32. ♕d2 ♖4c7 33. ♖a2 ♘c4 34. ♕e1 ♕a5
35. ♘g×e6 ♗×e6 36. ♘×e6 ♖e7 37. ♘f4
♖×e5 38. ♕d1 ♕b6 39. ♘×d5 ♕c5 40. ♘f4
♖e4 41. ♖e2 ♘e5 42. ♔g2 ♕c4 43. ♖×e4
♕×e4+ 44. f3 ♕e3 45. ♖c2 ♕b6 46. ♖e2
♘c4 47. ♕d7 ♖b8 48. ♘d5+– 1-0

☑ 46

Dvoiris – Gleizerov, *Hoogeveen 2000*

30. ♗×g6 h×g6 31. ♕e3 ♔f7 32. g5 ♕h8
33. g×f6 ♗×f6 34. ♗g5 ♗g7 35. ♕f4+ ♔g8
36. ♕g4 ♕h5 37. ♕×e6+ ♖f7 38. ♖c3+–
♗×d4 39. ♘×d4 ♕d1+ 40. ♔g2 ♕×d4
41. ♕e8+ ♖f8 42. ♕e6+ ♖f7 43. ♖f3 ♕g7
44. ♖f6 d4+ 45. f3 ♕f8 46. ♖×g6+ ♔h7
47. ♖h6+ ♔g8 48. ♖f6 ♗c8 49. ♕c4 ♗d7
50. ♖g6+ ♔h7 51. ♖h6+ ♔g8 52. ♕×d4 ♕g7
53. ♕d5 ♕b2+ 54. ♔g3 ♕b1 55. ♕a8+ ♖f8
56. ♖h8+ 1-0

☑ 47

Sveshnikov – Moskalenko, *Rostov on Don 1993*

13. ♗×g6 h×g6 14. ♕d3± ♔g7 15. ♘bd2
♗d7 16. c4 f×e5 17. c×d5 e×d5 18. ♕×d5
♗f5 19. ♕×e5+ ♕f6 20. ♖fe1 ♕×e5 21. ♖×e5
♖ae8 22. ♖×e8 ♖×e8 23. a5 ♗d8 24. ♘c4
♗f6 25. ♖d1 ♖d8 26. ♖×d8 ♗×d8 27. ♘d4
♗d7 28. f4 ♗e7 29. ♘e5 ♗c8 30. ♔f2
♗b4 31. ♘c4 ♗c5 32. ♔e3 ♗d7 33. b6
a×b6 34. ♘×b6 ♗c6 35. g3 ♗g2 36. ♔d3
♗b4 37. ♘b3 ♔f6 38. ♔c4 ♗e1 39. g4 h5
40. ♘d7+ ♔e6 41. ♘dc5+ ♔d6 42. ♘d3
♗d5+ 43. ♔d4 ♗h4 44. ♘bc5 h×g4
45. ♘e4+ ♗×e4 46. ♔×e4 g3 ½-½

☑ 48

Sveshnikov – Donchev, *Lvov 1983*

24. g4 ♖c7 25. ♘h4 g6 26. ♘g3 a5 27. f4
♘d8 28. f5 ♔e8 29. ♘f3 b4 30. a×b4 a×b4
31. ♖ef2 ♖a7 32. ♘g5 ♗b3 33. h4 ♗a2
34. f×e6 f×e6 35. ♗c2 ♗b3 36. ♗b1 ♗a2
37. ♗c2 ♗b3 38. ♗×b3 c×b3 39. c×b4 ♘ec6
40. ♘e2 h6 41. ♘h3 ♖b7 42. ♘hf4 g5
43. ♘d3 g×h4 44. ♔h2 ♖g8 45. ♔h3 ♘×b4
46. ♘df4 ♔d7 47. ♔×h4 ♔c8 48. ♖f3 ♘c2
49. ♘h5 ♖b4 50. ♘f6 ♖f8 51. ♖d1 ♘c6
52. ♖fd3 ♖f7 53. ♔h5 ♖a7 54. ♔×h6 ♖aa4
55. g5 ♘2×d4 56. ♘×d4 ♖×d4 57. ♖×d4
♘×d4 58. ♖×d4 ♖×d4 59. g6 ♖h4+ 60. ♔g5
1-0

☑ **49**
Sveshnikov – Luce, *Berlin 1989*

17. g4! ♘a5 18. ♖ec1 ♘b3 19. ♖f1! ♘a5 20. ♘e1 ♘c6 21. ♗e3 0-0-0 22. f4 g6 23. ♘g3 ♗e7 24. f5 ♖df8 25. ♖c1 ♗b3 26. ♖f2 ♘a4 27. ♗f3 ♖fg8 28. ♘g2 g×f5 29. g×f5 ♘×b2 30. ♖×b2 ♗×a3 31. ♖bb1 ♗×c1 32. ♖×c1 a5 33. ♘f4 ♘d8 34. ♘fh5 a4 35. ♘f6 ♖f8 36. ♘e2 ♘c6 37. ♘f4 ♘d8 38. ♔f2 ♖hg8 39. ♘×g8 ♖×g8 40. ♘h5 a3 41. ♗×h6 a2 42. ♖a1 e×f5 43. ♗c1 ♖h8 44. ♔g2 b4 45. ♘f4 b×c3 46. ♗×d5 ♔d7 47. ♘e2 c2 48. ♗g5 ♘e6 49. ♗×e6+ f×e6 50. ♘c3 ♔e8 51. h4 ♔f7 52. ♔f2 ♔g6 53. ♔e3 ♖b8 54. ♔d2 ♗a4 55. ♖×a2 ♖b1 56. ♘e2 ♗b3 57. ♘f4+! ♔f7 58. ♖a7+ ♔e8 59. ♘e2 ♖d1+ 60. ♔c3 ♖f1 61. d5 1-0

☑ **50**
Sveshnikov – Gofshtein, *Russian Championship, Rostov on Don 1976*

24. ♘g2!± ♕b3 25. ♘f4?

Instead 25. ♘e3± was correct, followed by the retreat of the bishop from f3, after which Black is helpless against the f2-f4-f5 advance.

25...♕c2 26. ♕e3 ♕f5 27. h4 f6? 28. e×f6 g×f6 29. ♗×h5+ ♖×h5 30. ♘×h5 f×g5 31. h×g5 ♗c2 32. ♖bc1 ♗×b2? 33. ♘f6+ ♔f7 34. g4! ♕g6 (34...♕d3 35. ♕f4±) 35. ♖fe1 ♗e4 36. ♕f4 e5 37. d×e5 ♔g7 38. ♖e3 ♘c6 39. ♖h3 ♗c5 40. ♖f1 ♕f7 41. ♕h2 ♗g6 42. ♖h8 ♕e7 43. ♖h7+ 1-0

☑ **51**
Ehlvest – Thompson, *San Francisco 2000*

17. g4 ♗g7 18. 0-0 ♖d8 19. ♘g5 0-0 20. ♕f3 ♘c6 21. ♖f2 ♕c7 22. ♖af1 ♕e7 23. ♘×f7 b6 24. ♘d3± (24. ♘×d8+- ♖×f3 25. ♘×c6 ♕c7 26. ♖×f3 b×c5 27. ♘a5 c×d4 28. e×d4) 24...♖a8 25. ♕e2 ♖×a3 26. ♕c2 (26. ♘d6±) 26...♖d8 27. ♘×d8

♕×d8 28. ♖×f8+ ♗×f8 29. ♖f6 ♗g7 30. ♖×e6?! (30. ♖f3±) 30...♕d7 31. ♘f4 g5 32. ♖d6 ♕×g4+ 33. ♘g2 ♖×e3 (33...♗f8!∞) 34. ♖×d5 ♗f8 35. ♖d8 ♖e2 36. ♕c6 ♖e1+ (36...♕f5!∓) 37. ♔f2 ♖e2+ 38. ♔f1 ♖b2? (38...♖d2! 39. ♕d5+ ♔g7 40. ♕d7+ ♕×d7 41. ♖×d7+ ♔g6⇄) 39. ♕d5+ ♔g7 40. ♕d7+ ♕×d7 41. ♖×d7+ ♔g6 42. ♖b7 ♗×b4 43. ♖×b6+ ♔f7 44. ♘e3± ♗a5 45. e6+ ♔e8 46. ♖b7 1-0

☑ **52**
Vorobiov – Volkov, *Moscow 2004*

23. ♘×e6

Here 23. h3!? also came into consideration, followed by g2-g4, maintaining the strong knight at c5, at least for the time being.

23...f×e6 24. ♘f4 ♕c7 25. g4 f×g4 26. ♕×g4 ♕f7 27. ♔h1 ♔h7 28. ♕h3 g5 29. ♘h5 ♗e7 30. f4 ♕f5 31. ♕g2 ♕g6 32. ♘g3 g×f4 33. ♗×f4 ♖f8 34. ♘e2 ♕×g2+ 35. ♔×g2 ♖f5 36. ♖h3 h5 37. ♗e3 ♖g8+ 38. ♔h1 h4 39. ♘f4 ♗g5 40. ♘×e6 ♗×e3 41. ♖×e3 ♖e8 42. ♘c7 ♖d8 43. ♖h3 ♖g6 44. ♖g1+ ♔h5 45. ♘e6 ♖d7 46. ♘g7+ ♖×g7 47. ♖×g7 ♘×d4 48. ♖h7+ ♔g5 49. ♖3:h4 ♖f1+ 50. ♔g2 ♖d1 51. ♖7h5+ ♔g6 52. ♖h6+ ♔f5 53. e6 ♖d2+ 54. ♔g3 ♔e5 55. ♖×d4 ♔×d4 56. ♖h4+ ♔c3 57. ♖e4 ♖d3+ 58. ♔g4 d×e4 59. e7 ♔d2 60. e8♕ e3 61. ♔f3 ♖×b3 62. ♕d8+ ♔e1 63. ♕d5 ♖a3 64. ♕c5 1-0

☑ **53**
Motylev – Potkin, *Russian League, Togliatti 2003*

21. g4!? ♘c4? (21...g×f4 22. ♖×f4 [22. ♘×f5!? e×f5 23. ♗×f4⩱] 22...♗g5 23. ♖f3⇄) 22. g×f5± ♘×d2 23. ♕×d2 g×f4 24. f×e6 ♗×e6 25. ♖×f4 ♗g5 26. ♖f3 ♕c7 27. ♕f2 ♕c3 28. ♘f5 ♖cf8 29. ♖f1 ♖f7 30. ♗b1 ♕c4 31. ♘d6 ♖×f3 32. ♕×f3 ♕×d4 33. ♘f7+ ♗×f7 34. ♕×f7 ♕h4 35. ♖g1 ♕h6 36. ♕×d5 ♖f8 37. ♕g2 ♗f4 38. e6 ♗e5 39. e7 ♖e8 40. ♕g8+ ♖×g8 41. ♖×g8+ ♔×g8 42. e8♕+ ♕f8 43. ♗×h7+ ♔×g7 44. ♕×e5+ ♔×h7 45. ♕h5+ ♔g7 46. ♕g5+ ♔h7

47. ♕h4+ ♔g6 48. ♔g2 ♕a8+ 49. ♔g3 ♕d5 50. ♕g4+ ♔h7 51. a4 ♕d6+ 52. ♕f4 ♕d3+ 53. ♔g4 ♕d1+ 54. ♔f5 ♕d7+ 55. ♔f6 ♕d8+ 56. ♔e6 ♕e8+ 57. ♔d5 ♕d7+ 58. ♕d6 ♕f5+ 59. ♔c6 ♕e4+ 60. ♔d5 ♕xa4 61. ♔b7 ♔g6 62. h4 ♕xh4 63. ♕e6+ ♔h5 64. ♕e8+ 1–0

☑ 54

Sveshnikov – Milos, *Budapest 1988*

8. ♗xc4 (a typical piece sacrifice) 8...dxc4 9. ♘xc4 ♕a6 10. ♘d6+ ♔d7 11. ♘xf7 ♖g8 12. ♕c2 h6 13. ♘d6 b5 14. 0–0 ♖b8 15. ♗e3 ♗b7 16. a4 b4 17. c4 ♘a5 18. ♘d2 ♗a8 19. ♕h7 ♔c7 20. ♘b5+ ♔d7 21. f3 ♘f5 22. ♗f2 ♗e7 23. ♕g6 ♗g5 24. ♘e4 ♗xe4 25. fxe4 ♘e7 26. ♕h5 ♘xc4 27. ♕e2 ♘d2 28. h4 ♘xf1 29. hxg5 hxg5 30. ♕xf1 ♖h8 31. ♕c4 ♖bc8 32. ♕xb4 ♕b7 33. ♕d6+ ♔e8 34. ♕xe6 ♕c6 35. ♘d6+ ♔d8 36. ♘f7+ ♔e8 37. ♕xc6+ ♖xc6 38. ♘xh8 ♔f8 39. d5 ♖h6 40. ♗xa7 ♔g8 1–0

☑ 55

Sveshnikov – Riazantsev, *St. Petersburg (Rapidplay) 2000*

17. ♘dxc4!? dxc4 18. ♘xc4 ♕b5 19. ♘d6 ♕a4 20. ♘xf7 (20. ♖b1!?±) 20...♕xa1 (20... ♖c8!? 21. ♖b1 ♖g8 22. ♘d6∞) 21. ♕xa4 ♗xa4 22. ♘xd8 ♘b3 23. ♗d2 ♗d7 24. ♘xb7 ♘d5 25. ♘d6 ♗xd6 26. exd6±, and White went on to win.

☑ 56

Shabalov – Bluvshtein, *Chicago 2003*

27. ♗xd5! exd5 28. ♘xd5 ♕e6 29. ♘xe7 ♕xe7 30. d5 ♗b5 31. e6 ♖d8 32. ♕d4+ ♔a8 33. ♖d2± ♕d6 34. e7 ♖de8 35. ♖e6 ♕d7 36. ♖de2 h6 37. ♕b6 ♔b8 38. gxh6 f4 39. f3 ♗a6 40. ♕d4 ♔a8 41. ♕b6 ♔b8 42. ♖2e4 ♔c8 43. ♕c5+ ♔b8 44. ♖xa6 bxa6 45. ♖e6 ♕c8 46. ♖c6 ♕b7 47. ♖b6 ♖xe7 48. ♖xb7+

♖xb7 49. ♔g2 ♖d8 50. ♕xc4 ♖c7 51. ♕xf4 ♖xd5 52. h7 ♖h5 53. ♕b4+ 1–0

☑ 57

Savić – Jeremić, *Budva 2003*

16...♘cxe5! 17. dxe5 (17. ♘xe5 ♘xe5 18. dxe5 ♗xb5 19. ♘xb5 ♖xc1 20. ♕xc1 ♕xb5∓) 17...♗xb5 18. ♘xb5 ♖xc1 19. ♘d6+ ♕xd6! 20. ♕xc1 ♕a6 21. ♕e3 0–0∓ 22. ♖c1 h6 23. ♗d4 b6 24. ♖c7 ♕a4 25. ♔g2 a5 26. ♖a7 ♕d1 27. bxa5 ♗g5 28. ♘xg5 ♕xg4+ 29. ♔f1 ♕d1+ 30. ♔e1 ♕xd4 31. ♘f3 ♕g4 32. ♕e3 bxa5 33. ♘e1 ♕c4+ 34. ♕e2 ♘xe5 35. ♖xa5 ♖b8 36. ♕xc4 ♘xc4 37. ♖a7 e5 38. a4 ♖b1 39. a5 d4 40. a6 d3 41. ♖a8+ ♔h7 42. a7 d2 43. ♖h8+ ♔g6 0–1

☑ 58

Movsesian – Berkes, *Budapest 2003*

18...♘dxe5 19. ♘xe5 ♘xe5 20. dxe5 d4 21. ♘a4 ♕b5 22. ♗xd4 ♕xa4 23. ♕e3?! (23. ♖fc1!±) 23...♖d5 24. ♖bc1 ♕d7! 25. ♗xa7 ♖d3= 26. ♕b6 ♗d8 27. ♕c5 ♖d5 28. ♕e3 ♖d3 29. ♕c5 ½–½

☑ 59

Sveshnikov – Chernin, *52nd USSR Championship, Riga 1985*

10...♘xd4 11. ♘xd4 ♗c5 12. ♘e2 ♗xf2+ 13. ♔f1 f6 14. ♗a4

14.♘bc3! fxe5 15. g3 ♘e7 16. ♔g2 ♗e3 17. ♖f1±.

14...fxe5 15. ♗xd7+? (15. ♘bc3!) **15... ♔xd7 16. ♕a4+ ♖c6 17. g3 ♘e7 18. ♔g2 ♘f5 19. ♘bc3 ♗xg3 20. ♘xg3 ♘h4+ 21. ♔f1 ♖f8+ 22. ♔e1 ♕f2+ 23. ♔d1 ♕xg3** 23...♖f3! 24. ♕b5□ ♖xg3 (24...♕xg3 25. ♕xb7+ ♖c7 26. ♕b5+ ♔e7 27. ♗d2) 25. ♕xb7+ (25. ♖f1 ♕d4+ 26. ♗d2 ♕b6∓) 25...♖c7 26. ♕b5+ ♔e7∓.

24. ♕xa7 ♕f3+ 25. ♔c2 ♕e4+ 26. ♔b3 ♕c4+

26...♛×h1!? 27. ♛×b7+ ♖c7 28. ♛b5+ ♔c8
29. ♛a6+ ♔b8 30. ♗f4 ♛×a1 31. ♗×e5 ♛f1!?
(31...♛g1 32. ♗×c7+ ♔×c7 33. ♘b5+ ♔b8
34. ♛d6+ ♔b7 35. ♛×f8 ♛e3+ 36. ♔a2∓)
32. ♛b6+ ♔a8 33. ♗×c7 ♛c4+ 34. ♔c2 ♘f5
35. ♛a5+ ♔b7 36. ♛b6+ ♔c8 37. ♛b8+ ♔d7
38. ♛×f8 ♛×c7∓.

**27. ♔c2 ♛e4+ 28. ♔b3 ♛c4+ 29. ♔c2
♛e4+ ½–½**

☑ 60

Jonkman – Smeets, *Groningen 2002*

13...g5! 14. ♗g3 (14. ♗×g5 ♛g7 15. ♛g4
[15. ♘f3 ♗×f3–+] 15...h6∓) **14...h5 15. h3
g4 16. h×g4 h4 17. ♗h2 h3 18. f4 h×g2
19. ♖f2 ♛g7 20. ♖×g2 ♗×g2 21. ♔×g2 ♛h6
22. ♗g3 ♛h3+ 23. ♔f2 ♘h6 24. ♗e2 ♗e7
25. ♘e4 ♗h4 26. g5 ♗×g3+ 27. ♘×g3 ♛h2+
28. ♔f3 ♘f5 29. ♘f1 ♖h3+ 30. ♔e4 d3 0–1**

☑ 61

Degraeve – Arencibia, *Guelph 2002*

**44...♘×g5 45. f×g5 ♖×g5!? 46. ♗×g5 ♗×g5
47. ♛d1 ♗f4 48. ♗e2 ♛b6 49. g4 h×g3+
50. ♔g2 ♗×e5 51. ♖h3 ♗b8 52. ♖gh1 e5
53. ♖h6 ♗c6 54. ♖f1 f4 55. d×e5 ♗×e5
56. ♗f3 ♖d8 57. ♛e2 ♗b8 58. ♖d1 ♖e8
59. ♛f1 ♛c5 60. ♖d4 ♗b5 61. ♛d1 ♗c4
62. ♖h5 ♛b6 63. ♛d2 ♗c7 64. ♖h7 ♛c5
65. ♛d1 ♔a7 66. ♛d2 ♖e3 67. ♛d1 ♛b6
68. ♖d2 ♗e5 69. ♛h1 0–1**

☑ 62

Najer – Volkov, *St. Petersburg 2004*

**22...♔d7 23. ♔g2 ♔c7 24. ♖c1 ♔b8
25. ♖c2 ♖g8 26. ♖c5 ♛b6 27. ♛h7 ♛d8
28. ♖c1 g6 29. ♛×f7 g×h5 30. ♛×h5 ♛b6
31. ♗×h6 ♖a2 32. ♗e3 ♘a5 33. ♛f7 ♖×g4+
34. ♔h3 ♘×b3 35. ♖c3 ♛×b4 36. ♛e8+
♔a7 37. ♖c8 ♖×f2 38. ♗×f2 ♖f4 39. ♔g3
♖f8 40. ♛d7 ♘c5 41. ♖×c5 ♗×c5 42. ♛×e6
♛b3 43. ♛g4 ♗b6 44. e6 ♗c7+ 45. ♔g2**

♗d6 46. ♘e5 ♖h8 47. ♗g3 ♛c2+ 48. ♗f2
♛b1 49. ♗g3 ♛b2+ 50. ♗f2 ♛c2 51. ♔g1
♛b1+ 52. ♔g2 ♛h1+ 53. ♔g3 ♖h2 0–1

☑ 63

Khamrakulov – Matamoros Franco, *Coria del
Río 2004*

16...e5!? (16...f5!?) **17. ♗×h7+ ♔h8 18. ♘h4
f5 19. g×f5 ♛h6 20. ♘g6+ ♘×g6 21. ♗×g6
e×d4 22. ♛d3 ♛h4+ 23. ♔d1 ♛g4+ 0–1**

☑ 64

Dvoiris – Korchnoi, *Beer Sheva 2004*

**16...♛d8! 17. ♔g2 g5 18. h×g5 h×g5 19. ♖h1
♖g8 20. ♛d3 ♔d7 21. ♗d2 ♛b6 22. ♔f1
f4 23. g×f4 g×f4 24. ♖h5 ♛a6 25. ♛×a6
b×a6 26. ♖h7 ♖ab8 27. b4 ♗g4 28. ♘eg1
♗f5 29. ♖×f7 ♔e6 30. ♖×e7+ ♔×e7 31. ♔e2
♗g4 32. ♔f1 a×b4 33. a×b4 ♘×b4 34. ♗×f4
♘c2 35. ♖c1 ♖b2 36. ♗g5+ ♔e6 37. ♗d2
♖f8 38. ♘g5+ ♔f5 39. f3 ♘×d4 40. f×g4+
♔×g4+ 41. ♔e1 ♖×d2 42. ♘h7 ♖g2 0–1**

☑ 65

Erenburg – Korchnoi, *Beer Sheva 2004*

**25...f5 26. ♗×b7 ♖b8 27. ♗a6 f×g4
28. ♛×c4 ♖×f4 29. ♖f2 ♛f5 30. d5 ♛b6
31. ♘×a4 ♛e3 32. ♖e2 e×d5 33. ♛c7 ♛×a3
34. ♛×b8+ ♘g8 35. ♖×f5 ♗×f5 36. ♗b2
♛×a4 37. b6 ♗c5+ 38. ♔g2 ♛×a6 39. ♖f2
♗e4+ 40. ♔g3 ♛d3+ 0–1**

☑ 66

Peng Xiaomin – Korchnoi, *Calcutta 2000*

19...♘×h4!? 20. ♘×h4 (20. ♗d2!?) **20...
♗×g5 21. ♛d1! ♗×c1 22. ♛×h5 ♗e8 23. ♗d3
f5**

The only move, after which the players
agreed a draw in view of the perpetual check
24. e×f6□ ♗×h5 25. ♖×g7+ ♔h8 26. ♖h7+
½–½

☑ **67**

Grischuk – Kolev, *34ᵗʰ Olympiad, Istanbul 2000*

14. ♘c2 ♖dg8 15. a3 g5 16. h×g5 ♘×g5 17. ♗×g5 ♗×g5 18. b4 ♗e7 19. ♗e4 c×b4 20. a×b4 ♘×b4 21. ♘×b4 ♗×b4 22. c5 ♗×c5 23. ♖b1 ♗b4 24. ♕c2+ ♗c6 25. ♗×c6 b×c6 26. ♖×b4 ♕×b4 27. ♕×c6+ ♔d8 28. ♖d1 ♔e7 29. ♕c7+ 1–0

☑ **68**

Grischuk – Kolev, *34ᵗʰ Olympiad, Istanbul 2000*

10. c4! d4 11. ♗d3 ♘f7 12. ♖e1 ♗e7 13. h4! 0–0–0 and so on, as in Position 67.

☑ **69**

Radulski – Oms Pallise, *Andorra la Vella 2002*

31. ♘h7 ♖de8 32. ♘g5 ♕c6 33. ♘h3 ♖e6 34. ♘f4 ♖d8 35. ♘×e6 ♕×e6 36. ♕f4 ♔b6 37. f3 ♖h8 38. ♕g5 ♔a5 39. ♕f6 ♖e8

40. ♕×e6 f×e6 41. ♔f2 ♖f8 42. ♔e3 ♔a4 43. ♔f4 a5 44. ♔g5 b4 45. a×b4 a×b4 46. ♔×g6 ♘a5 47. ♖a1+ ♔b5 48. ♔g7 ♖b8 49. g4 f×g4 50. f×g4 h×g4 51. ♖f1 ♘c6 52. ♖f8 ♖b7+ 53. ♖f7 ♖b8 54. h5 ♔a4 55. ♖c7 ♘a5 56. ♖a7 b×c3 57. b×c3 ♔b3 58. ♖e3 ♘c6 59. ♖c7 1–0

☑ **70**

Ubiennykh – Verevochkina, *Voronezh 2004*

23. b3! c×b3 24. ♘×b3 ♘×b3 25. ♕a2 ♘e7 26. ♖×b3 ♕a6 27. ♖db1 ♖d7 28. ♖b5 ♘f5 29. ♕b3 ♗e7 30. ♗f2 ♖c8 31. a4 ♖c4 32. ♖a1 ♖dc7 33. ♗e1 ♗g5 34. ♕d1 ♘h6 35. ♖b2 ♖d7 36. h4! ♗e7 (36...g×h3 37. ♕h5) **37. ♗d2 ♘f5 38. ♕×g4 ♖c8 39. ♖b5 ♖dd8 40. ♔f2 ♕c6 41. ♖ab1 ♖c7 42. h5 a6 43. ♖b6 ♕×a4 44. ♕e2 ♔a8 45. g4 ♗h4+ 46. ♔g2 ♘e7 47. ♔h3 f5 48. ♔×h4 f×g4 49. ♘e3 ♘f5+ 50. ♘×f5 e×f5 51. e6 ♖h8 52. h6 ♕e8 53. ♕e5 ♕e7+ 54. ♔g3 ♖hc8 55. ♕×d5 ♕a3 56. ♔g2 ♕a4 57. ♖×b7 1–0**

Appendix

I- indicates page numbers in Volume 1

II- indicates page numbers in Volume 2

Index of themes

A

attack
on both wings, I-69
on the dark squares, I-51
on the king, I-12, I-13, I-25, I-26, I-28, I-30, I-32, I-33, I-35, II-20, II-22, II-23, II-53
on the king on the queenside, I-105
on the kingside, I-69

B

blockade, I-69, II-24
Black's struggle against, II-16
for and against, I-71, II-13, II-15, II-21, II-24, II-29, II-30
in the endgame, I-127, I-128, I-129, I-130
of centre pawns, I-14, I-15
of king or entire wing, I-131
of one wing, I-62, I-124
of the squares e5 and d4, I-79, I-111, I-113, I-115, I-116, I-117
blockading knight, I-15, I-112, I-119, I-121, II-14, II-28

C

counterattack on the king, II-38
counterplay by Black, II-18
against the d4 pawn, I-77
against the e5 pawn, II-35, II-36
on the c-file, II-38
on the kingside, I-37, I-39, II-16, II-37
on the queenside, II-11

D

development advantage, I-42, I-60, I-61, II-23, II-25, II-33
for Black, II-13, II-17, II-38

E

endgame
transition into, I-42
typical, I-47, I-49, II-32, II-34

M

material advantage, converting, I-64, I-65

P

pawn break f7–f6, I-71, I-75, I-77
pawn centre, giving up, I-79
pawn sacrifice, II-16
by Black for the initiative, II-18
for lead in development, I-44
for the initiative, I-57, II-25, II-26, II-27, II-28
to establish blockade, I-68, I-125, I-126, I-127, I-133, II-21, II-29
piece sacrifice, typical, I-61
play on both wings, I-13, I-44, I-49, I-61, I-62, I-82, I-84, I-86, I-88, I-90, I-93, I-95, I-97, I-99, I-101, I-103, I-105, I-106, II-12, II-14, II-15, II-18, II-19, II-25, II-39, II-40, II-41, II-42, II-43, II-45, II-46, II-47, II-48, II-49, II-50, II-52, II-53
play on the c-file, II-33
play on the dark squares, I-33, I-35, II-22, II-41

S

space advantage, I-42, I-44, I-49, I-51, I-53, I-55, I-60, I-61, I-62, I-64, I-65, II-18, II-24, II-32, II-33, II-34

W

weak colour complex, I-122, I-123
weakness of the dark squares, I-12, I-68

Index of names

A

Agdestein, Simen I-11
Alapin, Semyon I-124
Alekhine, Alexander I-19, I-20, I-21, I-25, I-70, I-108, I-109, II-15, II-23
Anand, Viswanathan I-44, I-45, I-46, I-47, I-48
Anderssen, Adolf I-13
Atalik, Suat II-59
Azmaiparashvili, Zurab I-130

B

Balashov, Yuri I-40
Bareev, Evgeny ...I-6, I-11, I-29, I-64, I-65, I-88, II-6, II-115
Barsky, Vladimir I-9, II-9
Bogoljubow, Jefim I-108
Boleslavsky, Isaac I-13
Bondarevsky, Igor I-19
Botvinnik, Mikhail ..I-19, I-23, I-40, I-91, I-109, II-16, II-23, II-113
Bronstein, David I-106, I-126, II-11, II-23, II-30, II-36, II-106
Burn, Amos I-16

C

Capablanca, José Raoul I-19, I-119, I-128
Chernin, Alexander I-23
Chigorin, Mikhail I-13

D

Dreev, Alexey I-88, I-89
Dvoiris, Semion II-52

E

Eingorn, Viacheslav I-71
Erenburg, Sergey II-114
Euwe, Max I-19, I-20, I-21, I-108, II-15, II-23

F

Filipenko, Alexander II-88
Fine, Reuben I-116
Fischer, Robert I-110
Flohr, Salo I-108, I-119
Fominikh, Alexander I-86
Fritz II-108
Ftáčnik, Ljubomir I-98

G

Glek, Igor ...I-23, I-114, II-58, II-62, II-79, II-91, II-92, II-93, II-108, II-110

H

Hort, Vlastimil II-19, II-23

K

Kaidanov, Gregory II-62
Karpov, Anatoly I-7, I-11, I-60, I-70, I-110, II-7
Kasparov, Garry I-6, I-19, I-109, I-110, II-6, II-22
Keres, Paul I-16, I-19, I-20, I-88, II-27, II-58, II-60, II-61, II-107, II-112
Kharlov, Andrey II-80
Korchnoi, Victor I-11, I-22, I-23, I-96, I-119, I-120, I-121, II-19, II-20, II-23, II-66, II-113, II-114
Kupreichik, Victor I-21, I-22, I-23, I-33, I-71

L

Larsen, Bent I-110
Lasker, Emanuel I-18, I-19
Lempert, Igor II-73
Levenfish, Grigory I-16, I-19, I-71, I-112, II-16
Lputian, Smbat I-23, I-71, I-85, I-103, I-105, II-52
Lysenko, A. II-70

M

Malaniuk, Vladimir I-23
Maróczy, Géza I-16
Mestel, Jonathan I-106
Morphy, Paul I-13, II-13
Motylev, Alexander I-23

N

Nimzowitsch, Aaron I-13, I-14, I-15, I-16, I-17, I-18, I-19, I-20, I-21, I-57, I-63, I-108, I-109, I-110, I-111, I-112, I-113, I-115, I-116, I-117, I-124, I-126, I-127, II-16, II-112
Notkin, Maxim I-100, I-101, II-51

O

Oll, Lembit I-79

P

Pachmann, Ludek I-19
Paulsen, Louis ..I-13, I-14, I-15, I-16, I-18, I-23, II-20, II-112
Peng Xiaomin I-96
Petrosian, Tigran ...I-19, I-21, I-90, I-110, I-126, II-17, II-23
Piskov, Yuri II-92
Polgár, Judit I-120
Portisch, Lajos II-44, II-113
Potapov, Alexander I-129
Predojević, Borki II-65
Prokhorovich, Taras I-85
Psakhis, Lev I-23, I-35, I-55, I-90, II-51, II-65

R

Radjabov, Teimour I-80
Rauzer, Vsevolod I-19, I-20, I-21
Razuvaev, Yuri I-23, I-70, I-71, I-73, I-74, I-113, I-115
Romanishin, Oleg I-23
Romanovsky, Pyotr I-110
Rubinstein, Akiba I-16, I-17, I-18
Rublevsky, Sergey I-37
Réti, Richard I-110

S

Sakaev, Konstantin II-82
Salwe, Georg I-16, I-111
Sax, Gyula I-23
Schwarz, Adolf I-15
Shirov, Alexey ..I-23, I-44, I-45, I-46, I-97, I-98, II-85
Short, Nigel I-60, I-103, II-60
Sieiro González, Luis I-47
Smyslov, Vasily I-19, II-16
Spassky, Boris I-19, II-19, II-20, II-23
Spielmann, Rudolf I-108
Steinitz, Wilhelm I-11, I-15, I-16, I-18, I-108, I-113, II-23, II-112

Ståhlberg, Gideon I-108
Sveshnikov, Evgeny .I-6, I-7, I-23, I-37, I-40, II-6, II-7, II-97, II-116, II-119
Svidler, Peter I-23, I-55, I-56, II-38, II-65

T

Tal, Mikhail I-19, I-28, I-110, I-126, II-17
Tarrasch, Siegbert I-11, I-18, I-110, I-124
Timman, Jan I-60, I-61, II-51
Tseitlin, Mark II-115

U

Uhlmann, Wolfgang I-23, I-75
Ulibin, Mikhail II-70
Unzicker, Wolfgang I-13

V

Vaganian, Rafael I-8, I-33, I-82, II-8
Vaisser, Anatoly I-90
Vidmar, Milan I-111
Volkov, Sergey I-23, I-55, I-56, I-57

W

Wely, Loek van I-98, II-84

Y

Yakovenko, Dmitry I-129
Yusupov, Artur I-23

Z

Zaitsev, Igor ..I-21, I-22, I-23, I-42, I-106, I-113, II-47, II-110
Zlotnik, Boris I-26, II-63

Index of games

A page number in normal print means the first-named player had White; bold indicates that the player had Black; italic is used for games in the Encyclopaedia section. A page number between brackets means that a reference to this game can be found on the page indicated.

A

Abdul Satar, A. – Euwe **II-14**
Abrahamyan, Tatev – Shabalov **II-127**
Abramović, Bosko – Kosić *II-71*
Ács, Péter – Párkányi *II-70*
Adams, Michael – Epishin *II-76*
 – Illescas Cordoba *II-63*
 – Lputian *II-73*
 – Vaganian *II-73*, *II-82*
Adorján, András – Faragó *II-92*
Agrinsky, Vladimir – Sveshnikov **I-121**, *II-61*
Ahmed – Euwe **II-15**
Akobian, Varuzhan – Shabalov **I-151**
Akopian, Vladimir – Khalifman **I-29**, *II-73*
Alapin, Simon – Tarrasch I-124
Alavkin, Arseny – Driamin I-43
 – Motylev **[II-118]**
 – Sveshnikov **II-120**
Albert, Horacio – Sanguinetti **I-146**
Alekhine, Alexander – A. Marshall II-15
 – Euwe I-20, *II-60*
 – Muffang *II-71*
 – Nimzowitsch **II-15**, *II-59*
Alekseev, Evgeny – Ivanov [II-118]
 – Rustemov I-34, *II-67*
 – S. Ivanov *II-76*
Alekseev, Vadim – Boe Olsen *II-56*
 – Vysochin *II-56*
Alexandrescu, Gheorghe – Keres *II-58*
Alvarez Vila, Aroa – Karlovich *II-58*
Anand, Viswanathan – Gurevich *II-87*
 – M. Gurevich I-47
 – Nunn *II-80*
 – Rogers *II-57*
 – Shirov **I-44**, **(II-26)**, *II-65*, **(II-113)**
Anastasian, Ashot – Motylev **II-124**
Andersson, Ulf – Christiansen *II-73*
 – Hort *II-91*
Antić, Dejan – Savić **II-31**, *II-95*
Antonio, Rogelio – Lputian II-31, *II-95*
Antoshin, Vladimir – Kasparian I-151
 – Polugaevsky *II-58*
Apicella, Manuel – Grischuk *II-109*
 – Prié *II-110*
Araslanov, W. – Sveshnikov I-133
Arencibia, Walter – Degraeve **I-155**
 – Klinger **I-85**
Arizmendi Martínez, Julen – Tiviakov *II-73*
Aseev, Konstantin – Rustemov *II-62*

Asrian, Karen – Potkin *II-66*
Atalik, Suat – Popadić *II-59*
 – Sveshnikov **I-148**, *II-80*
Atanasov, Petko – Sveshnikov *II-78*
Azmaiparashvili, Zurab – Nisipeanu **I-130**

B

Bagamasbad, Efren – Torre **I-34**, **(I-43)**, *II-68*
Bagirov, Vladimir – Kupreichik *II-94*
Bagoly, János – Párkányi *II-87*
Baklan, Vladimir – Florath *II-107*
 – Moskalenko I-49, *II-98*
Balashov, Yuri – Belozerov I-49, *II-98*
 – Motylev **I-151**, *II-108*
 – Sveshnikov **I-39**, **I-40**, *II-77*, *II-109*
Baranov, Valentin – Yakhin *II-59*
Bareev, Evgeny – Benjamin *II-95*
 – Eingorn *II-62*
 – Grischuk **I-28**, **I-29**, **I-79**, *II-72*, *II-74*, *II-78*
 – Ivanchuk **I-30**, *II-103*, *II-109*
 – Ivanović **I-79**, *II-77*
 – Morozevich **(I-77)**, **II-36**, *II-100*, **(II-114)**
 – Ni Hua **I-75**, *II-110*
 – Sankovich *II-96*
 – Short *II-60*
 – Sveshnikov **I-64**, **I-65**, **(I-102)**, **(I-116)**, *II-73*, *II-100*, *II-101*, *II-102*, **(II-115)**, **[II-116]**, **II-131**
 – Topalov *II-95*
Barsov, Alexey – Charbonneau **I-97**, *II-85*
 – Degraeve **I-151**
 – Ehlvest *II-86*
 – Hadzimanolis *II-86*
 – Reefat *II-81*
Barua, Dibyendu – Sandipan **I-45**
Bashkov, Viacheslav – Sveshnikov *II-79*, *II-87*, *II-88*
Batchuluun, Tsegmed – Sveshnikov **II-132**
Bauer, Christian – Karpachev *II-95*
 – Lautier **II-50**, **(II-114)**
 – Najer *II-56*
 – Prié *II-56*
Becker, Albert – Maróczy *II-58*
Bednarski, Jacek – Hennings *II-56*
Beliakov, Alexander – Smirnov *II-93*
Beliavsky, Alexander – Illescas Cordoba *II-63*
 – Ivell *II-63*
 – Svidler *II-102*
Belkhodja, Slim – Morovic Fernandez II-50
Bellucco, G. – Longo I-146

Belov, Vladimir – Lisy I-147, *II-66*, II-120
Belozerov, Andrey – Balashov **I-49**, *II-98*
– Smirnov **I-50**, *II-98*
Benjamin, Joel – Bareev *II-95*
– Grétarsson *II-94*
– Gulko I-27, II-38, *II-79*, *II-80*, *II-86*
– Kavalek *II-57*
– Korchnoi *II-93*
– Lau *II-56*
Berend, Fred – Sveshnikov **II-127**
Bergstrom, Rolf – Kiriakov *II-85*
Berkes, Ferenc – Movsesian **I-154**
Bern, Ivar – Shirov **I-150**
Bertholee, Rob – Dvoiris *II-71*
Bisguier, Arthur – Westerinen *II-91*
Bjerke, Richard – Sveshnikov **I-123**
Blackburne, Joseph Henry – Paulsen **I-14**, *II-71*
Blasek, Ralph – Kishnev *II-92*
Blatný, Pavel – Gonzalez Rodriguez *II-58*
Bluvshtein, Mark – Charbonneau **I-31**, *II-106*
– Shabalov **I-154**
Bochkarev, Vasily – Sveshnikov **II-128**
Boe Olsen, Mads – Alekseev *II-56*
Bondarevsky, Igor – Botvinnik II-16, *II-60*
Borg, Geoffrey – Nikolić *II-91*
Borges Mateos, Juan – Bronstein **II-24**
Bosch, Jeroen – Lputian II-50
Botvinnik, Mikhail – Bondarevsky **II-16**, *II-60*
– Levenfish *II-60*
– Rabinovich *II-59*
Brenninkmeijer, Joris – Sax *II-87*
Bricard, Emmanuel – Degraeve *II-78*
Brinckmann, Alfred – Nimzowitsch I-125
Bronstein, David – Borges Mateos II-24
– Korchnoi *II-58*
– Kärner (I-36), II-23, *II-57*
– Mestel I-106, *II-107*
– Roos II-24, *II-106*
Brumen, Dinko – Sveshnikov **(I-38)**, **(I-107)**, **II-48**,
II-88
Brumm, Carsten – Teloudis I-148
Brunello, Sabino – Luther II-120
Buchnicek, Petr – Sebenik *II-106*
Bukal, Vladimir – Pavasović *II-70*
– Romero Holmes *II-72*
Bukhman, Eduard – Vasyukov **I-104**, **II-50**, *II-102*,
(II-114)
Burn, Amos – Steinitz **I-16**, *II-91*

C

Camara, Helder – Kharlov **I-124**
Camilleri, Henry – Uhlmann *II-96*
Campora, Daniel Hugo – Dreev *II-89*
Capablanca, José Raoul
– Flohr **I-119**, **I-127**
– Paredes II-14
Cardenas Serrano, Sergio – Garcia *II-61*

Carlsen, Magnus – Rustemov **I-34**, *II-68*
Casper, Thomas – Knaak I-75, *II-107*
– Möhring *II-93*
– Sveshnikov *II-110*
– Uhlmann I-75, *II-107*
Castro Rojas, Oscar – Korchnoi *II-93*
Charbonneau, Pascal – Barsov I-97, *II-85*
– Bluvshtein **I-31**, *II-106*
Charochkin, Michael – Kupreichik **I-147**, *II-70*
Chaumont, Adeline – Penalver *II-91*
Cherniaev, Alexander – Dzhakaev I-94, I-148, *II-86*
– Fernández Hernández *II-82*
– Harestad *II-109*
– Korniukhin II-30
– Korniushin *II-106*
– Mason II-123
– Pert *II-86*
– Sveshnikov *II-74*
Chernin, Alexander – Psakhis *II-71*
– Sveshnikov **(I-26)**, **I-154**, *II-72*, **II-76**
– Torre *II-98*
Christiansen, Larry – Andersson *II-73*
Cifuentes Parada, Roberto – Sokolov *II-84*
Circenis, Feliks – Katishonok II-27, *II-108*
Claesen, Pieter – Schürmans *II-96*
Clarke, Thomas – Hurley **I-78**
Cochrane, John – Staunton II-12
Conquest, Stuart – Pelletier *II-107*
Crosa, Martin – Leitão *II-60*
Csom, Istvan – Portisch I-148
Czebe, Attila – Nakamura I-130

D

Dambrauskas, Virginijus – Sveshnikov *II-65*
Damjanović, Mato – Dür **(I-53)**, **II-29**, *II-97*
Danielian, Oganes – Landa *II-102*
– Sveshnikov *II-66*
Darga, Klaus – Padevsky *II-92*
Degraeve, Jean-Marc
– Arencibia **I-155**
– Barsov I-151
– Bricard *II-78*
– Sokolov *II-105*
Del Rio Angelis, Salvador
– Saldano Dayer **I-78**
– Shirov **II-121**
Delchev, Alexander – Gurevich I-149, *II-85*
– Moreno Carnero I-151
– Volkov **(I-55)**, I-150, *II-65*
Deutsch, Eyal – Erenburg *II-57*
Dgebuadse, Alexandre – Hendriks **I-50**
Dimitrov, Vladimir – Prié *II-78*
Dittmar, Peter – Jonkman **I-49**
Dizdar, Goran – Grosar **I-93**, *II-85*, *II-88*
– Orak *II-86*
– Palleja *II-80*
– Stević *II-81*, *II-85*

– Sveshnikov **(I-38)**, **(I-107)**, **II-49**, **II-80**, **II-89**, **II-131**
Dobosz, Henryk – Krason **II-56**
Doda, Zbigniew – I. Zaitsev **II-25**
– Zaitsev **(II-38)**, **II-63**
Doesburgh, Gerrit van – Keres **II-58**
Doghri, Nabil – Matsuo I-126
Dokhoian, Yuri – Fedorowicz **II-100**
– Hector **II-59**
– Kamsky **II-100**
– Kharlov **II-80**
Dolmadian, Arshak – Inkiov **II-91**
Dolmatov, Sergey – Hertneck **II-87**
– Khalifman **(I-51)**, **(I-65)**, **(I-101)**, **II-22**, **II-101**, **(II-115)**
– Kharlov **II-77**
– Sandipan **II-122**
– Sveshnikov **I-27**, **(II-45)**, **II-85**
– Yemelin **I-102**, **II-101**, **(II-122)**
Donchev, Dimitar – Sveshnikov **(I-47)**, **I-152**, **II-32**, **II-110**
Donev, Ivo Hristov – Gärtner I-104
Doroshkevich, Vladimir – Sveshnikov **I-65**, **(I-77)**, **I-150**, **II-100**, **II-101**, **(II-115)**
Dražić, Sinisa
– Grosar **II-89**
– Sveshnikov **I-42**
Dreev, Alexey – Campora **II-89**
– Kharlov **I-40**
– Sax **II-63**, **II-81**
– Sveshnikov **I-37**, **I-88**, **II-88**
– Yagupov **II-88**
– Zaitsev **I-88**
Driamin, Dmitry – Alavkin **I-43**
Drosdovsky, Yuri – Rainfray **I-52**
Drvota, Antonin – Schmidt **II-94**
Dür, Arne – Damjanović **(I-53)**, II-29, **II-97**
Duhme, Alexander – Nimzowitsch **I-124**
Dukhov, Alexander – Sveshnikov **(I-64)**, **I-116**, **II-74**
Dvoiris, Semion – Bertholee **II-71**
– Eingorn **II-61**
– Gleizerov I-152, **II-80**
– Korchnoi I-155
– Naumkin I-149
– Sveshnikov **(I-101)**, **(I-104)**, **II-52**, **II-71**, **II-102**, **(II-114)**
– Vaganian **II-58**
– Willemze **II-86**
– Zakharevich **II-87**
Dzhakaev, Dshakai – Cherniaev **I-148**, **II-86**
Dzhakaev, Dzhakai – Cherniaev **I-94**

E
Edelman, Daniel – Glek **II-73**
Ehlvest, Jaan – Barsov **II-86**
– Minasian **II-84**
– Sveshnikov **[I-113]**, **[I-118]**, **II-66**

– Thompson I-153
– Vaganian **II-57**
Einarsson, Bergstein – Vlassov **I-77**
Eingorn, Viacheslav – Bareev **II-62**
– Dvoiris **II-61**
– Sveshnikov **I-61**, **I-62**, **II-105**, **II-109**, **II-110**
Enders, Peter – Uhlmann II-35, **II-106**
Epishin, Vladimir – Adams **II-76**
– Rozentalis **II-92**
– Sveshnikov **I-79**, **II-77**
Epstein, Esther – Saunina **II-96**
Erashchenko, Denis – Moiseenko **I-42**
Erenburg, Sergey – Deutsch **II-57**
– Gunnarsson **II-61**
– Korchnoi I-155
– Sangma **II-109**
Ermenkov, Evgeny – Spassov **II-86**
Euwe, Max – Abdul Satar II-14
– Ahmed II-15
– Alekhine **I-20**, **II-60**
– Graves **II-91**
– Kramer I-148, **II-93**
Evans, Larry – Sherwin **II-110**

F
Faragó, Iván – Adorján **II-92**
– Gobet **II-109**
– Hába **II-32**, **II-107**
– I. Zaitsev **I-105**
– Kupreichik **II-70**
– Psakhis **II-108**
– Sveshnikov **I-25**, **II-72**, **II-111**
– Zaitsev **(II-47)**, **II-111**
Fedorowicz, John – Dokhoian **II-100**
Feigin, Mikhail – Kupreichik **II-67**
Fernández Hernández, Gerardo – Cherniaev **II-82**
Filipenko, Alexander – Sveshnikov **II-28**, **II-95**
Filippov, Alexey – Sveshnikov **II-130**
Filippov, Valery – Potkin **I-77**, **II-100**, **(II-114)**
Fingerov, Dmitry – Vysochin I-147, **II-66**
Firman, Nazar – Ginzburg **II-56**
Flohr, Salo – Capablanca I-119, I-127
Florath, Patrick – Baklan **II-107**
Flores, Diego – Vallejo Pons I-95, **(I-104)**, **II-102**
Foisor, Ovidiu – Guido **II-45**, **II-80**
– Romanishin **I-72**
– Sveshnikov **II-88**
Fominikh, Alexander – Mukhametov **II-66**
– Sveshnikov **I-86**, **II-87**
Fressinet, Laurent – Halkias II-124
– Salaun **II-100**
– Shirov **I-147**
– Soćko **I-151**, **II-97**
Furlan, Miha – Grosar **I-149**
– Sveshnikov **II-84**
Furman, Semion – Kupreichik **II-71**

G

Gärtner, Guntram – Donev **I-104**
Gafner, Evgeny – Snatenkov I-50, *II-98*
Galdunts, Sergey – Gavrilov *II-63*
Gallagher, Joseph – Glek *II-74*
Galstian, Beniamin – Sveshnikov **II-129**
Galyas, Miklós – Predojević ***II-86***
García Fernández, Carlos – Rayo Gutiérrez *II-109*
Garcia, Jesus – Cardenas Serrano *II-61*
Gavrilov, Alexey – Galdunts ***II-63***
Gdański, Jacek
  – McShane **II-30**, ***II-95***
  – Owczarzak *II-110*
  – Przewoźnik *II-82*
Geller, Efim – Zaitsev **II-26**, ***II-65***
Genov, Petar – Sveshnikov I-148, ***II-92***
Gerbich, Vladimir – Wolf ***II-63***
Gershkovich, David – Petrosian *II-59*
Gertler, David – Polgar *II-105*
Ghane Gardeh, Shojaat – Sveshnikov **II-128**
Ginzburg, Mikhail – Firman *II-56*
Gleizerov, Evgeny – Dvoiris **I-152**, ***II-80***
  – Jerić ***II-70***
  – Kharlov ***II-98***
  – Nei ***II-59***
  – Rodríguez ***II-70***
  – Sveshnikov ***II-80***, ***II-85***
Glek, Igor – Edelman ***II-73***
  – Gallagher ***II-74***
  – Kogan ***II-60***
  – Krasnov ***II-92***
  – Maciejewski ***II-92***
  – Moroz ***II-108***
  – Sax ***II-71***
  – Schlosser ***II-73***
  – Short ***II-73***
  – Sveshnikov **I-64**, ***II-73***
  – Wempe **I-47**, ***II-87***
  – Yurtaev *II-79*
  – Zlotnik *II-91*
Gligorić, Svetozar
  – Sveshnikov **I-128**
  – Unzicker **I-14**
Gobet, Fernand – Faragó *II-109*
Gofshtein, Leonid – Sveshnikov **I-153**, **II-47**, ***II-110***
Goloshchapov, Alexander – Volkov *II-63*
  – Zakharevich *II-87*
Golovanov, Andrey – Sveshnikov **II-53**
Gonzalez Rodriguez, Jorge – Blatný ***II-58***
Gorelov, Sergey – Yudasin *II-100*
Gossell, Thomas – Shulman *II-92*
Graf, Alexander – Grischuk **(I-47)**, **I-99**, ***II-84***
  – Sveshnikov ***II-84***
Graves – Euwe *II-91*
Greco, Gioacchino – N.N. I-12, (I-25), **II-11**
Greenfeld, Alon – Sher *II-85*
Grétarsson, Helgi Áss – Benjamin ***II-94***

Griezne, Edvins – Prokhorov **I-149**
Grigoriev, Nikolai – Rauzer **I-19**, ***II-60***
Grischuk, Alexander – Apicella *II-109*
  – Bareev I-28, I-29, I-79, *II-72*, *II-74*, *II-78*
  – Graf (I-47), I-99, *II-84*
  – Gulko *II-80*
  – Gurevich (I-43), *II-68*, *II-86*
  – Kaidanov *II-87*
  – Kolev I-156
  – Korchnoi *II-108*
  – Kruppa *II-103*
  – Lputian I-101, *II-101*, (II-115)
  – M. Gurevich I-33, I-93
  – Najer I-29, *II-72*
  – Pelletier *II-107*
  – Pert *II-72*
  – Radjabov I-79, II-34, II-50, *II-77*, *II-78*, *II-103*
  – Sakaev I-102, *II-101*
  – Short *II-76*
  – Zhang Pengxiang I-102, *II-101*
Grosar, Aljosa – Dizdar I-93, *II-85*, *II-88*
  – Dražić *II-89*
  – Furlan I-149
  – Jelen *II-102*
  – Raičević I-148, *II-98*
  – Sulava I-150, *II-57*
  – Sveshnikov **(I-34)**, **I-42**, ***II-68***
  – Tabernig I-52
  – Weinzettl *II-97*
  – Zugaj I-42
Guido, Flavio – Foisor II-45, *II-80*
Gulko, Boris – Benjamin **I-27**, **II-38**, ***II-79***, ***II-80***, ***II-86***
  – Grischuk ***II-80***
  – Kupreichik ***II-78***
  – Sveshnikov **I-26**, ***II-76***, ***II-84***, ***II-86***
  – Vitolins *II-62*
Gunnarsson, Jón Victor – Erenburg *II-61*
Gurevich, Ilja – Motwani ***II-110***
Gurevich, Mikhail – Anand **I-47**, ***II-87***
  – Delchev **I-149**, ***II-85***
  – Grischuk **I-33**, **(I-43)**, **I-93**, ***II-68***, ***II-86***
  – Jonkman ***II-72***
  – Meessen ***II-82***
  – Movsesian **I-93**, ***II-84***
  – Sax ***II-73***
  – Seul ***II-60***
  – Shirov **I-149**, ***II-85***, ***II-103***
  – Sieiro González **I-47**, ***II-72***, ***II-87***
  – Spraggett ***II-61***
  – Sveshnikov **I-90**, ***II-88***
  – Wemmers **(I-93)**, **I-98**, ***II-84***
Gurgenidze, Bukhuti – Sveshnikov **I-88**
Gwaze, Robert – Summerscale *II-86*

H

Hába, Petr – Faragó II-32, *II-107*
  – Knaak *II-107*

– Kosić *II-103*
– Koutsin II-50
– Kupreichik **II-62**
– Mészáros *II-58*
– Potkin *II-76*
– Schmittdiel *II-110*
– Stojanov *II-97*
Hadzimanolis, Antonios – Barsov *II-86*
Halasz, Stefan – Soreghy II-26
Halkias, Stelios – Fressinet **II-124**
Hank, Holger – Klünter **II-66**
Hankipohja, Antti – Sorri *II-58*
Hansen, Curt – Timman **II-50, *II-102***
Hansen, Martin – Lovik I-146, *II-106*
Harestad, Hans Krogh – Cherniaev **II-109**
Hausner, Ivan – Hennings **II-108**
Hazenfuss, Wolfgang – Keres **II-60**
Heberla, Bartolomiej – Moskalik I-50, *II-98*
– Movsesian **I-49**, **II-98***
Hecht, Hans-Joachim – Karpov **II-62**
Hector, Jonny – Dokhoian *II-59*
Heinz, Timothee – Linder I-34
Hendriks, Willy – Dgebuadse I-50
Hengl, Christian – Luft *II-66*
Hennings, Artur – Bednarski *II-56*
– Hausner *II-108*
Hernandez, Gilberto – Vallejo Pons **I-149**
Hertneck, Gerald – Dolmatov **II-87**
– Kupreichik **II-96**
– Sandipan **II-84**
Hillarp Persson, Tiger – Vallejo Pons **[II-117]**
Hjartarson, Jóhan – Korchnoi *II-82*
Hoàng, Thanh Trang – Sveshnikov **I-42, (I-84)**, *II-97*
Hodgson, Julian – Morozevich *II-60*
– Ree *II-61*
Hoffman, Alejandro – Psakhis *II-62*
Honfi, Károly – Uhlmann I-75, *II-59*, *II-106*
Hort, Vlastimil – Andersson *II-91*
– Motylev **I-30**, ***II-106***
– Romanishin **II-81**
– Spassky II-21, (II-31), *II-95*
Howell, James – Mestel *II-63*
Hug, Werner – Makropoulos **II-58**
Hulak, Krunoslav – Sveshnikov **II-66**
Hurley, John – Clarke I-78
Huzman, Alexander – Kupreichik **I-117**, ***II-94***

I

Ibragimov, Ildar – Volzhin I-50, *II-98*
Ilinsky, Vladimir – Remizov **II-108**
Illescas Cordoba, Miguel
– Adams **II-63**
– Beliavsky *II-63*
– Speelman I-146
Ilyushin, Alexey – Kharlov **II-110**
– Vlassov **I-31**, ***II-106***
Inkiov, Ventzislav – Dolmadian ***II-91***

Ionescu, Konstantin – Nisipeanu **II-67**
Iruzubieta Villaluenga, Jesus – Korchnoi **(I-54)**, **II-33**, **II-97**
Iskusnykh, Sergey – Sveshnikov **II-81**
Iuldachev, Saidali – Kotronias I-149
Ivanchuk, Vasily – Bareev I-30, *II-103*, *II-109*
– Oll **I-79**, ***II-77***
– Romanishin **II-78**
– Short *II-79*
– Ye Jiangchuan **II-57**
Ivanov, Jordan – Motylev **II-78**
– Sveshnikov **I-115**
Ivanov, Sergey – Alekseev **II-76**, **[II-118]**
– Lastin **I-51**, **(I-77)**, **(II-50)**, ***II-101***
– Malysheva **I-52**
– Movsesian ***II-96***
– Shabalov **II-122**
– Sveshnikov ***II-93***
Ivanović, Bozidar
– Bareev I-79, *II-77*
– Levitt I-147
Ivell, Nicholas – Beliavsky *II-63*
Ivkov, Borislav – Sveshnikov **II-47**, ***II-110***
– Velimirović **II-26**, ***II-65***

J

Jelen, Iztok – Grosar **II-102**
Jeremić, Veljko – Savić **I-154**
Jerić, Simon – Gleizerov *II-70*
Jóhannesson, Ingvar – Timman **(I-93)**, **I-97**, ***II-85***
Jolles, Hajo – Sveshnikov **II-73**
Jonkman, Harmen – Dittmar I-49
– Gurevich *II-72*
– Sadvakasov I-29, *II-72*
– Smeets I-155, *II-78*
– Stellwagen *II-78*
– Stevanović I-49
– Uhlmann *II-95*
Jorgensen, Per Henrik Dorff – Kupreichik **II-70**

K

Kacheishvili, Giorgi – Kupreichik **II-70**
– Peng Xiaomin **II-87**
Kärner, Hillar – Bronstein **(I-36)**, **II-23**
Kaidanov, Gregory – Grischuk **II-87**
– Khalifman **II-73**
– Razuvaev I-113
Kalinichenko – Karmov **II-76**
Kalinin, Oleg – Sveshnikov **II-76**, ***II-105***
Kaminski, Marcin – Kupreichik **II-70**
Kamsky, Gata – Dokhoian *II-100*
Kantoris, Agris – Strauts **II-92**
Karer, Gregor – Sveshnikov **II-86**
Karlovich, Anastasia – Alvarez Vila *II-58*
Karmov, Mazhmudin – Kalinichenko *II-76*
Kärner, Hillar – Bronstein **II-57**

– Kiik **II-57**
– Zaitsev **II-57**
Karpachev, Alexander – Bauer *II-95*
– Lukov *II-71*
– Siedentopf *II-94*
Karpov, Anatoly – Hecht **II-62**
– Xie Jun **I-79**, **II-77**
Kasparian, Genrich – Antoshin **I-151**
Kasparov, Garry – Klimczok II-22
Katishonok, Nikolai – Circenis **II-27**, **II-108**
– Sveshnikov **II-76**
Kavalek, Lubomir – Benjamin *II-57*
Keres, Paul – Alexandrescu *II-58*
– Hazenfuss *II-60*
– Ståhlberg II-35, *II-60*
– van Doesburgh *II-58*
Khairullin, Ildar – Matlakov *II-102*
Khalifman, Alexander – Akopian I-29, *II-73*
– Dolmatov (I-51), (I-65), (I-101), II-22, *II-101*, (II-115)
– Kaidanov *II-73*
– Shirov **I-52**, **II-101**
Khamrakulov, Ibragim – Matamoros Franco I-155
Kharlov, Andrey – Camara I-124
– Dokhoian *II-80*
– Dolmatov *II-77*
– Dreev I-40
– Gleizerov *II-98*
– Ilyushin *II-110*
– Kuporosov *II-73*
– Sakaev *II-82*
– Sveshnikov **I-40**, **II-77**
– Zakharevich *II-77*
Khasanova, Elmira – Korbut **II-66**
Kholmov, Ratmir – Naumkin *II-110*
– Petrosian II-18
– Vasyukov *II-73*
– Velimirović **II-58**, **II-60**
Kholopov, Alexander – Sveshnikov **II-79**
Kiik, Kalle – Korchnoi I-95, (II-50), *II-101*, (II-115)
– Kärner *II-57*
Kindermann, Stefan – Movsesian **II-84**
– Vatter **II-80**
– Yanovsky **II-80**
Kiriakov, Peter – Bergstrom **II-85**
– Sveshnikov **(I-27)**, **II-45**, **II-85**
Kiselev, Mikhail – Sveshnikov **II-106**
Kishnev, Sergey – Blasek **II-92**
Kislov, Gennady – Vysochin II-31, *II-95*
Kivisto, Mikko – Tukmakov *II-61*
Klimczok, Krystian – Kasparov **II-22**
Klinger, Josef – Arencibia I-85
– Portisch *II-105*
Klünter, Wilhelm – Hank *II-66*
Knaak, Rainer – Casper **I-75**, **II-107**
– Hába **II-107**
– Sax **II-105**

Kogan, Artur – Glek *II-60*
Kolev, Atanas – Grischuk **I-156**
Komarov, Dimitri – Sveshnikov **(I-21)**, **(I-42)**, **I-57**, **II-59**, **(II-112)**
Kontić, Djordje – Ulibin I-72
Korbut, Ekaterina – Khasanova *II-66*
– Novikova *II-109*
Korchnoi, Victor – Benjamin **II-93**
– Bronstein **II-58**
– Castro Rojas **II-93**
– Dvoiris **I-155**
– Erenburg **I-155**
– Grischuk **II-108**
– Hjartarson **II-82**
– Iruzubieta Villaluenga (I-54), II-33, *II-97*
– Kiik **I-95**, **(II-50)**, **II-101**, **(II-115)**
– Kotsur I-53, *II-97*
– Kupreichik **I-21**, **(I-25)**, **II-57**, **II-94**
– Minasian **II-108**
– Peng Xiaomin **I-95**, **I-155**, **II-102**
– Romero Holmes **II-80**
– Sax **II-82**
– Spassky **(I-88)**, **(I-90)**, **II-19**, **II-20**, **II-21**, **II-87**
– Sveshnikov **I-119**
– Timman **II-96**
Korniukhin, Grigory – Cherniaev **II-30**
Korniushin, Grigory – Cherniaev **II-106**
Kosić, – Hába **II-103**
Kosić, Dragan
– Abramović *II-71*
– Pap **II-91**
Kosten, Anthony – Kupreichik **II-81**
– Lputian *II-95*
Kotronias, Vasilios – Iuldachev **I-149**
Kotsur, Pavel – Korchnoi **I-53**, **II-97**
Koutsin, Sergey – Hába **II-50**
Kovačević, Vlatko
– Kupreichik **[I-113]**, **[I-118]**, **II-61**
– Sveshnikov **I-69**, **[I-113]**, **[I-118]**, **II-61**
Kramer, Haije – Euwe **I-148**, **II-93**
Kramnik, Vladimir – Shirov **I-95**, **II-102**, **(II-114)**
Krapivin, Alexander – Zakharevich *II-65*
Krasnov, Sergey – Glek *II-92*
– Zaitsev **II-63**
Krason, Jozef – Dobosz *II-56*
Kristjánsson, Stefán – Ni Hua **II-86**
– Thorsson II-39
– Thorsteinsson *II-108*
Krizsány, László – Sveshnikov I-127
Kruppa, Yuri – Grischuk **II-103**
– Kupreichik **II-70**
Kuligowski, Adam – Sax **II-105**
Kun, Gábor – Szűk II-31
Kuporosov, Victor – Kharlov **II-73**
Kupreichik, Victor – Bagirov *II-94*
– Charochkin I-147, *II-70*
– Faragó *II-70*

– Feigin *II-67*
– Furman *II-71*
– Gulko *II-78*
– Hertneck *II-96*
– Huzman I-117, *II-94*
– Hába *II-62*
– Jorgensen *II-70*
– Kacheishvili *II-70*
– Kaminski *II-70*
– Korchnoi I-21, (I-25), *II-57*, *II-94*
– Kosten *II-81*
– Kovačević [I-113], [I-118], *II-61*
– Kruppa *II-70*
– Lautier II-41, *II-95*
– Levitt *II-81*
– Libeau *II-70*, *II-96*
– Lputian *II-96*
– Molnar II-38
– Nikolenko *II-70*
– Nikolić *II-82*
– Nun **II-91**
– Petrosian *II-56*
– Pilaj *II-86*
– Sveshnikov **I-124**
– Timoshchenko II-40, *II-61*
– Ulibin *II-96*
– Vaganian I-32, (I-42), (I-82), *II-56*, *II-57*, *II-58*
– Vasiljević *II-70*
– Zlotnik *II-61*
Kuzmin, Gennady – Lempert *II-96*

L
Laine, Panu – I. Zaitsev **II-29**
– Zaitsev **(I-50)**, *II-98*
Lalić, Bogdan – Sveshnikov *II-80*
Landa, Konstantin – Danielian *II-102*
Larsen, Bent – Menvielle Lacourrelle *II-79*
Lasker, Emanuel – Tarrasch **I-18**, *II-58*, **(II-112)**
Lastin, Alexander – Ivanov (I-77), (II-50), *II-101*
– Malakhatko I-95, *II-102*
– S. Ivanov I-51
Lau, Ralf – Benjamin *II-56*
Lautier, Joël – Bauer II-50, (II-114)
– Kupreichik **II-41**, *II-95*
– Prié *II-107*
Lavrov, Maxim – Sambuev II-122
Leitão, Rafael – Crosa *II-60*
Leito, Priit – Sveshnikov *II-81*
Lemmers, Oscar – Visser I-146
Lempert, Igor – I. Zaitsev **II-26**
– Kuzmin *II-96*
– Mukhametov *II-73*
– Zaitsev *II-65*, **(II-113)**
Leonhardt, Paul Saladin – Nimzowitsch **(I-19)**, **I-68**
Leuw, Micha – Witt II-122
Levenfish, Grigory – Botvinnik *II-60*
– Nimzowitsch **(I-71)**, **I-112**, *II-71*

Levitt, Jonathan – Ivanović **I-147**
– Kupreichik *II-81*
– Sveshnikov *II-109*
– Vasyukov *II-81*
Libeau, Rene – Kupreichik *II-70*, *II-96*
Liberzon, Vladimir – Timman *II-111*
Linder, Oliver – Heinz **I-34**
Lisitsyn, Georgy – Smyslov **II-16**, *II-59*
Lisy, Igor – Belov **I-147**, *II-66*, **II-120**
Ljubojević, Ljubomir
– Shirov **I-34**, *II-67*
– Timman *II-82*
Lobzhanidze, Davit – Volkov *II-62*
Longo, Maria – Bellucco **I-146**
Lovik, Lasse Ostebo – Hansen **I-146**, *II-106*
Lputian, Smbat – Adams *II-73*
– Antonio **II-31**, *II-95*
– Bosch **II-50**
– Grischuk **I-101**, *II-101*, **(II-115)**
– Kosten *II-95*
– Kupreichik *II-96*
– Malaniuk *II-72*
– Nevednichy **[II-118]**
– Romanishin **I-77**, **(II-114)**
– Savić *II-102*, **[II-117]**
– Short **(I-95)**, **I-103**, **(II-52)**, *II-102*, **(II-114)**
– Suetin *II-65*
– Sveshnikov **I-69**, **I-85**, **(I-101)**, **I-104**, **(I-113)**,
    (I-119), **II-50**, *II-61*, *II-72*, *II-95*, *II-97*, *II-102*
Luce, Sebastien – Sveshnikov **I-153**
Luft, Martin – Hengl *II-66*
Lukonin, Andrey – Voronovsky *II-87*
Lukov, Valentin – Karpachev *II-71*
Lunev, Andrey – Zaitsev *II-108*
Lupu, Mircea – Zaitsev *II-56*
Luther, Thomas – Brunello **II-120**
– Sveshnikov **(I-27)**, **II-33**, *II-81*
Lutsko, Igor – Sveshnikov *II-67*
Lutz, Christopher – Sveshnikov *II-110*

M
Maciejewski, Andrzej – Glek *II-92*
Makropoulos, Georgios – Hug *II-58*
Malakhatko, Vadim – Lastin **I-95**, *II-102*
Malaniuk, Vladimir – Lputian *II-72*
– Uhlmann *II-106*
Malysheva, Polina – Ivanov I-52
Manen, Gerber van – Stilling *II-108*
Margoline, Boris – Ulibin I-47
Marić, Rudolf – Velimirović *II-57*
Markarov, Arsen – Riazantsev *II-66*
Marković, Ivan – Sokolov *II-84*
Maróczy, Géza – Becker *II-58*
– Steinitz **I-16**, *II-96*
Marshall, A. – Alekhine **II-15**
Masip Rodriguez, Nuria – Rodriguez Boado *II-97*
Mason, Donald – Cherniaev **II-123**

Matamoros Franco, Carlos – Khamrakulov **I-155**
Matlak, Marek – Štoček *II-60*
Matlakov, Maxim – Khairullin *II-102*
Matsuo, Tomohiko – Doghri **I-126**
Matulović, Milan – Yukhtman *II-59*
Matveeva, Svetlana – Polovnikova *II-100*
   – Sveshnikov **II-46**, *II-66*
McConnell, James – Morphy I-150, II-13
McShane, Luke – Gdański II-30, *II-95*
   – Thórhallsson II-38
Mednis, Edmar – Wallyn *II-93*
Meessen, Rudolf – Gurevich *II-82*
Mencinger, Vojko – Sveshnikov **I-27**, *II-86*
Menvielle Lacourrelle, Augusto – Larsen *II-79*
Merenkov, Mikhail – Podlesny II-50
Meshkov, Yuri – Sveshnikov **I-75**, *II-107*
Mesropov, Konstantin – Zaitsev **I-29**, *II-72*
Mestel, Jonathan – Bronstein **I-106**, *II-107*
   – Howell *II-63*
Mészáros, Gyula – Hába *II-58*
Milić, Borislaw – Portisch **I-148**, **II-39**, *II-97*
Miljanić, Boro – Sveshnikov *II-102*
Milliet, Sophie – Zakurdjaeva I-147
Milos, Gilberto – Morozevich *II-100*
   – Rodríguez *II-78*
   – Sveshnikov **I-154**, *II-106*
Minasian, Artashes – Ehlvest *II-84*
   – Korchnoi *II-108*
Minev, Nikolai – Sveshnikov *II-65*
Mnatsakanian, Eduard – Monin *II-92*
Möhring, Günther – Casper *II-93*
   – Thormann *II-92*
Moiseenko, Vladimir – Erashchenko I-42
Molnar, Vojtech – Kupreichik *II-38*
Monakhov, Yuri – Sveshnikov *II-129*
Monin, Nikolai – Mnatsakanian *II-92*
Moor, Olivier – Pilaj *II-85*
Moor, Roger – Mukhametov **I-124**
Moreno Carnero, Javier – Delchev **I-151**
Morovic Fernandez, Ivan – Belkhodja *II-50*
Moroz, Alexander – Glek *II-108*
Morozevich, Alexander – Bareev (I-77), II-36, *II-100*, (II-114)
   – Hodgson *II-60*
   – Milos *II-100*
   – Movsesian *II-88*
   – Popchev *II-87*
   – Popov **I-47**
Morphy, Paul – McConnell **I-150**, **II-13**
Moskalenko, Victor – Baklan **I-49**, *II-98*
   – Sveshnikov **I-52**, **I-152**, *II-74*, *II-101*
   – Vasyukov *II-101*
   – Zaitsev *II-73*
Moskalik, Andrzej – Heberla **I-50**, *II-98*
Motwani, Paul – Gurevich *II-110*
Motylev, Alexander – Alavkin [II-118]
   – Anastasian II-124

   – Balashov I-151, *II-108*
   – Hort I-30, *II-106*
   – J. Ivanov *II-78*
   – Ponomariov *II-102*
   – Potkin I-153
   – Rustemov I-35, *II-56*
   – Rychagov I-49, *II-98*
   – San Segundo Carrillo *II-100*
Movsesian, Sergei – Potkin II-125
   – Yusupov II-126
Movsesian, Sergey – Berkes I-154
   – Gurevich I-93, *II-84*
   – Heberla I-49, *II-98*
   – Kindermann *II-84*
   – Morozevich *II-88*
   – Nikolić I-99, *II-79*
   – Priehoda *II-94*
   – Radjabov *II-109*
   – S. Ivanov *II-96*
   – Schlindwein *II-87*
   – Shirov I-97, *II-78*
   – Tibenský *II-57*
   – Ulibin *II-85*
   – Volkov II-38, *II-62*
Muffang, André – Alekhine *II-71*
Mukhametov, Eldar – Fominikh *II-66*
   – Lempert *II-73*
   – Moor I-124
   – Rechel I-52, *II-101*
   – Stojanović *II-82*

N

N.N. – Greco I-12, **(I-25)**, II-11
Najer, Evgeny – Bauer *II-56*
   – Grischuk **I-29**, *II-72*
   – Soćko I-49, *II-98*
   – Totsky I-49, *II-98*
   – Volkov I-155
Nakamura, Hikaru – Czebe **I-130**
   – Paschall *II-62*
Namyslo, Holger – Schuh *II-92*
Naumkin, Igor – Dvoiris **I-149**
   – I. Zaitsev **II-47**
   – Kholmov *II-110*
   – Sveshnikov **I-152**, **II-42**, *II-73*, *II-77*
   – Zaitsev *II-111*
Nei, Ivo – Gleizerov *II-59*
Nepomniashchy, Jan – Panarin **I-30**, *II-106*
Nevednichy, Vladislav – Lputian [II-118]
   – Sveshnikov **(I-42)**, **I-84**, *II-97*
   – Tugui I-130
Ni Hua
   – Bareev I-75, *II-110*
   – Kristjánsson *II-86*
Nikitin, Alexander – Ragozin *II-96*
Nikolaev, Sergey – Sveshnikov *II-74*, *II-88*
Nikolenko, Oleg – Kupreichik *II-70*

– Shur *II-76*
– Sveshnikov **II-71**, **II-110**
Nikolić, Predrag
– Borg **II-91**
– Kupreichik **II-82**
– Movsesian **I-99**, **II-79**
– Romanishin **II-82**
– Romero Holmes **II-82**
– Stević **(I-47)**, **I-149**, **II-84**
– Timman **II-82**
– Topalov **II-79**, **II-84**
Nimzowitsch, Aaron – Alekhine II-15, *II-59*
– Brinckmann **I-125**
– Duhme I-124
– Leonhardt (I-19), I-68
– Levenfish (I-71), I-112, *II-71*
– Rubinstein I-17
– Salwe I-111, *II-91*
– Spielmann *II-58*, *II-96*
– Székely *II-59*
Nisipeanu, Liviu-Dieter
– Azmaiparashvili I-130
– Ionescu *II-67*
Nogueiras, Jesus – Otero **I-77**
– Sax **I-53**, *II-97*
– Shabalov **I-149**
Novak, Ignacy – Popov **II-109**
Novikova, Anna – Korbut **II-109**
Nun, Jiří – Kupreichik *II-91*
Nunn, John – Anand *II-80*

O
Öchslein, Rainer – Tischer *II-92*
Olesen, Martin – Whiteley II-29
Oll, Lembit – Ivanchuk I-79, *II-77*
– Rustemov *II-66*
Oms Pallise, Josep – Radulski **I-156**
Orak, Ljubomir – Dizdar *II-86*
Ortega, Lexy – Sveshnikov **(I-91)**, **I-122**
Osmanović, Kemal – Sveshnikov **I-33**
Otero, Diasmany – Nogueiras I-77
Owczarzak, Jerzy – Gdański **II-110**

P
Padevsky, Nikola – Darga *II-92*
Pähtz, Thomas – Uhlmann I-75, (I-75), I-147, *II-107*
Palleja, Xavier – Dizdar *II-80*
Panarin, Mikhail – Nepomniashchy I-30, *II-106*
Panbukhian, Valentin – Sveshnikov **II-79**
Pap, Miša – Kosić *II-91*
Paramos Dominguez, Roberto – Sveshnikov **I-102**, **II-101**
Paredes, L. – Capablanca **II-14**
Párkányi, Attila – Bagoly *II-87*
– Ács **II-70**
Paschall, William – Nakamura **II-62**

Paulsen, Louis – Blackburne I-14, *II-71*
– Schwarz I-13, I-15, (I-25), (I-82), *II-71*
– Stern *II-95*
Pavasović, Duško – Bukal *II-70*
Pegoraro, Nicola – Salami *II-70*
Pelletier, Yannick – Conquest **II-107**
– Grischuk **II-107**
– Reefat **II-105**
– Vallejo Pons **II-107**
Penalver, Frédéric – Chaumont *II-91*
Peng Xiaomin
– Kacheishvili *II-87*
– Korchnoi I-95, I-155, *II-102*
– Soćko *II-97*
– Yusupov *II-79*
– Zhang Zhong I-93
Pert, Nicholas – Cherniaev **II-86**
– Grischuk **II-72**
Petrosian, Tigran – Gershkovich **II-59**
– I. Zaitsev **II-18**
– Kholmov **II-18**
– Kupreichik **II-56**
– Reshevsky **I-126**
– Tal **I-127**, **II-18**, *II-110*
Pilaj, Herwig – Kupreichik **II-86**
– Moor *II-85*
Pinski, Jan – Zontakh *II-59*
Pintér, József – Schmidt *II-108*
Piskov, Yuri – Sveshnikov **(I-42)**, **II-42**, *II-98*
– Yagupov **II-86**
Podlesny, Pavel – Merenkov **II-50**
Pokojowczyk, Jerzy – I. Zaitsev **I-22**, **(I-105)**, *II-108*
Polgár, Judit – Topalov *II-78*
Polgar, Zsuzsanna – Gertler **II-105**
Polivanov, Anatoly – Vysochin **I-102**, **II-101**, **(II-115)**
Poljakov, Sergey – Sveshnikov **II-97**
Polovnikova, Ekaterina – Matveeva *II-100*
Polugaevsky, Lev – Antoshin *II-58*
Ponomariov, Ruslan – Motylev **II-102**
Popadić, Dragan – Atalik *II-59*
Popchev, Roman – Morozevich *II-87*
Popov, Milko – Novak *II-109*
Popov, Roman – Morozevich I-47
Popović, Petar
– Sveshnikov **II-77**
– Vasyukov **II-73**
Portisch, Lajos – Csom **I-148**
– Klinger **II-105**
– Milić I-148, II-39, *II-97*
– Sveshnikov **II-43**, **II-94**, **II-96**, **(II-113)**, **(II-114)**
Potapov, Alexander – Sveshnikov **I-129**
Potkin, Vladimir – Asrian *II-66*
– Filippov I-77, *II-100*, **(II-114)**
– Hába **II-76**
– Motylev **I-153**
– Movsesian **II-125**
– Sveshnikov **I-95**, **(II-53)**, **II-103**, **(II-115)**

– Vysochin I-30, *II-109*
Prashnik, Anton – Yakimenko *II-106*
Praznik, Anton – Yakimenko I-61
Predojević, Borki
  – Galyas *II-86*
  – Wang Hao *II-110*
Prezerakos, D – Vysochin **II-102**
Prié, Eric – Apicella *II-110*
  – Bauer *II-56*
  – Dimitrov *II-78*
  – Lautier *II-107*
  – Villeneuve I-45
  – Walton I-146
Priehoda, Vitezslav – Movsesian **II-94**
Prokhorov, Alexander – Griezne I-149
Prudnikova, Svetlana – Salnikov **II-91**
Przewoźnik, Jan
  – Gdański **II-82**
  – Uhlmann *II-105*
Psakhis, Lev – Chernin *II-71*
  – Faragó *II-108*
  – Hoffman **II-62**
  – Sveshnikov I-88, *II-73*, *II-78*

R
Rabinovich, Ilja – Botvinnik *II-59*
Radjabov, Teimour – Grischuk I-79, **II-34**, **II-50**,
  II-77, **II-78**, **II-103**
  – Movsesian **II-109**
  – Sveshnikov (I-77), (I-95), (II-50), II-53, *II-103*,
  (II-115)
Radulski, Julian – Oms Pallise I-156
Ragozin, Viacheslav – Nikitin **II-96**
Rahman, Tahmidur – Reefat **II-26**
Raičević, Vladimir – Grosar I-148, **II-98**
Rainfray, Arnaud – Drosdovsky I-52
Rausis, Igors – Sveshnikov **I-132**
Rauzer, Vsevolod – Grigoriev I-19, *II-60*
Rayo Gutiérrez, Manuel – García Fernández **II-109**
Razuvaev, Yuri – Kaidanov **I-113**
  – Sveshnikov I-71, I-79, I-113, **II-76**, **II-78**, **II-86**,
  II-93, **II-96**, (II-131)
Rechel, Ralf – Mukhametov **I-52**, **II-101**
Ree, Hans – Hodgson **II-61**
  – Sax **II-105**
Reefat, Bin Sattar
  – Barsov *II-81*
  – Pelletier *II-105*
  – Rahman II-26
Rellstab, Ludwig – Unzicker [II-117]
Remizov, Yuri – Ilinsky *II-108*
Repkova, Eva – Sveshnikov **II-66**
Reshevsky, Samuel Herman – Petrosian I-126
Réti, Richard – Spielmann I-68
Riazantsev, Alexander – Markarov **II-66**
  – Sveshnikov **I-154**, *II-108*
Rodriguez Boado, Martin – Masip Rodriguez *II-97*

Rodríguez, Andrés – Gleizerov *II-70*
  – Milos **II-78**
Rogers, Ian – Anand **II-57**
  – Sribar II-39, *II-62*
  – Velimirović *II-100*
Rohde, Michael – Spraggett **II-72**
Romanishin, Oleg – Foisor I-72
  – Hort *II-81*
  – Ivanchuk *II-78*
  – Lputian I-77, (II-114)
  – Nikolić *II-82*
Romero Holmes, Alfonso
  – Bukal *II-72*
  – Korchnoi *II-80*
  – Nikolić *II-82*
Roos, Louis – Bronstein **II-24**, **II-106**
Rozentalis, Eduardas – Epishin *II-92*
  – Schmidt *II-62*
  – Züger *II-81*
Rubinchik, Leonid – Smolensky **I-148**
Rubinstein, Akiba – Nimzowitsch **I-17**
Rublevsky, Sergey – Sveshnikov I-37, **II-88**
Rustemov, Alexander – Alekseev I-34, **II-67**
  – Aseev **II-62**
  – Carlsen I-34, **II-68**
  – Motylev I-35, **II-56**
  – Oll **II-66**
  – Sveshnikov **II-130**
  – Svidler **II-57**
  – Ulibin **II-57**
  – Vysochin *II-105*
  – Yagupov **II-63**
Rychagov, Andrey – Motylev **I-49**, **II-98**
  – Yagupov **II-97**

S
Sadvakasov, Darmen – Jonkman **I-29**, *II-72*
  – Shirov **II-50**
Sæther, Øystein – Sveshnikov **II-79**
Sakaev, Konstantin – Grischuk I-102, **II-101**
  – Kharlov **II-82**
Salami, Marco – Pegoraro **II-70**
Salaun, Yann – Fressinet **II-100**
Saldano Dayer, Horacio – Del Rio Angelis I-78
Salem, Ghuloom – Volzhin *II-63*
Salnikov, Alexander – Prudnikova *II-91*
Salwe, Georg – Nimzowitsch **I-111**, **II-91**
Sambuev, Bator – Lavrov **II-122**
  – Vysochin **I-52**, **II-101**
San Segundo Carrillo, Pablo – Motylev **II-100**
Sandipan, Chanda – Barua I-45
  – Dolmatov **II-122**
  – Hertneck *II-84*
Sangma, Rahul – Erenburg **II-109**
Sanguinetti, Raul – Albert I-146
Sankovich, W. – Bareev *II-96*
Saunina, Ludmila – Epstein **II-96**

Savić, Miodrag
  – Antić II-31, *II-95*
  – Jeremić I-154
  – Lputian *II-102*, [II-117]
Savon, Vladimir – I. Zaitsev **II-25**
  – Sveshnikov **I-40**, *II-77*
  – Zaitsev *II-108*
Sax, Gyula – Brenninkmeijer *II-87*
  – Dreev *II-63*, *II-81*
  – Glek *II-71*
  – Gurevich *II-73*
  – Knaak *II-105*
  – Korchnoi *II-82*
  – Kuligowski *II-105*
  – Nogueiras I-53, *II-97*
  – Ree *II-105*
  – Short *II-57*
  – Speelman *II-79*
  – Uhlmann *II-105*
Schlindwein, Rolf – Movsesian **II-87**
Schlosser, Philipp – Glek *II-73*
Schmidt, Bodo – Drvota **II-94**
Schmidt, Włodzimierz
  – Pintér **II-108**
  – Rozentalis **II-62**
Schmitt, André – Short *II-58*
Schmittdiel, Eckhardt – Hába **II-110**
Schürmans, Robert – Claesen *II-96*
Schuh, Bernd – Namyslo *II-92*
Schwarz, Adolf – Paulsen **I-13**, **I-15**, **(I-25)**, **(I-82)**,
  II-71
Sebenik, Matej – Buchnicek **II-106**
Seirawan, Yasser – Shabalov **II-57**
Seul, Georg – Gurevich *II-60*
Shabalov, Alexander – Abrahamyan II-127
  – Akobian I-151
  – Bluvshtein I-154
  – Nogueiras I-149
  – S. Ivanov II-122
  – Seirawan *II-57*
  – Shirov *II-85*
  – Sveshnikov **(I-40)**, **I-152**, *II-77*
Sher, Miron – Greenfeld **II-85**
Sherwin, James – Evans *II-110*
Shilov, Yuri – Steinberg **II-26**, *II-65*
Shirov, Alexei – Del Rio Angelis II-121
Schirow, Alexey – van Wely *II-84*
Shirov, Alexey – Anand I-44, (II-26), *II-65*, (II-113)
  – Bern I-150
  – Fressinet **I-147**
  – Gurevich I-149, *II-85*, *II-103*
  – Khalifman I-52, *II-101*
  – Kramnik I-95, *II-102*, (II-114)
  – Ljubojević I-34, *II-67*
  – Movsesian **I-97**, *II-78*
  – Sadvakasov II-50
  – Shabalov *II-85*

  – Svidler **II-38**, *II-62*
  – Taddei I-102
  – Topalov *II-81*
  – van Wely I-97
Short, Nigel – Bareev *II-60*
  – Glek *II-73*
  – Grischuk *II-76*
  – Ivanchuk *II-79*
  – Lputian (I-95), I-103, (II-52), *II-102*, (II-114)
  – Sax *II-57*
  – Schmitt *II-58*
  – Vaganian *II-72*
Showalter, Jackson Whipps – Steinitz **I-16**, *II-59*
Shulman, Yuri – Gossell *II-92*
  – Sveshnikov *II-88*
Shur, Mikhail – Nikolenko *II-76*
Siedentopf, Daniel – Karpachev *II-94*
Sieiro González, Luis – Gurevich I-47, *II-72*, *II-87*
Skalkotas, Nikolaos – Sveshnikov **I-27**, *II-80*, *II-85*
Skoblikov, E. – Survila *II-94*
Slochevsky, Alexander – Sveshnikov *II-100*
Smeets, Jan – Jonkman **I-155**, *II-78*
  – Stellwagen *II-96*
Smirnov, Pavel – Beliakov *II-93*
  – Belozerov I-50, *II-98*
Smolensky, Yuri – Rubinchik I-148
Smyslov, Vasily – Lisitsyn II-16, *II-59*
Snatenkov, Vitaly – Gafner **I-50**, *II-98*
Soćko, Bartosz
  – Fressinet **I-151**, *II-97*
  – Najer **I-49**, *II-98*
  – Peng Xiaomin *II-97*
Sokolov, Ivan – Cifuentes Parada *II-84*
  – Degraeve *II-105*
  – Marković *II-84*
  – Timman *II-84*
Sokolsky, Alexey – Tal **II-17**
Soreghy, Janos – Halasz **II-26**
Sorri, Kari Juhani – Hankipohja *II-58*
Spassky, Boris – Hort **II-21**, **(II-31)**, *II-95*
  – Korchnoi (I-88), (I-90), II-19, II-20, II-21, *II-87*
Spassov, Ljuben – Ermenkov *II-86*
Speelman, Jonathan – Illescas Cordoba **I-146**
  – Sax *II-79*
Spielmann, Rudolf – Nimzowitsch *II-58*, *II-96*
  – Réti **I-68**
Spraggett, Kevin – Gurevich *II-61*
  – Rohde *II-72*
Sribar, C. – Rogers **II-62**
Sribar, Peter – Rogers **II-39**
Stamiris, Gerasimos – Vazelaki *II-70*
Starostits – Sveshnikov *II-101*
Staunton, Howard – Cochrane **II-12**
Steinberg, Mikhail – Shilov II-26, *II-65*
Steinitz, Wilhelm – Burn I-16, *II-91*
  – Maróczy I-16, *II-96*
  – Showalter I-16, *II-59*

– Tinsley II-13
Stellwagen, Daniel – Jonkman **II-78**
  – Smeets **II-96**
Stern, Adolf – Paulsen **II-95**
Stevanović, Vladan – Jonkman **I-49**
Stević, Hrvoje
  – Dizdar *II-81*, *II-85*
  – Nikolić (I-47), I-149, *II-84*
Stilling, Walter – van Manen *II-108*
Štoček, Jiří – Matlak *II-60*
Stojanov, Svetlin – Hába **II-97**
Stojanović, Mihajlo – Mukhametov **II-82**
Strauts, A. – Kantoris *II-92*
Ståhlberg, Gideon – Keres **II-35**, **II-60**
Subit, José – Vilela I-85
Suetin, Alexey – Lputian *II-65*
Sulava, Nenad – Grosar **I-150**, **II-57**
Suleimanov, Marat – Sveshnikov **II-72**
Summerscale, Aaron – Gwaze **II-86**
Survila, Rimvydas – Skoblikov *II-94*
Sveshnikov, Evgeny – Agrinsky I-121, *II-61*
  – Alavkin II-120
  – Araslanov **I-133**
  – Atalik I-148, *II-80*
  – Atanasov *II-78*
  – Balashov I-39, I-40, *II-77*, *II-109*
  – Bareev I-64, I-65, (I-102), (I-116), *II-73*, *II-100*,
    II-101, *II-102*, (II-115), [II-116], II-131
  – Bashkov *II-79*, *II-87*, *II-88*
  – Batchuluun II-132
  – Berend II-127
  – Bjerke I-123
  – Bochkarev II-128
  – Brumen (I-38), (I-107), II-48, *II-88*
  – Casper *II-110*
  – Cherniaev *II-74*
  – Chernin (I-26), I-154, *II-72*, *II-76*
  – Dambrauskas *II-65*
  – Danielian *II-66*
  – Dizdar (I-38), (I-107), II-49, *II-80*, *II-89*, II-131
  – Dolmatov I-27, (II-45), *II-85*
  – Donchev (I-47), I-152, II-32, *II-110*
  – Doroshkevich I-65, (I-77), I-150, *II-100*, *II-101*,
    (II-115)
  – Dražić I-42
  – Dreev I-37, I-88, *II-88*
  – Dukhov (I-64), I-116, *II-74*
  – Dvoiris (I-101), (I-104), II-52, *II-71*, *II-102*, (II-114)
  – Ehlvest [I-113], [I-118], *II-66*
  – Eingorn I-61, I-62, *II-105*, *II-109*, *II-110*
  – Epishin I-79, *II-77*
  – Faragó I-25, *II-72*, *II-111*
  – Filipenko *II-28*, *II-95*
  – Filippov II-130
  – Foisor *II-88*
  – Fominikh I-86, *II-87*
  – Furlan *II-84*

  – Galstian II-129
  – Genov I-148, *II-92*
  – Ghane Gardeh II-128
  – Gleizerov *II-80*, *II-85*
  – Glek I-64, *II-73*
  – Gligorić I-128
  – Gofshtein I-153, II-47, *II-110*
  – Golovanov II-53
  – Graf *II-84*
  – Grosar (I-34), I-42, *II-68*
  – Gulko I-26, *II-76*, *II-84*, *II-86*
  – Gurevich *II-88*
  – Gurgenidze I-88
  – Hoàng I-42, (I-84), *II-97*
  – Hulak *II-66*
  – Iskusnykh *II-81*
  – Ivkov II-47, *II-110*
  – J. Ivanov I-115
  – Jolles *II-73*
  – Kalinin *II-76*, *II-105*
  – Karer *II-86*
  – Katishonok *II-76*
  – Kharlov I-40, *II-77*
  – Kholopov *II-79*
  – Kiriakov (I-27), II-45, *II-85*
  – Kiselev *II-106*
  – Komarov (I-21), (I-42), I-57, *II-59*, (II-112)
  – Korchnoi I-119
  – Kovačević I-69, [I-113], [I-118], *II-61*
  – Krizsány **I-127**
  – Kupreichik I-124
  – L. Ortega I-122
  – Lalić *II-80*
  – Leito *II-81*
  – Levitt *II-109*
  – Lputian I-69, I-85, (I-101), I-104, (I-113), (I-119),
    II-50, *II-61*, *II-72*, *II-95*, *II-97*, *II-102*
  – Luce I-153
  – Luther (I-27), II-33, *II-81*
  – Lutsko *II-67*
  – Lutz *II-110*
  – M. Gurevich I-90
  – Matveeva II-46, *II-66*
  – Mencinger I-27, *II-86*
  – Meshkov I-75, *II-107*
  – Miljanić *II-102*
  – Milos I-154, *II-106*
  – Minev *II-65*
  – Monakhov II-129
  – Moskalenko I-52, I-152, *II-74*, *II-101*
  – Naumkin I-152, II-42, *II-73*, *II-77*
  – Nevednichy (I-42), I-84, *II-97*
  – Nikolaev *II-74*, *II-88*
  – Nikolenko *II-71*, *II-110*
  – Ortega (I-91)
  – Osmanović I-33
  – Panbukchian *II-79*

– Paramos Dominguez I-102, *II-101*
– Piskov (I-42), II-42, *II-98*
– Poljakov *II-97*
– Popović *II-77*
– Portisch II-43, *II-94*, *II-96*, (II-113), (II-114)
– Potapov I-129
– Potkin I-95, (II-53), *II-103*, (II-115)
– Psakhis I-88, *II-73*, *II-78*
– Radjabov (I-77), (I-95), (II-50), II-53, *II-103*, (II-115)
– Rausis I-132
– Razuvaev I-71, I-79, I-113, *II-76*, *II-78*, *II-86*, *II-93*, *II-96*, (II-131)
– Repkova *II-66*
– Riazantsev I-154, *II-108*
– Rublevsky I-37, *II-88*
– Rustemov II-130
– S. Ivanov *II-93*
– Savon I-40, *II-77*
– Shabalov (I-40), I-152, *II-77*
– Shulman *II-88*
– Skalkotas I-27, *II-80*, *II-85*
– Slochevsky *II-100*
– Starostits *II-101*
– Suleimanov *II-72*
– Sæther *II-79*
– Tarasov I-131
– Temirbaev *II-73*
– Timman (I-30), I-60, *II-106*, (II-113)
– Topi-Hulmi II-131
– Torre *II-76*
– Totsky I-151, I-152, *II-88*
– Tunik *II-72*
– Ulibin *II-80*, *II-85*, *II-88*
– Vaganian (I-42), I-82, *II-58*
– Vaisser *II-78*
– Volkov I-55, I-90, *II-65*, (II-114)
– Volzhin I-128
– Vysochin (I-33), II-26, *II-67*
– Yakovenko I-129
– Yanovsky *II-100*
– Yashtylov II-119
– Zaja I-129
– Zeller *II-61*
– Zhuravliov **II-37**, *II-73*
– Zlotnik I-88, *II-62*, *II-88*
Svidler, Peter – Beliavsky *II-102*
– Rustemov *II-57*
– Shirov II-38, *II-62*
– Volkov I-55, *II-65*
Székely, Jeno – Nimzowitsch *II-59*
Szűk, Balázs – Kun **II-31**

T

Tabernig, Bernhard – Grosar **I-52**
Taddei, Benoît – Shirov **I-102**
Tal, Mikhail – Petrosian I-127, II-18, *II-110*

– Sokolsky II-17
Tarasov, Mikhail – Sveshnikov **I-131**
Tarjan, James Edward – Zaitsev **II-78**
Tarrasch, Siegbert – Alapin **I-124**
– Lasker I-18, *II-58*, (II-112)
Teloudis, Angelis – Brumm **I-148**
Temirbaev, Serik – Sveshnikov **II-73**
Teske, Henrik – Uhlmann I-75, *II-107*
Thompson, Ian – Ehlvest **I-153**
Thórhallsson, Throstur – McShane **II-38**
Thormann, Wolfgang – Möhring **II-92**
Thorsson, Olafur – Kristjánsson **II-39**
Thorsteinsson, Thorsteinn – Kristjánsson **II-108**
Tibenský, Róbert – Movsesian **II-57**
Timman, Jan – Cu. Hansen II-50
– Hansen *II-102*
– Jóhannesson (I-93), I-97, *II-85*
– Korchnoi *II-96*
– Liberzon *II-111*
– Ljubojević *II-82*
– Nikolić *II-82*
– Sokolov *II-84*
– Sveshnikov **(I-30)**, **I-60**, **II-106**, **(II-113)**
Timoshchenko, Gennady – Kupreichik **II-40**, **II-61**
Tinsley, Samuel – Steinitz **II-13**
Tischer, Günter – Öchslein **II-92**
Tiviakov, Sergei – Arizmendi Martínez *II-73*
Topalov, Veselin – Bareev *II-95*
– Nikolić *II-79*, *II-84*
– Polgár **II-78**
– Shirov **II-81**
– van Wely **II-76**, **II-126**
Topi-Hulmi, Teemu – Sveshnikov **II-131**
Torre, Eugenio – Bagamasbad I-34, (I-43), *II-68*
– Chernin *II-98*
– Sveshnikov **II-76**
Totsky, Leonid – Najer **I-49**, **II-98**
– Sveshnikov **I-151**, **I-152**, **II-88**
Tregubov, Pavel – Tseitlin **II-109**
Tseitlin, Mark – Tregubov *II-109*
– Yusupov I-85
Tugui, Adrian – Nevednichy **I-130**
Tukmakov, Vladimir – Kivisto **II-61**
Tunik, Gennady – Sveshnikov **II-72**

U

Ubiennykh, Ekaterina – Verevochkina I-156
Uhlmann, Wolfgang – Camilleri **II-96**
– Casper **I-75**, **II-107**
– Enders **II-35**, **II-106**
– Honfi **I-75**, **II-59**, **II-106**
– Jonkman **II-95**
– Malaniuk **II-106**
– Przewoźnik **II-105**
– Pähtz **(I-75)**, **I-75**, **I-147**, **II-107**
– Sax **I-105**
– Teske **I-75**, **II-107**

Ulibin, Mikhail – Kontić **I-72**
 – Kupreichik *II-96*
 – Margoline **I-47**
 – Movsesian *II-85*
 – Rustemov *II-57*
 – Sveshnikov *II-80*, *II-85*, *II-88*
 – Westerinen *II-70*
Unzicker, Wolfgang – Gligorić I-14
 – Rellstab **[II-117]**

V

Vaganian, Rafael – Adams *II-73*, *II-82*
 – Dvoiris *II-58*
 – Ehlvest *II-57*
 – Kupreichik **I-32**, **(I-42)**, **(I-82)**, *II-56*, *II-57*, *II-58*
 – Short *II-72*
 – Sveshnikov **(I-42)**, **I-82**, *II-58*
 – Volkov *II-57*, **II-122**
Vaisser, Anatoly – Sveshnikov *II-78*
Vallejo Pons, Francisco
 – Flores **I-95**, **(I-104)**, *II-102*
 – Hernandez I-149
 – Hillarp Persson [II-117]
 – Pelletier *II-107*
Vasiljević, Dragan – Kupreichik *II-70*
Vasyukov, Evgeny – Bukhman I-104, II-50, *II-102*, (II-114)
 – Kholmov *II-73*
 – Levitt *II-81*
 – Moskalenko *II-101*
 – Popović *II-73*
 – Zaitsev **II-47**, *II-110*
Vatter, Hans-Joachim – Kindermann *II-80*
Vazelaki, Stamatia – Stamiris *II-70*
Velimirović, Dragoljub
 – Ivkov II-26, *II-65*
 – Kholmov *II-58*, *II-60*
 – Marić *II-57*
 – Rogers *II-100*
 – Züger *II-79*
Verevochkina, Elena – Ubiennykh **I-156**
Vescovi, Giovanni – Vučković *II-86*
Vilela, José Luis – Subit **I-85**
Villeneuve, Alain – Prié **I-45**
Visser, Bert Steffen – Lemmers **I-146**
Vitolins, Alvis – Gulko *II-62*
Vlassov, Nikolai – Einarsson I-77
 – Ilyushin I-31, *II-106*
Volke, Karsten – Zaitsev *II-73*
Volkov, Sergey – Delchev **(I-55)**, **I-150**, *II-65*
 – Goloshchapov *II-63*
 – Lobzhanidze *II-62*
 – Movsesian II-38, *II-62*
 – Najer **I-155**
 – Sveshnikov **I-55**, **I-90**, *II-65*, **(II-114)**
 – Svidler **I-55**, *II-65*
 – Vaganian *II-57*, II-122

 – Vorobiov **(I-55)**, **I-153**, *II-65*
 – Zviagintsev **I-55**, *II-65*, *II-67*
Volzhin, Alexander – Ibragimov **I-50**, *II-98*
 – Salem *II-63*
 – Sveshnikov **I-128**
Vorobiov, Evgeny – Volkov (I-55), I-153, *II-65*
Voronovsky, Dmitry – Lukonin *II-87*
Vučković, Bojan – Vescovi *II-86*
Vysochin, Spartak – Alekseev *II-56*
 – Fingerov **I-147**, *II-66*
 – Kislov **II-31**, *II-95*
 – Polivanov I-102, *II-101*, (II-115)
 – Potkin **I-30**, *II-109*
 – Prezerakos *II-102*
 – Rustemov *II-105*
 – Sambuev I-52, *II-101*
 – Sveshnikov **(I-33)**, **II-26**, *II-67*
 – Wojtaszek *II-93*

W

Wallyn, Alexandre – Mednis *II-93*
Walton, Alan – Prié **I-146**
Wang Hao – Predojević *II-110*
Weinzettl, Ernst – Grosar *II-97*
Wely, Loek van
 – Schirow *II-84*
 – Shirov **I-97**
 – Topalov *II-76*, II-126
Wemmers, Xander – Gurevich (I-93), I-98, *II-84*
Wempe, Joost – Glek I-47, *II-87*
Westerinen, Heikki – Bisguier *II-91*
 – Ulibin *II-70*
Whiteley, Andrew – Olesen **II-29**
Willemze, Jeroen – Dvoiris *II-86*
Witt, Rob – Leuw **II-122**
Wojtaszek, Radosław – Vysochin *II-93*
Wolf, J. – Gerbich *II-63*

X

Xie Jun – Karpov I-79, *II-77*

Y

Yagupov, Igor – Dreev *II-88*
 – Piskov *II-86*
 – Rustemov *II-63*
 – Rychagov *II-97*
Yakhin, Rashid – Baranov *II-59*
Yakimenko, Andrey – Prashnik *II-106*
 – Praznik **I-61**
Yakovenko, Dmitry – Sveshnikov **I-129**
Yanovsky, Sergey – Kindermann *II-80*
 – Sveshnikov *II-100*
Yashtylov, Anatoly – Sveshnikov **II-119**
Ye Jiangchuan – Ivanchuk *II-57*
Yemelin, Vasily – Dolmatov I-102, *II-101*, (II-122)

Yudasin, Leonid – Gorelov *II-100*
Yukhtman, Jacob – Matulović *II-59*
Yurtaev, Leonid – Glek *II-79*
Yusupov, Artur – Movsesian **II-126**
    – Peng Xiaomin **II-79**
    – Tseitlin **I-85**

    Z
Zaitsev, Igor – Doda II-25, (II-38), *II-63*
    – Dreev I-88
    – Faragó I-105, (II-47), *II-111*
    – Geller II-26, *II-65*
    – Krasnov *II-63*
    – Kärner *II-57*
    – Laine (I-50), II-29, *II-98*
    – Lempert II-26, *II-65*, (II-113)
    – Lunev *II-108*
    – Lupu *II-56*
    – Mesropov I-29, *II-72*
    – Moskalenko *II-73*
    – Naumkin II-47, *II-111*
    – Petrosian II-18

    – Pokojowczyk I-22, (I-105), *II-108*
    – Savon II-25, *II-108*
    – Tarjan *II-78*
    – Vasyukov II-47, *II-110*
    – Volke *II-73*
Zaja, Ivan – Sveshnikov **I-129**
Zakharevich, Igor – Dvoiris **II-87**
    – Goloshchapov **II-87**
    – Kharlov **II-77**
    – Krapivin **II-65**
Zakurdjaeva, Irina – Milliet **I-147**
Zeller, Frank – Sveshnikov **II-61**
Zhang Pengxiang – Grischuk **I-102**, **II-101**
Zhang Zhong – Peng Xiaomin **I-93**
Zhuravliov, Valery – Sveshnikov II-37, *II-73*
Zlotnik, Boris – Glek **II-91**
    – Kupreichik **II-61**
    – Sveshnikov **I-88**, **II-62**, **II-88**
Zontakh, Andrey – Pinski **II-59**
Zugaj, Fjodor – Grosar **I-42**
Zviagintsev, Vadim – Volkov I-55, *II-65*, II-67
Züger, Beat – Rozentalis **II-81**
    – Velimirović **II-79**

Index of variations

1. e4 e6
2. d4 d5
3. e5 c5
 3...b6 I-21, II-122
 3...♘e7 4. ♘f3 b6 I-32, I-82, II-130
 3...♗d7 4. c3 a6 I-35, II-23
4. c3
 4. d×c5 I-18, II-15
 4. ♕g4 I-57, II-16
 4. ♘f3
  4...♘c6 5. ♗d3 I-19, I-20, II-16
  4...♕b6 5. ♗d3 I-68, II-35
4...♘c6
 4...c×d4 I-12
 4...♘d7 II-15
 4...♘e7 5. ♘f3 I-69, I-118 (2), I-121, II-37
 4...♕b6 5. ♘f3 ♗d7
  6. ♘a3 II-40
  6. ♗e2 ♗b5 II-25, II-38
  6. a3
   6...♗b5 I-33, I-42, I-118, II-26, II-46
   6...a5 I-55, II-124
   6...c×d4 7. c×d4 ♗b5 II-120, II-124
5. ♘f3
 5. f4 II-12, II-13, II-14
5...♕b6
 5...f6 I-15, I-112, II-13
 5...c×d4 I-68
 5...♘ge7 6. ♘a3 c×d4 7. c×d4 ♘f5 8. ♘c2 I-25, I-122
 5...♘h6
  6. ♗d3 c×d4 7. ♗×h6 I-29
  6. d×c5 I-64, I-116, II-130
 5...♗d7
  6. a3 f6 II-120, II-126
  6. d×c5 I-39, II-14, II-42
  6. ♗e3 I-14, II-11, II-128
  6. ♗e2
   6...♖c8 7. 0-0 I-79, II-34, II-126, II-131
   6...♘h6 II-129
   6...♘ge7 7. ♘a3
    7...♘f5 I-86
    7...♘g6 I-99

7...cxd4 8. cxd4 ♘f5   I-26, I-37, I-47, I-88, I-90, I-93, I-97, II-19, II-38, II-45 (2), II-48, II-49, II-121, II-125

6. a3

6. ♗d3

6...cxd4 7. cxd4 ♗d7   I-17, I-113

6...♗d7   I-111, II-131

6. ♗e2

6...cxd4   I-16, II-18, II-22, II-43

6...♘ge7 7. ♘a3 cxd4 8. cxd4 ♘f5 9. ♘c2   II-24

6...♘h6   I-117, II-21, II-28, II-30, II-33, II-41

6...c4

6...f6   II-119

6...a5

7. ♗d3 ♗d7   I-44, II-17, II-20, II-21, II-26

7. b3   II-128, II-129

6...♗d7

7. ♗e2 ♘h6   I-71

7. b4 cxd4 8. cxd4

8...♘ge7 9. ♘c3   I-13

8...♖c8   I-49, I-53, I-84, II-29 (3), II-33, II-39, II-42

6...♘h6 7. b4 cxd4 8. cxd4 ♘f5   I-51, I-65, I-77, I-95, I-101, I-103, II-22, II-36, II-50, II-52, II-53, II-116 (2), II-117 (3), II-118 (3), II-122, II-123, II-127 (2), II-131

7. ♘bd2

7. ♗e2 ♗d7   I-61, II-18 (2), II-32

7. g3 ♗d7 8. h4   I-62

7...♘a5

7...♗d7 8.b3   I-30, I-60, I-61

7...f6   I-75, II-24, II-30, II-35

8. g3

8. ♗e2 ♗d7 9. 0-0   I-105, II-47

8. h4 ♗d7 9. h5   I-106

8. b4   II-27

8. ♖b1   II-32

8...♗d7   I-22, II-25, II-53, II-132